THE
AMERICAN
PRESIDENT

Robert E. DiClerico

West Virginia University

PRENTICE-HALL, INC., ENGLEWOOD CLIFFS, NEW JERSEY 07632

Library of Congress Cataloging in Publication Data

DiClerico, Robert E.
    The American President.

    Includes bibliographical references and index.
    1. Presidents—United States. I. Title.
JK16.D52   353.03'13   78-10305
ISBN 0-13-028555-2

Printed in the United States of America

10 9 8 7 6 5 4 3 2 1

Editorial/production supervision and interior design by Serena Hoffman. Cover
design by Edsal Enterprises. Manufacturing buyer Harry P. Baisley.

Prentice-Hall International, Inc., *London*
Prentice-Hall of Australia Pty. Limited, *Sydney*
Prentice-Hall of Canada, Ltd., *Toronto*
Prentice-Hall of India Private Limited, *New Delhi*
Prentice-Hall of Japan, Inc., *Tokyo*
Prentice-Hall of Southeast Asia Pte. Ltd., *Singapore*
Whitehall Books Limited, *Wellington, New Zealand*

FOR MY PARENTS

Contents

PREFACE   ix

INTRODUCTION   1
THE CONCERNS OF THIS BOOK 2
DIFFICULTIES IN STUDYING THE PRESIDENCY 4

1   THE SELECTION PROCESS   6
WHO CONTENDS, WHO IS NOMINATED 7
    Legal Criteria 7
    Informal Criteria 8
    The Future: More Contenders 17
TESTING THE CANDIDATES 18
    Intelligence 19
    Knowledge of the Issues 20
    Judgment 21
    Executive Ability 22
    Honesty 23
    Physical Stamina 24
    Mental Stability 25
    Testing the Candidates: The Merchandising Phenomenon 27
PROPOSALS FOR CHANGE 28

2   THE PRESIDENT AND FOREIGN AFFAIRS   32
SOME GENERAL CONSIDERATIONS:
   THE TWO PRESIDENCIES 32
THE WAR-MAKING POWER 35
    The Intent of the Founders 36
    Presidential War 37
    Congress Reacts: The War Powers Resolution 44
TREATIES AND EXECUTIVE AGREEMENTS 46
    Congress Reacts: The Case Act, 1972 47
THE CIA AND FOREIGN POLICY 49
THE SWING OF THE PENDULUM 52

THE PRESIDENT AND CONGRESS 57

THE PRESIDENT AND CONGRESS:
  A STRAINED RELATIONSHIP 58
    Separation of Powers 58
    Structure of Congress 59
    Different Constituencies 60
    Erosion of Support 61
THE LESSENING OR WORSENING OF THE ANTAGONISM:
  INTERVENING FACTORS 61
    Nature of the Times 62
    Public Prestige 62
    Legislative Leadership Style 63
    Party Control 68
THE ASCENDANCY OF THE PRESIDENT AS LEGISLATOR 73
    Congressional Reassertion 76
THE TOOLS AND TACTICS OF PRESIDENTIAL
  PERSUASION 83
    Status Conferral 84
    Legislative Assistance 84
    Program, Projects, and Patronage 85
    The Veto Power 86
    Campaign Assistance 87
    Appeal to the Public 87
RECENT STRAINS IN THE RELATIONSHIP: POCKET VETO,
  IMPOUNDMENT, EXECUTIVE PRIVILEGE 89
    Pocket Veto 89
    Impoundment 90
    Executive Privilege 92
THE ULTIMATE CONFRONTATION: IMPEACHMENT 96
    The Impeachment Process 97
    Impeachable Offenses 98
    The Impeachment Instrument: An Evaluation 99
CARTER, CONGRESS, AND THE FUTURE 102

THE PRESIDENT AND THE BUREAUCRACY 108

THE POWER OF APPOINTMENT 108
    Kinds of Choices 108
    Number of Choices 109
    Federal Regulatory Agencies 110
    Political Appointees: The Problem of
      "Going Native" 113
REORGANIZATION 124
    On the Need to Reorganize 119
    The Difficulties in Reorganizing 120
CENTRAL CLEARANCE 123
    The End Run 125
OTHER LIMITATIONS ON PRESIDENTIAL CONTROL 127
    Size and Complexity 127
    Lack of Clarity in Presidential Intent 129
RICHARD NIXON AND THE BUREAUCRACY:
  AN ATTEMPT AT GREATER CONTROL 130
    A Change in Approach 132
    The Results 134
INCREASING PRESIDENTIAL CONTROL OVER
  THE BUREAUCRACY 135
    Appointments 135
    Reorganization 140
    Civil Service Reform 142
    Zero-Base Budgeting 144

5 PRESIDENT, PUBLIC, AND PRESS 146

PUBLIC ATTITUDES TOWARD THE OFFICE:
  PRE-WATERGATE 147
    Importance of the Office 147
    The Office as an Object of Trust and Respect 149
    Attitudes About the Power of the Presidency 152
THE PUBLIC'S ATTITUDES TOWARD THE MAN 156
    The Inevitable Decline in Support 156
THE INTERPLAY OF PUBLIC ATTITUDES TOWARD THE MAN
    AND THE OFFICE: THE CASE OF WATERGATE 166
PRESIDENTIAL EFFORTS TO INFLUENCE PUBLIC
    OPINION 168
    The Media as Facilitators of Presidential Influence 170
    The Media as Complicators of Presidential Influence 180
    The Future of the President's Relationship With the
        Press 190
CONCLUSION 192

6 DECISION MAKING IN THE WHITE HOUSE 194

THE PARTICIPANTS 194
THE CABINET 195
    Cabinet Member Influence 199
THE EXECUTIVE OFFICE OF THE PRESIDENT 200
    National Security Council 201
    Council of Economic Advisers 205
    Office of Management and Budget 206
    Domestic Policy Staff 207
    The White House Staff 209
THE WHITE HOUSE STAFF AND THE PROBLEM OF
    PRESIDENTIAL ISOLATION 213
    Staff Organization 213
    Staff Attitudes Toward the President 217
    The President's Attitude Toward Staff 219
OUTSIDE ADVISERS 223
PRESIDENTIAL DECISION MAKING 225
FOUR CASES OF PRESIDENTIAL DECISION MAKING 228
    The Bay of Pigs Invasion 228
    The Cuban Missile Crisis 234
    The Vietnam War 239
    Shoe Import Quotas 248
MAXIMIZING THE FLOW OF INFORMATION TO THE
    PRESIDENT 253

7 PERSONALITY AND THE PRESIDENCY 258

    Conditions Conducive to the Expression of Personality 258
    The Analysis of Presidential Personality 259
    Barber's Analysis 261
LYNDON JOHNSON AS AN ACTIVE-NEGATIVE 263
    Johnson's Youth 263
    Johnson Enters Politics 266
    World View and Style 267
    The Johnson Presidency 269
RICHARD NIXON AS AN ACTIVE-NEGATIVE 274
    Nixon's Youth 274
    Nixon Enters Politics 277
    World View and Style 279
    The Nixon Presidency 282
FRANKLIN ROOSEVELT AS AN ACTIVE-POSITIVE 288
    Roosevelt's Youth 288

Entry Into Politics, World View, and Style 289
The Roosevelt Presidency 291
GERALD FORD AS AN ACTIVE-POSITIVE 294
Ford's Youth 294
Entry Into Politics, World View, and Style 295
The Ford Presidency 296
JIMMY CARTER: AN ACTIVE-POSITIVE? 298
PERSONALITY QUALITIES SUITABLE TO THE
PRESIDENCY 301
PREDICTING PRESIDENTIAL PERSONALITIES 304

THE PRESIDENCY AND EMERGENCY POWERS 308

THE FOUNDERS, THE CONSTITUTION,
AND EMERGENCY POWERS 310
ON THE NECESSITY FOR EMERGENCY POWERS 312
ON THE NECESSITY FOR SAFEGUARDS 313
Essential Safeguards 313
Emergency Powers and the Courts 320
RECENT CONGRESSIONAL ACTION ON EMERGENCIES 327

PRESIDENTIAL LEADERSHIP 330

EVALUATING PRESIDENTIAL LEADERSHIP:
THE PROBLEMS 331
Achievement Is in the Eye of the Beholder 333
The Situational Problem 333
The Problem of Perspective 336
The Matter of Unanticipated Consequences 337
Achievement versus Agenda Setting 338
The Matter of Who Gets Credit 339
QUALITIES OF LEADERSHIP 340
Empathy with the Public 341
An Ability to Communicate 342
Credibility 345
A Sense of Timing 347
Courage 351
Decisiveness 353
Vision 355
Flexibility 357
A Sense for Power 360
CONCLUSION 363

APPENDIX:
THE CONSTITUTION AND THE PRESIDENCY 364

ARTICLE I/SECTION 3 364
ARTICLE I/SECTION 7 365
ARTICLE II/SECTION 1 365
ARTICLE II/SECTION 2 366
ARTICLE II/SECTION 3 366
ARTICLE II/SECTION 4 367
AMENDMENTS 367
Amendment XII (1804) 367
Amendment XX (1933) 367
Amendment XXII (1951) 368
Amendment XXV (1967) 368

INDEX 370

Preface

Writing a book has proven to be an even more formidable undertaking than I had anticipated. At various stages in this lengthy process several individuals provided valuable assistance. My thanks go first to Bryce Dodson and Stan Wakefield of Prentice-Hall for encouraging me initially to undertake this project.

I am also indebted to many of my colleagues in the Political Science Department at West Virginia University. At one time or another, I must have called upon nearly all of them for information and advice. In particular, I wish to thank Allan Hammock, Herman Mertins, and Tom Ingersoll, for they suffered innumerable intrusions upon their time so that I might seek their judgment on matters of content, organization, and style. I am also grateful to the past (David Temple) and current (O.B. Conaway, Jr.) chairmen of my department, both of whom were more than accommodating in providing me with a reduced teaching load so that I might complete this project.

Colleagues at other institutions read all or portions of this manuscript. I am particularly grateful to Eric Uslaner, Lawrence Dodd, Lester Seligman, and James Soles, whose criticisms and suggestions were right on target. I also owe a very special debt of gratitude to Charles S. Hyneman, for even though he had no direct involvement with this book, nevertheless he greatly influenced my thinking about the broader context in which the Presidency must function.

On numerous occasions I was required to seek the assistance of individuals working in the federal government. While it is frequently alleged that getting answers from the federal bureaucracy is like trying to get water out of a turnip, I had no such experience. On the contrary, phone calls made by me to various department and agency officials were invariably returned, and the information I requested was happily provided. Robert Cunningham of the Office of Management and Budget was a model in this regard.

Thanks must also go to members of the editorial staff at Prentice-Hall. Copy editor Shirley Stone not only had a keen eye for detail, but also a remarkable ability to bring clarity to some of my more chaotic paragraphs. I am especially grateful to Serena Hoffman, who oversaw the entire editorial process. I have no doubt but that her efficient, thorough, and professional approach to this task improved the quality of this manuscript immeasurably.

While writing a book is an exciting intellectual experience, there is also much drudgery involved. Thus, I would finally like to thank those individuals who lightened this burden considerably. Several of my work study students (James Cassell, Bryan Dugan, and Pat Neal) conscientiously undertook chores ranging from typing permission forms to proofreading, running down sources, and cataloguing information. I was also most fortunate in having the services of a competent and hardworking secretarial staff (Lauren Heidelbach, Gloria Ashcraft, Susan Steve, and Sharon Orchard). Although they frequently had to type from a manuscript replete with abbreviations, arrows, and inserts, they somehow managed to produce an accurate finished copy. And despite the occasions when they were given deadlines to meet on short notice, they alway met them—all without so much as a sign of impatience on their part.

Robert DiClerico
West Virginia University

Introduction

An examination of the Presidency is appropriate at any time, for it is the focal point and energizing force in our government. Over the course of the last decade, however, this institution has been the subject of considerable controversy, and for this reason has proven to be an even more intriguing topic for study. While presidential action on several fronts contributed to this controversy, it was nurtured primarily by the role of the Presidency in the Vietnam War and the Watergate scandals. These two dramatic events in our national life brought with them equally dramatic reassessments of the Presidency. It was Senator William Fulbright who asserted in 1961 that "the price of democratic survival in a world of aggressive totalitarianism is to give up some of the democratic luxuries of the past . . . through the conferral of greatly increased authority on the President."[1] Yet nine years later, this same senator was warning us that in the conduct of foreign policy the American political system had moved "far along the road to an executive despotism."[2] Similar reversals in position were also evident in the scholarly community. Thus, for example, one eminent historian complained in 1965 that Congress was involving itself in the affairs of the Executive branch to such an extent as to increase its own power, while diminishing that of the President.[3] Just eight years later, however, he wrote a book entitled *The Imperial Presidency* in which he warned that the powers and pre-

[1] Cited in Theodore Sorensen, *Watchmen in the Night* (Cambridge, Mass.: MIT Press, 1975), p. 71.

[2] Address to the American Society of Newspaper Editors, April 16, 1971.

[3] Arthur Schlesinger, Jr., *A Thousand Days* (Boston: Houghton Mifflin Company, 1965), pp. 707–8.

rogatives of the President had grown so extensive that our cherished principle of balanced government was being seriously threatened.

As the full import of the Watergate scandals became known in 1974, more and more people joined the ranks of those who were calling for the reining in of presidential power. In some instances, the proposals for doing so included such drastic changes as the creation of a plural executive and providing Congress with the power to terminate a President's tenure through a vote of "no confidence." Yet even as these reforms were being advocated by some, others were cautioning us against overreacting to such abuses. Such overreaction, they argued, might lead to restrictions that would deny the office its capacity for creative leadership. Speaking to this point, one adviser to two presidents noted that "The single largest difficulty with curbing executive authority is that the power to do great harm is also the power to do great good"; a fact not fully appreciated by those who would "carelessly reshape or curb an office that over the long haul has served us well."[4]

In the aftermath of Watergate and Vietnam, the presidential office does indeed appear less formidable than it was during the Johnson and Nixon years. While several factors may be said to have ushered in the era of the postimperial Presidency, to a considerable extent the change resulted from a Congress determined to reassert is own authority. In the judgement of some, this development is viewed as a necessary corrective if we are to restore the proper balance between the executive and legislative branches. Others, however, have already begun to view this turn of events with some alarm, for they fear that the imperial Presidency is being replaced with an increasingly imperial Congress.

The Office of the Presidency has a significant impact upon all our lives, and consequently the current debate over its proper place in the American political system deserves our close attention. One hopes that the knowledge and perspectives gained from this text will better equip the reader to evaluate this debate.

THE CONCERNS OF THIS BOOK

While this text will address itself to a variety of specific topics, there are six major areas of concern that underly it:

1. *Presidential selection.* Operating on the assumption that what a President is depends in part upon how we get him, it is imperative to assess the process by which we go about choosing our President. Specifically, we shall be concerned with who can contend for this high office as well as how adequately this selection process tests the candidates on those qualities necessary to execute the responsibilities of the Presidency.

[4] Sorensen, *Watchmen in the Night,* pp. 75, 82.

Given the importance of the office, the process used for selecting its occupant could not be ignored under any circumstances. Given the recent abuses of Watergate, however, an examination of this process is rendered all the more compelling.

2. *Presidential power.* Although the Presidency is alleged to be the most powerful office in our government, indeed perhaps in the world, rarely have presidents ever thought they had enough power. Upon succeeding to this office, they begin to see more clearly than ever that they are not operating in a vacuum but rather must compete with other power centers in our political system. We shall examine their relationship with these other power centers (Congress, court, bureaucracy, the public, the press), emphasizing those factors that enhance and constrain the exercise of presidential power over them.

3. *Presidential accountability.* Any examination of presidential power must be accompanied by still another consideration, namely, to what extent is the President held accountable for the exercise of that power? Surely one of the most widespread criticisms currently directed against this institution is the absence of adequate accountability. We shall examine the validity of this criticism along with the desirability and/or feasibility of proposals that have been put forth to correct this defect.

4. *Presidential decision making.* While it may be argued that Presidents are elected to perform a variety of functions for the political system, in a fundamental sense we elect them to make decisions. The issues coming over a President's desk will all be important ones, and what he chooses to decide or not decide can have important implications for the country and possibly the world. Consequently, we shall spend considerable time examining the nature of the decision-making process in the White House. Specifically, we shall be concerned with who participates and with how much impact. Knowing how decisions get made may help us understand some of the great successes and failures in presidential decision making.

5. *Presidential personality.* If the Office of the Presidency influences the man who occupies it, it is also equally clear that the personality of the man helps to shape the Office. Accordingly, here we shall first consider how the personalities of various presidents have influenced the tone and style of their presidencies; second, we shall consider whether certain personality types may be more suited to the demands of the Office than others. While an inquiry into this aspect of the Presidency would be appropriate at any time, the scandals of Watergate render it an even more compelling topic for consideration.

6. *Presidential leadership.* This consideration will of necessity inject itself into the discussion at various points throughout the book, but it will also be treated by itself in the final chapter, since it draws upon and integrates much of the subject matter that precedes it. We tend to view leadership as being synonymous with the Presidency, yet experience has shown us that some have led better than others and some have

scarcely led at all. In addressing this matter we shall consider the requirements for effective leadership, given the nature of our political institutions and given also the problems we currently face as a nation.

DIFFICULTIES IN STUDYING THE PRESIDENCY

One respected student of the Presidency has remarked that "the eminence of the institution . . . is matched only by the extraordinary neglect shown to it by political scientists. Compared to the hordes of researchers who regularly descend on Congress, local communities, and the most remote foreign principalities, there is an extraordinary dearth of students of the Presidency, although scholars ritually swear that the Presidency is where the action is before they go somewhere else to do their research."[5] More recently, another political scientist began his assessment of the literature on the Presidency by remarking that "it reflects the worst of all possible worlds: it is neither empirically rich nor revealing about how the Presidency affects who gets what, when, and how in the United States."[6] The state of affairs suggested by these two remarks is in no small way due to the fact that the Presidency is in many ways the most difficult of our three national institutions to investigate with some degree of empirical rigor.

The proceedings on the floor of the House of Representatives and the Senate are, with rare exception, open to the public. In addition, a daily record is published of the previous day's proceedings on the floor of each House. To be sure, most of the important work done by the Congress takes place in committees and not on the floor, but it is also the case that most of the committees in each House have opened many of their proceedings to the public. In those cases where proceedings are not open, the scholar still has a variety of potential sources he can tap, such as committee members and their staffs, all of whom are far more accessible than the President.

The Supreme Court presents a greater problem. It consists of only 9 members in contrast to the 535 in Congress; thus, the potential sources of information are severely limited. And not only will the justices not discuss cases currently before the Court or sensitive issues that might come before it, but they are rarely willing to discuss its inner workings while they are members of the Court. At the same time, however, the Court's proceedings are partially open to public scrutiny, at least to the extent that the public and the press may observe what goes on in the courtroom itself. While it is true that the actual decision-making process takes place in utmost secrecy, nevertheless, each decision of the Court is published in the form of one or more opinions, and these opinions are likely to

[5]Aaron Wildavsky, ed., *The Presidency* (Boston: Little, Brown, 1969), p. ix.

[6]John F. Manley, "The Presidency, Congress, and National Policy-Making," in Cornelius Cotter, ed., *Political Science Annual,* vol. 5 (Indianapolis: Bobbs-Merrill, 1974), p. 228.

give a fairly accurate reflection of the issues discussed and the positions taken by the judges during the decision-making stage.

Unlike the Congress and the Court, the White House opens no part of the decision-making process to the public. Nor is a record published of the daily proceedings in the White House. Beyond this, the central figure in the Presidency is not accessible to the scholar. The President may from time to time grant interviews to members of the press, but the newspaper reporter's concerns are not likely to be those of the scholar. And although presidential papers provide a valuable source of information, much of what we need to know about the Presidency cannot be gained from reading correspondence and written statements. Many presidents upon leaving office write their memoirs, but those also must be viewed with caution. With the Court or the Congress, praise or blame must be apportioned among the total membership, but the success or failure of any given Presidency will be largely determined by an assessment of one man, the President himself. Presidents are acutely aware of this fact. Thus, in attempting to seek a favorable judgment from history, their memoirs are likely to present their own stewardship in the most favorable light possible.

Other sources of information about the Presidency include the recollections of individuals who have served under a given President. These also have their drawbacks, however. Some are written by speechwriters who may have participated at only one particular stage in the decision-making process. Others have been written by close aids to the President. Their proximity to the central figure would seem to put them in the best position to evaluate the inner workings of the White House. But it is just this fact that must put us on our guard, for those closest to the President are often likely to be his most ardent admirers, in awe of both the man and the office he holds. Finally, the number of people close to the President is relatively small indeed, and even they may not all decide to write about their White House experiences. This means that when accounts about the man or events differ, the scholar has few alternative sources to turn to in order to resolve such contradictions.

All of this is not to say that the Presidency cannot be studied. Rather, I am simply trying to point out that it cannot be studied easily—that when we examine this institution we will often be looking at it through a keyhole rather than an open door.

1

The Selection Process

The importance people attach to how someone is selected for a particular position is fundamentally determined by the nature of the job's responsibilities. We are probably not overly concerned with how the local community selects the dog catcher because his responsibilities are not likely to have a very significant impact upon the community. On the other hand, we must pay very special attention to the procedure by which we go about selecting our President precisely because his responsibilities are so great. He is responsible to more than forty different countries with which the United States has treaties or friendships; he is responsible for the actions of 2.5 million federal employees and for the lives of 2.5 million servicemen.[1] Not only do his actions have consequences for the more than 200 million Americans, but in this nuclear age his actions can affect the lives of everyone on this planet.

Given the awesome responsibilities of this high office, several observers of the American political system contend that we do not take sufficient care in the selection of our presidents. The process has been described by one eminent scholar as "the most ramshackle, the flimsiest method ever used to select the supreme leader of a nation."[2] Another political scientist notes the consequences that may follow from this allegedly haphazard process:

> In our system, there is nothing to prevent a man who is absolutely incapable of being President from becoming President. He runs in the primaries; if he has money, if he has charisma, he can win the nomination,

[1] Theodore Sorensen, *Decision-Making in the White House* (New York: Columbia University Press, 1963), p. 11.

[2] Herman Finer, *The Presidency* (Chicago: University of Chicago Press, 1960), p. 23.

and move into the Presidency as an absolutely untried character. They usually come out of the legislature now, which means they have very little administrative experience as a rule. And there is no way you can assure that through this rather haphazard selection system you are always going to get men of competence and integrity.[3]

These two remarks address themselves to the selection process and the vital and direct impact it has upon the Presidency. The question is, does it provide us with qualified individuals? The remainder of this chapter will be devoted to this central issue.

WHO CONTENDS? WHO IS NOMINATED?

Simply because someone may decide that he wants to seek the Presidency, it does not necessarily follow that this candidacy will be taken seriously by party influentials, by the press, and by the public. There are a variety of factors operating in the selection process that serve to include and exclude individuals from serious consideration. To the extent that a candidate is included, his nomination is facilitated, though not guaranteed.

Legal Criteria

The pool of potential contenders is restricted at the very outset by three constitutional requirements. An individual must be at least thirty-five years of age, a requirement which obviously excludes millions from consideration. In addition, the President of the United States must be a natural-born citizen. This means, then, that no current American citizen who was born as a citizen of another country can hold the presidential office. As of 1970, there were 6,198,173 such individuals in our population. The precise meaning of this particular requirement became a minor issue with respect to the candidacies of Barry Goldwater in 1964 and George Romney in 1968. Goldwater was born in the Arizona Territory before it became a part of the United States, while George Romney was born to American parents in Mexico. Were they in fact natural-born American citizens? The issue still remains unresolved since the Court has never rendered a definitive judgment on this question. Finally, in order to be eligible for the Presidency, an individual must have resided in the United States for at least fourteen years.

The intent behind these constitutional provisions seems clear. Both the age and fourteen-year-residency requirements were designed to insure that presidents would be sufficiently knowledgeable and experienced. The average age

[3] James Sundquist, "What Happened to Our Checks and Balances?" in Charles Roberts, ed., *Has The President Too Much Power?* (New York: Harper's Magazine Press, 1974), p. 110.

of presidents has in fact been considerably beyond the thirty-five years. Excluding vice presidents who succeeded to the Presidency following a President's death, the average age of incoming presidents has been fifty-three.[4] The insistence on a natural-born citizen was intended to prevent the election of a president whose loyalties might be divided between the United States and the country of his birth. While all of these legal requirements make some sense, it may also be argued that they unduly restrict the number of presidential possibilities. Furthermore, some might contend that whether or not an individual is qualified is a judgment that should be determined by the voters and not predetermined by constitutional restrictions.

Informal Criteria

In addition to the constitutional requirements for holding the office of President, there also exist informal criteria that serve to include some and exclude others from serious contention. While they are not written down anywhere, they are nevertheless equally important.

Governmental Experience. Those individuals with some previous governmental experience in either an elected or appointive capacity appear to be viewed most favorably for presidential consideration. In examining the contenders in our two major political parties from 1868 to 1972, we discover that only four lacked any governmental experience whatsoever. More importantly, only four of the major party nominees during this period were without previous governmental experience.[5] It should not be surprising that both contenders and nominees have served in government, for not only is such experience considered by many to be a requisite for the Presidency, but also government positions are likely to provide their occupants with some degree of national recognition.

If the experience of public office adds to a candidate's prospects for being viewed as a serious contender, it is equally clear that some government positions provide a better route to the nomination than do others. As Table 1-1 indicates, from 1868 to 1956 the governorship provided the best springboard to the Presidency, followed by federal appointive office. Note that the House and the Senate provided relatively few nominees (four) during this period.

A very different picture emerges, however, when we examine the period from 1960 to 1972. Not only did most of the contenders come from the Senate, but so did 50 percent of the nominees. If one includes Lyndon Johnson, who succeeded to the Presidency upon the death of President Kennedy, then the

---

[4]Laurence Urlang, ed., *CBS News Almanac 1976* (Maplewood, N.J.: Hammond Almanac, 1975), p. 147.

[5]Robert Peabody and Eve Lubalin, "The Making of Presidential Candidates," in Charles Dunn, ed., *The Future of the American Presidency* (Morristown, N.J.: General Learning Press, 1975), p. 37.

TABLE 1-1. CAREER PATTERNS OF MAJOR PARTY PRESIDENTIAL NOMINEES, 1868-1956

Last Office Held Prior to Nomination	Percent of Nominees	Number of Nominees
Governor	40	12
Federal appointive office	20	6
None	13.4	4
House	6.7	2
Senate	6.7	2
Statewide elective office (exclusive of governorship)	3.3	1
Succession to presidency and renomination	10	3

SOURCE: Adapted from Robert Peabody and Eve Lubalin, "The Making of Presidential Candidates," in C. Dunn, ed., *The Future of the American Presidency* (Morristown, N.J.: General Learning Press, 1975), p. 33. Reprinted by permission of Silver Burdett Company.

other 50 percent of our nominees during this period came from the vice presidency.[6] It should also be noted, however, that Nixon, Johnson, and Humphrey all came to the vice presidency via the Senate. Of course this 1960–72 period covers too brief a time span to allow us to state confidently that the Senate rather than the governorship now appears to be the best springboard to the Presidency, but we can note several developments that suggest that such a trend is likely to continue.

In the past, governors exercised considerable influence over their state party organizations. Such influence often allowed them to control their state's delegation to the national nominating conventions. Thus governors from large states especially could take their presidential candidacies to the national convention with firm blocks of delegate votes behind them. The disintegration of party organization, along with convention reforms, has largely eroded this advantage. Another former advantage of governors was the analogy drawn between the Presidency and the governorship. Although on a much smaller scale, governors, like presidents, are chief executives. They must preside over a bureaucracy and contend with a legislature. With the increasing importance of foreign policy and national defense, however, senators have been judged more qualified than governors to deal with these matters. Nor do the advantages of senators end here. Senators have achieved a much greater degree of national visibility through television, which focuses its attention primarily on the national level. The bias of television in favor of senators is suggested by the frequency with which the networks' public-interest programs invite them to appear as guests. For example, from 1964 to 1974 senators appeared on "Meet the Press" and "Face the Nation" a total of 288 times, while governors appeared only 100 times. In 1973

[6]Ibid., p. 40.

alone, senators appeared on these two programs 26 times, but not one governor appeared.[7]

Since senators are elected to a six-year term, not only do they have a longer time to build a national reputation but they come up for reelection in presidential years only half the time, and thus they can run for the Presidency without having to surrender their Senate seats. On the other hand, governors have over the years been highly vulnerable to defeat in their reelection attempts, and consequently their relatively short tenure in office does not provide them with sufficient time to establish national reputations.[8] Furthermore, a governor who comes up for reelection in a presidential year is faced with having to surrender the office in order to seek the Presidency. Finally, senators can absent themselves more easily from their jobs than governors. The major work of the Senate occurs from Tuesday through Thursday, which provides them with a good long weekend that can be devoted to their presidential candidacies. And while one senator out of one hundred is not likely to be missed, a governor's frequent absences from his state would not go unnoticed.

At this point, the reader might perhaps be disturbed by the fact that our nominees have recently been drawn almost exclusively from the ranks of the Vice Presidency and the Senate. With respect to the Vice Presidency, individuals selected for this position are often picked not so much for their qualifications as for their ability to attract more votes to the ticket. Richard Nixon, for example, appears to have been picked as Eisenhower's running mate primarily because he was young, conservative, and from the state of California. Similarly, while Nixon's personal preference for a running mate in 1968 was his good friend Robert Finch, he ultimately gave the nod to a little-known governor from Maryland—Spiro Agnew. He did so in the belief that Agnew would be able to attract votes from the border states.

That the Vice Presidency has become an increasingly important springboard to the presidential nomination may also cause us some concern, in view of the haphazard procedure that frequently surrounds the selection of a vice presidential running mate. Since presidential contenders are concerned primarily with securing their own nomination, they rarely have time to engage in a systematic search for a running mate prior to the convention. Moreover, since the vice presidential nominee is usually picked on the day after the selection of the presidential nominee, the presidential nominee and his staff have very little time to screen potential running mates. In addition, both the nominee and his staff are likely to be thoroughly exhausted following the fight to secure the presidential nomination. The choice of Senator Eagleton as George McGovern's running mate may serve as a case in point. McGovern found himself in a tough fight with Hubert Humphrey for the presidential nomination in 1972. Thus, neither before nor at the convention was there any time for him to con-

---

[7] Arthur Hadley, *The Invisible Primary* (Englewood Cliffs, N.J.: Prentice-Hall, 1976), p. 179.

[8] Peabody and Lubalin, "Making of Presidential Candidates," p. 48.

sider the question of a running mate. Only after winning the nomination did McGovern get his staff together in the early morning hours and begin the task of finding someone for the number two spot. After a few hours of discussion, Eagleton was selected. Had McGovern and his staff had more time, they may well have discovered Eagleton's past emotional problems *before* rather than after he was offered the vice presidential place on the ticket. As it was, McGovern was put in the embarrassing position of dropping Eagleton and later replacing him with Sargent Shriver.

It is worth pointing out that Walter Mondale's selection as Jimmy Carter's running mate constitutes a notable exception to the haphazard approach usually taken in selecting vice presidential candidates. Carter's staff devoted well over a month to screening the backgrounds of prospective candidates, and Carter himself held lengthy talks with each of those who appeared on the final list of possibilities. Whether Carter's approach to the vice presidential selection process will be emulated by future presidential contenders remains uncertain, however. Carter, after all, had the nomination safely in hand before he even went to the convention, and thus both he and his staff had the time to make a careful search for a running mate. Unfortunately, however, those presidential contenders who find themselves in a close contest for the nomination will not have the luxury of being able to shop around for a running mate.

Perhaps we should also be concerned that our nominees have come increasingly from the Senate. While foreign policy is undoubtedly an area of great concern to a President, it could be argued that only those few senators on the Senate Foreign Relations Committee are likely to have any in-depth knowledge in this area. More important, one might assert that the major problems facing this country today make a governor's experience more desirable in the Presidency. All of the candidates in the 1976 election campaign made much of the issue of big government and its unmanageability. Coping with this problem calls for managerial talents on the part of our President. Governors would seem to be especially qualified in this regard since they must preside over their own state bureaucracies. The nation faces other major problems in the areas of race relations, energy, pollution, unemployment, fiscal responsibility, and transportation, and governors more than senators are likely to have had first-hand experience in dealing with the consequences of these problems.

Some would argue that we should not only include governors but must cast the net even more widely so that individuals in private as well as public life are considered for the Presidency: "In private life, the people who have the jobs most nearly comparable to the U.S. President's are those who head corporations, banks, universities, labor unions, and large civic or public service institutions."[9] Like presidents, they must be able to recruit and organize talent, mediate among conflicting constituencies, oversee a complex organization, and withstand enormous pressures. While there is considerable merit to this line of argument, it should also

---

[9] "New Places to Look for Presidents," *Time,* December 15, 1975, p. 19. Reprinted by permission from *Time,* The Weekly Newsmagazine; copyright Time Inc., 1975.

be noted that there are certain advantages to recruiting nominees from among those individuals who have held elective public office. Voters have an opportunity to evaluate how the candidate performed in a public capacity, a situation in which he is required to face the judgment of the people. Secondly, not only is the performance of an elected official to a considerable extent a matter of public record, but such a record is likely to be more easily evaluated by and relevant to the concerns of the voter than is the record of a university or corporation president. Finally, an individual who has taken his or her candidacy directly to the people, who has rubbed elbows with them and listened to their problems, may very well develop a feel for and sensitivity to public moods that cannot be so easily gained in a corporation board room.

Before we turn to other factors that serve to include some and exclude others from serious contention for the Presidency, one additional matter deserves mention here. Clearly the nomination of Jimmy Carter runs contrary to the major argument being made in this section, namely, that governorships no longer appear to be a very fruitful route to the presidential nomination. What factors, then, appear to have accounted for Carter's success? In the first place, his presidential bid was carefully conceived, with the initial planning having begun as early as 1972. Second, Carter managed to get himself placed in charge of the Democratic Party's 1974 campaign fund drive. In this position, he was able to establish contacts with state party leaders and with heads of important interest groups representing organized labor, farmers, consumers, and so on; he took full advantage of these contacts once he started campaigning. Third, although Carter did indeed serve one four-year term as Governor of Georgia, he did not hold this position at the time he was seeking the nomination; consequently, he was able to devote all of his time to campaigning. On the other hand, Carter's most formidable opponents—Congressman Morris Udall and Senator Henry Jackson—were campaigning for the presidential nomination while holding public office. Thus their time had to be divided between campaigning and meeting their responsibilities in Washington. Finally, and perhaps most important of all, Carter appears to have benefited greatly from the "anti-Washington" sentiment that pervaded the country in the aftermath of Watergate. While the lack of any direct connection with Washington would normally have been a disadvantage, the politics of 1976 were such that Carter's "outsider" image worked in his favor. Should this anti-Washington sentiment prove to be more than a passing public mood, then the governorship could prove to be a viable avenue to the Presidency in the future.

Money. It is often asserted that if you do not have a lot of money, then you cannot run for the Presidency. While there is considerable truth to this remark, it oversimplifies a rather complex issue.

Unlike governmental experience, the importance of money does not derive from the fact that it is considered a necessary quality for presidents to have in order to more effectively execute their responsibilities. Rather, the increasing importance of money is a consequence of certain developments in our political system. Although the increase in population, party competition, and inflation have all contributed to rising campaign expenditures, it is campaign technology itself that has been primarily responsible. With the advent of television, polling, computer mailings, and political consultants, the costs of seeking the Presidency have skyrocketed. In 1968, Richard Nixon spent over $12 million dollars in his campaign for the presidential nomination, and Hubert Humphrey spent over $4 million, a figure that would have been much higher had he not been a sitting Vice President.[10] McGovern's successful bid for the nomination in 1972 cost him $11 million.[11] The following specific expenditures graphically illustrate the high cost involved in the new campaign technology. On polling alone, Nixon and Humphrey spent $384,102 and $261,521 respectively in their 1968 election campaigns.[12] In the election campaigns of 1968 and 1972, money allocated to radio and television constituted the single largest expenditure: 1968—Nixon, $12.6 million, Humphrey, $6.1 million; 1972—Nixon, $4.3 million; McGovern, $6.2 million. And between August 1973 and September 1974, the Wallace campaign paid $800,000 to a company specializing in direct mailings.[13]

While it is true that several men of considerable personal wealth have run for the Presidency in recent times (e.g., Stevenson, Stassen, Kennedy, Symington, Rockefeller, Scranton, Romney, Shapp, Bentsen), such men have been the exception rather than the rule. Nor is it likely that these individuals were viewed as serious contenders merely because of their great personal wealth. All of them occupied positions of visible success in our society, and it is this fact rather than their money that put them in contention. Of course, the wealth, and in some cases the social backgrounds, of many of these candidates may have played an important part in helping them to attain these positions of visible success.[14]

If great personal wealth is not a requisite for seeking the Presidency, *access* to big money is a necessity for most candidates. Even this statement must be qualified, however, for there have been several dramatic examples of strong nomination campaigns waged largely from small contributions. In his bid for the Republican nomination in 1964, Barry Goldwater was able to raise $5.5 million from 300,000 contributors.[15] In 1968, Eugene McCarthy was able to raise $11 million in his attempt to challenge Lyndon Johnson for the presidential nomination of the Democratic party. While some of this money came from a few large

[10]Herbert Alexander, *Money in Politics* (Washington, D.C.: Public Affairs Press, 1972), pp. 60, 66.

[11]David Adamany and George Agree, *Political Money* (Baltimore: Johns Hopkins University Press, 1975), p. 19.

[12]Alexander, *Money in Politics,* p. 90.

[13]*Dollar Politics,* vol. 2 (Washington, D.C.: Congressional Quarterly, 1974), pp. 52, 61.

[14]Kenneth Prewitt and Alan Stone, *The Ruling Elites* (New York: Harper & Row, 1973), pp. 131–58.

[15]Alexander, *Money in Politics,* p. 31.

donations, the bulk of it came from 150,000 small contributions.[16] Between February and October of 1968, George Wallace reported raising $6.7 million, and 85 percent of this total came from contributions of $100 or less.[17] It is important to note, however, that each of these candidates represented highly committed constituencies on the left or right of the political spectrum. More moderate candidates appeal to more moderate voters, who are likely to be lacking the strong commitment that would motivate them to give.

Those with great personal wealth or with access to big money enjoy certain advantages in the selection process. These advantages are likely to be greatest at the nominating stage, for at this point the candidates cannot receive financial assistance from their parties but must instead rely on their own sources. Consider the candidate who is unknown nationally and who does not enjoy great personal wealth or access to such wealth. He may experience considerable difficulty in meeting the "start-up" costs of a campaign and consequently may be forced to withdraw before there has even been an opportunity to get his campaign off the ground. On the other hand, the unknown candidate with access to his own or other people's wealth is in a position to meet those important start-up costs. As the nominating contest progresses, a candidate's campaign may falter, perhaps as a consequence of a defeat in one or more of the primaries. When that happens, contributions are harder to come by. At such times, however, the personally wealthy candidate may still be able to maintain an active candidacy through the use of his own money, while the individual who lacks wealth may be forced to withdraw. It should also be noted that the very nature of money itself provides certain advantages because, unlike other political resources, money is convertible. It can be used to buy other political resources, such as manpower and television time. Finally, the role of money in the selection process is cause for concern not only because of the advantage it gives, but also because of the consequences that may follow from its use. Individuals who must rely upon their access to big money in order to make a run for the Presidency may, upon being elected, feel special obligations to those who heavily financed their candidacy. The revelations concerning Richard Nixon's 1972 reelection campaign provide ample confirmation of this fear.

If money provides some candidates with an initial advantage at the starting gate and at certain points around the track, it is far less clear that having it is sufficient to insure nomination. Were that the case, we would expect the candidacies of people like Rockefeller, Stassen, Symington, and Scranton to have met with greater success. More than money, such factors as a candidate's image, past record, and issue positions are far more critical in determining whether or not he will capture the nomination. If, like John Kennedy, he is judged favorably on these factors and also enjoys considerable personal wealth, then he is in a very advantageous position indeed. If he is lacking in personal wealth but is viewed

[16] Ibid., p. 72.

[17] Adamany and Agree, *Political Money*, p. 30.

favorably on these other factors I have mentioned, then his financial support is likely to be forthcoming. Finally, if he lacks a favorable image, an impressive record of accomplishment, and acceptable issue positions, then his money alone is not likely to save him.

Before concluding this section, it is necessary to note one fairly recent development in American electoral politics that should help to diminish the importance of money in presidential nominating politics. I refer to the Federal Election Campaign Act of 1974. Under the provisions of this act, an individual's annual contribution to a candidate for federal office is limited to $1,000 for each election. (Primaries, run-offs, and general elections are defined here as separate elections.) In addition, an individual's contributions to *all* federal candidates cannot exceed $25,000. While the act also originally provided that no person could spend more than $1,000 *on behalf of* a candidate, this provision was declared unconstitutional by the Supreme Court (*Buckley v. Valeo,* 1976) on the grounds that it constituted an infringement upon an individual's right of free speech. For the same reason, the Court also declared unconstitutional another provision of the act that would have prevented a presidential candidate from spending any more than $50,000 of his *own* money on his whole campaign (primaries and general election included). Accordingly, presidential candidates continue to be free to spend as much of their own money as they wish, as long as they finance their campaigns exclusively from *private* contributions.

Perhaps the most important provision of this act as it bears on the nominating process is that candidates may now receive partial funding of their nomination campaigns from the government. Specifically, the government will match the money raised by a candidate up to a limit of $5 million. In order to qualify for these matching funds, however, a candidate must first raise $5,000 in each of twenty states for a total of $100,000. Finally, candidates who opt to receive funds from the government can spend no more than $10,000,000 in their campaign for the nomination; on the other hand, candidates who choose to finance their campaigns without matching funds from the government can spend as much as they are able to raise. It should be clear that this act—especially given the Supreme Court's rulings on it—does not so much curb the influence of the wealthy as it assists the candidate who is not.

Ideology. Not only do prior governmental experience and money serve to include and exclude individuals from consideration for the nomination, but so too do the political beliefs of a candidate. The major goal of any political party is usually to nominate a candidate who can win in November, and such a candidate is likely to be someone whose political beliefs coincide with those of a majority of Americans. Most Americans do not locate themselves on the far left or the far right of the political spectrum, but rather situate themselves somewhere in the broad middle. Consequently, those candidates will be favored whose political beliefs place them in the middle also. This is not to say that the middle of the political spectrum will always remain in one spot. It may move to the left or to the right, depending upon changing moods in the population. Thus, for example, in 1968 Americans tended to move in a conservative direction. Richard Nixon detected this movement, moved with them, and that is precisely why he won.[18]

There have of course been some startling exceptions to the rule that moderates will be favored for the nomination, but these exceptions also point up the necessity—from the party's point of view—for following this rule. In 1964 the Republicans did nominate a candidate (Barry Goldwater) who was considerably to the right of center, and in 1972 the Democrats awarded their nomination to a candidate who was considerably left of center. While Goldwater maintained his position on the right throughout his campaign, McGovern moderated his position, but not enough to convince rank and file Democrats that he was not a radical. Both candidates not only lost but lost badly, with Goldwater carrying only six states and McGovern only one.

Background Factors. In the past, a variety of factors related to background also served to include and exclude individuals from serious consideration for the Presidency. These factors include one's race, sex, religion, and geographical location. Candidates were favored who were male, white, Anglo-Saxon, Protestant, and from a large northern state. Many of these factors seem to be receding in importance, however. In recent years, not only have contenders been of the Catholic, Jewish, and Mormon faiths, but we nominated and elected a Catholic in 1960, and nominated a candidate of Jewish background (Goldwater) in 1964. We have not yet nominated candidates who were either female or black; nor for that matter have there been any serious contenders who fall into these two categories. To the extent that race and sex still operate as important exclusionary factors in the nominating contest, we severely restrict the pool of potential contenders, for as of 1975 the U.S. Bureau of the Census estimated that there were 47,125,000 women and 8,120,000 blacks who were thirty-five years of age or older. However, there are some encouraging signs that even race and sex may be receding in their importance as exclusionary factors. While in 1958 only 38 percent of the population said they would be willing to vote for a qualified black man for President, in 1971, 70 percent of the American people expressed a willingness to do so.[19] If responses on such a sensitive issue can be believed, they certainly suggest progress, though not enough. Women in our society also have experienced a marked improvement in their status and that has carried over into the political arena as well. As of 1977, 11,318 women were holding elective public office.[20]

Finally, the importance of coming from a large state is also likely to decline.

[18]Richard Scammon and Ben Wattenberg, *The Real Majority* (New York: Coward, McCann & Geoghegan, Inc., 1970) pp. 72–81, 209.

[19]George Gallup, *The Gallup Poll: Public Opinion, 1935-1971*, vols. 2 & 3 (New York: Random House, 1972), pp. 1575, 2327.

[20]Figures provided by Center for the American Woman and Politics, Rutgers University.

As mentioned earlier, the governorship was in the past the primary recruiting ground for the Presidency. Governors from large states were especially favored, not only because their states had a large number of electoral votes, but also because they had achieved a higher visibility. The recruiting pool has now shifted to the Senate, however, where a state's size has very little bearing on the ability of its senator to attain public visibility.

The Future: More Contenders

It is no mere coincidence that an unusually large number of individuals declared themselves candidates for the Presidency in 1976. Included among the ranks of Democratic Party contenders were: six senators, three governors, two former governors, one congressman, one former federal appointee. On the Republican side, a sitting president was seriously challenged by a former governor.

Several developments would suggest that this proliferation of candidates is likely to continue. Certainly one of the most important is the Federal Election Campaign Act of 1974. As stated earlier, this act eases the financial burden of contenders since they may now gain partial funding of their campaigns from the government. Such assistance is not only likely to increase the number of contenders in the out party but also could render incumbent presidents somewhat more vulnerable to challenge than they have been in the past.

The increase in the number of primaries may also have an impact. While there were only eighteen primaries in 1960, there were thirty in 1976, and almost 70 percent of the delegates to the Democratic National Convention were selected from these thirty primaries. Since the primaries allow an individual to take his or her candidacy directly to the people, the power of the party bosses is reduced considerably. Consequently, the increased number of primaries may serve to encourage more insurgent candidates.

For the 1976 nominating process the Democrats also introduced important procedural changes in the selection of delegates to their national convention, which may also have contributed to the increase in the number of contenders. For example, they eliminated the winner-take-all primary.[21] Formerly, in a state such as California which used this form of primary, the candidate who received the most popular votes also received all of the votes cast by the California delegation at the Democratic National Convention. In 1972 California's delegates totalled 271, a sizeable number indeed. Given the primary's winner-take-all character, candidates were reluctant to expend the vast amount of energy and money required in a state of this size unless they felt they had some chance of winning. In 1976, however, California's primary was run as a proportional primary. Thus, the number of California delegate votes cast for a candidate at the convention was proportional to the percentage of the popular vote

---

[21] There was one exception to this; namely, states were permitted to select their delegates on a winner-take-all basis if they chose them at the district level rather than statewide.

he or she received in the state. This rule of proportionality was also applied to the caucus-convention procedure, which is used by some states for selecting some or all of their delegates. However, in order to qualify for proportional representation—be it under the primary or the convention-caucus system—a candidate had to attain a minimum base of support which was set at 15 percent.

Having pointed out that public financing, the increasing number of primaries, and the Democratic rule of proportionality all serve to encourage a greater number of contenders, we should also note that, as of this writing, the Democratic National Committee is considering a new set of proposals for 1980 which, if implemented, could have precisely the opposite effect. Specifically, in 1978 the party's Commission on Presidential Nomination and Party Structure recommended first of all that the delegate selection process be reduced from twenty-one to thirteen weeks. Such a change, it is argued, would both cut down on voter boredom and reduce wear and tear on the candidates. Whether or not voters are bored by the current length of the primary season is open to question. However, it hardly seems likely that confining the primaries and caucus-convention process to thirteen weeks will prove to be any less grueling for the candidates. Moreover, shortening the delegate selection process will put the less known candidates at a considerable disadvantage since they will now have less time to establish national visibility. The Commission is also proposing that this thirteen-week period be divided into trimesters. For primaries held in the first trimester, a candidate would have to get at least 15 percent of the vote in a state's primary in order to get a proportional share of that state's delegates. This same base of support would be necessary to gain delegates selected under the convention-caucus system during this first trimester. In the second trimester, the miminum threshold would be raised to 20 percent, and in the third trimester, to 25 percent. The purpose of this sliding threshold is to avoid having the delegates divided among so many candidates that no one would arrive at the convention with a majority, or close to it. On the other hand, it may also be argued that the threshold requirements might serve to arbitrarily eliminate some contenders prematurely. In addition, with the threshold set at 25 percent in the third trimester—which incidentally is when nearly 60 percent of the delegates would be chosen—it would be extremely difficult for a latecomer to enter the race. Finally, it is worth noting that both of the proposals mentioned here would favor an incumbent President. Consequently, it should come as no surprise that the primary impetus for them has come from the Carter White House. Whether the Democratic National Committee decides to adopt them remains to be seen.

TESTING THE CANDIDATES

Thus far our discussion has been concerned with identifying those factors that include and exclude individuals from serious consideration for the Presidency. We now turn our attention to another matter, namely, to what extent do the nominating and campaign stages of this process test candidates on the essential qualities we are looking for in a President? To the extent that they do not, we are less well equipped to estimate a candidate's potential performance in the Presidency. Even if they do, however, we are no better off unless we are watching to see how candidates meet these tests.

One is not likely to find universal agreement on what qualities are desirable in a President, nor on the importance that should be attached to each one. I think it is fair to say, however, that most would probably regard the following as essential: *intelligence, knowledge of the issues, judgment, executive ability, honesty, physical stamina,* and *mental stability.*

The very length of the selection process alone would seem to lend itself to a vigorous testing of the candidates. Indeed, in no other Western democracy does the process extend over such a long period of time. In 1976, for example, the nominating process got under way with the Iowa caucus on January 19 and continued through to the nominating conventions, which for the Democrats was July 12 and for the Republicans, August 16. Thus, voters had approximately six months to observe the contenders and during this time the coverage of their activities was relatively intense. There was an even longer opportunity to observe some of the contenders, for some of them made their intentions informally known as early as a year prior to the start of the primaries. Add to this the fact that voters had the chance to scrutinize some of the contenders in previous election years as well. In the last thirty-six years, 60 percent of the Republicans and one third of the Democrats mentioned in the polls as presidential possibilities had also been considered presidential possibilities in one or more previous nominating contests.[22] As for the nominees themselves, the public had the opportunity to assess their candidacies on an intensive basis from the start of the nominating process in January up to the day of the election in early November—more than nine months. Of course, the length of the selection process becomes significant only to the extent that candidates are truly being tested during this long period of time. We now turn to this matter.

Intelligence

Heavy demands are placed upon the intellect of the person who occupies the White House. One former presidential advisor has noted that a President must be "at home with a staggering range of information."[23] That is strain enough. The burden is made all the heavier by the fact that much of this information is necessarily of a highly complex nature, dealing with the intricacies of such matters as economics and defense. Finally, while the President cannot be expected to provide instant solutions to all the problems the nation faces, his mind must nevertheless have the analytical power to recognize what questions need to be

[22] Donald Matthews, "Presidential Nomination: Process and Outcomes," in James Barber, ed., *Choosing The President* (Englewood Cliffs, N.J.: Prentice-Hall, 1974), p. 40.
[23] Sorensen, *Decision-Making,* p. 38.

asked if we are to move toward those solutions. In short, a President must be an individual of considerable intelligence.

Although there is no guarantee, it seems unlikely that individuals of merely average intellect will be successful in capturing the Presidency. As noted earlier, presidential aspirants most frequently have held a high public office prior to their decision to seek the Presidency. When serving in such a capacity, they are required to come to grips with a vast array of complex public issues; they are required to think on their feet in public, matching their wits against opponents, an inquiring press, and interested publics. Their performance is watched by fellow politicians, as well as other political observers, and those lacking the necessary quickness of mind are not likely to be mentioned as presidential timber by either group. In his quest for the Presidency, the presidential aspirant faces many similar tests, which are more intense, more constant; at such time, even closer scrutiny is given to how he measures up.

Knowledge of the Issues

We also seek a President who is well informed. Although a keen intelligence may facilitate the accumulation of knowledge, there is no guarantee that the bright will also be knowledgeable. Specifically, we are looking for individuals who have a grasp of the pressing problems confronting the nation and also have an informed understanding of what options are available for dealing with them. The nature of our selection process allows it to do a reasonably good job of testing the candidates on this criterion.

Throughout the nomination and election campaigns, candidates are probed day after day on a variety of foreign and domestic issues. On the domestic side, they must be cognizant of local as well as national issues. In 1968, for example, candidates campaigning in the Wisconsin primary discovered that voters were concerned with hearing their views on the property tax, while in the Florida primary they found people preoccupied with busing. A candidate's position on the issues are dissected by the press, public officials, opponents, and interested voters. Inconsistencies, unfounded assumptions, or the absence of any position at all are likely to be detected and exposed. Thus, in 1968 it became apparent that George Romney's knowledge of foreign affairs was rather limited, and this weakness received considerable attention in the news media. Pressed continually for his position on the Vietnam War, it became apparent that he did not have one, and that proved to be a major handicap in his unsuccessful bid for the Republican nomination. George McGovern has acknowledged that one of his costly mistakes in the 1972 election was the "inadequate preparation" he gave to his proposal for a $1,000 guaranteed annual income.[24] The weaknesses of this plan did not go unnoticed by the press and his opponents. In 1976, Ronald Reagan found the voters, press, and opponents questioning whether or not he

---

[24] Cited in *New York Times,* October 26, 1975, p. 41. ©1975 by The New York Times Company. Reprinted by permission.

fully appreciated the implications of his plan to cut $90 billion from the federal budget.

At this point, what I have said thus far must be qualified in one important respect. While I have tried to argue that the selection process can serve as a test of how informed the candidates are, it should be noted that such testing can be frustrated to *some* extent by the candidate himself. For example, from early 1967 until shortly before the election, Richard Nixon did not permit himself to be interviewed on such public interest television programs as "Meet the Press" and "Face the Nation." Rather, he confined his television appearances to those forums that he could directly control. While the format of some of these programs permitted questioning of Nixon by a panel, the members of the panels were selected by the Nixon staff. On another occasion, Nixon bought time for a telethon, and listeners were invited to phone in their questions. Here again, the questions were screened, and even rephrased, by his staff before being passed on to candidate Nixon for his response.[25] Most presidential candidates, however, will gleefully accept the opportunity to appear on almost any television program because it provides them with free television exposure. The luxury of being able to refuse such exposure lies only with the candidate who has enough money to pay for his own.

Judgment

That we seek judgment in a President seems obvious enough. Given the enormous consequences of his action, we must have a person in the White House who knows what words and actions are appropriate to any given set of circumstances.

In the assessment of judgment, a candidate's issue positions become a relevant consideration. For example, many began to question the judgment of Barry Goldwater in 1964 when he suggested that the decision to use tactical nuclear weapons in wartime be left with the NATO field commanders.[26] Similarly, George McGovern's judgment came into question when he proposed a $32 billion cut in the defense budget, stated that he would go to Hanoi and beg for the return of American prisoners, and equated Richard Nixon with Adolf Hitler.[27]

In addition to the anticipated issues that present themselves in a campaign, we may also get some indication of a candidate's judgment by his reaction to unanticipated issues. There is no guarantee that such issues will materialize, but the length of the selection process certainly increases the prospects. In 1952, for example, Eisenhower suddenly found himself confronted with the accusation that his vice-presidential running mate harbored a secret "slush fund" while

[25] Joe McGinniss, *The Selling of the President, 1968* (New York: Pocket Books, Division of Simon & Schuster, Inc., 1970), pp. 137, 153, 154.

[26] Theodore White, *The Making of the President, 1964* (New York: Atheneum, 1965), p. 23, pp. 295–300.

[27] Theodore White, *The Making of the President, 1972* (New York: Atheneum, 1973), pp. 117, 127, 217; Nelson Polsby and Aaron Wildavsky, *Presidential Elections,* 4th ed. (New York: Scribner's, 1976), p. 174.

serving as a United States senator. The money in this fund was given to Senator Richard Nixon by a California businessman and was to be used by Nixon to pay for political expenses.[28] During the presidential nominating campaign of 1960, the contenders were also required to address themselves to a major but unexpected event, namely, the shooting down of an American U-2 pilot over the Soviet Union. Later on in the 1960 campaign, the nominees of both parties were confronted with yet another unforeseen event when Martin Luther King was jailed while participating in a civil rights march. More recently, George McGovern was taken by surprise when he discovered that the man he picked as his running mate had a previous record of mental illness. In each of these cases, the voters had an opportunity to assess a candidate's reactions to unforeseeable situations.

A President must be able to judge people as well as events. He cannot preside over the government of our nation by himself and thus must bring with him people of integrity, intellect, and knowledge who can assist him in this task. In order to find individuals with such qualities, however, he must first be able to recognize them as such. We can get some indication of his ability to judge people by observing the company he keeps during the selection process. I refer specifically to his campaign staff, most of whom will accompany him to Washington if he is elected. Unfortunately, the degree to which a candidate measures up on this test of judgment will be discernible only to those who are intimately involved in the campaign. Thus one chronicler of American election politics, who has followed Richard Nixon's career for twenty years, notes that he constantly heard him criticized for the quality of the people he surrounded himself with.[29] Yet in the 1968 election, it is highly doubtful that a vast majority of Americans were familiar with the names, let alone the characters, of H. R. Haldeman and John Ehrlichman, even though they both occupied important positions on Nixon's campaign staff. That is not altogether surprising, for campaign aids do not occupy positions of high visibility during the campaign, and consequently they are not deemed newsworthy. While the abuses of Watergate highlighted the importance of the men around presidential candidates, it was not apparent that campaign aids received more careful scrutiny by the press during the 1976 selection process.

Executive Ability

Presidents must preside over an ever-burgeoning bureaucracy and White House staff. As noted earlier, it is an impossible undertaking for one man alone. Consequently, he must recognize and attract talent that can assist him in this task. Furthermore, he must organize it and delegate to it. And as the man at the top, he must also be able to act decisively on those matters that cannot be delegated. To do all of this successfully requires executive ability.

[28] Theodore White, *Breach of Faith* (New York: Atheneum, 1975), p. 68.
[29] Ibid., p. 68.

This quality is tested to some degree in the selection process. A contender must set up a campaign organization in most of the fifty states, and the nominees do so in every state. While the candidates themselves are not likely to be directly involved in this chore, they must nevertheless put together a campaign staff that will be. In organizing this staff, the candidate must delegate tasks and establish a hierarchy of command. The Kennedy campaign of 1960 was a model of efficiency and organization in this regard.[30] By contrast, in 1972 the McGovern campaign organization gradually deteriorated into "disorganization and staff squabbling," with the candidate apparently unable to exert the necessary leadership to eliminate it.[31] His failure to do so took a heavy toll among those associated with his campaign:

At his Washington headquarters, by the second half of October, when the upturn had failed to come, a condition had set in which I had never known before; it was not the condition of bleak despair, or the black-humor surliness of the Goldwater headquarters in 1964; it was a condition that passed disloyalty. Men and women I had known for over a year as disciples now despised their own candidate. They were not disaffected with the cause, but contemptuous of the man; betrayed not by his beliefs, which they still shared, but by the absence of that hard quality of leadership which they sought.[32]

Nor, according to the candidate himself, was the dissaffection limited to staff workers alone. It also spread to the voters themselves, who rejected what "they perceived to be confusion and uncertainty of leadership."[33]

Honesty

We need not belabor the necessity for honesty in the Presidency. The many abuses that have come to be associated under the rubric of Watergate clearly demonstrate the high price we pay when it is lacking.

In several respects, the very nature of the electoral process serves to discourage complete candor. All candidates wish to win, and in an effort to do so, they will accentuate the positive. At the same time, however, if a candidate himself chooses to ignore those factors from the past that could adversely affect his candidacy, it is certain that every effort will be made by his opponents and the press to see that they are revealed. And given the crisis of integrity in our government spawned by Watergate, we can expect the press to be especially attentive to a candidate's past record in both his public and his private life.

Political expediency may also encourage less than total candor on some of

[30] White, *Making of the President, 1960,* pp. 63–73, 174–206.

[31] *New York Times,* October 26, 1975, p. 41.

[32] White, *Making of the President, 1972,* p. 338.

[33] Cited in *New York Times,* October 26, 1975, p. 41.

the issues in the campaign. There is a tendency for candidates to develop a calculated ambiguity, especially on those issues that divide the population. If the candidate is sufficiently vague, he not only reduces the risk of alienating any significant portion of the electorate but also avoids providing his opponents with issue positions specific enough to attack. Of course, if pushed too far, such a strategy will leave him open to the charge that he is indecisive or else not sufficiently informed to develop a clear position. Also, it is doubtful that he can sustain such a strategy of equivocation throughout our lengthy selection process. Finally, with voters attaching increased importance to issues, they are likely to be less tolerant of such ambiguity in the future.[34]

The operations of the selection process hardly provide us with foolproof tests for ascertaining honesty. To be sure, overt acts of dishonesty are more likely to be detected. With members of the press following a candidate as he travels about the country, he cannot easily get away with presenting one image to one part of the population and a completely different image to another part. But even overtly dishonest acts may occasionally go undetected. In his 1960 campaign for the Presidency, John Kennedy told the voters that the United States had fallen dangerously behind the Soviet Union in missile procurement, even though he knew that was not so.[35] The population was not in a position to assess the validity of this charge, and for reasons of national security, the Eisenhower administration could not release figures to refute it. It is in the nature of campaign oratory to exaggerate realities, but Kennedy was alleging a reality that did not exist at all.

Covert acts of dishonesty are by their very nature more difficult to detect. While they may ultimately be uncovered, they may not be discovered at the time we need to know about them. The illegal contributions to Nixon's reelection campaign and the "dirty tricks" employed by his campaign staff against other candidates testify to this fact.

Physical Stamina

Unfortunately for a President, the problems and crises he faces do not conveniently adjust themselves to a nine-to-five day, five-day week. He is President twenty-four hours a day, seven days a week. Even in the absence of crises, his daily schedule will be filled with meetings and speeches, to say nothing of

[34] See, for example, Arthur Miller et al., "A Majority Party in Disarray: Policy Polarization in the 1972 Election" (Paper delivered at the 1973 Annual Meeting of the American Political Science Association, New Orleans), p. 69; Norman Nie, "Mass Belief Systems Revisited: Political Change and Attitude Structure, *Journal of Politics* 36 (August 1974), 540–91; Gerald Pomper, "From Confusion to Clarity: Issues and American Voters, 1956–1968," *American Political Science Review* 66 (June 1972), 415–28.

[35] Taken from Lewis Paper, *The Promise and the Performance* (New York: Crown, 1975), pp. 136, 137. © 1975 by Lewis J. Paper. Used by permission of Crown Publishers, Inc.

frequent trips around the country and abroad. Thus, physical stamina is essential. There can be little doubt that the selection process severely tests the candidates on this quality. From early morning until late at night, their schedules consist of meetings, speeches, interviews, handshaking, and constant travel about the country, moving from one primary to the next. Senator Muskie has described his schedule for just one week during his 1972 bid for the presidential nomination: "The previous week I'd been down to Florida, then I flew to Idaho, then I flew to California, then I flew back to Washington to vote in the Senate, and I flew back to California, and then I flew into Manchester [New Hampshire] . . . ."[36] For those candidates who manage to secure the nomination of their party, this frenzied activity continues up to the day of the election. It is small wonder that candidates have described the route to the Presidency as "crushing," a "torture trail," a process where the nomination goes to "the last survivor."[37]

Mental Stability

The strain on a President is mental every bit as much as it is physical. He is burdened with the realization that his actions could conceivably involve the United States, and indeed the world, in a nuclear holocaust. He must cope with living what is almost a totally public existence, where his every word and action will be watched and analyzed. He must be prepared to endure severe public attack on his person, family, and policies. Consequently, presidents need the emotional stamina to sustain such constant pressures. To be sure, presidential candidates are not subject to all the pressures of a President, but the pressures are there nevertheless. They must live constantly with the sad fact that months of grueling work may result in defeat, not victory. Like presidents, they must cope with close public scrutiny of their every utterance, realizing that a wrong word or a certain inflection of the voice may prove damaging to their candidacies. Finally, they are required to bear up under attacks directed toward their families, their character, and their policies.

Some candidates have found the strain too great. George Romney, for example, proved quick to anger whenever his good faith was called into question.[38] Similarly, the pressures of the selection process took their toll on Senator Muskie in 1972. Appearing in New Hampshire outside the building of a newspaper whose editorials had severely criticized his wife, he characterized the newspaper's owner as a "liar" and a "gutless coward." In the process of doing so, he ultimately broke down and cried. While the impact of this event is not known, it is clear that Muskie felt he had damaged himself greatly: "It changed people's minds

[36]White, *Making of the President, 1972*, p. 81.

[37]*Newsweek*, January 12, 1976, pp. 27, 28.

[38]White, *Making of the President, 1968*, p. 40.

about me, of what kind of guy I was. . . . They were looking for a strong, steady man, and here I was weak."[39]

At least in the context of the Presidency, mental stability must mean something more than the ability to control one's emotions. Individuals may outwardly be able to subdue their anger and frustration yet still be psychologically unfit for the office. It has been argued, for example, that we must be wary of those who have a low sense of self-esteem, for they may try to compensate for it by seeking the power of the Presidency.[40] Such individuals may view criticism as an attack upon their self-esteem and thus attempt to deal with their adversaries through the ruthless exercise of presidential power. Furthermore, they may become rigid in their behavior, refusing to abandon ill-conceived policies because to do so would further damage their self-esteem.[41] We must also be on our guard against those individuals who view the world around them with hostility and suspicion.[42] They are likely to isolate themselves from this "hostile" environment, thus restricting the public's ability to find out about their President as well as inhibiting his ability to learn about them. As we shall see later in this book, Richard Nixon exhibited both of these dispositions, and his administration reflected the negative consequences that may follow from them.

Unfortunately, a candidate's performance during the course of the selection process may not necessarily provide a good reading of his personality. According to one authority in this area, the full repertoire of an individual's personality is likely to come into play after attaining the Presidency rather than prior to it. In his quest for the office, he is likely to conform "more closely to the expectations of those around him."[43] Thus, he argues that the best clues to his psychological make-up are to be found by studying his childhood. At this point, however, we are confronted with several formidable difficulties. How confident can we be of inferences made about a candidate's personality based upon his childhood experiences? How confident can we be that everyone would draw the same conclusions from the evidence? What group is to be entrusted with pursuing this task? Surely such an undertaking could be subject to great abuse. In 1964, for example, *FACT* magazine published an article that asserted that Barry Goldwater was psychologically unfit to be President. This finding was based upon questionnaire responses from 2,417 psychiatrists. The article was repudiated not only by the American Medical Association but also by the American Psychiatric Association, which characterized it as "a hodge-podge of personal political opinion rather than professional diagnosis."[44] Finally, even if

[39] White, *Making of the President, 1972*, p. 82.

[40] James Barber, *The Presidential Character: Predicting Performance in the White House*, 2nd ed. (Englewood Cliffs, N.J.: Prentice-Hall, 1977), pp. 141, 142.

[41] Ibid., p. 347.

[42] Erwin Hargrove, "What Manner of Man?" in *Choosing the President*, p. 19.

[43] Barber, *Presidential Character*, p. 99.

[44] Alexander George, "Assessing Presidential Character," in Aaron Wildavsky, ed., *Perspectives on the Presidency* (Boston: Little, Brown, 1975), p. 93.

these problems could be overcome, it is questionable whether the findings could be presented to the population in a manner that would be comprehensible.

Testing the Candidates: the Merchandising Phenomenon

In my discussion thus far I have tried to argue that the selection process tests certain essential presidential qualities rather well and others only imperfectly. It matters little, however, that the selection process tests candidates on these qualities unless the population is also using such qualities as standards for judgment in assessing the candidates. In an era of mass media, it is argued that candidates are being sold to the public like soap. We are encouraged to form our judgments based upon images that have been carefully contrived by public relations experts and then marketed on television. Such tactics smack of manipulation, and that is precisely what they are. But that is nothing new in American politics, for all campaigns throughout our history have, to a greater or lesser degree, tried to manipulate the voter. What is new, however, is the principle instrument by which such manipulation is being attempted, namely, television. Being a visual medium, it accentuates appearance rather than substance and invites the voter to do likewise in forming judgments:

> This development can only have the worst possible effect in degrading the level and character of our political discourse. If it continues, the result will be the vulgarization of issues, the exaltation of the immediately ingratiating personality and, in general, an orgy of electronic demagoguery. You cannot merchandise candidates like soap and hope to preserve a rational democracy.[45]

While the merchandising of candidates is not a heartening development in the selection process, we should not attribute greater significance to its impact than it deserves. In the first place, those who seek to create an image for a candidate must be able to control the voters' information about him. However, those candidates who are initially unknown to the voters are not likely to have the financial resources to gain national exposure through a controlled nationwide political advertising campaign. Consequently, they must try to secure this exposure any way they can get it, such as on television news and interview programs, none of which can be easily controlled by the image makers. To be sure, the candidate who is already nationally known is in a better position to let his political advertisers sell his image when and where they choose. At the same time, however, the well-known candidate already has an image, and it cannot be significantly altered through political advertising. Nixon's presidential candidacy in 1968 is a case in point. By presenting him on television in carefully controlled

---

[45] Cited in Harold Mendelsohn and Irving Crespi, *Polls, Television, and the New Politics* (Scranton, Pa.: Chandler, 1970), p. 290.

situations, his public relations experts attempted to mold a "new Nixon" image. Although he won the election, the evidence suggests that his image campaign had very little to do with it.[46]

Among the individuals who pay greatest attention to the mass media are those with a strong sense of party identification.[47] The strength of this identification makes it extremely difficult to move them away from the candidate of their party.[48] One objection that has been raised to this argument, however, is that party identification has no importance at the nominating stage of the selection process since all the presidential candidates a voter chooses from in the primaries are of the same party. True enough, but those voting in the primaries are also more educated and more active politically than the average voter and thus less susceptible to being manipulated.[49] A second argument claims that party identification is less potent than it used to be as a shield against manipulation because the number of voters who identify with a party has declined markedly. We now live in an era of ticket splitters. But it is important to note that ticket splitters are both more educated and more active politically than the average member of the population, and while they rely to a great extent upon the media for their information, they depend primarily on those media formats that cannot be controlled by the candidate.[50]

Not only do party identifiers and ticket splitters pay greater attention to the media, but so do the more educated and politically interested individuals in the population. Consequently, we can expect them to be more discerning and critical in their evaluation of political advertising. By the same token, although the apathetic and uninterested are most susceptible to manipulation by the "merchandising phenomenon," they are only moderately exposed to it. Although even moderate exposure may be enough to influence their vote, it is precisely these individuals who are *least* likely to vote.[51]

PROPOSALS FOR CHANGE

The major proposals for change in the selection process grow out of two rather divergent concerns. On the one hand, there are those who argue that the manner in which we go about selecting our presidents is not democratic enough. On the other hand, there are also those who contend that we may have moved too far

---

[46]William Flanigan, *Political Behavior of the American Electorate,* 3rd ed. (Boston: Allyn & Bacon, 1975), pp. 123, 124.

[47]Ibid., p. 163.

[48]Dan Nimmo, *The Political Persuaders* (Englewood Cliffs, N.J.: Prentice-Hall, 1970), pp. 173, 174.

[49]Austin Ranney, "Turnout and Representation in Presidential Primary Elections," *American Political Science Review* 66 (March 1972), 27.

[50]Walter DeVries and V. Lance Tarrance, *The Ticket-Splitter* (Grand Rapids, Mich.: William B. Eerdmans, 1972), pp. 61, 77.

[51]Flanigan, *Political Behavior,* pp. 163, 164.

in the direction of democratizing the selection process. We will now look more closely at these two criticisms as well as the proposals designed to accommodate them.

It has been argued in several quarters that our selection process is lacking in democratic character to the extent that the people do not participate *directly* in the selection of the nominees for President. If the population can vote for President, why should they not also be able to decide who their choices are going to be? Their opportunity to do so under the current system is limited by several factors. In the first place, not all states hold primaries. Second, in a few of the states that do hold primaries, the delegates chosen are not bound to cast their votes in accordance with the preferences expressed by the state's voters. Third, those who vote in the primaries do not necessarily have the opportunity to choose from among all of the presidential contenders. This results in part from the fact that most candidates usually enter the primaries selectively; in part, it is also the consequence of some contenders getting knocked out early and others entering the contest late. In 1976, Bayh, Jackson, Shriver, and Shapp, for example, all dropped out of the running at a point when a majority of primaries were yet to be held; Church and Brown both entered the race fairly late, and thus those voting in the earlier primaries had no opportunity to vote for them. All of these problems would be solved, it is argued, if we instituted a *national primary* in which the rank-and-file members of each party selected the candidate to represent their party in the general election.[52]

Upon first inspection this proposal seems eminently reasonable and practical. It suffers from several drawbacks, however. Under a national primary, candidates would be required to campaign on a nationwide basis, thus giving an advantage to the candidate who is already known as well as to the one who has money. Second, the necessity of reaching all or most of the nation might bring with it greater reliance upon television, a discouraging development for those who already view television's influence as objectionable. Third, the national primary would introduce an element of rigidity into the nominating process with respect to the number of entries into the race, for there would presumably have to be a filing deadline. Under our current system, it is at least possible for candidates to get into the contest right up to the time the vote is taken at the national convention. Fourth, what are we to do if no one receives a majority of the vote in this primary? Presumably this would necessitate a runoff. Thus, the selection process would occur in three stages: a national primary, a national primary runoff, and finally the general election itself. Three separate nationwide elections would not only be an expensive proposition, but would also impose a severe physical strain upon the candidates. One may also question whether the voting population has the ability to sustain interest over such an extended period of intensive politicking. Finally, the ability of a candidate to raise money depends on whether or not he or she looks like a winner. Under our current system,

---

[52]The various proposals for a national primary can be found in *Congressional Quarterly Weekly Report,* July 8, 1972, pp. 1650–54.

the primaries provide an early test of a candidate's potential. Under a national primary, however, candidates would be expected to raise large sums of money *before* there had been any dramatic test of their vote-getting ability.

A variation on the national primary proposal is the idea of holding a series of regional primaries. This proposal would certainly be easier on the candidates, for they could confine their campaigning to one geographical area for a certain period of time instead of constantly hopping about the country, as they must do under our current system. Like the national primary, however, regional primaries would also advantage the well-known and the monied. Thus a candidate with limited funds and name recognition would have an easier time establishing himself in New Hampshire alone, for example, than he would in all of the New England states. Moreover, since the first of the regional primaries would involve several states instead of just one, the outcome would take on much greater significance; consequently, the losers might be prematurely forced out of the nominating contest altogether.

If some seek to open the selection process up to even greater public participation, others fear that we have already moved too far in this direction. As they see it, we have lost an element of quality control over the selection of our nominees due to the declining influence of party leadership in the nominating process. Nelson Polsby speaks to this point:

> I must say I'm getting terribly pessimistic about the presidential selection process because what we are losing—slowly, but at an accelerated rate it seems to me—is the ability of the party organizations to insert a screen which reflects elitist values about candidates. By that I mean whether people who know each of the various candidates intimately think that he can do a decent job, or that he's smart enough, or that he has enough character. My view is that more and more this screen has been pulled apart and disintegrated.[53]

Those in the party organization are more politically informed, more likely to have first-hand knowledge of the candidates, and presumably more apt to apply higher standards in judging candidates' qualifications for the Presidency. It is argued that their ability to exercise this expertise has been greatly diluted by the proliferation of primaries, which has taken the nominating process out of the hands of the party and put it into the hands of "small primary electorates manipulated by money and publicity."[54] And according to another political scientist, "This primary system has given us too many emotional cripples, too many cases for psychohistory, too many Freudian misfits."[55]

[53] "American Political Institutions After Watergate—A Discussion," *Political Science Quarterly* 89 (Winter 1974–75), 737.

[54] Ibid., p. 738.

[55] Michael Robinson, "An Idea Whose Time Has Come," *Presidential Studies Quarterly* 5 (Fall 1975), 49.

The ability of the party organization to protect us from candidates of marginal ability presumes that the organization's preferences may be different from those of the voting population. The evidence does not convincingly demonstrate that this is so. The proliferation of primaries has taken place since 1968. Yet prior to 1968, when the national conventions were more firmly in the grips of the party leadership, there was not a marked difference between the preference of the conventions and that of the voters. For the time period of 1936–72, with only one exception, the candidate leading in the polls prior to the convention has also been the candidate who received the nomination of his party.[56] This fact suggests two possible conclusions. Either the rank-and-file voters are fully as discerning as their party leadership, in which case we need not fear expanded public participation through the primaries; or the party leadership is just as unenlightened as the rank-and-file voter of their party, in which case we have nothing to gain by reducing the number of primaries.

---

[56]William Ludy, "Polls, Primaries, and Presidential Nominations," *Journal of Politics* 35 (November 1973), 837.

2

The President
and
Foreign Affairs

SOME GENERAL CONSIDERATIONS:
THE TWO PRESIDENCIES

For analytical purposes, we can divide the impact of presidential actions into two broad areas, the foreign and the domestic. In the past, presidents have enjoyed much greater freedom of action and support in foreign, as opposed to domestic, affairs, This is evidenced by the fact that between 1948 and 1964 presidential legislative proposals in foreign affairs met with congressional approval approximately 70 percent of the time, as opposed to a 40 percent approval rate for proposals related to domestic matters.[1] Let us now look at those factors that give the President greater leverage in the area of foreign affairs.

Information is power, and in foreign affairs the President has more information at his disposal than does either the Congress or the public. He is constantly being informed of international developments by the Bureau of Intelligence and Research in the State Department, the Defense Intelligence Agency at the Defense Department, and finally the Central Intelligence Agency. Neither the Congress nor the public have any comparable sources of information, and consequently they are largely dependent upon the Executive branch and the press for learning about what is happening outside the United States. To the extent that the President has a monopoly on such information, he is free to define for the public and the Congress the nature of important developments in the area of foreign affairs. He enjoys no such advantage in the domestic area, however. Many issues, such as inflation, energy, and busing, have a very direct

[1] Aaron Wildavsky, "The Two Presidencies," in Aaron Wildavsky, ed., *The Presidency* (Boston: Little, Brown, 1969), p. 231.

impact upon American society, and the experience of the public and the Congress with the effects of these issues provides both with an information base independent of the President.

The presidential advantage in foreign affairs derives not only from his near monopoly of information but also from the fact that on many issues in foreign affairs people have no preexisting opinions, a condition that no doubt results from a lack of knowledge or interest, or both. Lacking such, they are highly susceptible to having their opinions on a given issue shaped by the President. However, even where public opinion is firm on a foreign policy issue, the President may still prove successful in altering it. For example, Americans have for many years held rather hostile attitudes toward the People's Republic of China. When asked in 1968 to rate China on a scale running from most favorable to least favorable, only 5 percent of the American people gave it any kind of a favorable rating.[2] In 1973, however, following President Nixon's initiation of "détente" and his trip to China, 49 percent of the population gave China a favorable rating.[3] The public's inclination to bring its opinions into line with the President's foreign policy position reflects its willingness to trust the judgment of the President in the area of foreign affairs.

In the past, presidents have also been able to exert greater leverage in foreign, as opposed to domestic, affairs because there are fewer interest groups attempting to exert influence over foreign policy matters. Many of those groups that do enter the foreign policy arena are temporary, arising as a result of a particular issue and then dissipating after the issue has been resolved. Among the most active interest groups in foreign policy are American ethnic associations, which seek to influence the government's policy toward their homelands. Cuban Americans, for example, have long sought the continuation of a hard-line policy toward Castro's Cuba. American Jewish organizations have been active in attempting to influence the United States' role in the Arab-Israeli conflict. Similarly, the Greek lobby in this country has been exerting considerable pressure on the Congress in the recent dispute between Greece and Turkey over the island of Cyprus. These organizations, however, do not even approach in number the many interest groups seeking to influence our domestic policy. In nearly every area of domestic life there are a formidable number of powerful organizations that represent the interests of various groups within our population, such as the business community, farmers, labor, and consumers. To the extent that a President must compete with many more alternative power centers in domestic affairs, he will find it more difficult to get his way. To take just one example, the Kennedy Administration was repeatedly frustrated in its attempts to gain congressional approval for Medicare because of an alliance of powerful interest groups consisting of the American Medical Association, the U.S. Chamber of

[2] *The Gallup Opinion Index,* February 1968, p. 24.
[3] *The Gallup Opinion Index,* June 1973, p. 15.

TABLE 2-1: PERCENTAGE APPROVING THE WAY A PRESIDENT IS HANDLING HIS JOB AND PERCENTAGE DISAPPROVING

Before Event	Event	After Event
June 1950 37 pro/45 anti	U.S. enters Korean War (Truman)	July 1950 46 pro/37 anti
July 1958 52 pro/32 anti	U.S. sends Marines to Lebanon (Eisenhower)	August 1958 58 pro/27 anti
May 1960 62 pro/22 anti	U-2 incident, summit meeting collapse (Eisenhower)	Early June 1960 68 pro/21 anti
March 1961 73 pro/7 anti	Bay of Pigs invasion (Kennedy)	April 1961 83 pro/15 anti
October 1961 61 pro/24 anti	Cuban missile crisis (Kennedy)	December 1961 74 pro/5 anti
March 1970 53 pro/30 anti	Cambodian invasion (Nixon)	May 1970 57 pro/31 anti
March 1972 53 pro/37 anti	Mining of Haiphong Harbor (Nixon)	May 1972 61 pro/32 anti
May 1975 40 pro/43 anti	*Mayaguez* incident (Ford)	June 1975 51 pro/33 anti

SOURCES: Hazel Gaudet Erskine, ed., "A Revival: Reports from the Polls," *Public Opinion Quarterly,* 25 (Spring, 1961), 135–137; *Gallup Opinion Index* (Princeton: American Institute of Public Opinion, 1972), p. 3; *Gallup Opinion Index* (Princeton: American Institute of Public Opinion, 1976), p. 12.

Commerce, the National Association of Manufacturers, and the American Farm Bureau Federation.[4]

Finally, in his conduct of foreign policy, the President benefits from what may be characterized as the "us against them" syndrome. There is a natural inclination on the part of the population to rally around the President when he is acting against what is perceived as an outside threat to the interests of the United States. As is evident in Table 2-1, approval of the President inevitably increases after he has faced an international crisis of any kind. Note also that this support increases even after the President's or the government's actions have resulted in a major foreign policy blunder, such as when an American U-2 plane was shot down over the Soviet Union, or when President Kennedy ordered the abortive Bay of Pigs invasion of Cuba.

In domestic affairs, however, the President is not likely to receive this kind of support, for domestic crises usually "divide popular opinion and thereby dilute support for presidents who act decisively."[5]

Whether or not the President will continue to enjoy all of the advantages described in the preceding pages is open to some question. The reason for doubt

[4] Arnold Rose, *The Power Structure* (New York: Oxford University Press, 1967), p. 401.
[5] Erwin Hargrove, *The Power of the Modern Presidency* (New York: Alfred A. Knopf, 1974), p. 111.

arises from our experience in Vietnam. Not only was this war a costly failure but it has become apparent that the government was less than candid with the American people about our role and goals in this conflict. Since the Presidency must bear much of the blame for both of these mistakes, the public may in the future be less inclined to trust either the President's judgment or the truthfulness of his assessments on matters of foreign policy. Presidents may also find that their freedom of action is restricted in the future to the extent that they must now compete with an increasing number of interest groups in the foreign policy arena:

> . . . in the future, there is likely to be an increasing emphasis on *non-defense* foreign policy issues, most of which will have a great impact on *domestic* politics and great attraction for domestic interest groups. Problems with the monetary system, trade deficits and surpluses, energy policy, and the import or export of things such as inflation, unemployment, technology, and pollution will consume more and more of the foreign policy effort. This will occur, not merely because the prominence of security issues may be declining relatively with the evolution of détente, but because these nondefense issues will have a greater absolute impact on American society.[6]

We have already seen, for example, that farm groups took a keen interest in supporting the Ford Administration's decision to sell wheat to the Soviet Union. At the same time, however, the AFL-CIO and the Longshoreman's Union temporarily prevented this agreement from being implemented by refusing to load the grain until the Soviet Union agreed to allow it to be transported on American rather than Soviet ships. The Ford Administration also encountered resistance over its decision to allow the British and French supersonic planes to land at American airports. Several environmental interest groups contended that the Concorde jet would expose various parts of our country to unacceptable air and noise pollution, and consequently, they decided to fight the government's decision in the courts. While they ultimately lost their case in the courts, their efforts did cause a lengthy delay in granting landing rights to the Concorde, a delay which caused the Ford Administration more than a little embarrassment.

THE WAR-MAKING POWER

In no area have the actions of recent presidents evoked greater controversy than by their involvement in war making. Acting in their capacity as Commander in Chief, Lyndon Johnson committed the United States to a protracted war in Vietnam and Richard Nixon committed air and ground forces in Cambodia.

---

[6]Donald Peppers, "The Two Presidencies: Eight Years Later," in Aaron Wildavsky, ed., *Perspectives on the Presidency* (Boston: Little, Brown, 1975), pp. 463–464.

These actions were responsible for much of the political and social upheaval in our society during the late sixties and early seventies, as individuals in and outside of government asked by what authority these two recent presidents justified the commitment of our human and material resources to such undertakings. We must consult history in order to gain a proper perspective on their actions specifically and on the President's war-making power generally.

The Intent of the Founders

The Founding Fathers were not at all ambiguous on the matter of who should possess the war-making power. In their judgment, prudence clearly dictated that this power should be given to the Legislative branch. In the words of James Madison, "The Constitution supposes, what the History of all Govts. demonstrates, that the Ex. is the branch of power most interested in war, & most prone to it. It has accordingly with studied care vested the question of war in the Legisl."[7] The Constitutional Convention did qualify this grant of power in one respect, however. The first draft of the Constitution stated that Congress would have the power to "make war." This was later changed to "declare war," in recognition of the fact that swiftness of action would be a necessity in the event of a sudden attack on the United States. Since the President would be better able to act with dispatch under such circumstances, they expected him to repel sudden attacks without having to receive the prior approval of Congress. While under the Constitution the President was accorded the power to act as Commander in Chief of the armed forces, it is clear that the Founders did not intend for this role to confer any authority upon him to wage war. Rather, as Alexander Hamilton noted, "It would amount to nothing more than the supreme command and direction of the military and naval forces, as first general and admiral of the confederacy."[8] In short, the President was to be in charge of the armed forces once committed to battle, but the decision on whether or not to commit them was to rest solely with the Congress.

That war making must rest with the Congress was recognized and scrupulously adhered to by our early presidents. When in 1793 George Washington declared that the United States would remain neutral in the war between Britain and France, it was argued by many that his declaration in effect prevented Congress from exercising its right to side with France in the conflict and declare war against Britain. Washington ultimately agreed, stating that "it rests with the wisdom of Congress to correct, improve, or enforce the neutrality."[9] Thereafter, declarations of neutrality rested with the Congress.

From 1798 to 1800, the United States was involved in a limited maritime war

---

[7]Cited in Arthur Schlesinger, Jr., *The Imperial Presidency* (Boston: Houghton Mifflin, 1973), p. 5. Copyright © 1973 by Arthur Schlesinger, Jr. Reprinted by permission of Houghton Mifflin Company.

[8]Jacob Cooke, ed., *The Federalist* (New York: World, 1961), p. 465.

[9]Cited in Schlesinger, *Imperial Presidency,* p. 20.

with France. When the trouble began, President Adams called Congress into secret session in order to determine what measures would be appropriate on the part of the United States. While Congress never officially declared war on France, they nevertheless passed legislation authorizing Adams to wage a limited war against France.

Americans encountered further difficulty on the high seas during the administration of Thomas Jefferson, when an American schooner was attacked in the Mediterranean by a cruiser from Tripoli. Although the cruiser was captured and disabled by the American schooner, both the ship and its crew were released because the American commander, as Jefferson told the Congress, "was unauthorized by the Constitution, without the sanction of Congress, to go beyond the line of defense."[10] He then asked Congress if they would authorize measures to allow American forces to take offensive action against the ships from Tripoli. Alexander Hamilton thought that in this particular instance Jefferson was being overly sensitive to the right of Congress to declare war. In his judgment, once someone declared war on you, a state of war automatically existed, and thus a congressional declaration of war became unnecessary.

Nor did James Monroe share Jefferson's view when he became President. In 1817, when Seminole Indians conducted raiding parties into American territory, President Monroe ordered General Andrew Jackson to chase them back into Spanish Florida, and Jackson did so with great relish. Monroe gave this order to send American troops into foreign territory without consulting Congress. This doctrine of "hot pursuit" would be invoked by later presidents to justify certain military actions in Korea and Laos.[11] Andrew Jackson, however, behaved a good deal more cautiously as President than he did as general. During his administration, he ordered an armed American ship to South America to protect American ships there from Argentine raiders. While he did so without first seeking congressional approval, he immediately went before Congress and asked them for the "authority and means" to protect "our fellow citizens fishing and trading in these seas."[12] Both in this case and in future instances, Congress was apparently willing to allow presidents to commit American forces into situations where armed hostilities might result, provided that protection of American lives and property was the justification for doing so—a justification that would be subject to considerable abuse by future presidents.

Presidential War

It was during the Presidency of James Polk that the first of several blows was struck against the war-making power of Congress. In 1846 he ordered American soldiers into the hotly disputed territory between Texas and Mexico. Not un-

---

[10] Ibid., p. 22.

[11] Louis Fisher, "War Powers: A Need for Legislative Reassertion," in Rexford Tugwell, ed., *The Presidency Reappraised*, 1st edition (New York: Praeger, 1974), pp. 64, 65.

[12] Cited in Schlesinger, *Imperial Presidency*, p. 28.

expectedly, Mexican soldiers attacked the Americans, whose presence they viewed as an invasion of their territory. Polk immediately asked Congress to recognize that a state of war now existed between the United States and Mexico. This event clearly demonstrated that while Congress had the exclusive power to declare war, the President could nevertheless precipitate a set of circumstances that would make war unavoidable, thus giving Congress little choice in the matter. Several members of Congress challenged the constitutionality of Polk's actions, with Congressman Abraham Lincoln among the President's most vocal critics. Indeed two years later, the House passed a vote of censure against Polk, but the Senate refused to go along with it.

Lincoln's perspective on the war-making power changed substantially once he ascended to the Presidency. Without calling Congress into session, Lincoln ordered a naval blockade of the Confederacy. His authority to do so was ultimately challenged in the courts in a series of suits known as the *Prize* cases. It was argued that a naval blockade constituted an act of war under international law and since Congress had not declared war in this instance, Lincoln had no right to institute the blockade. The Supreme Court did not agree, and instead ruled than an "invasion or insurrection created a state of war as legal fact" and thus the President did not have to wait for a congressional authorization before responding.[13] While Lincoln's action has been cited as a precedent for presidential war making, this claim is in error, for the Court specifically stated that such action could only be constitutional in times of invasion or rebellion. Also worth noting is the fact that Lincoln never claimed that the right to take the nation into war was a routine power of the President. Rather, he repeatedly maintained that he was justified in exercising this power only because the very survival of the nation was at stake.

At the turn of the century the Presidency further eroded the war-making power of Congress. In 1900, President William McKinley ordered five thousand American soldiers to China in order to help put down the Boxer Rebellion. While he alleged that the purpose of our intervention was to protect American lives and property, in fact his motives were purely political. Although the approval of Congress was never sought by McKinley, Congress did not see fit to raise any objections, in spite of the fact that China promptly declared war upon the United States. This event is a significant one because it marks the first time that an American President unilaterally committed troops to combat against another sovereign state outside of the Western Hemisphere.

The need to protect lives and property was also used by Theodore Roosevelt and Woodrow Wilson as a pretext for intervening militarily in the political affairs of several Caribbean countries, and doing so without consulting Congress. Since most of the Congress supported such actions, they chose not to dwell on their legality. Lyndon Johnson would resort to the same justification in 1965 when he sent 22,000 American soldiers to the Dominican Republic, although he admitted

[13] Ibid., p. 64.

privately that the real reason for doing so was to avoid a Communist takeover of its government.[14]

The congressional war-making power suffered further setbacks during the Presidency of Franklin Roosevelt. The boldness of his actions, however, may well have been encouraged by a Supreme Court decision in the *Curtiss-Wright* case, which was handed down at the end of his first term. The central issue in the case had no bearing at all upon the war-making power. On the contrary, it was concerned with the right of the President to regulate foreign commerce. After disposing of this immediate issue, however, the Court's majority opinion launched into a general discussion of the role of the President in foreign affairs, arguing that he had the right to exercise certain powers in this area, even though they were not specified in the Constitution. They contended that this *inherent authority* must be accorded the President in foreign affairs because only he had adequate knowledge in this area. Just exactly what these powers were, the Court never made clear, but future presidents would draw on this inherent authority as one of their justifications for committing American troops into hostilities. Whether or not they were entitled to do so is open to serious question, since the issue in this Court case did not involve the war-making power; and secondly, since the point at issue was not whether the President could act without congressional authorization, but rather whether Congress had the right to delegate to the President its own power to regulate foreign commerce.

Prior to our entry into the Second World War, President Roosevelt undertook several actions of doubtful constitutionality, the most dramatic of which was his "shoot at sight" order given to American naval forces, which were convoying military materiel to a beleaguered Great Britain. This order grew out of a prior incident in which the U.S.S. *Greer* had two torpedoes fired at it by a German submarine while cruising in waters off the coast of Iceland. In relaying the news of this incident to the Congress and the public, however, Roosevelt failed to note that the *Greer* was not cruising innocently off the coast of Iceland. On the contrary, "It had been systematically trailing the Nazi submarine and broadcasting its position to a British warplane overhead."[15] Nor did he note that no injury had been done to either the ship or its personnel. Finally, he issued his order to attack German vessels without seeking any prior authorization from the Congress; indeed, the formal declaration of war by Congress did not come until three months later, following the attack on Pearl Harbor. Thus, as one distinguished historian has noted, "From the date of the *Greer* incident, 4 September 1941, the United States was engaged in a de facto naval war with Germany on the Atlantic Ocean."[16] Roosevelt himself acknowledged that he was uncertain about the constitutionality of his order when he informed Congress that his ac-

---

[14] Ibid., p. 178.

[15] Emmet John Hughes, *The Living Presidency* (New York: Coward, McCann & Geoghegan, 1973), p. 239. Copyright © 1973 by Emmet John Hughes. Reprinted by permission of Coward, McCann & Geoghegan.

[16] Cited in Merlo Pusey, *The Way We Go to War* (Boston: Houghton Mifflin, 1969), p. 3.

tions "whether strictly legal or not were ventured upon under what appeared to be a popular demand and a public necessity; trusting then as now that Congress would readily ratify them."[17] Once again, Congress raised no objections.

It was under the Presidency of Harry Truman that the congressional war-making power was dealt one of its severest blows. Two days after Truman was informed that the North Koreans had invaded South Korea, he ordered American air and naval forces to the area to support the South Koreans. While he did summon congressional leaders to the White House, it was not to seek their advise and consent but rather to inform them of the decision he had already made. The boldness of Truman's actions takes on greater significance when one considers, first, that Truman gave the order even before South Korea made any request for such assistance, and second, that the United States was not bound by any mutual defense pact to come to the aid of South Korea.[18] Indeed, one year prior to the Korean conflict, the Secretary of State did not even mention South Korea when discussing those countries in the Pacific that were deemed vital to our national security.[19] Finally, although the United Nations Security Council did pass a resolution recommending that armed force be used to repel the North Korean attack, this resolution came the day *after* Truman issued his order.[20]

Several days after his initial commitment of air and naval forces to the area, Truman made the decision to commit ground forces as well. In a meeting with congressional leaders to inform them of these developments, it was suggested that he ask Congress for a joint resolution giving approval to his actions. Truman replied that he would take this request under advisement, but after consulting with his advisors, he concluded that no such approval was necessary. Rather, he argued that his role as Commander in Chief provided him with the necessary authority to commit armed forces into combat.[21] Thus, for the first time in our history, a President of the United States was asserting that his responsibilities as Commander in Chief provided him with the constitutional authority to take the country into a major war against another sovereign state thousands of miles away from home. While some members of Congress questioned Truman's authority in this regard, they were overwhelmed by the vast majority who aquiesced. Once again, Congress had willingly surrendered its constitutional authority to the President.

Given the more restrained view that Eisenhower took toward the powers of the Presidency, it is not surprising that he sought advance congressional approval for committing American troops to combat. Thus, he asked for and received joint resolutions from Congress authorizing him to employ the armed forces in

---

[17]Schlesinger, *Imperial Presidency,* p. 112.

[18]Hughes, *Living Presidency,* p. 244.

[19]Ibid.

[20]Louis Fisher, *President and Congress* (New York: MacMillan Publishing Co., Inc., 1972), p. 195.

[21]Schlesinger, *Imperial Presidency,* p. 132.

defense of Formosa and the Pescadores, and to thwart Communist aggression in the Middle East.[22] One factor related to these resolutions, however, demonstrates how low the Congress's concern for its war-making power had fallen. Prominent members of both the House and the Senate were in fact denying that Eisenhower even needed to seek congressional approval on these matters. Lyndon Johnson, who was Senate Majority Leader at the time, asserted that "we are not going to take responsibility out of the hands of the constitutional leader and try to arrogate it to ourselves."[23] In a similar vein, the Speaker of the House stated that "if the President had done what is proposed here without consulting with the Congress, he would have had no criticism from me."[24] Such statements undoubtedly would have shocked the Founding Fathers.

Two years into his administration, President Kennedy found himself confronted with a grave crisis when he learned that the Soviet Union was in the process of installing missile bases in Cuba. He ordered American naval forces to set up a blockade around the island so as to prevent Soviet ships from reaching it. As he knew only too well, this action could have resulted in a military confrontation with the Russians on the high seas, one that could ultimately have led to a nuclear war. Yet he gave the order without any prior advice or consent from the Congress. However, unlike the other examples we have discussed in this chapter, here was a situation in which both secrecy and a swift response seemed a necessity. To have consulted Congress might well have denied Kennedy the opportunity to act with both dispatch and surprise. Congress agreed, although many argued that he had not acted forcefully enough.

We now consider an event in our history—the Vietnam War—that would ultimately force Congress to reassess the desirability of presidential encroachment upon its war-making power. This reconsideration grew not only out of the apparent futility of our policy in Vietnam, but also out of the deception with which this policy had been undertaken. It was reported to Congress that in August of 1964 two torpedoes were fired at the U.S.S. *Maddox* while it was cruising in the Gulf of Tonkin off the coast of North Vietnam. The Secretary of Defense stated that this attack was "deliberate and unprovoked."[25] At the request of President Johnson, Congress responded to this event by passing the Tonkin Gulf Resolution, authorizing the President "to take all necessary measures to repel any armed attack against the forces of the United States and to prevent further aggression."[26] Only two members of Congress voted against this resolution. Not until several years later did the Congress discover that the circumstances surrounding this incident may have been different from what they were told earlier. For example, Congress learned that the commander of the

---

[22] Ibid., pp. 160, 161.

[23] Ibid., p. 160.

[24] Ibid., pp. 160, 161.

[25] Hughes, *Living Presidency,* p. 236.

[26] Cited in Schlesinger, *Imperial Presidency,* p. 179.

U.S.S. *Maddox* had sent the following cable back to the Defense Department immediately after the "incident":

> Review of action makes many recorded contacts and torpedoes fired appear doubtful. Freak weather effects and overeager sonarman may have accounted for many reports. No actual visual sitings by *Maddox*. Suggest complete evaluation before any further action.[27]

Yet despite the uncertainty of the situation as evidenced by the content of this cable, President Johnson ordered fifty bombing strikes against North Vietnam. Congress also learned later that the U.S.S. *Maddox* was not lying inoffensively in the waters of the Tonkin Gulf. On the contrary, it was a spy ship "collecting military intelligence and collaborating operationally with South Vietnamese patrol boats shelling the northern coast."[28] Had Congress been in possession of all this information when they considered the Gulf of Tonkin Resolution, they might well have withheld their approval of it. Unfortunately, however, at the time the incident allegedly took place, they had no source of information other than the President himself. This event clearly emphasizes a point made earlier in this chapter—the great information advantage the President enjoys in the area of foreign affairs. In this particular case, his monopoly of information allowed him to define the Tonkin Gulf incident as he wished.

While Johnson did see fit to seek the approval of Congress for his actions, it seems clear that he did so for political rather than constitutional reasons. Four years after Congress passed the Gulf of Tonkin Resolution, he expressed the following view: "We stated then, and we repeat now, we did not think the resolution was necessary to what we did and what we're doing."[29] Rather, he based his action partly on precedents set by previous presidents, and more importantly, on the right of the President to repel a sudden attack. Although the Founding Fathers intended that presidents should be able to respond to a sudden attack, they clearly had in mind an attack upon the United States itself. The Johnson Administration, however, was arguing that in this day and age the security of the United States could be threatened by events occurring thousands of miles away from our shores, in this case, Vietnam. In essence then, it appeared that a President could commit American troops to combat anywhere and at any time he thought the security of the United States was threatened. As one student of this subject has noted, "Under this theory it is hard to see why any future President would ever see any legal need to go to Congress before leading the nation into war."[30]

---

[27]Cited in Charles Hardin, *Presidential Power and Accountability* (Chicago: University of Chicago Press, 1974), p. 103.

[28]Hughes, *Living Presidency*, p. 237.

[29]Cited in Schlesinger, *Imperial Presidency*, p. 180.

[30]Ibid., p. 184.

Richard Nixon came into the Presidency inheriting the Vietnam War from his predecessor, and his attempts to deal with it proved equally controversial. During the course of American troop reductions in Vietnam, he ordered American soldiers into the neighboring country of Cambodia in order to eliminate enemy sanctuaries there. It was his judgment that these sanctuaries were inhibiting the safe withdrawal of American soldiers. This decision to invade a neutral country with which we were not at war was made without any consultation with Congress either before or after the order was given. Nixon justified his actions on grounds that as Commander in Chief he had a responsibility to protect the lives of American men, a responsibility that superseded his obligation to Congress:

> . . . in the modern world, there are times when the Commander in Chief . . . will have to act quickly. I can assure the American people that this President is going to bend over backward to consult the Senate and consult the House whenever he feels it can be done without jeopardizing the lives of American men. But when it is a question of the lives of American men or the attitudes of people in the Senate, I am coming down hard on the side of defending the lives of American men.[31]

This justification had a hollow ring to it, however, not only because the enemy sanctuaries had been in Cambodia for years but also because they had been largely evacuated by the time Nixon ordered the invasion.

Equally controversial was the President's decision to conduct bombing raids on Cambodia. These raids were begun as early as 1969 without any prior consultation with the Congress. Indeed, Congress was not even informed of them after the fact.[32] Since the enemy quite obviously knew that such raids were taking place, the inescapable conclusion was that these raids were being kept secret in order to prevent the Congress and the public from finding out about them. Equally puzzling was the fact that these bombing raids were accelerated in March of 1973, after American forces had already been withdrawn from Vietnam. Since the President's justification for these bombings in Cambodia was the protection of American troops, how could their continuance be justified when there were no longer any American soldiers there? In responding to queries by congressmen on this question, one State Department official finally replied: "The justification is the reelection of President Nixon."[33] Thus it appeared that if an individual could get himself elected to the Presidency, he was free to do as he wished. The justification for presidential war making had finally reached its farthest point.

While President Nixon's actions could be challenged on constitutional

---

[31] Cited in Ibid., p. 189.

[32] Louis Koenig, *The Chief Executive,* 3rd ed. (New York: Harcourt Brace Jovanovich), p. 218.

[33] Cited in Schlesinger, *Imperial Presidency,* p. 198.

grounds, so also could those of many other presidents. Where Nixon differed was not so much in what he did, but rather the manner in which he did it. Franklin Roosevelt had at least acknowledged that his actions might be unconstitutional and thus asked Congress to approve them after the fact. While Truman did not feel any constitutional responsibility to consult with Congress on going into Korea, he did not keep any of our military actions secret from them. Even though Lyndon Johnson did not feel congressional approval was necessary for taking us into the Vietnam War, the fact is he asked for their approval anyway. President Nixon, however, sought the advice and consent of Congress neither before nor after he committed American troops into hostilities thousands of miles from home. And with respect to the secret bombings in Cambodia, he chose not even to *inform* the Congress after the fact.

Congress Reacts: the War Powers Resolution

Although the erosion of the congressional war-making power was a gradual process, it ultimately became complete. The Founding Fathers saw the role of Commander in Chief as nothing more than the "first general and first admiral" of the armed forces. Yet a succession of later presidents would expand upon this role until it was finally viewed as empowering presidents to lead the United States into major undeclared wars in various places around the world. If such actions were questionable on constitutional grounds, it is clear that presidents could not have undertaken them successfully if Congress had not been a willing accomplice. Indeed, only after our experience in Vietnam did Congress begin to reassess its own role and that of the President with regard to the war-making power. This reassessment led in 1973 to passage of legislation known as the War Powers Resolution. The major provisions of this act are summarized below:

1. The President *in every possible instance* shall *consult* with Congress before introducing United States Armed Forces into hostilities, or into situations where imminent involvement in hostilities is clearly indicated by the circumstances.
2. Within *forty-eight hours* after introducing troops into hostilities or into a situation where hostilities are imminent, the President shall *submit a report* to Congress explaining his actions.
3. Within *sixty days* after the report is submitted, the President *shall terminate the use of such armed forces* unless Congress has: (1) declared war; (2) or extended the sixty-day period; (3) or cannot meet because of an armed attack upon the United States.
4. *Notwithstanding anything said* in the above provisions, *at any time* the United States Armed Forces are engaged in hostilities outside the United States *without a declaration of war or specific statutory author-*

zation, such forces *shall be removed* by the President if the *Congress so directs* by a concurrent resolution.[34]

Note that the President is not absolutely required to consult Congress before introducing armed forces into combat. Rather he is to do so "in every *possible* instance." Whether or not it is "possible" will be left up to the President to decide. Furthermore, the term "consult" is not clearly defined in the act. Does it mean that he merely informs Congress, or is he to seek their advice? Of course even if it is the latter, he is still free to ignore it. In short, the War Powers Resolution now gives the President the legal authority to commit troops into hostilities without the prior approval of Congress. The reasons for doing so, however, are not without merit. First of all, Congress realized that under emergency conditions, a President may not have time to gain the approval of Congress. Second, they also recognized that the conditions surrounding the commitment of troops to combat are not likely to provide the necessary climate for careful evaluation. As stated earlier, the public is likely to unite behind the President at such times, and thus their support might possibly stampede the Congress into giving its approval also. They were also aware that at the time of the initial crisis, they would have to rely almost exclusively upon the President for information. And as they learned from the Gulf of Tonkin incident, a President may not always be completely candid in apprising Congress of the circumstances surrounding a given crisis. Thus they concluded that rather than giving their initial approval on the basis of possible misinformation, it would be better to let the President go ahead and commit troops on his own. Then, after Congress had had more time and more information with which to assess the situation, they would be able to render a more considered judgment concerning the President's actions.[35] The problems here, however, are whether or not Congress will be able to find alternative sources of information, and whether they can do so before we become so deeply involved in hostilities that withdrawal is not possible.

The now famous *Mayaguez* incident provided the first instance in which a President had to act in accordance with the provisions of the War Powers Resolution. After the ship *Mayaguez* was seized by the Cambodians off their coast, President Ford ordered marine and naval forces into the area in order to secure its release. While the evidence suggests that the President did not seek the advice of Congress on this matter, he did inform them. And two days later, he submitted a report to Congress detailing the circumstances of the incident and justifying his actions. Whether or not his actions were constitutional in this particular case is still open to some question, since in 1973 legislation was signed

---

[34] Adapted from the Appendix to Cedric Tarr, "The War Powers Resolution and the Problem of Information" (Prepared for delivery at the Annual Meeting of the American Political Science Association, Chicago, Ill., August 29–September 2, 1974).

[35] Ibid., p. 8.

into law prohibiting all combat activity in Indochina after August 15 of that year. However, this delicate issue was not raised by Congress at the time of the *Mayaguez* incident.

TREATIES AND EXECUTIVE AGREEMENTS

The Founding Fathers sought to involve both the Executive and Legislative branches of government in treaty making. They felt that if the President were not involved, he would not enjoy sufficient respect among foreign governments. Beyond this, they also believed that treaties would often have to be negotiated with secrecy and dispatch, and these were conditions that could be better met by the President than by the Congress. At the same time, however, the Founding Fathers recognized the possibility that a President might be corrupted by foreign governments, and thus they decided to give the Senate the power to ratify treaties negotiated by the President.[36]

Agreements with foreign governments have not been arrived at solely through treaties. Indeed, since the time of George Washington, such arrangements have also been made through what have come to be known as *executive agreements*. These are agreements made by the President of the United States with a foreign government. While they enjoy the same *legal* status as treaties under international law, they do *not* have to be ratified by the Senate. The right of a President to enter into such agreements was never entirely clear. In 1817, for example, James Monroe made an executive agreement with the British which was designed to reduce the number of American and British naval forces on the Great Lakes. He asked the Congress whether or not he had the right to make such an agreement, but Congress never provided him with an answer. They simply gave their approval and then one year later formalized the agreement by a treaty. However, the President's right to make such agreements was firmly established in 1937 by a Supreme Court ruling in the *Belmont* case. Their decision, however, did not do much to resolve the confusion over what matters were appropriate for negotiation by treaty on the one hand and executive agreement on the other.[37] As Table 2-2 indicates, over the years treaties have been gradually replaced by executive agreements.

Most of these executive agreements have been of a routine and uncontroversial nature, dealing with such matters as food deliveries and custom enforcements. Some, however, have involved rather extensive United States commitments—military and otherwise—to other countries. Although Congress passed a law in 1950 requiring the Secretary of State to publish annually all executive agreements entered into during the previous year, the Executive

[36] Cooke, *The Federalist,* pp. 505-507.
[37] Schlesinger, *Imperial Presidency,* p. 104.

TABLE 2-2. TREATIES AND EXECUTIVE AGREEMENTS, 1789-1977

Period	Treaties	Executive Agreements
1789–1839	60	27
1839–1889	215	238
1889–1939	524	917
1940–1970	310	5,653
1971–1977	110	2,062
Total	1,219	8,897

SOURCES: Louis Fisher, *President and Congress* (MacMillan Publishing Co., Inc., 1972), p. 45. ©Copyright 1972 by MacMillan Publishing Co., Inc.; used by permission. Figures for 1971–77 provided by Department of State, Washington, D.C.

branch has in fact withheld those agreements that it considered sensitive to our national security.[38] The impact of such secret agreements was impressed upon Congress when they were told that our commitment to the South Vietnamese grew in part out of executive agreements made between American presidents and the South Vietnamese government.[39] This startling revelation persuaded the Congress to set up a special committee in 1969 to investigate the nature of American commitments abroad reached through executive agreements. The investigation turned up several important commitments that they were not previously aware of. These commitments included American military support for the Ethiopian army, apparent commitments to the defense of Thailand and the Phillipines, and a commitment to defend the Franco regime in Spain against *internal* uprisings.[40] Perhaps most startling of all was the revelation that as a result of agreements reached between the Executive branch and the Laotian government, the United States had been secretly assisting the government of Laos in fighting Communist insurgents in that country since 1964. This assistance took the form of the training of Laotian soldiers by American advisers as well as bombing raids by American planes against Communist insurgents in Laos.[41]

Congress Reacts: the Case Act, 1972

The chairman of the House International Relations Committee voiced the growing concern among members of Congress that the Legislative branch had been excluded from participating in decisions involving major American commitments: "In recent years Presidents of both parties have resorted increasingly to executive agreements in place of treaties, involving the United States in far-reaching commitments abroad. This practice has abridged Congress's foreign

[38]*Congressional Quarterly Weekly Report,* August 2, 1975, p. 1713.

[39]Schlesinger, *Imperial Presidency,* p. 201.

[40]*Congressional Quarterly Weekly Report,* January 1, 1971, p. 24.

[41]Ibid., p. 23.

affairs power under the Constitution."[42] In an attempt to achieve some control in this area, Congress passed the Case Act, which was signed into law by the President in 1972. The provisions of this act require first that the President transmit all executive agreements to the Congress within sixty days after they have been negotiated. It states further that Congress must be informed of all executive agreements in effect at the time this act was passed. Finally, only the House International Relations Committee and the Senate Foreign Relations Committee need be informed of secret executive agreements. Several members of Congress did not think this act went far enough. Senator Sam Irvin, for example, thought the Congress should also have the power to reject any such agreement that it found unacceptable and introduced a bill to that effect. It did not receive much support, however, because President Nixon made it clear that he would veto any bill containing such a provision.

Whether or not the Case Act has accomplished its purpose is open to serious question. The major weakness of the act was its failure to define what it was in fact attempting to control, namely, executive agreements. The consequence of this omission is that the Executive branch has informed Congress only of those accords that fall under its own definition of executive agreements. Thus in 1975 Congressman Les Aspin of Wisconsin estimated that since the Case Act was passed, the Executive branch had entered into between 400 and 600 accords with foreign governments, none of which had been reported to the Congress.[43] The most dramatic recent example of such an accord was President Nixon's letter to President Thieu of South Vietnam in which he stated that the United States would "respond will full force should the settlement (i.e., the Paris Peace Agreement) be violated by North Vietnam."[44] Senator Clifford Case, author of the Case Act, has contended that this secret commitment by President Nixon constituted an international agreement, which should have been transmitted to the Congress.[45] Nixon's failure to do so proved extremely embarrassing to the United States, for the Congress ultimately refused to provide the South Vietnamese government with additional assistance, following North Vietnam's renewed invasion of the South in 1975.

Several proposals have been introduced in Congress that are designed to correct the weaknesses of the Case Act. These proposals not only seek to clarify what constitutes an executive agreement, but also provide that Congress may, if it wishes, reject such agreements within sixty days after they have been concluded. Any legislation along these lines is likely to face stiff opposition from the President, however. Presidents have argued with some justification that they cannot be effective negotiators if they are denied the right to make firm com-

---

[42] *Congressional Quarterly Weekly Report,* August 2, 1975, p. 1712.

[43] *New York Times,* April 17, 1975, p. E2.

[44] *Congressional Quarterly Weekly Report,* August 2, 1975, p. 1714.

[45] Ibid.

mitments with foreign governments. Moreover, they also point out that delicate compromises might well come undone while waiting for Congress to approve or reject such agreements.[46]

THE CIA AND FOREIGN POLICY

Only recently has it become generally known how important the Central Intelligence Agency is as an arm of presidential foreign policy. Revelations of the last few years have shown, for example, that much of the United States involvement in the secret war in Laos was coordinated by the Central Intelligence Agency.[47] The CIA also engaged in assassination attempts upon heads of foreign governments, with Fidel Castro among those targeted for elimination. In Chile, the CIA sought to destabilize the Marxist government of President Salvadore Allende by supporting various groups within the country who were opposed to him.[48] Whether or not any or all of these activities constitute legitimate goals of American foreign policy has been the subject of considerable debate both in and outside of government. Legitimate or not, however, these activities are of such magnitude and gravity that Congress has concluded they ought to be informed of them. That they have lacked such knowledge in the past is due both to their own laxity and to the nature of the activities themselves.

The Central Intelligence Agency was created under a provision of the National Security Act of 1947. While this act did not foresee that the CIA would perform any activity other than intelligence gathering, the vague wording of the legislation was used by the CIA as a justification for expanding its role to include military and political interventions in other countries.[49] Congress also saw fit to pass legislation in 1949 exempting the CIA from disclosing to the Congress information that is normally required of all other agencies. Specifically, the CIA was not required to divulge information regarding the organization of the agency, its functions, or the number of people it employed. Furthermore, its budget was not made public, nor was it made available to most of the Congress. Rather, its annual budget requests were to be concealed in the budget requests of other agencies. Finally, the agency was also exempted from statutory limits on spending.

All this is not to say that Congress completely surrendered its control over the activities and budget of the CIA. In theory, two subcommittees in the Senate

[46] Ibid., p. 1716.

[47] Edward Kolodziej, "Congress and Foreign Policy: The Nixon Years," in Harvey Mansfield, ed., *Congress Against The President* (New York: The Academy of Political Science, 1975), p. 177.

[48] Victor Marchetti and John Marks, *The CIA and the Cult of Intelligence* (New York: Alfred Knopf, 1974), pp. 18, 19.

[49] Harry Ransom, "Congress and the Intelligence Agencies," in Mansfield, *Congress Against,* p. 158.

and two in the House were charged with overseeing the activities of the agency. In actual fact, these four subcommittees did not prove very effective in monitoring the activities of the CIA. In part, this was due to the fact that information on many CIA operations was relayed only to the subcommittee chairmen, who were usually highly sympathetic to the agency and did not inform the rest of their subcommittee membership of the more controversial activities undertaken by the CIA.[50] In addition, these subcommittees had very few staff workers attached to them, and consequently, systematic oversight of the agency was not possible.[51]

Since 1947, over two hundred bills have been proposed by members of Congress in an attempt to bring the CIA under closer congressional control. Only one has been passed, however, and this was in response to the revelations regarding the CIA's secret political and military activities. Enacted in 1974, this legislation states that no money can be spent

> by or on behalf of the Central Intelligence Agency for operations in foreign countries, other than activities intended *solely for obtaining necessary intelligence,* unless and until the President finds that each such operation is important to the *national security* of the United States and *reports, in a timely fashion,* a description and scope of such operation to the appropriate committees of the Congress. (Italics supplied by author.)[52]

This legislation also provided that two more committees, the House International Relations Committee and Senate Foreign Relations Committee, now be informed of CIA activities. In the judgment of many, this legislation has not proved effective because of the stipulation that the President must inform Congress *in a timely fashion* of those CIA activities that go beyond foreign intelligence gathering. This phrase was never clearly defined, and the President and the CIA have interpreted it to mean that Congress need not be informed of these activities until after they have already taken place.[53]

In the years 1975–77, the CIA was subjected to intense scrutiny by both the Executive and Legislative branches. In 1975 President Ford created a special commission to inquire into the agency's activities. Based upon their recommendations, he issued an Executive Order in February 1976 prohibiting the CIA from engaging in further assassination plots. In addition, he established an Intelligence Oversight Board composed of civilians who were charged with monitoring the activities of the CIA. Shortly after assuming office, President Carter ordered his own review of United States intelligence operations and subsequently made several sweeping changes through a series of Executive Orders.

---

[50] *New York Times,* February 1, 1967, p. E1.

[51] Ransom, "Congress and the Intelligence Agencies," p. 160.

[52] *New York Times,* July 20, 1975, p. E3. © 1975 by The New York Times Company. Reprinted by permission.

[53] Ibid.

First, in order to ensure greater coordination and accountability, he gave the Director of the CIA responsibility for all United States intelligence operations (Defense Intelligence Agency, National Security Agency, the intelligence divisions of the Army, Navy, and Air Force, the FBI's counter-intelligence unit, and the Department of Energy's research and development unit). Specifically, he was charged with preparing the budgets of the entire intelligence community and given the authority to assign tasks to all intelligence units except those housed in the Department of Defense. The latter would remain under the authority of the Secretary of Defense. Carter also ordered other changes designed to increase oversight of the intelligence community; these included, first, giving the Attorney General the authority to veto covert CIA activities directed against American citizens living at home or abroad. This was designed to check the use of such clandestine practices as electronic surveillance and the opening of mail. Second, Carter decided to retain the Intelligence Oversight Board created by President Ford, but in addition, he also established a Special Coordination Committee within the National Security Council. Chaired by the President's adviser for national security affairs, this committee has responsibility for assessing the CIA's operations and its methods of gathering information. Finally, Carter also reaffirmed the right of the Senate and House intelligence committees to be supplied with any information they might request from the CIA. Nothing was said, however, about informing the appropriate congressional committees of covert CIA operations in advance of their occurrence.

Efforts to make the CIA more accountable came from the Congress as well as the White House. Both the House and the Senate conducted separate inquiries into the agency's activities and concluded that the Congress must make a more concerted effort to monitor intelligence operations. Accordingly, a new Select Committee on Intelligence was established in both the Senate and the House. Both committees are empowered to demand information from the various intelligence agencies, compel testimony, review budgets, and receive reports. In addition, the Senate Committee was given a staff of fifty people and the House Committee, a staff of twenty-two. This represents a substantially greater commitment of resources than Congress was willing to make in the past.

To date, the Senate Select Committee on Intelligence appears to be carrying out its responsibilities more vigorously than its counterpart in the House. It has, for example, sent staff members overseas to inquire into some agency activities. It has also released a report challenging the CIA's assessment of Soviet energy needs in the 1980s. Finally, in early 1978 the Senate Select Committee on Intelligence submitted to the Senate several legislative proposals relevant to the organization and activities of the intelligence community. Some of these are designed to put into statute what Ford and Carter already did by Executive Order, while others go beyond their actions. These proposals include: (1) establishing a Director of National Intelligence who would oversee all of the government's intelligence activities; (2) requiring court orders for CIA activities that involve searches, electronic surveillance, and the opening of mail of U.S. citizens;

(3) prohibiting political assassinations, the overthrow of democratic governments, and the use of terrorism; (4) requiring that the President inform Congress of all covert operations before they occur; (5) establishing an Intelligence Oversight Board; (6) requiring all intelligence agency personnel to report any illegal acts to their superiors; (7) directing the Attorney General to ensure that "whistle-blowers" do not suffer any reprisals. As of this writing, all of these proposals are still under consideration by the Senate.

THE SWING OF THE PENDULUM

For most of this century the President has enjoyed almost total preeminence in foreign affairs. Time and again American soldiers were committed to combat, agreements with foreign governments were made, covert military and political actions were undertaken, all without any prior approval from Congress; and in some cases, Congress was not even informed of such activities after the fact. Congressional willingness to let the pendulum swing so far in the direction of presidential discretion was due to several factors: (1) a recognition on the part of Congress that the President had superior information in the area of foreign affairs; (2) a desire to provide the President with the necessary flexibility in dealing not only with the Nazi threat of the forties, but also with the threat of Communist aggression during the Cold War period of the fifties and early sixties; (3) the development of a congressional state of mind that simply became accustomed to presidential dominance; in other words, the more initiatives the President undertook, the more appropriate it seemed for him to do so. What the Congress failed to appreciate, however, was that the discretion it was willing to accord presidents under certain circumstances would ultimately be seen by Presidents as their *right* under any circumstances. In short, they failed to recognize that presidential discretion feeds upon itself.

Only with our involvement in Southeast Asia did the Congress come to see the consequences of its permissiveness. One President took us into Vietnam claiming that he needed no congressional authorization for his actions. His successor extended the war into Cambodia and asserted that it was wholly within his power to do so. But the issue here was not simply the arrogance with which they claimed their authority but also their judgment. While Congress had in the past usually acceded to the President's superior expertise in foreign policy, Vietnam proved to be a case where his judgment was questionable. Neither Congress nor the public was ultimately convinced that our security was so threatened by events in Southeast Asia that we were required to make such a vast commitment of human and material resources.

The question was not whether Congress had the power to rein in the President's power in foreign affairs, but rather whether it had the will to do so. Vietnam provided the catalyst for congressional reassertion in a variety of areas concerned with foreign affairs. As noted earlier, in 1972 Congress passed legislation to increase its role in executive agreements. In 1973, the Congress passed and the President reluctantly signed a bill that prohibited the use of any funds to finance further combat activity in Indochina after August of that year. As a result of this legislation, President Nixon was forced to halt bombings in Cambodia. Not long afterwards Congress also passed the War Powers Resolution over a presidential veto.

Congress also began wielding its budgetary power in an increasingly independent fashion on matters related to foreign affairs. While in the past the State Department, Peace Corps, and United States Information Agency were given appropriations for several years, Congress has now decided to fund them on an annual basis. They have also become increasingly less inclined to support presidential requests for foreign aid. For example, between 1950 and 1968 Congress cut presidential foreign aid requests by 19 percent,[54] but from 1969 through 1974 foreign aid requests were cut back by an average of 28 percent.[55] Most notable among these cutbacks were the restrictions on military and economic aid to Vietnam and Turkey. In spite of strong objections from both President Ford and Secretary of State Henry Kissinger, the Congress reduced the 1974 aid request for Vietnam from $1.45 billion to $700 million. Nor did Congress act on President Ford's request in 1975 for an additional $522 million in aid for Vietnam. Furthermore, to the chagrin of the President and Secretary of State, Congress declined to grant additional military aid requests to Turkey and temporarily suspended current military aid following their invasion of Cyprus.

In the area of trade, the Congress not only denied trade concessions to members of the international oil cartel (OPEC) but also refused to go along with the 1972 Nixon-Brezhnev agreement in which the Soviet Union was to be accorded "most favored nation" status in its trade relations with the United States. The refusal to do so resulted from the Soviet Union's unwillingness to permit greater freedom to Soviet Jews.[56] Both of these actions were taken despite strong warnings from President Ford that our relations with oil-producing countries and the Soviet Union would be seriously damaged. Finally, the Congress also passed legislation that now requires the President to gain congressional approval before selling nuclear equipment to other nations.

That Congress had been able to reassert itself in foriegn affairs during the Nixon and Ford presidencies was undoubtedly due not only to its own determination but also to a weakened adversary. Engulfed in the scandals of his Presidency, Richard Nixon was in no position to challenge or change congressional will. His successor also operated from a diminished power base not only because he was an unelected president but also because he had succeeded to an office whose prestige was seriously eroded by the scandals of Watergate. Whether Con-

[54] *Congressional Quarterly Almanac* (Washington, D.C.: Congressional Quarterly, Inc., 1968), p. 605.

[55] Kolodziej, "Congress and Foreign Policy," p. 175.

[56] *New York Times,* January 25, 1975, p. E1.

gress would exhibit the determination to reassert itself against future and perhaps stronger presidents remained to be seen. The Majority Leader of the Senate clearly thought it would:

> I believe that Congress will retain the momentum. There will be a slow and deliberate effort by Congress to reassert its own power. Of course, we have to be sure the pendulum doesn't swing too far in the other direction. But the President will not continue to accumulate more power at the expense of Congress. There will be no more Vietnams.[57]

If the behavior of Congress during the first part of the Carter Administration is any indication, then one would have to conclude that the prediction of the former Senate Majority Leader seems to be correct. Clearly the now famous DeConcini reservations, with one attached to each of the Panama Canal Treaties, demonstrated the Senate's willingness to exercise its *own* judgment as to what is in the national interest of the United States. But congressional assertiveness showed itself in other areas as well, notably, foreign aid, arms sales, troop withdrawals from overseas, and the recognition of countries.

In 1977 President Carter narrowly averted a major setback to his foreign aid program. More specifically, the House voted overwhelmingly to reduce the United States contributions to international lending agencies (e.g., World Bank, Asian Development Fund, International Development Association) if they lent any portion of their United States contributions to Vietnam, Cambodia, Cuba, and several countries in Africa and South America. Since the United States is the major contributor to these agencies, and since these agencies cannot accept contributions with strings attached, passage of this legislation could have had a disastrous effect upon the World Bank and other such agencies. While the House ultimately backed off from this legislation, they were able to extract a promise from President Carter in return; namely, that the United States representatives to these international lending agencies would be instructed to vote against aid to the countries singled out by the House. It should also be noted that both the House and Senate did approve a provision in the Foreign Assistance Act (1977) which would prohibit the United States from giving any *direct* aid to Cuba, Vietnam, Laos, Mozambique, Cambodia, and Angola.

Carter's difficulties with Congress were also evident in the area of arms sales. Like his predecessor, Carter implored the Congress to lift its arms embargo against Turkey—imposed after Turkey used American arms in its 1974 invasion of Cyprus. (In retaliation for the embargo, the Turkish government closed United States intelligence and military installations located in its country.) While Congress's past opposition to lifting the embargo was undoubtedly influenced by the powerful Greek lobby, two other considerations loomed large as well: first, the law mandated a suspension of United States arms to any country

---

[57]*New York Times,* March 28, 1976, p. 44. © 1976 by The New York Times Company. Reprinted by permission.

that used them for aggressive purposes; second, the arms embargo constituted the only significant leverage the United States could exert to pressure Turkey into resolving its differences with Cyprus. The Carter Administration, however, was now arguing that the strategy of exerting pressure through the embargo had clearly not worked. Moreover, the administration also expressed the fear that a continuance of our present policy could precipitate Turkey's withdrawal from NATO and encourage it to come to terms with the Soviet Union. In the summer of 1978, the issue once again came to a vote in the Congress, but this time Congress voted to lift the embargo. No doubt, this change of heart resulted not only from the President's extraordinary lobbying effort, but also from the increased strain in United States/Soviet relations. It should be pointed out, however, that the President's victory was a very narrow one indeed, for in the House the vote to repeal carried by a margin of only three votes.

Carter also experienced difficulty with Congress on arms sales to other countries. It took several months, for example, to gain the necessary approval to sell an air defense system to one of our strongest allies in the Middle East, namely, Iran. And to facilitate Senate passage of his arms package to Egypt, Saudi Arabia, and Israel, the President reversed himself and agreed to increase the number of F-15s going to Israel.

Even in areas of foreign policy that clearly fall within the scope of the President, the Congress made its views known in a more assertive fashion. One such area concerned the movement of United States troops. Not long after assuming office, President Carter announced his intention to begin a gradual withdrawal of the 40,000 American troops stationed in South Korea. Despite the fact that the Senate Foreign Relations Committee recommended that the Senate give a vote of support to Carter's decision, none was forthcoming. In fact, only through the efforts of Majority Leader Robert Byrd was the Carter Administration able to head off a resolution condemning the proposed troop withdrawal. But even the Byrd compromise amendment, which ultimately won Senate approval, stated that troop reductions should be "carried out in regular consultation with the Congress." On another occasion, the Senate narrowly defeated an amendment that called for a halt in the movement toward restoring diplomatic relations with Cuba until it had made further concessions. Of course, had the Senate passed this amendment, or for that matter the one condemning Carter's troop withdrawal from South Korea, neither of these would have been binding on the President. As Commander in Chief, he is free to move American troops as he wishes (excepting those restrictions imposed by the War Powers Resolution), and his constitutional power to appoint and receive ambassadors gives him the authority to recognize other countries. Yet the fact that both amendments received considerable support in the Senate clearly indicated that its membership would now be taking a closer look at the President's actions in these areas.

Following years of deference to the President in foreign affairs, the willingness of Congress to play a more active role in this area represents a healthy development. At the same time, however, we would do well to bear in mind that, while excessive deference to the President in this area has had distinct drawbacks, so too may excessive involvement on the part of Congress. Foreign policy, after all, requires the direction of one hand—a reality appreciated only too well by our Founding Fathers. With a membership totalling five hundred and thirty-five individuals, the Congress is ill-suited to developing a coherent and integrated approach to foreign policy matters. Nor is this problem of size mitigated to any significant extent by organization, for fourteen of the fifteen standing committees in the Senate and seventeen of twenty-two standing committees in the House all have at least some jurisdiction over matters related to foreign affairs. Given such a wide dispersal of responsibility, coordination of policy understandably becomes extremely difficult. Finally, to a far greater extent than the President, Congress is susceptible to the pleadings of special interests, and this too inhibits its ability to take a holistic view of foreign policy matters. These limitations are not meant to indicate that Congress should keep hands off, but they are meant to suggest that congressional involvement should be directed toward more vigorous oversight of foreign policy, rather than toward attempts to determine the details of it.

3

The President and Congress

Much of what a President wishes to accomplish must be done in partnership with the Legislative branch. Establishing and maintaining this partnership is, as presidents have inevitably discovered, one of the great frustrations of the Office. One adviser to three presidents speaks to this point: "I suspect that there may be nothing about the White House less generally understood than the ease with which a Congress can drive a President quite out of his mind and up the wall."[1] Theodore Roosevelt gave vent to his frustrations on one occasion when he remarked, "Oh, if I could only be President and Congress too for just ten minutes." Even Gerald Ford, who was a long-time member of the congressional establishment, was not in the Presidency very long before he acknowledged some frustration with his former home:

> The only thing that is disappointing—I guess any President has this. The President thinks he has the right answers. The facts of history are that he doesn't always—but he thinks he does. And he would like to implement, he'd like to execute—to get things done. But under our system, the Congress has a very definite partnership. Right now we are going through an extraordinary trauma in the relationship between the Congress and the President. I understand that. I've been on the other end of it. But if there was one part which I would really like to change, it would be the speed with which you could make decisions and carry them out.[2]

[1] Emmet John Hughes, *The Living Presidency* (New York: Coward, McCann & Geoghegan, 1973), p. 208. Copyright © 1973 by Emmet John Hughes. Reprinted by permission of Coward, McCann & Geoghegan.

[2] *New York Times Magazine,* April 20, 1975, pp. 112, 113. © 1975 by The New York Times Company. Reprinted by permission.

In this chapter we shall examine this critically important relationship between the Executive and Legislative branches, noting those factors that make for antagonism as well as those that can serve to mitigate it. We shall also consider how and why the relationship between these two branches has changed over the years.

THE PRESIDENT AND CONGRESS: A STRAINED RELATIONSHIP

Shortly after he took over the reins of the Presidency, Gerald Ford spoke before a joint session of Congress and stated that he wanted their relationship to be "a marriage, not a honeymoon." While such words expressed an admirable sentiment, a man of his long-time Washington experience surely knew that he was asking for the impossible. There exist a variety of factors that make it inevitable that the relationship between the President and the Congress will be a less than harmonious one. These factors are rooted in the very structure of our political system and thus they are ever present. To be sure, other factors can help to reduce this antagonism, but it is just that—reduction rather than elimination.

Separation of Powers

Under our constitutional system, the Executive and Legislative branches were created as two organically distinct components of the government. Each has a strong sense of its own responsibilities and importance in the scheme of things; each has powers, which if exercised, can frustrate the will of the other. Consequently, it is not surprising that an institutional rivalry develops between the two branches. In order to impress upon Congress that it was he who was running the government, Franklin Roosevelt would on occasion ask his aids for "something I can veto."[3] Richard Nixon likewise exhibited this same sense of institutional rivalry between the two branches when he remarked, "The moment that a President is looking over his shoulder down to Capitol Hill before he makes a decision, he will then be a weak President."[4]

The old adage "What one sees depends upon where one stands" is applicable here. The separation of powers principle locates the President and Congress at different points in our political system. They each have different responsibilities and face different pressures, and consequently they may not always view matters from the same perspective. As a congressman from Illinois, Abraham Lincoln was horrified by President James Polk's misuse of power when he took the

[3] Richard Neustadt, *Presidential Power* (New York: John Wiley, 1960), p. 84.

[4] Cited in Theodore Sorensen, *Watchmen in the Night* (Cambridge, Mass.: MIT Press, 1975), p. 89.

United States into war against Mexico. Yet as President, Lincoln was not at all reluctant to take actions that far exceeded his constitutional powers. Similarly, in 1950 Congressman Richard Nixon voted in favor of a House resolution designed to prevent presidents from making executive agreements with heads of state. President Nixon, however, not only made frequent use of executive agreements, but also announced that he would veto pending legislation that sought to restrict this power. Likewise, when President Truman invoked executive privilege and thus refused to hand over certain information requested by a congressional committee, Congressman Nixon objected strenuously, arguing that Truman's actions simply "cannot stand from a constitutional standpoint."[5] As President, however, Richard Nixon defended and extended the use of executive privilege to a greater degree than any other American President.

Structure of Congress

The very structure of Congress itself insures that the President will not have an easy time of getting what he wants. Congress is first of all divided into two different bodies, thus requiring the President to gain the support of two different leadership groups. Power is dispersed still further as a consequence of the committee system. There are fifteen standing committees in the Senate and twenty-two in the House. Moreover, power in the House has become dispersed even more widely since 1973, when the Democratic Caucus voted to give subcommittees—of which there are approximately 150—greater autonomy over their own operations.

Since virtually all important legislation must be referred to committees for study, committee chairmen occupy a very strategic position in the legislative process. They may prevent a piece of presidential legislation from even being considered by their committee, which means that it will most likely die quietly there. Or a chairman and his committee may decide to report the bill out of committee with a favorable recommendation but not before they have made substantial changes in it. President Johnson felt the sting of a committee chairman's power when Wilbur Mills, chairman of the powerful House Ways and Means Committee, singlehandedly held up the President's tax surcharge legislation for almost two years.[6] President Kennedy humorously took note of Mills's extraordinary power when visiting the congressman's district to dedicate a federal project: "I read in the *New York Times* this morning that if Wilbur Mills requested it, I'd be glad to come down here and sing 'Down By The Old Mill Stream.' I want to say that I am delighted."[7]

Finally, the rules and procedures of Congress serve to diffuse power still

[5] Cited in Arthur Schlesinger, Jr., *The Imperial Presidency* (Boston: Houghton Mifflin, 1973), pp. 42, 151, 154.

[6] Joseph Califano, *A Presidential Nation* (New York: W.W. Norton, 1975), p. 56.

[7] Dale Vinyard, *The Presidency* (New York: Scribner's, 1971), p. 111.

further. In the Senate especially, the rules permit a minority of one or more senators to frustrate the passage of legislation. While such obstructionist tactics may ultimately be stopped by the rest of the membership, extraordinary majorities (three fifths) are usually required to do so.

In summary, the point to be made here is simply this: to the extent that the President must deal with a large number of independent power centers within Congress, the task of gaining acceptance for his legislative proposals is rendered all the more difficult.

Different Constituencies

In the past, one traditional source of conflict between the President and Congress has stemmed from the fact that each was elected by different constituencies. Thus, to the extent that the presidential prize depends upon winning the large northern industrialized states—each having a large share of electoral votes—presidents are likely to be more responsive to the urban minority groups who reside there. Congress, on the other hand, has traditionally overrepresented the rural areas of the country, which tend to be more conservative. While reapportionment of congressional districts has greatly reduced the rural bias of the House, this change may not eliminate its conservatism altogether. Substantially fewer people vote in congressional as opposed to presidential elections. It may be argued, therefore, that congressmen are more responsive to this "smaller, more stable, better organized, and probably more satisfied electorate than the President, who seeks to mobilize numbers of people largely untouched by politics."[8] Meanwhile, the Senate appears to have become increasingly liberal and cosmopolitan, a change that can perhaps be explained by the fact that urbanization has spread to virtually all the states in the Union.[9] Accordingly, conservative presidents may in the future find the Senate to be a greater stumbling block to securing support for their policy initiatives, while more liberal presidents will continue to find greater opposition to their programs in the House.

The precise impact of constituency on presidential behavior is difficult to assess in cause and effect terms. It seems likely, however, that Lyndon Johnson as President felt he could take a more visible and assertive role in favor of civil rights than he could as a senator who represented only the conservative and southern states of Texas. Similarly, it is worth pondering whether or not President Ford would have introduced even his limited amnesty program had he continued to represent only his conservative congressional district in Michigan.

[8] Erwin Hargrove, *The Power of the Modern Presidency* (New York: Alfred A. Knopf, 1974), p. 207.

[9] Ibid., p. 206.

Erosion of Support

While the ability of the President to get his way with Congress fluctuates a good deal throughout his tenure in office, nevertheless he appears to enjoy greater success earlier as opposed to later in his term. Lyndon Johnson was acutely aware of this fact:

> We'll have nine, eh, maybe even eighteen months before the Hill turns around on us. We have that much time to get it all through. . . . you can have anything you want for a time. . . . No they'll be glad to be aboard and to have their photograph taken with you and be part of all that victory. They'll come along and they'll give you almost everything you want for a while and then they'll turn on you. They always do. They'll lay in waiting, waiting for you to make a slip and you will. They'll give you almost everything and then they'll make you pay for it.[10]

Presidents come into office on a wave of good will, which has often been characterized as the "honeymoon period." There is a natural inclination on the part of those in and outside of Congress to unite around and cooperate with the newly elected leader of the nation. This reservoir of good will does not last for long, however. A President must inevitably expend his political capital in attempting to accomplish his goals. Nearly every major decision he makes will irritate some, even while pleasing others. Over the course of his Presidency, such dissatisfactions are likely to accumulate, thus making it increasingly difficult for him to work his will on Congress. As one longtime congressman has noted, "The rule here is to forgive—and remember."[11] This erosion of support is made still worse for a President who is ineligible to run again, for as he moves through his final term of office, he is likely to become increasingly less persuasive with those who realize his days are numbered.[12]

LESSENING OR WORSENING OF THE ANTAGONISM: INTERVENING FACTORS

Up to this point, I have discussed certain *ever-present* factors that serve to frustrate the development of a harmonious relationship between the President and Congress. We now consider another set of factors, which may or may not be present. To the degree that they are, the President's relationship with Con-

---

[10] David Halberstam, *The Best and the Brightest* (New York: Random House, Inc., 1969), p. 516.

[11] Ralph Huitt, "White House Channels to the Hill," in Harvey Mansfield, ed., *Congress Against the President* (New York: Academy of Political Science, 1975), p. 83.

[12] Harold Laski, *The American Presidency* (New York: Universal Library, 1940), p. 138.

gress is made easier. To the extent that they are absent, his dealings with it are likely to be even more difficult.

Nature of the Times

Not surprisingly, Congress is much more disposed toward cooperating with the President during times of crisis. Under such conditions decisive leadership is required, and Congress recognizes that a single man can provide it more effectively than can a legislative body composed of five hundred and thirty-five individuals. Franklin Roosevelt was accorded considerable freedom of action and strong support by the Congress in fighting the Great Depression as well as in waging war against Germany and Japan. Similarly, when Lyndon Johnson succeeded to the Presidency upon the death of President Kennedy, he initially received extraordinary support for his legislative programs. While his success was undoubtedly enhanced by his own persuasive skills and his thorough understanding of congressional politics, he also benefited from a desire on the part of Congress and the public to unite around their new President at this critical time.

Later in his Administration Johnson would again seize upon another domestic crisis—the assassination of Martin Luther King—in order to work his will on Congress. In 1966, he had proposed a bill to Congress known as the Fair Housing Act, the purpose of which was to prevent discriminatory practices in housing. It was defeated. He reintroduced the bill again in 1967 and early 1968, but the Congress failed to pass it both times. Immediately following the assassination of Martin Luther King on April 4, 1968, Johnson realized that the mood of the Congress would now be more hospitable to his housing bill. Accordingly, he introduced the bill once again, and this time it passed both Houses of Congress. The Fair Housing Act was signed into law by the President on April 10, 1968, just six days after the King assassination.

Public Prestige

Presidents who are fortunate enough to enjoy considerable support from the population are likely to encounter less resistance from the Congress. While the absence of such support does not by any means render presidents powerless to act, their freedom of action is nevertheless likely to be restricted:

> The weaker his apparent popular support, the more his cause in Congress may depend on negatives at his disposal like the veto. . . . He may not be left helpless, but his options are reduced, his opportunities diminished, his freedom of maneuver checked in the degree that Washington conceives him unimpressive to the public.[13]

This is not to say that the congressional mood will respond to any sudden and temporary decline or increase in the President's public prestige. Rather, the

[13]Neustadt, *Presidential Power,* p. 90.

Congress is more likely to react to the long-run trends in a President's popularity. Throughout most of Truman's second term in office, his public approval rating declined steadily from around 80 percent down to as low as 23 percent. In the case of Lyndon Johnson, his public approval rating went from 71 percent in 1965 all the way down to 36 percent in 1968.[14] Richard Nixon suffered a similar fate as the Watergate scandals gradually unraveled before the American public. In January of 1973, his approval rating was at 51 percent but fell all the way to 24 percent by August of 1974.[15]

For each of these presidents, the persistent erosion of public support was also accompanied by a general decline in his ability to get the legislation he wanted from the Congress. While it would be incorrect to presume that these declines in legislative success were due exclusively to decreasing popular support, they surely played a role.[16]

It should be noted, however, that the blow of decreasing public support may be cushioned to some extent by other factors. Lyndon Johnson, for example, was quite adept at exercising leadership over the Legislature. In addition, he also benefited from the fact that his party controlled both Houses of Congress. Had both of these factors been absent, his declining success with Congress would most likely have accelerated. Eisenhower, on the other hand, did not have Republican majorities in control of Congress for most of the time he was in office, and he was not especially effective as a legislative leader. At the same time, however, his public approval rating never dropped below 49 percent during his whole eight years as President.[17] If his success rate with Congress was not outstanding, neither was it disastrous; but it might have been had he not enjoyed such widespread public support. Lyndon Johnson, who was then the powerful Senate Majority Leader, was keenly aware of Eisenhower's popularity in Texas. Accordingly, during his frequent radio broadcasts to his Texas constituents, Senator Johnson never passed up an opportunity to remind them of how many times he had supported President Eisenhower on several important issues.[18]

Legislative Leadership Style

If the President wishes favorable consideration of his legislative proposals, then he must be willing to involve himself in the legislative process. He must

[14] John Mueller, *War, Presidents and Public Opinion* (New York: John Wiley, 1973), pp. 199, 201.

[15] *The Gallup Opinion Index,* January 1974, p. 3; *The Gallup Opinion Index,* September 1974, p. 11.

[16] For a discussion of the influence of public prestige upon the President's legislative success see George Edwards, "Presidential Influence in the House: Presidential Prestige as a Source of Presidential Power," *American Political Science Review* 70 (March 1976), 101–13.

[17] Mueller, *War, Presidents and Public Opinion,* p. 202.

[18] Booth Mooney, *LBJ: An Irreverent Chronicle* (New York: Thomas Y. Crowell, 1976), pp. 19, 32. Copyright © 1976 by Booth Mooney. Reprinted by permission of Thomas Y. Crowell.

make a special effort to cultivate the good will of members of Congress. He must be willing to press his advantages in dealing with them. By virtue of their interest, temperament, and political astuteness, some presidents have proven more adept at this task than others.

Among our earlier presidents, Jefferson was by far the most assertive in seeking congressional support, and he did so in a manner unmatched by those who preceded or came after him. While the Congress was in session, he held White House dinners for legislators on an almost nightly basis. To insure an intimate atmosphere, no more than twelve were invited at any one time, but almost all were invited more than once while Congress was in session. Invitations were written personally by Jefferson and were often accompanied by an additional note. A round dinner table was used for the occasion, "thus avoiding a place of precedence for the President and putting him among his peers, at the same time that it prevented separate, private conversations."[19] In an effort to encourage frank and open conversation, Jefferson did not permit any servants to be present, but instead had a dumbwaiter installed from which he personally served the dinner. The good food and wine, the informal atmosphere, and free and easy conversation, all helped to make such dinners the talk of Washington. Nor can their importance be underestimated in explaining why Jefferson enjoyed such extraordinary support among members of his party in Congress.

Jefferson had the luxury of occupying the Presidency at a time when fewer demands were made upon it and also when Congress was considerably smaller than it is today. Although twentieth-century presidents lack the time to cultivate the Congress in the manner to which Jefferson was accustomed, they do attempt to establish a working relationship in other ways. Harry Truman was the first President to officially designate certain members of his staff as a legislative liaison. Eisenhower went further by establishing within his staff an Office of Congresssional Relations, which has been continued under subsequent presidents. Eisenhower himself, however, did not assume a very assertive role in his dealings with Congress, for his conception of the Presidency as well as his personal style were not suited to such a role. Beyond making his views known to the Congress, he did not think it appropriate for the Presidency to intrude itself into the legislative process. In addition, he made it quite clear that he found distasteful the role of a President as a partisan politician, prodding and cajoling the members of Congress: "I think it is quite apparent that I am not very much of a partisan. The times are too serious, I think, to indulge in partisanship to the extreme."[20]

This refusal to politick with the Congress was clearly demonstrated in Eisenhower's response to the death of Senator Robert Taft, the Republican Majority Leader in the Senate. The top contender to succeed Taft was Senator William Knowland of California, a Republican who had strongly opposed Eisenhower's

[19] James Young, "The Presidency and the Hill," in Aaron Wildavsky, ed., *The Presidency* (Boston: Little, Brown, 1969), p. 418.

[20] David Broder, *The Party's Over* (New York: Harper & Row, 1971), p. 6.

presidential candidacy. Since support by the Majority Leader is of considerable importance to the success of the President's legislative program, it was expected that Eisenhower would fight to prevent the selection of Senator Knowland. Thus, it came as quite a surprise when the President announced to his Cabinet that "This Administration has absolutely no personal choice for new Majority Leader. *We* are not going to get into *their* business."[21] Knowland ultimately was selected, and he did indeed prove to be unsympathetic to many of Eisenhower's programs. The President's reluctance to involve himself in partisan politics is not altogether surprising, for he had very little training for it. As he himself noted, he had been isolated "from boyhood from nearly all politics."[22]

John Kennedy took a more activist view of the Presidency and was committed to the belief that such activism included presidential involvement in partisan politics: "Legislative leadership is not possible without party leadership. . . . No President can escape politics."[23] He retained the Office of Congressional Liaison, but unlike Eisenhower, who kept it out of politics, he staffed it with a group of strong Democratic partisans headed by Larry O'Brien. He was not in the Presidency very long before he vigorously asserted his office into congressional affairs. Sensing that his liberal legislative programs were destined to be killed by the powerful and conservative House Rules Committee, he pressured the Democratic House leadership to push for an expansion of the House Rules Committee so that more liberals could be placed on it. After a long legislative battle, the plan was ultimately approved by a slim margin of eight votes.

Kennedy was equally willing to bestow presidential favors upon members of Congress as payment for past or future support. There were limits to his assertiveness, however. When push came to shove, he was reluctant to use high-pressure tactics. According to Senator Everett Dirksen, he preferred to persuade by relying "entirely on the intrinsic merits of the request."[24] This assessment is confirmed by Kennedy's chief legislative liaison, who recalls that the President would make his case in a rational fashion, hoping that a given congressman would see the issue as he did, but that he "rarely asked a member for his vote on a specific piece of legislation."[25] His reluctance to do so is perhaps explained by the fact that his relationship with members of Congress was correct rather than friendly. In the words of a former aid, "Kennedy's Congressional relations were marked by a formality and stiffness, which I believe stemmed from the fact that he never really felt comfortable as a member of the legislature, nor did he

---

[21] Hughes, *Living Presidency,* p. 63.

[22] Broder, *Party's Over,* pp. 5, 6.

[23] Cited in Broder, *Party's Over,* p. 34.

[24] Taken from Lewis Paper, *The Promise and the Performance* (New York: Crown, 1975), p. 262. © 1975 by Lewis J. Paper. Used by permission of Crown Publishers, Inc.

[25] Ibid., p. 261.

personally identify with it. He was unwilling to pay the dues, so to speak, and felt something of an aloofness, if not disdain, for the legislative body."[26]

Among recent presidents none exercised presidential leadership over the Congress with greater skill, energy, and success than did Lyndon Johnson. Twenty-three years of experience in Congress—eight of which were spent as Senate Majority Leader—undoubtedly provided him with an invaluable opportunity to gain a thorough understanding of the process and its people. And he was determined to make every use of this advantage. Moreover, unlike his predecessor, Johnson was genuinely fascinated by the legislative process, and consequently his involvement with it was undertaken with great relish. Furthermore, he had an abiding respect for the abilities of its membership, frequently reminding his advisers that "not all the patriotism and wisdom reside in the Executive branch. They [Congress] will change our bills and often as not, they will improve them."[27] Acutely aware of Congress's importance in the policy-making process, Johnson went to extraordinary lengths to cultivate their support. His instructions to staff aids conveyed his determination to do so: "The most important people you will talk to are senators and congressmen. You treat them as if they were President. Answer their calls immediately. Give them respect. . . . they are your most important clients."[28]

To an unprecedented degree, Johnson also sought to involve the Congress in the formulation of legislation. He put congressmen and senators on task forces that were charged with identifying problem areas in need of legislative solutions. When it actually came time to begin drafting a piece of legislation, Johnson dispensed his aids to Capitol Hill, where they met secretly with those congressmen and senators who had a special interest in the legislation. The purpose of these meetings was to incorporate their suggestions into specific provisions of the bill. Finally, on the eve of formally introducing the bill before Congress, Johnson would hold a White House dinner meeting with congressional leaders to consider last-minute suggestions for changing the bill and also to plan legislative strategy once the bill was before Congress.

Johnson's meticulous efforts to include Congress in the process of formulating legislation greatly enhanced the possibility that his programs would be favorably received by the Legislative branch.[29] When additional pressure was needed, however, Johnson was not at all reluctant to intervene personally. Whereas Kennedy tried to convince primarily on the merits of the case, Johnson went further—he begged, flattered, and twisted arms when necessary. On one occasion he even went so far as to contact a senator's mistress to see if she could persuade the

[26] Ibid., pp. 260, 261.

[27] Cited in Huitt, "White House Channels," p. 73.

[28] Jack Valenti, *A Very Human President* (New York: W.W. Norton, 1975), p. 178.

[29] Doris Kearns, *Lyndon Johnson and the American Dream* (New York: Harper & Row, 1976), pp. 222-32.

senator to vote in favor of closing off a filibuster that was being waged against the 1964 civil rights bill.[30] Such high-pressure tactics ultimately produced considerable resentment and resistance among members of Congress, but not before Johnson had produced one of the most remarkable legislative records of any President in our history.

In several respects, Richard Nixon provided a marked contrast to his predecessor. While Johnson was genuinely fascinated by the legislative process, Nixon found it singularly uninteresting. And whereas Johnson felt an abiding respect for the institution, his successor regarded Congress as a nuisance. One explanation for these attitudes may be the fact that his own experience in Congress was not an altogether happy one. In the House he functioned as a loner, and as a senator never gained entry into the Senate's inner club of influentials.[31]

Although Nixon did appoint a highly respected political pro by the name of Bryce Harlow to head his legislative liaison office in the White House, Harlow's efforts to develop a working relationship with the Congress were largely nullified by Nixon's two closest advisers, H. R. Haldeman and John Ehrlichman. Having never had any Washington experience themselves, these two Nixon aids failed to appreciate the delicate nature of the relationship between the President and the Congress. Indeed, the latter was viewed by them as an "awkward and obnoxious obstacle, a hostile foreign power."[32] Accordingly, members of Congress experienced great difficulty in gaining access to the President. Phone calls to the White House by long-time supporters went unanswered, and appointments with the President were hard to come by. And, apparently, not even the Republican leadership in Congress was consulted on legislative matters as evidenced in a complaint voiced by the Republican Minority Leader of the Senate: "They never invite me for the take-offs but they damned well want me there for the crash landings."[33] While Nixon was not at all reluctant to assert himself in his relations with Congress, his actions usually took the form of negative as opposed to positive action. Unlike Johnson, he did not enjoy face-to-face bargaining with legislators; nor did he make a strenuous effort to gain their support, especially on domestic matters:

> . . . Nixon did not seem to want anything from Congress. To be sure, he initiated domestic programs and proclaimed priorities, but he seemed to lose interest in them quickly. In fact, Congress found itself upbraiding him for not really trying to get what he said he wanted, which many members wanted more than he did.

[30]Califano, *Presidential Nation,* p. 215.

[31]Rowland Evans, Jr., and Robert Novak, *Nixon in the White House* (New York: Vantage Books, 1971), p. 106.

[32]Ibid., p. 109.

[33]Cited in Randall Ripley, *Congress: Process and Policy* (New York: W.W. Norton, 1975), p. 233.

Trying to oppose Nixon on domestic programs was, as some congressmen put it, "like pushing on a string." There was no resistance.[34]

Rather his assertiveness took the form of frequent condemnations of the Congress as irresponsible, frequent use of the veto, and refusal to spend money that had been duly authorized and appropriated by the Congress. Needless to say, presidential action of this sort served only to further aggravate an already strained relationship.

Party Control

The natural antagonism between a President and Congress is likely to increase or decrease depending upon whether his own party is in control of Congress. Thus, while Lyndon Johnson's persuasive skills were considerable, his extraordinary legislative record in 1964-65 was greatly facilitated by the fact that his party enjoyed such substantial majorities in the House (239-140) and the Senate (69-32) during this time. And conversely, in addition to the fact that Richard Nixon's leadership style served to create antagonism between himself and Congress, he was further disadvantaged because his party did not control either House of Congress during the entire time he occupied the Presidency.

Of course, it should be emphasized that while any President would prefer to have his party in control of Congress, such a state of affairs is by itself no guarantee that he will get all that he wants from it. From 1962 to 1968, for example, the Democrats controlled both the House and the Senate. The average support among Senate Democrats for Johnson's legislative programs over this period was 59 percent; among House Democrats it was 72 percent. Nor can a President count on the full support of his party when it is in the minority in Congress. As already noted, Republicans lacked majorities in both Houses while Richard Nixon was in office. During this time House Republicans supported his stands on legislation 63 percent of the time and Senate Republicans, 62 percent of the time.[35]

It should be apparent from the discussion in the previous section that a President's leadership style can help to explain his failure to gain the full support of his party. Other factors also include the possibility that congressmen or senators may be philosophically opposed to the President's position on a given issue; or they may be under strong pressure from their constituencies to vote against one of his programs. As Lyndon Johnson aptly observed, "It is day dreaming to assume that any experienced congressman would ignore his basic instincts or his constituents' deepest concerns in quaking fear of the White House." Finally, a congressman's failure to support his party's President is undoubtedly encouraged by the fact that he pays little penalty for withholding

[34] Cited in Huitt, "White House Channels," p. 76.

[35] Frank Sorauf, *Party Politics in America,* 3rd ed. (Boston: Little, Brown, 1976), p. 356.

such support. He is not likely to suffer any sanctions within Congress nor, more important, is his reelection likely to be seriously jeopardized. Members of Congress are not easily defeated. In fact, in the seven elections from 1954 to 1966, for example, 92.8 percent of the House members and 88.2 percent of the Senate membership were reelected.[36] To be sure, a disloyal congressman may suffer the displeasure of the President, but even this is likely to be only temporary, for the President will most certainly have to enlist his support on some future occasion.

The impact of party on the relationship between the President and Congress has been a source of concern in some parts of the scholarly community for quite some time. This concern grows out of the belief that our political parties contribute to the immobilization of presidential leadership, not so much in foreign policy where a tradition of bipartisanship exists, but rather in domestic policy. In the words of one political observer, "Our government has suffered from crippled leadership, from a slowdown of decision making, an impairment of its vital processes. The result has been an accumulation of unresolved problems and a buildup of public frustration. . . . "[37]

This government by stalemate results from two factors. First, under our constitutional arrangements it is possible for the Presidency to be controlled by one political party while the opposition party controls *one* or *both* Houses of Congress. This possibility has in fact become a frequent, rather than a rare, occurrence. In approximately half of the elections in this century, presidents have faced a situation in which one of the two Houses of Congress was controlled by the opposition party. More important, during fourteen of the last twenty-seven years presidents have faced a Congress in which *both* Houses were controlled by the opposition party. Gerald Ford was the most recent President to face such a frustrating situation. In a Congress where the Democrats enjoyed an overwhelming 60 to 39 advantage in the Senate and a 291 to 144 advantage in the House, Ford found the Congress repeatedly unsympathetic to his attempts to control inflation and deal with the energy problem. Indeed, Congress's support for his legislative positions in the year 1975 was only 61 percent, the lowest support score for a second-year President in twenty-three years.[38]

The immobilization of presidential leadership is not only the consequence of presidents having to face a Congress controlled by the opposition party. It is also argued that party discipline is almost totally lacking; that is, members of the President's party who fail to support his programs suffer no penalties from his party's leadership in Congress. Accordingly, even if a President is fortunate enough to have his own party in control of Congress, he still has no guarantee of

---

[36]Warren Kostroski, "Party and Incumbency in Postwar Senate Elections," *American Political Science Review* 57 (December 1973), 1217.

[37]Broder, *Party's Over,* p. xvii.

[38]Congressional Quarterly, *Presidency 1975* (Washington, D.C.: Congressional Quarterly, 1976), p. 42.

their full cooperation. On paper, for example, John Kennedy enjoyed healthy Democratic majorities in both the House (263-174) and the Senate (64-36) when he assumed the Presidency. These figures are deceiving, however, for 99 of the Democrats in the House and 21 of the Senate Democrats were from the Old Confederacy.[39]

In order to avoid alienating these conservative southern Democrats, Kennedy postponed for two years his campaign promise to seek civil rights legislation. Even this tactic did not prevent southern Democrats from frequently uniting with conservative Republicans to defeat or seriously alter several of Kennedy's key legislative initiatives. Noting his frustration with Congress, Kennedy on one occasion remarked that he and British Prime Minister Harold Macmillan had both decided on a tax cut for their respective countries at approximately the same time. Yet the Prime Minister had gotten his proposal through Parliament in six weeks, while the President had still not succeeded in gaining congressional approval of his tax cut at the end of three years. Both heads of government enjoyed party majorities in their respective legislatures. Macmillan succeeded where Kennedy failed, however, because there exists a high degree of party discipline in the British Parliament. Except under rare circumstances, the Prime Minister is assured of receiving full support from members of his party.

Lyndon Johnson enjoyed much greater legislative success with Congress than did John Kennedy, but we paid a price for it. Taking advantage of the overwhelming Democratic majorities in both houses of Congress, Johnson pushed through one piece of legislation after another at a record-breaking pace. Complaints by legislators that Johnson was pushing too much at them too quickly proved of no avail. The result of this frenetic legislative pace was 181 new programs passed into law in 1965-66.[40] Quantitatively this was one of the most remarkable legislative records of any Congress in our history. Qualitatively, however, many of these programs left much to be desired. Congress simply lacked the time to consider them all carefully, and consequently several programs proved to be ill-conceived. Governors criticized the President for failing to consult the state and local officials who would be charged with implementing all this new legislation. They also pointed out that his programs were being enacted so quickly that state and local officials did not have adequate time to gain an understanding of their complexities.[41] The point to be made here, however, is that Johnson felt compelled to move quickly with Congress because he did not feel that he would be able to sustain the continued support from members of his party: "I keep hitting hard because I know this honeymoon won't last. Everyday I lose a little more political capital. That's why we have to keep at it, never letting up."[42] Had he felt assured that some members of his party

[39] Broder, *Party's Over,* p. 30.

[40] Califano, *Presidential Nation,* p. 20.

[41] Broder, *Party's Over,* p. 64.

[42] Valenti, *Very Human President,* p. 144; see also Broder, *Party's Over,* p. 58.

would not abandon him, he may well have pursued his legislative program at a slower pace, thus allowing for more careful and deliberate action.

To recapitulate briefly, it is argued by some observers that presidential leadership has become immobilized, first, because the Presidency and Congress are often controlled by different political parties, and second, because there is a general lack of party discipline within the Congress itself.

Some scholars have argued that we could eliminate the stalemate in government by adopting a model known as responsible party government. While this model entails a variety of proposals, we shall concern ourselves only with those that have a direct bearing upon the relationship between the President and Congress. In the first place, it is proposed that each national political party adopt clear, programmatic platforms on which their respective candidates would run. Second, the nomination of candidates would be placed exclusively in the hands of each party in order to insure that only individuals who supported the platform would be nominated. Third, a system of rigid party discipline would be instituted in Congress to insure that a congressman or senator voted in accordance with his party's position as it is reflected in his party's platform. Where the platform failed to address a given policy issue, his party's position would presumably be determined by its membership within the Congress, unless his party controlled the White House. In this case, his party's position would be determined by the President. Those members of Congress who failed to support their party's position would be subject to disciplinary measures. These measures might take the form of a loss of seniority or a failure to be renominated by the party at the next election. Finally, it is proposed that the *entire* House of Representatives and *one half* of the Senate be elected *with* the President every four years, thereby increasing the term of a congressman to four years and that of a senator to eight years.[43] The purpose of this last proposal is to maximize the possibility of a President's taking into office on his coattails a majority of congressmen and senators from his own party.

The implementation of these proposals would have two salutary effects. First, the President would now have the capacity to implement his programs over a four-year period because he would be supported by a *disciplined majority of his own party* in Congress. Second, accountability would be substantially increased. With one party in control of both the Executive and Legislative branches, the population could better assess which party is responsible for what happened over the preceding four years. Such an assessment is rendered more difficult under our current system where the Presidency and Congress are often controlled by two different parties.

While these proposals have much to recommend them, some scholars have

---

[43] For a discussion of these proposals see Sorauf, *Party Politics,* pp. 385–410; Evron Kirkpatrick, "Toward a More Responsible Two-Party System: Political Science, Policy Science, or Pseudo-Science?" *American Political Science Review* 55 (December 1971), 965–90; Stephen Bailey, *The Condition of Our National Political Parties* (Santa Barbara, Calif.: Fund for the Republic, 1959), p. 15.

serious doubts about their feasibility. For one thing, the makeup of both the Republican and Democratic parties is so diverse that it is highly doubtful whether candidates would be able to support all the planks in their respective party's platform. Second, given the decentralized nature of our party system and the consequent wide dispersion of power within it, there is no central disciplinary authority that would be able to compel candidates to support the party platform.[44] Third, given the increased tendency on the part of the population to split their tickets, it is far from certain that election of the President, the House, and one-half of the Senate simultaneously would substantially increase the chances of the President's party gaining control of Congress.[45]

Even if these proposals were feasible, however, their desirability is still questionable. In the first place, to put the nomination of candidates exclusively in the hands of each party would necessitate eliminating the *direct primary,* a mechanism that allows voters themselves to select their nominees directly. Second, some are offended by the fact that under a rigid system of party discipline, congressmen and senators would be committed to fixed party positions, thus taking away their ability to exercise their own independent judgment. Under this system, for example, it seems less likely that William Fulbright, Democratic Senator and one-time chairman of the Senate Foreign Relations Committee, would have challenged Lyndon Johnson's Vietnam policy by having his committee hold public hearings on the war.[46] Third, a President supported by a disciplined majority in Congress could implement programs with little regard for the views of the minority party or skeptics within his own party. The lack of compromise that results from such circumstances could produce marked discontinuities in policy. Thus, the Democrats could gain control of the government for four years and pass legislation that was wholly unacceptable to the Republicans. If the Republicans then gained control of the government for the next four years, they would undoubtedly seek to dismantle the legislation enacted by the Democrats. Under our current system where a President is not always assured of the support of his own party members in Congress, he is often forced to strike compromises among skeptics within his own party, or else seek out support in the opposition party, a strategy that also necessitates compromise on his part. The legislation that results from such compromises will probably satisfy very few *completely.* At the same time, however, it is likely to be *totally* unacceptable to few, if any. Fourth, the proposal to increase the terms of congressmen and senators to four and eight years, respectively, also has its limitations, for less frequent elections would make Congress less reflective of changes in the public mood. Finally, all of the proposals outlined above would

---

[44] Sorauf, *Party Politics,* p. 391.

[45] For a discussion of the ticket-splitting phenomenon, see Walter DeVries and V. Lance Tarrance, *The Ticket-Splitter* (Grand Rapids, Mich.: William B. Eerdmans, 1972).

[46] Hargrove, *Modern Presidency,* p. 291.

serve to increase the President's independence from Congress, an unsettling prospect for those who view the Presidency as too powerful already.

THE ASCENDANCY OF THE PRESIDENT AS LEGISLATOR

While in this day and age we readily accept as a given the role of the President as an initiator of legislation, his ascendancy in this area represents one of the most profound changes in the relationship between the President and Congress. Accordingly, we shall now consider this development in some detail.

In drawing up the Constitution, the Founding Fathers did provide that the President "shall from time to time give the Congress Information on the State of the Union, and recommend to their Consideration such Measures as he shall judge necessary and expedient." Notwithstanding this provision, however, the primary function of the Executive was to execute the legislation that was proposed and passed by Congress. Even the veto power was intended as a mechanism to be used by the President chiefly against legislation that threatened the constitutional rights of his office.[47] While such presidents as Jefferson, Jackson, and Lincoln did inject themselves into the legislative process, these initiatives were clearly the exception rather than the rule. Indeed, the predominant view was one voiced by Congressman Abraham Lincoln: "Were I President, I should desire the legislation of the country to rest with Congress, uninfluenced in its origin or progress, and undisturbed by the veto unless in very special and clear cases."[48] Although as President, Lincoln did not see fit to follow his own advise, his successors did. Indeed, for the three decades following the Civil War the Congress exercised a virtual monopoly over the legislative agenda, prompting one observer of the time to comment:

> . . . the president's wishes conveyed in a message have not necessarily any more effect on Congress than an article in a prominent party newspaper, and in fact the suggestions which he makes, year after year, are usually neglected even when his party has a majority in both Houses . . .[49]

Congressional domination in this area slowly began to change during Theodore Roosevelt's first term. Believing that the President should be an active force in the political system, he submitted a great number of legislative proposals to Congress. He trod gingerly, however, on one occasion warning a frustrated adviser of the "extreme unwisdom of irritating Congress by fixing the details of

[47] Alexander Hamilton, "Federalist Paper No. 73," in Jacob Cooke, ed., *The Federalist* (Cleveland: World, 1961), p. 497.

[48] Cited in Robert Dahl, *Pluralist Democracy in the United States* (Chicago: Rand McNally, 1967), p. 98.

[49] Cited in Harold Laski, *The American Presidency* (New York: Grosset and Dunlap, 1940), pp. 126, 127.

a bill concerning which they are very sensitive."[50] Woodrow Wilson went one step further than Roosevelt. He not only submitted legislative proposals for consideration but also went so far as to make personal appearances before the Congress to speak on behalf of his legislation.

The growth in the role of the President as a legislative initiator continued to a greater or lesser degree under subsequent presidents and came to full fruition under President Truman, who established the presidential practice of submitting an entire, integrated legislative program at the beginning of each session of Congress. That Congress had come to accept this executive initiative was reflected in its reaction to Eisenhower's failure to promptly submit a legislative program to Congress after he became President. Holding to a strict view of the President's responsibilities under the Constitution, Eisenhower was extremely reluctant to intrude into the legislative process. He changed his mind, however, when the Republican leadership in Congress complained about having no legislative agenda to act on. The point was made clearly by one Republican committee chairman in his remarks to an administration spokesman: ". . . don't expect us to start from scratch on what you people want. That's not the way we do things here—*you* draft the bills and *we* work them over."[51] Such an admission by a member of Congress would undoubtedly have shocked the Founding Fathers.

The ascendancy of the President in the legislative area should not be construed to mean that Congress no longer performs an important legislative function. On the contrary, it still makes valuable contributions, which take the form of criticizing and amending presidential proposals. As one student of Congress has observed, however, the fact remains that a President now defines "the bulk of the legislative agenda for Congress with his various annual and specific messages. Thus, even before specific actions are taken, the President, in effect, decides what is and is not most important for Congress to consider."[52]

Several factors are responsible for this change. In the first place, much of the twentieth century has been marked by periods of domestic and international crisis. The Presidency has been more suited to exercising the necessary leadership at such times, for unlike Congress, it speaks with one voice. Equally important was the fact that during these times of war and economic crisis, the Presidency was usually occupied by individuals whose conception of the office embodied vigorous leadership. Accordingly, they took the initiative in proposing legislative solutions to many of the nation's pressing problems. Finally, presidential dominance of the legislative agenda has been enhanced by the complexity of the problems we faced as an advanced industralized nation. Information and expertise are required in order to formulate legislative solutions to these problems. In the past, however, Congress has found itself lacking the necessary information

[50] Cited in John Johannes, *Policy Innovation in Congress* (Morristown, N.J.: General Learning Press, 1972), p. 3.

[51] Ibid.

[52] Ripley, *Congress,* p. 249.

and expertise, primarily because it has been woefully understaffed. In 1972, for example, the number of staff members attached to House committees totalled 992, and the number working for House members came to 5,727. While a comparable breakdown is not available for the Senate, nevertheless, the *entire* Senate staff in 1972 came to 4,700 (including clerks, secretaries, and maintenance).[53] This rather meager staff arm of the Congress had to compete with the Executive branch, whose analysts and experts number in the hundreds of thousands.

The problem is further compounded by the fact that Congress has lacked the analytic capability that computer technology provides. Specifically, it has less than a half dozen computers, which is equivalent to the computer capacity of the First National Bank of Kodoka, South Dakota.[54] The Executive branch, on the other hand, has several thousand computers which are manned by more than fifty thousand individuals, at a cost in excess of $2.7 billion a year.[55] Because of the vastly superior information base that computers give to the Executive branch, Congress is frequently forced to rely upon it for facts and figures. For example, when the House Ways and Means Committee was considering the financial impact of various proposals for welfare reform, it was compelled to turn to the Department of Health, Education and Welfare and its computers for the needed information. As Vice President Walter Mondale points out, however, such assistance from the Executive branch is not always forthcoming: "I recall hearings on legislation dealing with multi-billion dollar education programs where we asked the Executive branch for computer assistance. We received either no help at all or information that was often useless. But the congressional backers of Administration positions received full and very valuable support as well as computer assistance."[56] To the extent that Congress must rely upon the information and expertise of the Executive branch, it is hampered in its ability to make an independent evaluation of presidential programs, let alone present alternatives to them.

In discussing the dominant role of the President in initiating legislation, special mention must be given to the federal budget, which is the most important piece of legislation submitted to the Congress. Presidential ascendancy over the budgetary process had its genesis in the Budget and Accounting Act, which was passed by Congress and signed into law by President Harding in 1921. This act gave to the President the responsibility for submitting an Executive budget to the Congress every January. Prior to this act, each department and agency in the Executive branch submitted its own budget estimates directly to the Congress, a procedure that created considerable confusion and inefficiency.

---

[53]These figures were provided to the author by the Office of the Clerk of the House and the Office of the Secretary of the Senate.

[54]William Mullen, *Presidential Power and Politics* (New York: St. Martin's Press, 1976), p. 79.

[55] Walter Mondale, *The Accountability of Power* (New York: David McKay, 1975), p. 126.

[56]Ibid., pp. 126, 127.

While Congress has been free to make any changes it wishes in the President's budget, its handling of this important piece of legislation has in the past been ineffective. In the first place, no group in Congress ever examined the budget in toto. Rather, each congressional committee would deal only with that portion of the budget which came directly under its jurisdiction. For example, those committees charged with recommending the authorization and appropriation of money related to agriculture would concern themselves only with those parts of the budget related to agriculture. The result of this procedure was that no committee knew how its own budgetary recommendations affected the total budget expenditure. Secondly, Congress had put itself in a position of reacting to the President's budget rather than generating its own budget as an alternative to it. This state of affairs was hardly surprising, given the piecemeal fashion in which the Congress approached the budget. Equally important, however, was the fact that Congress lacked the staff capability possessed by the President on budgetary matters. In drawing up his budget, the President is assisted by an arm of the Executive branch known as the Office of Management and Budget, which is staffed with over six hundred individuals. Populated by budget analysts and possessed with a formidable computer capacity, the OMB has provided the President with an analytic capability that the Congress simply could not match. Thus, in conducting its own analysis of the budget, Congress often has been compelled to rely on the OMB for needed facts and figures.

Congressional Reassertion

In the last several years Congress has taken several important steps designed to increase its capacity for policy initiation. Under the Legislative Reorganization Act of 1970, committee staffs have been expanded, with an emphasis upon hiring individuals who are policy analysts. To assist these analysts, Congress is also increasing its own computer capacity. This act also allows committees to contract out for the assistance of groups with special expertise, such as the National Academy of Sciences and the National Academy of Engineering. In 1972, the Congress also passed legislation known as the Technology Assessment Act, which created an Office of Technology Assessment. The purpose of this office was to provide the Legislative branch with its own independent source of expertise in analyzing complex policy questions. As Senator Edward Kennedy points out, the Congress had lacked such a capacity in the past:

> Over the past two decades the Executive branch's capability in science and technology has grown immensely, while the ability of Congress to evaluate such programs has stumbled along at a snail's pace. Thus in recent years we have witnessed great controversies over the technical facts involved in programs such as the SST, the space shuttle, the use of chemical pesticides, and food and drug additives, the impact on human health of air pollution

and waste disposal, not to mention the enormous number of questions regarding the current energy crisis. In such cases, the Congress has not had a reliable source of technical expertise on which it could draw to provide an independent technical appraisal of the various alternatives under consideration.[57]

As of 1978, the Office of Technology Assessment was working on policy options related to such matters as energy conservation, nutrition, environmental contaminants, railroad safety, technology and world trade, and the societal impact of national information systems. In addition to the creation of this office, Congress has also sought to expand its information base by increasing the number of policy analysts and computers in the Congressional Research Service.[58]

The passage of the Budget Control and Impoundment Act of 1974 is of greatest potential significance in helping Congress to gain greater control over the policy-making process. This act is designed to correct the rather haphazard manner in which Congress has approached the budget in the past. Specifically, it established a budget committee in each House of Congress, and these two committees are charged with recommending spending limits for each of the seventeen major categories in the federal budget. This process must be completed by April 15 of each year. Each House must then act upon the recommendations of its budget committee, and if the two Houses should differ in their spending limits, a compromise is then worked out in a conference committee. The adoption of these spending limits must be completed by May 15. Once these limits have been established, the appropriate congressional committees then proceed to allocate funds for specific items within each of the budget's major categories. By September 15 the Congress must approve a second budget resolution, which may retain or alter the broad spending limits set down in the first resolution. Also provided for in the Budget Control and Impoundment Act was the establishment of a Congressional Budget Office. Staffed with budget analysts who are assisted by computers, this office is intended to provide congressional committees with the analytic capability necessary for better evaluating the President's budget recommendations as well as proposing alternatives to them. In short, it represents the legislature's counterpart to the President's Office of Management and Budget.

It is still too early to assess the full impact of these reforms upon the congressional role in the budget process. Even if they succeed, however, Congress's problems are far from over. The Executive branch has often taken advantage of certain appropriations and spending practices that permit it to circumvent the congressional will as it is reflected in the budget. These include *contingency funds, transfer authority, reprogramming, covert financing, full funding,* and

---

[57] *New York Times,* January 9, 1974, p. E2. © 1974 by The New York Times Company. Reprinted by permission.

[58] Richard Pious, "Sources of Domestic Policy Initiatives," in Harvey Mansfield, ed., *Congress Against the President* (New York: Academy of Political Science, 1975), pp. 107, 108.

impoundment. We shall now briefly examine each of these practices, with the exception of impoundment, which is treated later in this chapter.

Contingency Funds. Congress often provides the President and Executive departments with funds that are not earmarked for any specific purpose. Rather they are to be used for urgent and unforeseen matters. While it certainly makes sense to provide the Executive with such *contingency funds,* they are also subject to abuse, for the Executive branch may use them to finance projects of which Congress does not necessarily approve. In 1959, for example, the Congress refused to fund an Eisenhower Administration proposal that called for the establishment of an Incentive Investment Program. The Administration then proceeded to implement the program anyway and financed it out of a contingency fund.[59] Similarly, in 1973 Congress appropriated $25 million for a foreign aid contingency fund which was to be used for disaster relief and matters related to national security. President Nixon, however, proceeded to use $10 million of this fund for a "Bahamas and Livestock Research Project." Upon investigating this project, Congress discovered that it had no relation to either disaster relief or national security.[60] When and if Congress discovers such abuses, it can of course either eliminate the fund, or else specify that it may not in the future be used for the purposes to which it was put. The problem with responses of this kind is that they amount to locking the door after the horse has already left the barn.

Transfer Authority. Department and agency heads within the Executive branch are given statutory authority to *transfer funds* from one account to another. The Secretary of Defense, for example, may transfer up to $600 million dollars a year between accounts that come under the juridisction of his department.[61] Congress grants such authority for reasons of efficiency. Thus, if circumstances are such that one program requires more money than Congress had anticipated, while another requires less, it makes sense to allow a department head to transfer some money from the overfunded to the underfunded program. If he lacked such authority, much of Congress's time would be consumed by having to act upon a multitude of requests for supplemental appropriations. Like contingency funds, however, transfer authority may be used by the Executive branch to finance programs that Congress may not support. In 1970, for example, President Nixon financed military aid to Cambodia by having $110 million transferred from an account which was earmarked for aid to Taiwan, Turkey, Greece, and Vietnam. Congress did not learn of this action until one year later when the President asked them to restore funds for aid to these four countries.[62]

---

[59] Louis Fisher, *Presidential Spending Power* (Princeton: Princeton University Press, 1975), p. 67. Copyright © 1975 by Princeton University Press. Used by permission.

[60] Ibid., p. 69.

[61] Timothy Ingram, "The Billions in the White House Basement," in Stanley Bach and George Sulzner, eds., *Perspectives on the Presidency* (Lexington, Mass.: D.C. Heath, 1974), p. 334.

[62] Ibid., p. 335.

Subsequently, Congress took steps to restrict the President's use of transfer funds for military aid to Cambodia, but there was little it could do about the funds that had already been spent.

Reprogramming. Still another procedure by which the Executive branch manipulates appropriations to its own advantage is *reprogramming.* It differs from transfer authority in two important respects. The latter involves shifting funds from one account to another, whereas reprogramming is concerned with shifting funds *within* a given account. Secondly, transfer authority is granted to department heads in statutes passed by Congress. Department heads, however, are not given statutory authority to reprogram funds. Accordingly, before doing so they must inform *or* receive prior approval from appropriate members of Congress. Usually if reprogramming involves relatively small amounts of money, then a department head need only inform the relevant members of Congress, but if it involves a large sum of money, then he must receive the prior consent of these members. These relevant members of Congress customarily involve only four individuals, namely, the chairmen of the authorizing committees in the House and Senate and the chairmen of the appropriate subcommittees of the House and Senate Appropriations Committees.

Reprogramming is used extensively by the departments and agencies of the Executive branch. The Defense Department, for example, reprograms an average of $2 billion a year.[63] This procedure once again allows the Executive to substitute its own wishes for those of Congress as a whole. A given department may seek appropriations for a program that it knows Congress will support. Then, after the program has been funded, a department head may reprogram those funds into a project that Congress would not have supported.

Although such actions may in theory be prevented by the requirements that call for notification *or* prior approval of relevant members of Congress, these stipulations have not always proved satisfactory. Sometimes Congress is simply not notified of reprogramming. In 1973, for example, the General Accounting Office discovered that the Internal Revenue Service had reprogrammed $42.7 million over a three-year period without informing the appropriate congressional committees.[64] The prior approval requirement also suffers from drawbacks, for an incestuous relationship often develops between a department and the chairmen of those congressional committees having jurisdiction over it. Thus, a committee chairman may approve a departmental request for reprogramming large amounts of money without even consulting the rest of the members of his committee and without the knowledge of Congress as a whole.

A dramatic example of this particular kind of behavior occurred in 1969 when the Navy requested $275 million to build six F-14 fighters. The House Appropriations Committee reduced this figure to an amount that would per-

---

[63] Fisher, *Presidential Spending Power,* p. 87.

[64] Ibid., p. 80.

mit the Navy to construct only one experimental fighter. This decision was influenced by the fact that the Air Force had recently purchased a substantial number of bombers whose performance standards were disgraceful. Therefore it seemed prudent to have the Navy build just one test model of the F-14, and if it worked, it would then be appropriate for Congress to finance the building of additional ones. It came as quite a surprise to Congress when, nine months later, it discovered that the Navy had gone to the chairman of the defense subcommittee on appropriations and received permission to reprogram $517 million to build not one, or even the six asked for in the original request, but rather twenty-six F-14 bombers.[65]

In the last few years the Congress has taken some steps to bring reprogramming under closer control. The Defense Appropriation Act of 1974 contained a provision that prohibits the Defense Department from reprogramming funds into a project for which Congress has previously denied funds. While this provision represents a step in the right direction, it would also seem desirable to subject all the other Executive departments to the same restriction. In addition, the House Appropriations Committee has decided to open some of its hearings on reprogramming requests and to publish the transcripts of them. These actions alone are not sufficient, however. Given the large amounts of money involved in reprogramming requests, the number of congressmen who participate in this process should be expanded. Thus, rather than simply having the relevant committee chairmen act upon reprogramming proposals, the full membership of these committees should make the decision. Furthermore, all such proposals should be made a matter of public record before these committees act upon them. In this way, Congress would have an opportunity to stop those requests that a majority of its members do not support.[66]

Covert Financing. Yet another opportunity for the Executive branch to spend funds in ways not always in keeping with the wishes of Congress is *covert financing.* This form of financing may be broken down into two broad categories, the first of which is known as *confidential funds.* While these funds appear as items in the budget, the use to which the money is put is kept secret from both Congress and the public. So too is the auditing of expenditures from these funds. The Congress has seen fit to permit such secretiveness because the funds are used for matters of a sensitive nature. The FBI, for example, has a confidential fund which is used to pay informers. As of 1973, there were twenty different confidential funds appearing in the budgets of various departments and agencies of the Executive branch, and four of these came under the direct jurisdiction of the President himself.[67] One was labelled the White House Special Projects Fund and could be used by the President for any purpose he wished. President Kennedy used it to finance an emergency guidance counselor program

---

[65] Ingram, "White House Basement," p. 340.

[66] Fisher, *Presidential Spending Power,* pp. 94–98.

[67] Ibid., p. 207.

to deal with the problem of high youth unemployment during the summer of 1962.[68] Watergate investigations revealed that President Nixon may have used this same fund to help finance some of the activities of the notorious White House Plumbers. In pursuing this matter, Congress asked the President to supply it with vouchers and expenditures from this account, but President Nixon refused to honor the request.[69]

Secret funding constitutes the second major type of covert financing, and it is used in appropriating money for U.S. intelligence operations. Unlike confidential funds, secret funds do not even appear as items in the budget but instead are hidden in other budget requests. The budget of the Central Intelligence Agency, for example, is hidden in the various items of the Defense Department budget, and the location of these items is known only to the House and Senate intelligence subcommittees. After the Defense Department budget has been approved, the funds are then transferred over to the CIA. In many instances these funds have been used for activities that are highly questionable in nature. They include financing private organizations, domestic intelligence gathering, and covert military operations abroad. In the past, the congressional subcommittees charged with overseeing the CIA did not do a very effective job of monitoring how the agency spent its money. In part this was the fault of subcommittee chairmen who rarely called meetings and failed to pass relevant information on to the rest of the members. Also at fault was the agency itself, which did not always come forth with information in a timely fashion. Hopefully, the newly created House and Senate Select Committees On Intelligence will play a more vigorous oversight role in this area.

It is estimated that confidential and secret funds constitute between $10 billion and $15 billion of the federal budget.[70] Obviously a serious question of accountability arises here if Congress does not know *what* the money is being appropriated for nor *how* it is being spent. Only recently has it begun to take steps to correct this problem. Some confidential funds have been reduced or eliminated. For example, following President Nixon's refusal to detail expenditures from the White House Special Projects Fund, Congress decided not to fund it any longer. In addition, Congress has decided to allow some confidential funds to be audited by the General Accounting Office. With respect to secret funding, legislation has been proposed that would make public the overall budget figure of the United States intelligence community, and the Carter Administration has gone on record as supporting this legislation. The Congress, however, is of two minds on the matter. In 1977 the Senate Intelligence Committee agreed to support the proposal by a vote of 9 to 8; in April of 1978 its counterpart in the House voted against disclosing the overall budget figure. In order for this figure to be made public, it is only necessary that one House give its approval. At this

---

[68] Sorensen, *Watchmen in the Night,* p. 76.

[69] Fisher, *Presidential Spending Power,* pp. 211–13; See also Ben Roberts, "Tying the Imperial Purse Strings," *Washington Monthly* 7 (September 1975), 27–30.

[70] Fisher, *Presidential Spending Power,* p. 228.

writing, however, the Senate leadership has still not called up the bill for consideration by the entire membership.

Full Funding. One final budgetary procedure must be mentioned which also poses difficulties for Congress in its attempt to hold the Executive branch accountable for what it spends. It is known as *full funding.* Most appropriations are for one year only and at the end of this time any funds remaining in a given account automatically revert back to the federal Treasury. In some cases, however, Congress makes a multiyear appropriation for those programs and projects that take several years to complete. An aircraft carrier, for instance, takes seven or eight years to build. Thus, rather than making an annual appropriation for the carrier for each of the seven years, Congress fully funds its construction at the time of inception. The advantages of such a procedure are, first, that it allows Congress to know the full costs of such expensive projects, and second, that it frees it from having to make appropriations each year until the project is completed.

The amount of money that accumulates from multiyear appropriations is considerable. Indeed, it was estimated that at the end of 1976 there was approximately $502.4 billion of carryover funds in the pipeline as a consequence of multiyear appropriations which had been made prior to this time.[71] Unfortunately, these carry-over funds make it difficult for the Congress to regulate spending levels. In 1971, the Senate felt the full impact of this problem when it defeated a foreign aid bill, only to discover that there was already $4.7 billion in carry-over funds for foreign aid; a figure, incidentally, that was one and a half times the amount contained in the bill they had just defeated.[72] There also exists the problem of departments and agencies using these carry-over funds for purposes other than those intended by Congress. Aware of this possibility, Senator Fulbright voiced his doubts as to the ability of Congress to put a restriction on aid to Laos in October of 1971: "I have never figured out how [Defense Managers] are able to spend money that has neither been authorized nor appropriated. They have ways of drawing on unexpended funds. I imagine that there is at least $50 billion of unexpended funds in the pipeline as a reserve for the Pentagon. So I would not be sure that even with a prohibition against appropriation of any money, they could not find some in a very short time."[73]

In conclusion, it does little good for the Congress to reassert its control over the formulation of the federal budget if its will can be circumvented by the Executive branch during the spending process. To be sure, all of the appropriations and spending practices discussed above were instituted by Congress, and thus it can eliminate them at any time. But to do away with these practices simply because they have been abused by the Executive branch would be analogous to

---

[71] Ibid., p. 138.

[72] Ingram, "White House Basement," p. 338.

[73] Ibid., p. 337.

throwing out the baby with the bath water. The fact of the matter is that most of these procedures can make for greater administrative efficiency in the spending of money appropriated by the Legislative branch. Consequently, the solution lies not in abandoning them but rather in establishing within Congress both the *will* and the *ability* to discover when they are abused. As one scholar has noted, however, the will has often been lacking.

> The weakness of legislative oversight in the spending area is part of a long-standing paradox. Legislators derive credit and satisfaction from the steps needed to enact a bill. To pursue its implementation is regarded as tedious and frustrating, as indeed it is, and of little value in advancing in committee ranks or in being reelected.[74]

There are indications that Congress is now willing to assume a more active role in holding the Executive branch accountable for its spending practices. It must now develop the capacity to do so more effectively. Much of the information related to transfers, contingency funds, reprogramming, and full funding is already accessible to the Congress in the form of agency reports of one kind or another.[75] Given the size of the Executive branch, however, the sheer volume of this information is overwhelming. What Congress needs, therefore, is an institutional mechanism that can systematically gather all of this data, digest it, and present it to Congress in a manageable form. Once the Executive branch is aware that Congress is possessed with both the will and the ability to discover spending abuses, departments and agencies will be less inclined to engage in them.

TOOLS AND TACTICS OF PRESIDENTIAL PERSUASION

Although the President now sets the legislative agenda of Congress, it does not necessarily follow that his agenda will receive their ready approval. Indeed, sufficient support for passing a presidential proposal is rarely present initially. Some congressmen may be indifferent to it; others may have philosophical objections to it; and still others may be under pressure from constituents or special-interest groups to vote against it. Accordingly, if a President wants favorable action on his legislative programs, he usually has to work for it. We shall now consider the specific tools and tactics employed by a President in seeking to persuade members of Congress to see things his way. It is important to note here that these tools and tactics are not reserved exclusively for those occasions when the President needs the support of a legislator on a given bill. They are also used in order to build up a reservoir of good will that the President hopes to be able to tap when the specific need arises.

[74] Fisher, *Presidential Spending Power,* p. 258.
[75] Ibid., p. 263.

Status Conferral

Presidents are not unaware that the office they occupy enjoys extraordinary status in our political system. They also recognize that members of Congress, like most politicians, are individuals with considerable egos. Accordingly, shrewd presidents will often attempt to persuade by using the status of their office to flatter the egos of congressmen and senators. This tactic may take a variety of forms, such as an invitation to a legislator to have his picture taken with the President, a personal letter written by the President asking for a congressman's support, an invitation to dine with the President in the family quarters of the White House, or a phone call from the President. In all of these examples, the President is conferring some of his own status upon the individual he is seeking to persuade or to thank. And as one congressman notes in the following passage, this kind of personal treatment is not without its effects:

> You know, I was sitting in my office and the phone rang telling me it was the president calling. I damn near collapsed right on the spot. Sure enough, it was the president. He said, "Silvio, this is Lyndon Johnson, and I just wanted to thank you on behalf of this nation for your vote. You stood up and you were counted at the right time. I am mighty grateful to you." It's the only time since I have been in Congress that a president called me. I will never forget it. [76]

This tactic of status conferral was frequently used by President Kennedy to secure the good will of Harry Byrd, the powerful and conservative senator from Virginia. Indeed on Byrd's birthday, the President even went so far as to arrive by helicopter on the front lawn of the senator's Virginia estate. He got out and wished him a happy birthday. Senate Minority Leader Everett Dirksen received similar kinds of attention from Kennedy, one of the favorites being special rides in the presidential helicopter.

Legislative Assistance

A President also uses his considerable influence and power to assist congressmen with their own pet legislation. Such a favor is rendered with the understanding—sometimes implicit and sometimes explicit—that the legislator will reciprocate by supporting some current or future legislative proposal of the President's. Legislative assistance may take several forms. The President may agree to sign a given bill even though he may not be strongly supportive of it. Kennedy, for example, was once approached by one of his legislative aids and advised to sign a particular bill in order to maintain the continued support of a given congressman. After reading the bill, Kennedy turned to his aid and

[76] Valenti, *Very Human President,* p. 194.

remarked, "Chuck, I just want you to be sure you understand that this bill is a goddamn boondoggle." As the aid nodded his agreement, the President went ahead and signed it anyway.[77]

Presidential assistance may also take the form of helping a congressman to get his own legislation passed by Congress. Any legislator recognizes that it is a great asset to have the prestige and resources of the White House thrown behind one of his bills. Finally, presidents may decide to alter their own legislative proposals in order to accommodate the wishes of a congressman or senator. President Kennedy made use of this tactic in his dealings with Senator Robert Kerr of Oklahoma, who was regarded by many as the most powerful man in the Senate. The Kennedy Administration initially intended to push for legislation that would create a publicly owned communications satellite corporation. Senator Kerr, however, felt very strongly that the corporation should be under private ownership. Kennedy recognized that passage of many of his own legislative proposals depended upon having the future support of the powerful senator from Oklahoma. Consequently, in spite of his reservations about a privately owned satellite corporation, the President introduced a bill that accommodated the wishes of Senator Kerr. The full resources of the Administration were used to get it through Congress.[78] After a difficult fight, the legislation was finally passed and signed into law by the President. This tactic paid off, for shortly thereafter President Kennedy introduced to Congress one of the most important pieces of legislation of his entire administration, namely, the trade expansion bill. There on the floor of the Senate leading the successful fight for its adoption was Senator Kerr of Oklahoma.[79]

Programs, Projects, and Patronage

In their efforts to persuade members of Congress, presidents are armed with several inducements such as economic assistance, federal contracts, post offices, court houses, dams and jobs, all of which may be channelled into a congressman's district in return for his support. While civil service laws have reduced the number of federal jobs that can be handed out by a President, he still has effective control over approximately 6,700 of them. Among these are 3,500 positions in the Executive branch, 140 ambassadors, 523 federal judges, 93 U.S. attorneys, 94 U.S. marshals, and approximately 2,100 part-time positions on various commissions and boards.[80]

In his attempt to win the favor of conservative Democrats, President Kennedy saw to it that southern states were made the beneficiaries of numerous defense contracts, military bases, federal judgeships, etc. Similarly, in disbursing funds

[77]Paper, *Promise and Performance,* p. 270.

[78]Ibid., p. 272.

[79]*Congressional Quarterly Weekly Report,* September 21, 1962, p. 1556.

[80]Ripley, *Congress,* p. 229.

for the Model Cities Program, Lyndon Johnson took pains to see to it that they were funneled into the hometowns of powerful committee chairmen in Congress. Nor was he reluctant to point out that presidential rewards would not be forthcoming if a legislator failed to see things his way on matters of special importance. On one occasion, for instance, Senator Frank Church presented Johnson with a newspaper column written by Walter Lippmann which he felt made some constructive criticisms of the President's Vietnam policy. Johnson's pointed response to the senator was, "All right, the next time you need a dam for Idaho, you go ask Walter Lippmann."[81] The bestowal of patronage is not without its drawbacks, however, for there are likely to be several congressmen seeking a piece of the patronage pie. Consequently, when a President gives it to one congressman, he is of necessity denying it to several others. President Taft astutely pointed out this presidential dilemma when he remarked that patronage decisions create "nine enemies and one ingrate."

The Veto Power

The President's veto power is not only an effective tool for voiding congressional action after the fact, but can also be highly useful as an instrument for preventing Congress from passing certain legislation in the first place. As Table 3-1 clearly demonstrates, the potency of the veto as a persuasive tool lies in the fact that it is extremely difficult to override.

The President may employ the threat of a veto as a means of persuading Congress to make changes in legislation which in its present form is clearly unacceptable to him. President Nixon's warning that he would veto any congressional legislation authorizing Congress to approve executive agreements persuaded members of Congress to drop that provision from their legislation. On another occasion, he informed Congress that he was displeased with the Senate version of a bill titled the Family Assistance Plan and made it known that unless Congress passed the House version of the bill instead, he would veto it. In the words of Vice President Walter Mondale, who was a strong supporter of the Senate bill, "The practical and predictable result of this action was that no family assistance bill passed the Senate."[82]

It should be noted, however, that Congress is not powerless to thwart the use of the presidential veto. In addition to overriding a veto, Congress can also make use of another tactic. Under its operating procedures, the Senate may attach an irrelevant amendment to a given piece of legislation. Such amendments are known as riders. In 1959, for example, a rider that called for extending the life of the Civil Rights Commission was attached to a foreign aid bill. In effect, this rider mechanism allows the Senate to attach an amendment that the Presi-

---

[81] Louis Koenig, *The Chief Executive,* 3rd ed. (New York: Harcourt Brace Jovanovich, 1975), p. 125.

[82] Mondale, *Accountability of Power,* p. 82.

TABLE 3-1. PRESIDENTIAL VETOES AND OVERRIDES, 1932-76

Presidents	Number of Bills Vetoed	Number of Times Overridden
Roosevelt	631	9
Truman	250	12
Eisenhower	181	2
Kennedy	21	0
Johnson	30	0
Nixon	41	5
Ford	61	12

dent is against to a bill that he supports. Since the President's veto power does not permit him to veto only those parts of a bill he dislikes, he is faced with a dilemma: either he must veto the entire bill, including those provisions he supports, or he can veto none of it, in which case the objectionable rider becomes law along with the rest of the bill. Needless to say, presidents do not like to be faced with such a dilemma, and consequently they will attempt to use their influence to prevent the addition of objectionable riders to an otherwise acceptable piece of legislation.

Campaign Assistance

A President recognizes that one of the common preoccupations of all politicians is securing their reelection. Accordingly, he may decide to assist a congressman who is facing an especially tough fight in an upcoming election. Such assistance may result in the President's taking special steps to insure that a congressman receives generous financial support from the party treasury. Or he may go further and offer to come into the congressman's district and campaign on his behalf. Any congressman will welcome such an offer—provided the President is popular in his district—for the Chief Executive's presence will insure large crowds and extensive media coverage. Like the other tactics we have discussed, this one may be used by presidents to reward past support or to lay the groundwork for future support.

Appeal to the Public

With the exception of the veto power, all of the tactics and tools of presidential persuasion discussed thus far are primarily geared toward influencing an individual congressman or senator. But the President may also resort to a tactic designed to bring pressure to bear upon the Congress as a whole. He does so by going over the heads of the congressmen and taking his case directly to the American people. The hope, of course, is to generate enough public enthusiasm for his proposal so that Congress will feel compelled to support it also. In an attempt to draw public attention to his Medicare program, President Kennedy addressed a mass rally of Medicare supporters in Madison Square Garden. In addition, he dispatched several high administration officials to address other rallies held in thirty-one major cities throughout the country. Presidents may also choose to focus in upon those publics who are especially affected by his proposed program and whose political clout could be of great assistance in getting it through Congress. Thus, when Kennedy introduced his trade expansion bill to Congress, he made a personal appearance before the National Association of Manufacturers and the AFL-CIO where he asked for and received their support.[83]

Finally, a President may also decide to take his case to the people through a nationwide address. Since frequent use of such a tactic would reduce its dramatic effect, it is likely to be reserved only for those issues that are of special importance to the President. No other elected office in our government is so well suited to making such a nationwide appeal. The visibility and prestige of the Presidency guarantees the President an attentive audience, and his unequalled ability to command the use of the public airwaves insures that he will be addressing a wide audience. Franklin Roosevelt proved a master at mobilizing public support for his programs through the use of a series of "fireside chats" with the American people on radio. On several occasions both Johnson and Nixon made televised addresses to the American people asking for their support on matters related to economic policy and the Vietnam War. Gerald Ford twice did the same in an effort to put public pressure on a Democratic Congress that proved unreceptive to his proposals for dealing with the problems of energy and recession. An appeal to the nation, however, does not in and of itself guarantee that a President will gain the public support he needs. Rather, the ultimate success of this tactic will hinge on his public prestige at the time, the nature of what he has to say, and his ability to communicate it effectively. President Carter's attempt to mobilize the American people behind his energy policies may serve to illustrate this point. After assuming office, he addressed the nation three different times regarding the energy crisis. Yet a Gallup poll taken in April of 1978 indicated that he had not made any significant progress in educating the American people to the reality of this crisis.[84] To be sure, Carter was faced with a formidable task, since the "crisis" nature of the energy problem is not readily apparent. But it is just this fact that necessitates appeals to the public that are clear and inspiring. Unfortunately, the President's addresses to the nation lacked both these qualities; consequently, he was not able to mobilize the public behind his energy proposals. This explains, in part, why they languished so long in Congress.

---

[83] Randall Ripley, *Kennedy and Congress* (Morristown, N.J.: General Learning Press, 1972), p. 15.

[84] Cited in *Washington Post,* April 30, 1978, p. A15.

MORE RECENT STRAINS IN THE RELATIONSHIP:
POCKET VETO, IMPOUNDMENT, EXECUTIVE PRIVILEGE

As noted earlier in this chapter, the relationship between the President and Congress is always a strained one. During the Nixon Presidency, however, this customary strain took on an unusual severity. While the President's style of legislative leadership was a contributory factor, the major cause was something more fundamental. Specifically, the Congress concluded that Richard Nixon was engaged in a calculated effort to exercise certain of his powers and prerogatives in such a way as to preempt the ability of Congress to exercise its own constitutional powers. To understand why Congress ultimately felt compelled to take steps to protect these powers, it is first necessary to examine how the President's actions served to undermine them.

Pocket Veto

After a bill has been passed by Congress and comes to the President, he has *ten days* (excluding Sundays) to act on it. He may sign the bill, in which case it becomes law. Or he may veto the bill, in which case it is returned to Congress, which then has an opportunity to try to override it by a two-thirds vote. Or, finally, he may do nothing. In this case, the bill automatically becomes law without his signature after the ten days have passed. But if Congress should adjourn during this ten-day period, and if the President has taken no action on the bill, then it does *not* become law. This procedure is known as a pocket veto, and it was first used by President James Madison in 1812. The pocket veto is a potent presidential weapon, for since Congress is no longer in session, it cannot override a veto of this kind.

The use of the pocket veto has been the subject of litigation in the past, and the courts have ruled that it may be used at the end of a session of Congress as well as at the end of a Congress itself. Increasingly, however, the Congress has also been adjourning for brief periods *within* a given session. Prior to the Nixon Presidency the pocket veto had been used only sixty-four times during intrasession adjournments. And it is also important to note that bills pocket vetoed under this circumstance were all of minor importance. In addition, all but one of these intrasession adjournments were for periods of at least one month. The one exception was a pocket veto by President Johnson during a nine-day intrasession adjournment. Even here, however, the bill pocket vetoed was a private rather than a public bill.[85]

Richard Nixon differed from his predecessors in that he was willing to use the pocket veto on *major* pieces of legislation during *brief* adjournments for holidays. For example, on December 14, 1970, Congress sent to the President a bill

[85] Schlesinger, *Imperial Presidency,* p. 243.

known as the Family Practice of Medicine Act, which authorized $225 million to be given to hospitals and medical schools with programs in family medicine. On December 22, both Houses adjourned for Christmas. Before leaving, however, the Senate authorized the Secretary of the Senate to receive any veto messages from the President during their absence. President Nixon recognized that if he vetoed the bill, it would surely be overriden, for the Senate had passed it by a margin of 64-1, and the House by a margin of 345-2. Accordingly, he declined to veto the bill outright. Instead, he decided to consider Congress's five-day Christmas break as an adjournment and thus returned the bill to them on December 26 as a pocket veto.[86] In effect, the President had taken away the constitutional right of the Legislative branch to override his veto. Although this was not the first time he had employed this tactic, it was apparently the straw that broke the camel's back. Senator Edward Kennedy decided to challenge the President's actions in the courts. The U.S. District Court found in favor of the Congress, and this decision was upheld by the U.S. Court of Appeals the following year. The judge ruled that the intrasession adjournment did not prevent the President from vetoing the bill and returning it to Congress because prior to adjourning, Congress had made arrangements to have the Secretary of the Senate receive any veto messages from the President. Thus, the President's use of the pocket veto in this instance was invalid, and consequently, the Court ruled that the Family Practice of Medicine Act would become law on December 25, 1970. President Nixon decided to accept this decision instead of appealing it to the Supreme Court. Until such time as the Supreme Court is asked to rule on the matter, however, it cannot be said that the use of the pocket veto has been settled definitively. Thus, Gerald Ford pocket vetoed five bills when Congress recessed for the election campaign in 1974, and he did so because he did not think that a President should surrender a power whose constitutionality has not yet received a definitive judgment from the Supreme Court. Although Senator Kennedy vowed to take the President into court once again, he never followed through on it.

Impoundment

Impoundment is a practice by which the President temporarily or permanently withholds the spending of funds that have been appropriated by the Congress. The practice dates all the way back to Thomas Jefferson, who at one time refused to spend money appropriated for gunboats on the Mississippi River. Several justifications have been given for the impoundment power. For one thing, circumstances may arise that render the spending of money unnecessary or inappropriate. Thus, in Jefferson's case, he impounded the money for gunboats because the purchase of the Louisiana Territory rendered them unnecessary. Congress agreed. Similarly, at the end of World War II Congress appropriated a

[86] *Congressional Quarterly Weekly Report,* November 18, 1972, p. 3039.

substantial sum of money to build veterans' hospitals. Truman temporarily impounded the money, believing that it would be better to wait until the veterans returned home and settled down, thus enabling the government to better determine where the hospitals should be located. In some instances, Congress itself provides the President with statutory authority to impound funds. Such was the case with the 1964 Civil Rights Act, which allows the President to withhold funds from federally financed programs in which discrimination is being practiced. Similarly, when President Truman impounded funds that had been appropriated by Congress to expand the size of the Air Force, he was simply exercising an option specifically provided to him in the bill.[87] It is worth noting here that Congress has been especially willing to provide the President with broad spending discretion on appropriations related to national defense because of his constitutional role as Commander in Chief. Finally, presidents have justified impoundment on the grounds that it is necessary to stop inflation. Lyndon Johnson invoked this justification when he temporarily withheld funds totalling $5 billion in order to dampen the fires of inflation resulting from the Vietnam War.

Richard Nixon's use of the impoundment power differed from his predecessor's in two important respects. First, he impounded $18 billion, which far exceeded the amount impounded by any President in our history.[88] Second, he sought to eliminate completely programs to which he was opposed by withholding all of the funds appropriated for them. In most cases previous presidents had withheld funds only temporarily, or else had cut back on the funds appropriated for a given program. In those few cases where they withheld all funds from a program, they did so because the legislation was written in such a way as to provide them with this option. Finally, it should be noted that President Nixon undertook these impoundments in spite of an advisory opinion from his Attorney General that questioned the constitutionality of such actions: "With respect to the suggestion that the President has a *constitutional* power to decline to spend appropriated funds, we must conclude that the existence of such a broad power is supported neither by reason nor precedent."[89]

When the Founding Fathers were dispersing power among the three branches of government, they gave the power over the purse strings to that branch which most directly represented the people, namely, the Legislature. As James Madison remarked, they did so because "This power over the purse may in fact be regarded as the most effectual weapon with which any Constitution can arm the immediate representatives of the people for obtaining a redress of every grievance and for carrying into effect every salutary measure." Richard Nixon's use of the impoundment power represented a fundamental assault against this most

---

[87] Schlesinger, *Imperial Presidency,* p. 236.

[88] Allan Schick, "The Battle of the Budget," in Harvey Mansfield, ed., *Congress Against the President* (New York: Academy of Political Science, 1975), p. 62.

[89] Cited in Schlesinger, *Imperial Presidency,* p. 237.

potent of legislative powers. And the power was wielded with unusual arrogance, as evidenced when John Ehrlichman put Congress on notice that "the Administration will not spend money it considers wasteful even if Congress appropriates the funds over a presidential veto."[90] This was not an idle threat. In 1972 the Congress overwhelmingly passed a $5 billion water pollution bill, and it was promptly vetoed by the President. Within twenty-four hours the Congress overrode his veto by an overwhelming margin. Indeed, the President received only twelve Senate votes and twenty-three House votes in favor of sustaining his veto. Yet in spite of this action, the President announced that he would impound $3 billion out of the $5 billion that had been appropriated in the bill. Reaction to the Nixon impoundments finally came from both the courts and the Congress. Members of Congress as well as private citizens brought suit against the Executive branch in order to compel the release of the impounded funds. In most of the cases the courts ruled that the President's impoundments violated the expressed will of Congress, and thus ordered their release.

Congress also sought to restrict the use of this power by passing the Budget Control and Impoundment Act of 1974. This legislation stipulates, first, that the President must inform Congress in writing of any intentions to defer *or* permanently terminate the expenditure of funds for any program. Second, in those cases where the President makes known his intention to *defer* the spending of funds, he can be compelled to spend them if either House passes a resolution ordering him to do so. Third, the President cannot *terminate* the funds for a program unless Congress passes a bill of recision—within forty-five days after the President makes known his intention—permitting him to do so. While this act has only been in effect for a relatively short time, the evidence so far indicates that Congress is taking a hard line on presidential impoundments, especially those dealing with the termination of funds. Between September 1974 and February 1975, President Ford made several proposals for termination of funds which altogether totalled nearly $2.5 billion. Congress, however, agreed to less than 15 percent of this total.[91]

Executive Privilege

One of the major responsibilities of Congress is to inquire into the operation of the Executive branch. It does so for several reasons: to determine the effectiveness of the programs it has passed, to make sure that the Executive branch is implementing legislation in keeping with congressional intent, and finally, to determine possible abuses of authority by the Executive branch. The ability of Congress to exercise this investigative role is predicated upon its being able to

---

[90] Quoted on "The Advocates," a program telecast on February 16, 1973, by the Public Broadcasting Service. This quote appears on p. 22 of the written transcript from this program.

[91] Schick, "Battle of the Budget," p. 64.

secure the necessary information from the Executive branch. Presidents, however, have not always been forthcoming in this regard, believing as they do that it is not in the public interest to disclose certain kinds of information to the Congress. In refusing to do so, they have invoked what has come to be known as *executive privilege.* While there is in fact no specific provision in the Constitution that accords them this right, presidents since the time of Washington have argued that the exercise of executive privilege is implied in the constitutional powers granted to the Executive branch.

In the past presidents have invoked this privilege on matters concerning (1) foreign policy, (2) military security, (3) investigative files related to law enforcement, and (4) intragovernmental communications that are advisory in nature.[92] Washington, for example, argued that an element of secrecy must be maintained during delicate foreign policy negotiations. The same argument was made by presidents on matters related to national security. With respect to the third category, earlier presidents such as Jefferson and Tyler argued that release of investigative files related to law enforcement could damage innocent persons as well as compromise the integrity of the law enforcement process itself. Finally, presidents since the time of Jackson have viewed their personal communications with cabinet members and aids as privileged from congressional scrutiny on grounds that confidentiality is essential if presidents are to be assured of receiving frank and honest advice. Under the Eisenhower Administration, however, this final category was greatly expanded to cover intragovernmental communications within the *entire* Executive branch. Specifically, the umbrella of executive privilege extended to such Executive branch communications as "interdepartmental memoranda, advisory opinions, recommendations of subordinates, informal working papers, material in personnel files."[93] Given this expanded view of executive privilege, it is hardly surprising that it was invoked more often during the Eisenhower Administration than in the entire first century of American history.[94]

Neither Kennedy nor Johnson shared Eisenhower's broadsweeping view of this privilege. Indeed, each invoked it only twice during their administrations. While President Nixon's statements on the subject indicated that he shared the view of his two predecessors, his actions demonstrated otherwise. In his first term alone, he invoked the privilege four times personally. In addition, members of his administration refused congressional requests for information fifteen times.[95] Nor do these figures tell the whole story, for there were numerous occasions when members of the Executive branch simply refused to hand over

[92] Robert Dixon, "Congress, Shared Administration, and Executive Privilege," in Harvey Mansfield, ed., *Congress Against the President* (New York: Academy of Political Science, 1975), p. 135.

[93] Cited in Schlesinger, *Imperial Presidency,* p. 156.

[94] Ibid., p. 158.

[95] Dixon, "Congress and Executive Privilege," p. 134; Schlesinger, *Imperial Presidency,* p. 247.

information to Congress without even bothering to invoke the doctrine of executive privilege. According to one Senate subcommittee study, between 1964 and 1974 there were 225 occasions when agencies of the Executive branch refused to supply the Congress with requested information, and over 90 percent of these came during the Nixon Administration.[96]

The difficulty experienced by Congress in securing information from the Executive during the Nixon Presidency was compounded by the President's refusal to permit his White House aids to testify before Congress. Although previous presidents had set restrictions on what their staff aids could say to Congress, they did not set down a blanket prohibition against appearing. President Nixon, however, prevented his staff aids from testifying on any subject whatever, including substantive policy questions.[97] In the past, Congress rarely had any need to question White House aids on policy matters because policy making rested more with department heads whom Congress was empowered to call for testimony. Under recent presidents, however, policy making has moved away from department heads and into the White House, and this tendency was accelerated during the Nixon Presidency. For example, during Nixon's first term the major force in shaping American foreign policy was not Secretary of State William Rogers, but rather the President's special assistant for national security affairs, notably, Henry Kissinger. Yet since Kissinger was a member of the White House staff, he was prohibited from testifying before Congress. Thus Congress was denied the opportunity to probe the mind of the one man who, aside from the President, had the greatest impact upon the substance of American foreign policy.

Throughout our history conflicts arising between the President and Congress over disclosure of information were ultimately resolved through a process of negotiation and accommodation. Such was not to be the case with the Nixon Presidency. As the Watergate scandals unfolded, investigations began on three fronts. First, the Senate created a special Select Committee on Presidential Campaign Practices. Under the chairmanship of Senator Sam Ervin, this committee was charged with investigating alleged campaign abuses during the 1972 election. As pressure mounted from both the Congress and the public, the President also decided to appoint a Special Prosecutor to inquire into possible wrongdoing by members of the Executive branch. And finally, as it began to appear that the President himself might be implicated in the Watergate scandals, the House Judiciary Committee also began an inquiry to determine whether there were possible grounds for impeachment. All three of these investigative bodies repeatedly requested that the President provide them with information that was judged relevant in determining wrongdoing by members of the Executive branch. The President refused to comply with certain of these requests, arguing that he

[96] Sorensen, *Watchmen in the Night,* p. 104.

[97] Schlesinger, *Imperial Presidency,* p. 251.

alone had the ultimate right to determine what information could appropriately be turned over to the Congress and the Special Prosecutor. Confrontation thus proved inevitable.

The House Judiciary Committee decided against taking the President into court because it felt the Court had no constitutional role to play in the impeachment proceedings. Instead, the Committee cited as one of the grounds for his impeachment the President's repeated refusal to comply with committee subpoenas for information. No other President in our history had ever claimed that executive privilege could be used to withhold information requested in connection with an impeachment proceeding. Had the House Judiciary Committee acceded to this claim, it is clear that impeachment would have been rendered a meaningless instrument.

The Senate Watergate Committee, however, did decide to take the President into court over the issue of executive privilege. This was an act of considerable historical importance since never before had Congress gone to court over this issue. The U.S. Appeals Court ruled that presidential conversations must be presumed to be privileged unless it can be shown that such information is "demonstrably critical to the performance of the committee's functions." In this particular case, the Court concluded that the Ervin Committee had not made such a showing. While the Court acknowledged that the Senate Watergate Committee had a legitimate "oversight" function with respect to the Executive branch, it maintained that in this instance this function had been preempted by the House Judiciary Committee. Furthermore, while the Court recognized that the committee's inquiry constituted a necessary part of its "legislative function," it concluded that such a function did not extend to "limitless fact finding."[98]

The Special Prosecutor also took the President into court because of his refusal to supply certain of the White House tapes that were deemed relevant in determining possible illegal activities in the Executive branch. Since the lower courts ruled that the President was required to hand over the tapes in question, the President appealed his case all the way to the Supreme Court. On July 24, 1974, the Supreme Court handed down its historic decision concerning the issue of executive privilege. It ruled first that the President does indeed have a right of executive privilege. This in itself was a significant statement, for up to this time it had not been definitively established that the President enjoyed such a right. But the Court went on to say that this right was not absolute, as President Nixon had claimed, but rather it was a "qualified privilege"; that is, the President's need for confidentiality had to be balanced against other compelling interests. In this particular case, the Court concluded that the need for the tapes in a criminal court proceeding outweighed the President's need for confidentiality. The Court did imply, however, that it might well have

[98] Dixon, "Congress and Executive Privilege," pp. 136, 137.

ruled differently if the President had based his claim of executive privilege on the "need to protect military, diplomatic or sensitive national security secrets."[99] While this decision was a resounding defeat for President Nixon, it might be argued that it was a victory for the Presidency, for it established that a President does have the right of executive privilege, and also that the Court may well defer to this right when it is exercised on sensitive matters related to military and foreign affairs. It is important to note, however, that the Court's ruling dealt only with the President's right to withhold information from the courts. The right to withhold information from Congress has still not been firmly determined, for the Supreme Court has never been asked to rule on this question.

Executive privilege became a controversial issue once again during the Ford Presidency, but Congress took a more assertive position in responding to it. On one occasion, Secretary Kissinger refused to supply the House Select Committee on Intelligence with documents related to American covert operations abroad since 1961. The Secretary argued that revealing such documents would violate the confidentiality of Executive branch deliberations. In addition, former CIA Director William Colby refused to supply this same committee with subpoenaed documents dealing with the 1968 Tet offensive in Vietnam.[100] The House Select Committee on Intelligence made it clear that it was prepared to recommend that the House of Representatives find Kissinger and Colby in contempt of Congress. In theory, such a finding could have resulted in the House instructing its Sergeant-at-Arms to apprehend both secretaries and place them in the District of Columbia jail.[101] As has been the case throughout most of our history, however, direct confrontation was avoided through mutual accommodation. The House Intelligence Committee permitted Secretary Kissinger to give an oral report on the contents of the documents it had requested. Similarly, Director Colby agreed to hand over CIA documents in exchange for the committee's assurance that such documents would be held in the strictest confidence. This form of compromise will likely persist as a means for resolving disputes over executive privilege, for neither side wants to take the matter to the courts and risk the possibility of an adverse ruling. Although President Nixon's decision to take his case to the Supreme Court constitutes an exception to this tradition of compromise, it is important to note that he had no other viable option, since the tapes were clearly incriminating.

THE ULTIMATE CONFRONTATION: IMPEACHMENT

The Founding Fathers were fully cognizant of the fact that power may corrupt those who exercise it. Accordingly, in Article II, Section 4 of the Constitution they provided that "The President, Vice President and all civil Officers of the

[99] *New York Times,* July 28, 1974, p. 2E.

[100] *New York Times,* December 14, 1975, p. 3E; *Congressional Quarterly Weekly Report,* October 4, 1975, p. 2097.

[101] Raoul Berger, "Congressional Subpoenas to Executive Officials," *Columbia Law Review* 75 (June 1975), 889.

United States shall be removed from Office on Impeachment for and Conviction of, Treason, Bribery, or other High Crimes and Misdemeanors." Whether or not a President ought to be impeached was to be decided by the House of Representatives. Whether or not he should be convicted was to be determined by the Senate. In our entire history, only thirteen officers of the federal government have been impeached and they included a President, a cabinet officer, a senator, and ten federal judges. Only four were convicted, and they were all federal judges. The infrequent use of this formidable congressional power prompted Woodrow Wilson to refer to it as "little more than an empty menace." Lord Bryce, writing before the turn of the century, acknowledged that impeachment was indeed a formidable instrument, but maintained that it was precisely this fact that made it awkward to use:

> [It is] the heaviest piece of artillery in the congressional arsenal, but because it is so heavy, it is unfit for ordinary use. It is like a hundred-ton gun which needs complex machinery to bring it into position, an enormous charge of power to fire it, and a large mark to aim at.[102]

That Congress ultimately felt compelled to employ this rarely used "piece of artillery" against President Richard Nixon suggests the gravity of the scandals surrounding his Presidency.

The Impeachment Process

Any member of the House of Representatives may introduce articles of impeachment against the President of the United States. Following such introduction, the common practice has been to refer the charges to the House Judiciary Committee for study, although the Speaker of the House may create a special committee for this task if he wishes. After examining the charges, the Judiciary Committee makes a recommendation to the full House. In the case of Richard Nixon, for example, the committee recommended that the House vote to impeach on only three of the five charges filed against him. Impeachment of a President requires only a *simple* majority of those present and voting. If the House does vote to impeach, the Senate is immediately informed so that preparations can be made for the trial. In the meantime, the House selects several of its members to prosecute its case against the President in the Senate. Although these individuals are the only House members who participate in the Senate trial, the entire membership of the House may sit in on the proceedings as observers.

When federal officers other than the President are being tried, the President of the Senate—who is also the Vice President—presides over the proceedings. When the President is on trial, however, the Chief Justice of the Supreme Court must preside. In terms of procedure, the Senate trial differs from a normal courtroom trial in two important respects. Whereas in a civil court proceeding

[102] Cited in Schlesinger, *Imperial Presidency*, p. 75.

lawyers can disqualify prospective jurors because of possible prejudice in the case, no senator may be disqualified from voting on the guilt or innocence of a President. During Andrew Johnson's impeachment trial, for example, his son-in-law was serving as one of the senators from the state of Tennessee, and he understandably voted against conviction of his father-in-law. Secondly, in a civil court proceeding the presiding judge rules on matters of procedure and admissability of evidence. In a Senate trial, the Chief Justice may initially rule on these questions, but his decisions can be overturned by a vote of the Senate.

In order to remove a President from office, two-thirds of those senators present and voting must vote to convict. Should they do so, they must then vote on whether they want to prohibit the President from holding any federal office in the future. Finally, it should be noted that even after he is removed from office, a President is still subject to possible trial and punishment in the civil courts for his actions.

Impeachable Offenses

One of the major controversies concerning the impeachment process centers upon the question of what constitutes an impeachable offense. The Constitution states that a President may be impeached for "Treason, Bribery, or other High Crimes and Misdemeanors." While there is little dispute over the meaning of treason and bribery, there has been considerable disagreement over the meaning of "High Crimes and Misdemeanors." Echoing the argument made by others before him, Richard Nixon's defense lawyer contended that this phrase refers exclusively to *criminal* offenses, and not to *political* crimes. To interpret the phrase to include the latter, he argued, would mean that Congress could virtually impeach a President for anything it wished.

Opposing this view are those who assert that the Founding Fathers fully intended High Crimes and Misdemeanors to include political as well as criminal offenses. They had, after all, borrowed the phrase from the British, who gave the term just such a meaning. This position is certainly buttressed by historical precedent, for less than one-third of the eighty-three articles of impeachment drawn up by the House over the years have "explicitly charged the violation of a criminal statute or used the word 'criminal' or 'crime' to describe the conduct alleged."[103] Rather, most of the charges cited behavior that served to undermine public confidence in the office. Finally, it should also be noted that a restriction of the phrase "High Crimes and Misdemeanors" to mean *only* criminal activity would leave the Congress powerless to act against certain kinds of presidential behavior. For example, upon assuming office a President might decide to grant a free and open pardon to all individuals currently serving in federal

---

[103]Congressional Quarterly, *Impeachment and the U.S. Congress* (Washington, D.C.: Congressional Quarterly, 1974), p. 32.

prisons. Clearly, he would be doing nothing criminally wrong, for the Constitution empowers the President with the right to grant pardons. Yet most would agree that such an irresponsible act would constitute an extraordinary abuse of his constitutional powers.

In considering the charges against Richard Nixon, most of the members of the House Judiciary Committee adopted the broader view of the phrase "High Crimes and Misdemeanors," thus viewing it as encompassing political as well as criminal offenses. They ultimately passed three articles of impeachment against him. Article I charged him with *obstruction of justice.* He was accused of encouraging perjury, destruction of evidence, and making false and misleading statements. Article II cited him for *abuse of power.* Specifically, it was charged, first, that he authorized agencies within the government (FBI and IRS) to harass private citizens for his own political advantage; second, that he established a secret investigative unit within the White House, the purpose of which was to engage in unlawful and covert activity against private citizens; and third, that he used the powers of his office to cover up these abuses. The final Article of Impeachment charged the President with *contempt of Congress.* The grounds for this charge were his continued refusal to comply with Judiciary Committee subpoenas for tapes and documents relevant to its impeachment investigation. Two additional articles were proposed, but the Judiciary Committee declined to vote in favor of them. One called for the President's impeachment because of the secret bombing initiated in Cambodia. This was rejected because some members of the Judiciary Committee felt that the President had authority to order such actions in his capacity as Commander in Chief. Others felt the charge was unjustified since Congress has acquiesced in the bombings. The other article rejected by the committee accused the President of income tax evasion. The reasons for voting down this charge were varied. Some believed that the improper tax deductions were made by the President's lawyers, without the knowledge of the President himself. Other committee members felt that impeachment should be used for crimes against the integrity of the political system. In their judgment, tax evasion did not qualify as such a crime. Still others felt that enough was enough.

The Impeachment Instrument: An Evaluation

Our recent experience with the impeachment process clearly demonstrates that it suffers from several severe limitations. In the first place, the process consumes a great deal of time. More than nine months had passed from the time the House Judiciary Committee first began its inquiry until the day Richard Nixon resigned from office. If the President had permitted the process to run its full course, with a vote of impeachment on the House floor and a trial in the Senate, the process would probably have consumed an additional six months. The problem here is that the government is thrown into a state of paralysis over this extended period of time. Given the gravity of such an undertaking, Congress is not in a position to consider anything else. In addition, a President is severely weakened politically during this time and thus unable to exert the necessary leadership over national affairs. Nor for that matter is he likely to be concerned with matters other than those related to his impeachment. Department heads not only complained about being unable to see the President, but also pointed to lack of direction from the White House in important policy areas. Moreover, it now appears that during the President's final year in office, his chief of staff acted as a surrogate President on many matters.[104]

That the impeachment process leads to a protracted paralysis of governmental leadership is serious enough. Equally disturbing is the possibility that foreign governments may attempt to take advantage of this paralysis. During the week of October 14-20, 1974, Richard Nixon had to contend with a war in the Middle East, the firing of Archibald Cox as Special Prosecutor, and an impeachment inquiry in the House. It was also during this week that the Soviet Union contemplated committing troops to the Middle East, a plan that compelled the United States to put its armed forces on "Red Alert." It is worth pondering whether the Soviet Union may have considered such a dramatic move in part because it concluded that a weakened and preoccupied President would not be able to respond.

Our procedure for removing presidents from office also suffers from another drawback, namely, that impeached presidents are likely to be rendered incapable of exerting political leadership, even if they are not convicted. Let us suppose, for example, that Richard Nixon had been impeached in the House but had narrowly escaped conviction in the Senate by three or four votes. The country would have been left with a President whom a majority of both the House and the Senate deemed guilty of impeachable offenses. Such a President would scarcely be capable of leading the Congress under such circumstances. Nor is it likely that he would enjoy the confidence of the American people.

A further problem with the impeachment process is that presidents who perceive that they are likely to be convicted may feel a strong urge to resign as Richard Nixon did. This is certainly not surprising, for since no President in our history has ever been convicted and removed from office, it seems likely that any President would want to avoid being the first. But there is also a more practical reason for resigning, namely, a financial one. Presidents convicted of impeachable offenses lose their nearly $60,000 a year pension as well as an additional sum awarded to them for transition expenses. In Richard Nixon's case, this latter item amounted to $100,000. While a resignation prior to impeachment or conviction has the benefit of shortening the agony for all concerned, the failure of the process to run its full course may raise an element of doubt as to the President's guilt or innocence. And especially among the diehard supporters

---

[104]Theodore White, *Breach of Faith* (New York: Atheneum, 1975), pp. 9, 13; see also Bob Woodward and Carl Bernstein, *The Final Days* (New York: Simon and Schuster, 1975), pp. 323, 324.

of a President, this uncertainty of guilt could lead to charges that he was railroaded out of office.

Finally, it should be noted that the impeachment process is an extraordinary ordeal for presidents. Not only is the process prolonged, but presidents must also live with the prospect of being nationally disgraced and condemned by history. When these pressures are combined with the normal burdens of the office, one may well question the ability of some presidents to function rationally under such circumstances. Much has been written about Richard Nixon's state of mind during his last months in office, with his chief of staff allegedly telling the Special Prosecutor that "the President was unstable—in fact, out of control."[105] The Secretary of Defense was so concerned over the President's emotional state during his last week in office that he took the unprecedented step of issuing an order to all U.S. military commands around the world, instructing them to accept no direct orders from the White House unless they had been countersigned by the Secretary of Defense himself.[106] All of this is to suggest that if the impeachment process can impose such a severe emotional strain upon the occupant of the White House, then the country is in a very precarious position indeed during this period. Accordingly, it may be argued that a swifter method of removal is necessary.

As is so often the case, however, identifying weaknesses in our current constitutional arrangements is far easier than coming up with solutions to remedy them. Throughout our recent impeachment ordeal many looked longingly at the British parliamentary system where, if the Prime Minister receives a vote of no confidence in the House of Commons, Parliament is dissolved, elections are held, and a new government installed. The entire process is consummated in seventeen days (excluding Saturday and Sundays). Taking their cue from the British example, some have proposed that a President be removed if two-thirds of the Congress give him a vote of no confidence. Thereupon, a new election would be held for the Presidency and both houses of Congress within thirty to sixty days following the no-confidence vote.[107]

The swiftness of the process makes it highly appealing, but herein also lies its danger. Although Richard Nixon would probably have been removed much sooner under such a system, it is also possible that Harry Truman would have been thrown out of office for his unpopular firing of General Douglas MacArthur. In short, the procedural ease with which a President could be removed from office would subject him to the whims and passions of the moment. The no-confidence proposal also fails to take into account some important distinctions between the British political system and our own. In the first place, while a Prime Minister is assured of having a majority of his own party in control of Parliament, a President has no guarantee that his own party will control the

[105]Cited in Woodward and Bernstein, *Final Days,* p. 249.
[106]White, *Breach of Faith,* p. 23.
[107]Cited in Hargrove, *Modern Presidency,* p. 317.

Congress. A vote of no confidence would be considerably more likely for those presidents who faced a Congress controlled by an unfriendly majority of the opposition party. Furthermore, in removing the Prime Minister, the British are only getting rid of the head of government. The Queen still remains as the Head of State, and as such, represents an important symbol of continuity. In removing a President from office, however, we are losing both the chief of state and the head of government. Finally, holding new elections in Britain is managed with relative ease because of the country's small size. Given the size of the United States, elections constitute a formidable undertaking. It is highly questionable whether candidates could be nominated, campaign organizations created, adequate money raised, and an election held, all within the thirty to sixty days following the removal of a President.

On occasion, it has been proposed that it might be appropriate for the Congress to take action against a President that falls short of impeachment. For example, Congress might pass a joint resolution calling upon the President to resign his office. This hardly seems practicable, for a President who was independent enough to arouse the wrath of Congress would probably also be independent enough to decline its request for his resignation. A variant of this proposal is a vote of censure against a President. A vote of censure was used by the Senate against Andrew Jackson following his decision to remove the government's bank deposits from the Second Bank of the United States. Such a tactic is of questionable benefit, however, for it is not clear what kinds of actions would merit censure as opposed to impeachment. As Andrew Jackson pointed out to the Senate, if it were in fact censuring him for actions that were impeachable, then the Congress was failing to meet its constitutional responsibilities.[108]

As one ponders the alternatives, our current impeachment process seems less unappealing. Unlike a British Prime Minister, who is selected by his party, the President is selected by the people themselves. Accordingly, it may be argued that any process that attempts to revoke the choice of a popularly elected Chief Executive should not be made easy. Moreover, the slow and somewhat cumbersome nature of impeachment enhances—even if it does not guarantee—the possibility that the Congress will act with care and deliberation. Finally, the length of the process allows adequate time for the population to become educated to the nature and persuasiveness of the charges brought against a President.

CARTER, CONGRESS, AND THE FUTURE

Jimmy Carter's relationship with Congress in 1977 did not get off to a very auspicious start. It began with the Senate refusing to confirm Theodore Sorensen, the man first nominated by Carter to be Director of the CIA. Prior to this, the

[108]Schlesinger, *Imperial Presidency,* pp. 411, 412.

Senate had rejected only eight Cabinet rank nominees in our entire history, the most recent occurring in 1925 when it refused to approve Calvin Coolidge's nominee for Attorney General. Not long after Carter suffered this rebuff, a Senate resolution condemning his pardon of Vietnam draft evaders was narrowly defeated in the Senate by a vote of 49 to 45—a surprisingly narrow victory for a newly elected President whose party was firmly in control of both Houses of Congress.

Neither did Congress prove overly hospitable to the new President's legislative program in 1977. While it did approve Carter's reorganization proposals, it failed to pass the centerpiece of his legislative program: his energy bill. In addition, Congress declined to act on the President's proposals for election reform, refused to go along with his proposal to prop up the Social Security program with general revenue funds, failed to take action on his welfare reforms, and passed a $12 billion farm bill which proved to be considerably more than the President had recommended. Finally, it took no action on his hospital cost containment legislation nor on his proposal to create a Consumer Protection Agency.

In seeking to account for Carter's limited success with Congress during his first year, part of the blame must certainly be laid at his own doorstep. Having arrived in Washington as an "outsider," he had few personal contacts in Congress and little understanding of how it operates. The same was true of his staff members, one of whom he placed in charge of the White House Office of Congressional Liaison. This inexperience led to several tactical blunders by the President and his staff. For example, the Carter Administration sometimes drafted legislation without making any effort to consult members of Congress on the bill's substance. Both his energy and water projects legislation suffered as a result of this oversight. Nor did the President always consult the legislators when he decided to change his mind on legislation. Several congressmen who went out on a limb to support Carter's $50 rebate all of a sudden found the proposal scrapped without so much as a word of warning from the President.

Another tactical blunder made by the White House was its failure to follow up on legislation after it was introduced in Congress. Thus, although Carter's energy legislation was reported out of the House largely intact, the White House failed to anticipate the chilly reception the bill received in the Senate. Similarly, the President's politically delicate voter registration reform was introduced into the House before any consideration was given to forging a coalition that would support it.

In addition to inadequate consultation and follow-up, the President's legislative program suffered from an excess of proposals. In a relatively short span of time, Carter sent to the Hill legislation dealing with such matters as energy, election and welfare reform, government reorganization, the Panama Canal Treaties, Social Security, and agriculture. In so doing he failed to provide Congress with any indication of what should take priority. As one congressman noted, "With almost no exceptions every issue that has come down from the White House or agency has been viewed as THE big issue."[109] Moreover, by thrusting all of this legislation upon Congress—most which was highly controversial—the President was forced to deal with opposition from many different quarters all at once.

Finally, Carter also failed to make adequate use of some important tools of persuasion. For example, rather than keeping hold of the patronage lever, he gave his department heads the responsibility for filling appointive positions in government. In many instances, congressmen and senators suggested individuals for positions in the government, only to have them ignored by department heads. Needless to say, this kind of treatment does not serve to build up a store of congressional good will toward the administration. Carter's apparent insensitivity to the importance of such presidential carrots as patronage and projects stems from an aversion to the LBJ style of wheeling and dealing. In the words of the House Majority Leader, "He does not like to indulge in quid pro quo. . . . I think he came to the office thinking there was something a bit corrupt about the political give-and-take of Washington."[110]

As the Carter Administration moved into 1978, there were some indications that it had learned from its mistakes. Although he submitted legislation on tax reform and government reorganization, for the most part the President was content to let Congress digest what he had given it the previous year. Moreover, the administration's handling of the critically important Panama Canal Treaties reflected not only more careful planning and consultation with members of Congress, but also a willingness to trade presidential favors in return for votes, something the President and his aids had been reluctant to do previously.[111]

Having noted that Carter's difficulties with Congress have to a considerable extent been a consequence of his own doing, we must acknowledge that he was also disadvantaged by circumstances over which he had no control. For one thing, although he enjoyed substantial majorities in both the House and Senate, we must remember that he was dealing with Democrats who, during the eight years of the Nixon and Ford presidencies, had become used to acting independent of White House leadership.

Second, Carter came into office with a Congress that was substantially different from those faced by Kennedy and Johnson. Of the members elected to the House in 1976, 159 were freshmen; moreover, over half the House members serving in 1977 had been elected since 1970. In the Senate, 30 new members were elected in 1976; 59 of the senators serving in 1977 had been elected since 1970. These newer members, most of whom were Democrats, exhibited a higher than usual degree of independence from the leadership within their own Houses.

---

[109] *Washington Post,* November 13, 1977, p. B12.

[110] Hedrick Smith, "Problems of a Problem Solver," *New York Times Magazine,* January 8, 1978, p. 36. © 1978 by The New York Times Company. Reprinted by permission.

[111] See, for example, F.T. Merrill, Jr., "How Carter Stopped Playing Politics and Started Having Trouble with Congress," *The Washington Monthly,* 9 (July/August, 1977), pp. 28–30; *Washington Post,* March 28, 1978, p. B15.

According to an administrative assistant to House Speaker O'Neill, "In the old days the congressmen followed the reports of the committee and voted the way the committee wanted them to vote. Now members are young, bright, highly educated, independent. . . . It makes it infinitely harder for the leadership."[112] Since the congressional leadership of his party is one of the principal instruments by which a President attempts to mobilize support for his programs, a leadership with less clout makes this task all the more difficult.

Third, Carter has had to compete—often unsuccessfully—with a growing number of highly organized and well-financed special interest groups. Moreover, to a far greater extent than ever before, these groups are focusing their energies and resources on Congress. In part, this development reflects the realization that Congress is now playing a more active role in the policy-making process. In part, it is also a consequence of campaign finance reforms, for with optional public financing of presidential nomination and election campaigns, the role of special interest contributions at this level has now been greatly reduced. The members of Congress, however, have not yet seen fit to provide for public financing of their own elections; thus, it is not surprising that special interest groups are funnelling more and more of their financial resources into senatorial and congressional elections, where their contributions continue to be gratefully received.

Finally, of course, Jimmy Carter came into the Presidency facing a Congress that has become accustomed to asserting itself. In the words of the House Minority Leader, "Congress has gotten used to kicking presidents around and they don't care whose president it is."[113] While this remark overstates the point, it is nevertheless clear that Congress is insisting on playing an active role in all policy making. Of course, it may be that some of the edge will be taken off this assertiveness as the memory of the Johnson and Nixon presidencies grows dimmer. But even if one allows for this, the fact remains that Congress has increased its role in the budgetary process and is gradually expanding its policy expertise. These developments alone make it likely that future presidents will face a Congress that speaks with a louder and more confident voice.

[112]*Washington Post,* May 23, 1977, p. 1.

[113]*New York Times,* October 9, 1977, p. 31. © 1977 by The New York Times Company. Reprinted by permission.

4

The President
and
the Bureaucracy

While the President is admittedly the most important figure in the Executive branch, he is by no means its sole member. The Executive is composed of eleven separate departments (see Table 4-1) and some 120 separate agencies, which together employ nearly three million civilian employees. As such, it constitutes the largest and most complex entity in the federal government. Its size is a function of its responsibilities in the governmental process. These include administering a myriad of federal programs—currently about 1,400 in number—which have an impact upon nearly every aspect of our national life. This function takes on added significance since the legislation enacting these programs is often written in rather general language. Consequently, the bureaucracy can exercise considerable discretion in deciding how such programs should be implemented. In addition to being an implementer of legislation, the bureaucracy is also a proposer. Indeed, most of the legislation annually submitted to Congress by the President is planned and drafted by the various departments and agencies in the Executive branch. Finally, the bureaucracy also functions as a provider of information to both the President and the Congress. Its constant involvement in the day-to-day administration of federal programs, its abundance of trained experts in all policy areas and its formidable capacity for data collection, all provide the bureaucracy with an unequalled capacity to inform decision makers.

As noted in the previous chapter, the President experiences considerable frustration in his dealings with Congress. This is understandable, for the separation of powers and checks and balances serve to encourage a certain degree of antagonism. Each branch is organically distinct from the other; each exercises powers that can frustrate the will of the other; and each is elected by different constituencies and thus is subject to different pressures and expectations. On the

TABLE 4-1. EXECUTIVE DEPARTMENTS AND CIVILIAN EMPLOYEES, 1977

Departments	Civilian Employees
Agriculture	110,601
Commerce	38,055
Defense	993,516
Energy	18,295*
Health, Education and Welfare	156,582
Housing and Urban Development	16,537
Interior	77,496
Justice	53,429
Labor	16,459
State	35,838
Transportation	74,845
Treasury	127,345

SOURCE: U.S. Bureau of the Census, *Statistical Abstract of the United States* (Washington, D.C.: Government Printing Office, 1977), p. 270.

This figure is for 1978 and was provided by the Department of Energy.

other hand, the bureaucracy and the President are both members of the same branch of government. And even more important, it is the President who sits at the head of it. Thus one might expect the President to encounter little difficulty in gaining the cooperation of those under him. Such an expectation would not be grounded in fact, however. Indeed, all of our more recent presidents have attested to the resistance they encountered from this vast bureaucracy over which they preside:

The Treasury is so large and far-flung and ingrained in its practices that I find it almost impossible to get the action and results I want—even with Henry [Morganthau] there. But the Treasury is not to be compared with the State Department. You should go through the experience of trying to get any changes in the thinking, policy and action of the career diplomats and then you'd know what a real problem was. But the Treasury and State Department put together are nothing compared with the N-A-V-Y. The admirals are really something to cope with—and I should know. To change anything in the N-A-V-Y is like punching a feather bed. You punch it with your right and you punch it with your left until you are finally exhausted, and then you find the damn bed just as you left it before you started punching.

Franklin Roosevelt

I thought I was the President, but when it comes to these bureaucracies, I can't make them do a damn thing.

Harry Truman

Yea. One of the reasons, George, that you got to act on that SBA (Small Business Administration) guy—I don't care if he's a guy with eighteen

kids—is that we have no discipline in this bureaucracy. We never fire anybody. We never reprimand anybody. We never demote anybody. We
always promote the sons-of-bitches that kick us in the ass. That's true in
the State Department. It's true in HEW. It's true in OMB, and true for ourselves, and it's got to stop. This fellow deliberately did not—I read the
memorandum—he did not carry out an order I personally gave. I wrote
the order out [unintelligible]. And the son-of-a-bitch did not do it. Now,
I don't care what he is. Get him out of there.

Richard Nixon

Before I became president, I realized and was warned that dealing with the
federal bureaucracy would be one of the worst problems I would have to
face. It has been even worse than I had anticipated.

Jimmy Carter

Although these remarks serve to highlight his sense of impotence in dealing with
the bureaucracy, the President does have ways of exercising a measure of control
over it. These include the power of *appointment,* the power to *reorganize the
Executive branch,* and the use of a coordinating procedure known as *central
clearance.* As we shall see, however, these instruments of leverage are not absolute. Some are subject to constitutional, statutory, and political limitations.
Moreover, none of these instruments is exercised in a vacuum, for the bureaucracy also has resources of its own, such as *expertise, permanence,* and *alliances*
in and outside government, all of which may be used in an effort to countervail
those resources of the President. To the extent that it is able to do so successfully, the President is precluded from being the master of his own house.

THE POWER OF APPOINTMENT

Kinds of Choices

Quite obviously a President is not able to administer and supervise the operations of the Executive branch by himself. Thus he chooses what he believes to be
a group of competent administrators to assist him in this task. These political
appointees include department heads and those serving immediately under them,
the members of independent agencies and regulatory commissions, and some
bureau chiefs. While the power to fill these upper-level positions in the bureaucracy is surely an important one, it is also subject to several limitations. For one
thing, presidents may not always be able to get the people they want. Some do
not choose to leave a high-paying job in the private sector in order to take a
government job at a much lower pay scale; and others simply cannot afford to do
so. Second, in filling these top positions, the President must take into account
views other than his own. The Senate, for example, has the constitutional

responsibility for approving or rejecting the President's nominees to these posts. Thus, he is not likely to nominate an individual who enjoys little support among the Senate membership, for failure to win their approval would prove embarrassing both to him and his nominee. Sometimes, of course, presidents will miscalculate, as Jimmy Carter did when he was forced to withdraw the nomination of Theodore Sorensen to be Director of the Central Intelligence Agency. In this particular case, Carter's staff had apparently failed to gauge the degree of opposition to Sorensen in both the liberal and conservative wings of the Senate. Various publics may also take a keen interest in a President's prospective appointment to a particular position, and their views cannot be easily ignored. It would be politically unwise, for example, were a President to nominate as Secretary of Labor a man who was thoroughly unacceptable to the major labor unions. Similarly, he would be reluctant to fill the position of Secretary of the Treasury with an individual who did not enjoy the confidence of the business and financial interests in the country.

Number of Choices

The limitations on the presidential appointment power extend not only to the kinds of choices a President is able to make but also to the number of people he can appoint. In actuality, he has effective control over approximately 3,500 positions in the bureaucracy. The occupants of these positions serve at the pleasure of the President, which means they are subject to removal at his discretion. His right to do so was established by a Supreme Court ruling in the case of *Myers* vs. *United States* (1926), and as we shall see shortly, it has been modified only slightly since then. The remaining positions in the Executive branch, however, are held by career civil servants. They are not appointed by the President, but rather are selected in accordance with standards of merit determined by the Civil Service Commission. Nor are they subject to removal by him except for malfeasance, neglect of duty, or inefficiency. While most of these career bureaucrats do not have policy-making responsibilities, approximately twenty-eight thousand have at least some, and nearly four thousand of these have considerable responsibilities in this area.

These individuals constitute part of the permanent government. They remain in their jobs while administrations come and go, and consequently, their loyalties are likely to lie with their particular department or agency rather than with any given President. They are not likely to react favorably to presidential policies that seek to alter long-established agency procedures or that adversely affect the programs their agencies administer. Since it is these high-level career bureaucrats who are charged with the actual implementation of a President's policies, they may use their positions to frustrate rather than facilitate his wishes. Such resistance may take a variety of forms: delaying tactics, complying with the letter but not the spirit of a presidential policy, failing to pass along an order received from above, "leaking" embarrassing information to the press, stirring up opposition to presidential policies among members of Congress and interest groups.

Since the major expansions in the bureaucracy have occurred as a result of massive social programs enacted under Democratic administrations, Republican presidents have long suspected that the career bureaucracy manifests a pronounced Democratic bias. Acting upon this conviction, President Eisenhower sought to have a substantial number of high-level career positions reclassified to policy-making positions so that he could fill them by political appointment. As we shall see later in this chapter, Richard Nixon also attempted to employ this same tactic as well as other, more ingenious, ones in order to bring the career bureaucracy more directly under his control.

Republican suspicions of the pro-Democratic bureaucracy are not entirely without foundation. Indeed, a recent study of some eighteen government agencies revealed that among supergrade career bureaucrats working in these agencies, 17 percent classified themselves as Republicans, 47 percent as Democrats, and 36 percent as independent. Furthermore, those bureaucrats classifying themselves as independent exhibited attitudes that were more often characteristic of Democrats than of Republicans.[1] And as Table 4-2 indicates, an overwhelming majority of these high-level career civil servants favor maintaining or increasing the current level of government-provided social services. Given the fact that the Republican party has traditionally taken a more conservative view on government spending than the Democratic party, it is not surprising that a Republican President such as Richard Nixon would encounter strong bureaucratic resistance when attempting to cut back on massive federal spending in the area of social services.

Federal Regulatory Agencies

Within the Executive branch there exist several agencies that are charged with the responsibility of regulating various aspects of our national life. The first of these, the Interstate Commerce Commission, was created by the Congress in 1787. Several others have been established since that time, with the total number currently standing at twelve. Their importance lies in the fact that they establish and administer regulations as well as adjudicate disputes in such areas as communication, transportation, commerce, energy, finance, and labor relations (see Table 4-3). The Civil Aeronautics Board, for example, regulates the air routes, safety standards, and prices charged by airlines. The Federal Maritime Commission performs similar regulatory functions for the shipping industry.

Although the President is vested with the power to appoint the members of

---

[1] Joel Aberbach and Bert Rockman, "Clashing Beliefs Within the Executive Branch: The Nixon Administration Bureaucracy," *American Political Science Review* 70 (June 1976), 461.

TABLE 4-2. ATTITUDES OF CAREER SUPERGRADE CIVIL SERVANTS ON GOVERNMENT PROVISION OF SOCIAL SERVICES

For Much More Government Provision of Social Services	For Some Additional Government Provision	For Present Balance	For Less Government Provision	For Much Less Government Provision
32%	22%	25%	12%	10%*

SOURCE: Adapted from Joel Aberbach and Bert Rockman, "Clashing Beliefs within the Executive Branch: The Nixon Administration Bureaucracy," *American Political Science Review,* 70 (June 1976), 461.

Totals do not equal 100% because of rounding.

TABLE 4-3. MEMBERSHIP, TERMS, AND PARTISAN BALANCE OF THE FEDERAL REGULATORY AGENCIES

Agency	Number of Members	Term (Years)	Partisan Balance
Civil Aeronautics Board	5	6	Not more than 3 members from one political party
Consumer Product Safety Commission	5	7	Not more than 3 members from one political party
Federal Communications Commission	7	7	Not more than 4 members from one political party
Federal Maritime Commission	5	5	Not more than 3 members from one political party
Federal Energy Regulatory Commission	5	4	Not more than 3 members from one political party
Federal Reserve Board	7	14	No statutory limitation on political party membership
Federal Trade Commission	5	7	Not more than 3 members from one political party
Interstate Commerce Commission	11	7	Not more than 6 members from one political party
National Labor Relations Board	5	5	No statutory limitation on political party membership
National Mediation Board	3	3	Not more than 2 members from one political party
Nuclear Regulatory Commission	5	5	Not more than 3 members from one political party
Securities and Exchange Commission	5	5	Not more than 3 members from one political party

these important regulatory agencies, this power is once again circumscribed in a variety of ways. In the first place, the terms of service in these agencies range from a minimum of three years to a maximum of fourteen. Moreover, the terms within each of the agencies are staggered. Both of these factors insure that when a new President takes office, he will find many of the positions in the regulatory agencies held by individuals who were appointed by his predecessor. Under normal circumstances, for example, Jimmy Carter would only be able to fill forty-three of the sixty-eight positions on the regulatory agencies during his first four years in office. (In his particular case, however , the number will be slightly higher because the Democratic Congress withheld its approval of President Ford's nominees to fill those terms that expired in December 1976 and early January 1977.) Of course, if a President is fortunate enough to serve two terms, his impact upon the regulatory agencies will be greater. During his five and a half years in office, for example, Richard Nixon was able to name every member in eight of the twelve agencies.[2]

Even when a President has the opportunity to fill vacancies, however, he is still constrained by the requirement that nearly all agencies must reflect some kind of partisan balance (see Table 4-3). Moreover, agency members usually assume a highly independent posture once they have been appointed. In the early sixties, for example, the clearly stated position of the White House was that competition in the railroad and airline industries ought to be increased, and yet the Civil Aeronautics Board and the Interstate Commerce Commission went ahead and approved railroad and airline mergers that served to reduce competition.[3] Lyndon Johnson likewise felt the sting of agency independence in 1965 when the Federal Reserve Board Chairman, William MacChesney Martin, increased the discount rate over strong objections from the President. The President's irritation was all the greater since he had not only reappointed Martin to another fourteen-year term on the board, but had also designated him as chairman. The independence of agency members is encouraged essentially by two factors—first, the rather lengthy terms that characterize most agency positions, and second, the fact that members of the federal regulatory agencies do not serve at the pleasure of the President and thus cannot be arbitrarily removed by him.

The basis for this limitation on the President's power was a ruling by the Supreme Court in the case of *Humphrey's Executor* vs. *United States* (1935). In 1931 President Hoover reappointed William Humphrey to another seven-year term on the Federal Trade Commission. Shortly after becoming President, however, Franklin Roosevelt sought to remove Humphrey on grounds that the goals of his administration could best be served by allowing him to pick the membership of the FTC. Roosevelt's reasons were in fact purely political, for he

---

[2] *Congressional Quarterly Weekly Report,* August 24, 1974, p. 2281.

[3] Peter Woll and Rochelle Jones, "Bureaucratic Defense in Depth," in Michael Sego, ed., *Political Leadership in America* (Cleveland: Regal Books/King's Court Communications, 1974), p. 198.

did not want a man of Humphrey's conservative views serving on the commission. The Court ruled that Congress had the right to establish agencies independent of executive control, and in this case, the statute establishing the Federal Trade Commission had indeed specified that its members could not be removed except for malfeasance, neglect of duty, or inefficiency. Thus the President's dismissal of Humphrey for political reasons was in violation of the law.[4] The scope of the President's removal power became an issue once again in the fifties, when President Eisenhower removed an individual from the War Claims Commission solely for political reasons. In this case, however, the circumstances were different since the statute creating the War Claims Commission did not specify the grounds for removing its members. The Supreme Court nevertheless ruled that since the War Claims Commission performed a judicial rather than an executive function, the President had no authority to remove its members (*Wiener* vs. *United States,* 1958).[5]

The independent character of the regulatory agencies continues to be a subject of some controversy. Those who support their current structure point out that the lengthy terms of service not only increase the expertise of agency members but also provide for continuity in policy. In addition, they argue that decision making "provides both a barrier to arbitrary or capricious actions and a source of decisions based on different points of view and experience."[6] Finally, given the powerful political influence of the industries regulated by these agencies, it is absolutely essential that an agency be insulated from partisan influences. Critics are quick to point out, however, that agency independence often results in a lack of policy coordination between the President and the agencies on important economic matters. Furthermore, since many of the members in these agencies are in fact recruited from the industries that the agencies are supposed to regulate, the claim to agency impartiality is more fiction than fact. This charge was confirmed by a two-year congressional investigation (1975–76) of nine regulatory agencies, which concluded that agency commitment to the interests of the regulated industries took precedence over their commitment to the public interest.[7]

Political Appointees: the Problem of "Going Native"

Thus far, our discussion has noted that the President's appointment power is limited by the availability of people willing to serve, by the acceptability of his nominees to groups in and outside governments, by the relatively small number

---

[4] *Rathbun (Humphrey's Executor)* vs. *United States,* 295 U.S. 602 (1935).

[5] *Weiner* vs. *United States,* 375 U.S. 349 (1958).

[6] This statement is taken from the report of the first Hoover Commission and cited in Emmette Redford, "The Arguments For and Against the Commission System," in Samuel Kristov and Lloyd Musolf, eds., *The Politics of Regulation* (Boston: Houghton Mifflin, 1964), p. 124.

[7] *New York Times,* October 3, 1976, p. 21.

of people he is able to place in the bureaucracy, and finally, by the restrictions upon his ability to remove some of them once they get there. His problems do not end here, however, for even those who serve at the pleasure of the President may not always be thoroughly supportive of his policies. Speaking to this point, Vice President Charles Dawes once remarked that "Cabinet members are the natural enemies of the President."[8] To be sure, this remark is an exaggeration, but like all overstatements, there is a kernel of truth in it. Even though the President's political appointees may assume their positions with every intention of expediting his policy goals, they soon discover that they must give an attentive ear to other voices besides that of the President. These voices emanate from three major constituencies: the *career bureaucrats* within their own department, *members of Congress,* and various *organized interests* within the society. Over-responsiveness to these groups by Cabinet and sub-Cabinet officials have frequently prompted White House aids to charge that Cabinet officials "go off and marry the natives." We shall now consider why this happens.

As was noted earlier in this chapter, the loyalties of career bureaucrats tend to lie with the agency or department they work in. Thus, they are not likely to be receptive to presidential policies that threaten their jobs, the agency's programs, or its organizational structure. Moreover, they will make every effort to impress their own views upon the head of their department or agency. And as one former White House aid notes, they are often successful:

> The major problem is the lack of any identification [on their part] with the president's program priorities. At State they try to humor the president but hope he will not interfere in their complex matters and responsibilities. It is equally a problem with civil servants and Cabinet types. It is amazing how soon the Cabinet people get captured by the permanent staffs. Secretary _____ under Nixon, for example, was captured within days . . . and Nixon's staff didn't even try to improve things. They just assumed there was a great problem. Personally, I think you can't expect too much from the bureaucracy. It is too much to expect that they will see things the president's way.[9]

Given the formidable administrative task Cabinet secretaries face, it is not altogether surprising that they and their assistant secretaries come to rely heavily upon the career bureaucracy within their departments. Using the Department of Commerce as an example—and it is a relatively small department at that—the Secretary of Commerce is ultimately responsible for the actions of the following subunits within his department: Business and Defense Services Administration, Maritime Administration, Economic Development Administration, Environ-

[8] Cited in Harold Seidman, *Politics, Position and Power* (New York: Oxford University Press, 1970), p. 72.

[9] Cited in Thomas Cronin, *The State of the Presidency* (Boston: Little, Brown, 1975), p. 161.

mental Services Administration, Office of Business and Economics, Office of Field Services, Bureau of the Census, Bureau of International Commerce, National Bureau of Standards, United States Travel Agency.

And if the size and complexity of a department were not burden enough, his managerial task is further complicated by the fact that most of his time must be spent on other matters: "He spends 30 to 40 percent of his time testifying or meeting with Congress; the next block of his time meeting with constituency groups, speechmaking, etc.; the next block of time in committees—that leaves him about 10 percent of his time to devote to departmental matters if he's interested in doing so."[10]

Nor do these constitute all of his limitations, for a Cabinet appointee and his assistant secretaries frequently have very little expertise in the substantive concerns of their department. Furthermore, they are not likely to remain in their positions long enough to develop this expertise nor, for that matter, long enough to grasp thoroughly the internal operations of their department. Of the eighty-seven Cabinet members serving from 1953 to 1976, for example, over half (forty-six) served for a period of approximately one to two years. Similarly, a study made of undersecretaries and assistant secretaries during the Kennedy and Johnson administrations and the first four years of Nixon's revealed that nearly one-fifth served under twelve months and less than half served more than two years.[11] Consequently, Cabinet secretaries and their assistants are forced to rely heavily upon the career bureaucrats, whose customarily long service in a department has provided them with a sophisticated understanding of the policy issues confronting it, as well as a thorough mastery of the department's internal operations.

In addition to the career bureaucrats within his department, the head of a department or agency must also be attentive to the views of Congress, especially those congressional committees having oversight responsibilities for his department. Their judgments as to what programs and goals the department should pursue may not always accord with the President's. Moreover, since these committees are charged with authorizing programs and recommending appropriations for the departments, their policy preferences cannot easily be dismissed.

Finally, organized interests within the society constitute still another constituency requiring the attention of a Cabinet secretary. Each of the domestic departments within the Executive branch (Agriculture, Energy, Interior, Labor, Commerce, Transportation, Health, Education and Welfare, Housing and Urban Development) provides services to one or more groups in the population. Quite

[10] Remarks by Harold Seidman in Douglas Fox, ed., "A Mini-Symposium: President Nixon's Proposals for Executive Reorganization," *Public Administration Review* 34 (September/October 1974), 490.

[11] *Watergate: Its Implications for Responsible Government,* a Report Prepared by a Panel of the National Academy of Public Administration at the Request of the Senate Select Committee on Presidential Campaign Activities (New York: National Academy of Public Administration, 1974), p. 107.

understandably, these groups expect a department head to be an advocate for their own interests. Their expectations take on added importance because they are likely to have powerful support within the Congress. Consequently a Cabinet secretary who chooses to ignore their pleas is likely to encounter rough going.

At the start of his second term in the Presidency, for example, President Nixon appointed the determined and conservative Caspar Weinburger to replace Elliot Richardson as the Secretary of Health, Education and Welfare. Weinburger's marching orders were to cut back, as well as cut out, many of the expensive social service programs being administered by HEW. The new Secretary soon made it clear that he was opposed to several of the department's goals and programs. Among them were higher Social Security payments, several forms of aid to elementary schools, federal grants used to train medical researchers, social workers and educators, and direct programs of federal medical care.[12] His statements sparked a storm of opposition from medical school deans, college presidents, high school principals, social scientists and other professional groups long served by these programs. While Weinberger was not powerless to act, his actions were largely confined to what administrative discretion would permit, such as tightening of eligibility requirements for federal grants and impounding a portion of the funds appropriated for certain programs (most of these impoundments were successfully challenged in the courts, however). But most of the cutbacks he sought to make required congressional approval, and Congress refused to cooperate. Indeed, even when Weinburger attempted to use his administrative authority to close eight Public Health Service hospitals, the Congress promptly passed legislation revoking such authority. The opposition of both organized interests and their supporters in Congress ultimately forced Weinburger to abandon many of his original goals and to turn instead to a policy of conciliation. He announced that HEW would increase aid to elementary and secondary schools by $500 million. An expensive vocational rehabilitation program opposed by the Nixon Administration earlier in the year was soon signed into law by the President. In addition, HEW was now at work on a national health insurance plan, which was considerably more generous than the one earlier proposed by the Nixon Administration. Finally, the Secretary also announced that he was interested in lightening the Social Security tax burden on the poor. These reversals in position prompted one close observer of HEW affairs to comment that "they do show that even the most convinced conservative finds HEW's built-in pressures for activism hard to resist and the support of his constituents important, if not indispensable."[13]

Department and agency heads must thus perform a delicate balancing act among a variety of constituencies, only one of whom is the President. Of course, when and if a President concludes that the balancing is frustrating his own policy goals, he can remove his political appointees. But even here he does not

[12] *Wall Street Journal,* November 13, 1973, p. 26.
[13] Ibid.

have a completely free hand, for what he can do legally, he may not be able to do politically. Some of his political appointees may be astute enough to build up strong bases of support within Congress as well as among various elements of the public. Accordingly, the President may incur high political costs if he removes them. On numerous occasions, for example, Franklin Roosevelt's Secretary of Commerce adopted policy positions that were in direct conflict with the President's. Yet Secretary Jones's excellent rapport with the Congress and his strong support among powerful interests in the business community led Roosevelt to conclude that he stood to lose more by firing him than by keeping him on.[14]

J. Edgar Hoover is perhaps the classic example of a political appointee whose overwhelming support in and outside government rendered him invulnerable to presidential removal. Indeed, he was customarily the first individual to be reappointed by a succession of newly elected presidents. While of late the reputation of the Federal Bureau of Investigation has been tarnished, nevertheless for most of Hoover's long tenure as Director, the bureau enjoyed a reputation as the most professional law-enforcement agency in the world. It was this reputation, established under his leadership, that afforded Hoover the ability to engage in independent political actions which presidents felt compelled to tolerate. In 1964, for example, the United States and the Soviet Union signed a Consular Treaty which failed to receive Senate approval until three years later. One of the major obstacles to immediate ratification was none other than Mr. Hoover. Without consulting either his immediate superior in the Justice Department (the Attorney General) or the President of the United States, the Director appeared before a congressional committee and warned them that approval of the treaty would allow the Soviet Union to expand their intelligence operations in the United States. In September 1966, Secretary of State Rusk released his correspondence with Hoover, which revealed the Director's refusal to entertain the Secretary's request that he withdraw his opposition to the treaty. An editorial in the *New York Times* noted the significance of this exchange of letters:

> There can be few, if any, precedents for the spectacle that correspondence presents: the Secretary of State, in effect, asking a Federal police official of sub-Cabinet rank to stop blocking United States foreign policy, and then receiving a reply so cryptic and ungracious that it can only further encourage opponents of the Administration's policy. It is a reminder of the magnitude of Mr. Hoover's power with implications that go far beyond the immediate issue.[15]

Not all political appointees have enjoyed a base of support as broad as

---

[14] Randall Ripley and Grace Franklin, *Congress, the Bureaucracy, and Public Policy* (Homewood, Ill.: Dorsey Press, 1976), p. 35.

[15] *New York Times,* January 23, 1967, p. 42. © 1967 by The New York Times Company. Reprinted by permission.

Hoover's, however. President Ford's dismissal of Defense Secretary James Schlesinger produced only minimal repercussions, for the Secretary's aloof and sometimes arrogant style had not endeared him to very many members of Congress. Likewise, when Interior Secretary Hickel openly criticized President Nixon's administrative style, his swift removal was assured by the fact that he lacked any substantial following either in or outside government.

REORGANIZATION

While the Constitution accords to Congress the responsibility for establishing, altering, or abolishing departments and agencies in the Executive branch, for some time now the primary initiative in this area has rested with the President. The impetus for this change came during the Presidency of Franklin Roosevelt. Concerned about the ability of the Executive branch to function efficiently, Roosevelt created the Committee on Administrative Management, which has since come to be known as the Brownlow Committee. Acting upon the Brownlow Committee's recommendation that sound management required substantial reorganizations within the Executive branch, the Congress passed the Reorganization Act of 1939. This act empowered the President to transfer, abolish, or consolidate government agencies unless such plans were vetoed by *both* Houses of Congress within *sixty days* after they were submitted to it. Following the substantial increase in the size of the bureaucracy during the New Deal and the Second World War, another study of the Executive branch was commissioned under the chairmanship of former President Hoover. The first Hoover Commission's recommendations culminated in congressional passage of the Legislative Reorganization Act of 1949, which not only gave the President authority to reorganize government agencies, but also granted him the power to create Cabinet-level departments. Congress still maintained its ultimate control over Executive reorganization, however, by stipulating that any reorganization plan could be killed if *either* House vetoed it within sixty days after it was submitted. The act has since been renewed periodically by the Congress with only one major change. In 1964, Congress amended it to prevent the President from using the reorganization initiative to create or abolish departments. The act last expired in 1973, at which time the Congress declined to renew it because of the scandals then breaking around the Nixon Presidency. At the request of President Carter, however, in 1977 it was once again extended for another three years.

The reorganization initiative can be of great assistance to a President. For example, by bringing under the control of one agency a variety of programs that were formerly administered by several agencies, he can achieve greater coordination over a particular policy area, eliminate possible duplication of effort, and more clearly establish lines of authority. These reasons undoubtedly accounted for President Carter's desire to combine all federal energy programs under one newly created Department of Energy. The reorganization initiative can also assist a President in other ways. If he has just implemented a new program and fears that it may become bogged down in the bureaucratic intransigence of an already existing agency, he may create a new one. That is in part why Lyndon Johnson decided to set up a special agency (Office of Economic Opportunity) to administer many of his Great Society programs and—to highlight its importance— located it in the White House. Of course, reorganization may be used to downgrade as well as elevate the importance of an agency and its programs. Richard Nixon had little use for many of President Johnson's expensive social programs and thus moved the Office of Economic Opportunity out of the White House and into the large and cumbersome Department of Health, Education and Welfare. Finally, if an agency in a given department is proving resistant to presidential policies, the President may seek to transfer its functions to a department that is more controllable. That was the motivation behind President Nixon's unsuccessful attempt to eliminate the Interstate Commerce Commission and transfer its functions to the Department of Commerce.

On the Need to Reorganize

It is fair to say that the reorganization plans of recent presidents have been designed to bring greater coordination, accountability, and economy to the operations of the Executive branch. Presidents have felt compelled to undertake such reorganizations because past decisions on where to locate new programs have not always been guided by a concern for efficient management.

> The decisive factor in situating a new program in a particular department or agency often has little to do with rational concepts of management. One congressional committee may be considered more receptive to a proposed idea than another, or simply be less busy than another. One cabinet or agency head may have more influence with the President, the White House staff, or the Congress; another may be more able as an administrator than those of his peers vying for the same program.[16]

These and other considerations have been responsible for locating programs and agencies in the most unexpected places. At various times in the past, for example, the Public Health Service, the Bureau of Narcotics, and the U.S. Coast Guard all came under the jurisdiction of the Treasury Department. Similarly, the government's current water-pollution control program is not to be found in the Department of Interior but rather in the Department of Health, Education and Welfare. This kind of irrationality on occasion has made victims even of those who are closest to it. Thus, not long after the Congress passed legislation permitting the

---

[16] Joseph Califano, *A Presidential Nation* (New York: W.W. Norton, and Co., Inc., 1975), p. 21.

President to declare certain areas of the country "wilderness areas," President Johnson decided he wanted to draw national attention to this project by making a public announcement of the first group of areas to be set aside. Accordingly, he instructed one of his aids to summon the Secretary of the Interior to the White House to brief members of the press on the project and announce the first selection of wilderness areas. After the press briefing, the President's aid received a phone call from Orville Freeman, the Secretary of Agriculture. With considerable irritation, Freeman inquired, "What in hell is going on over there? I just saw the wire service tickers saying that you and Udall briefed the press on the new wilderness areas. Wilderness areas fall within the jurisdiction of the Agriculture Department."[17] Yet neither the President of the United States, nor his aid, nor even the Secretary of the Interior was aware of this fact.

When functionally related programs are strung out over a variety of different departments and agencies, the President faces formidable difficulties in attempting to establish policy coordination and accountability. The following data should provide some appreciation of the problem: in 1977 nine different departments and twenty independent agencies administered programs related to education; seven departments and eight independent agencies dealt with health-related programs; three departments were involved in water resources; four agencies in two departments were involved in managing public lands; six agencies in three different departments were involved in federal recreation programs; seven agencies were involved in water and sewer systems; six departments were charged with compiling economic information; seven departments were involved in the area of international trade; seven departments and three independent agencies administered between twenty and thirty manpower programs.[18]

Difficulties in Reorganizing

Recent presidents have commissioned groups of distinguished citizens to study the bureaucratic structure and come up with recommendations for making it more coherent and manageable. President Johnson established two task forces, with the first recommending the creation of a Department of Natural Resources and a Department of Housing and Community Development, and the second calling for the establishment of a Department of Natural Resources and Development, a Department of Economic Affairs, and a Department of Social Services. Richard Nixon also established an Advisory Council on Executive Organization, whose recommendations proved to be considerably more ambitious. Acting upon the belief that the federal government should be organized according to functions and goals rather than program, they recommended retaining the departments of Justice, Defense, State, and the Treasury. At the same time, the remaining seven departments (Interior, Commerce, Labor, Agriculture, Transpor-

[17]Ibid., p. 22.
[18]*National Journal,* May 8, 1971, p. 978.

tation, Housing and Urban Development) were to be reorganized into the following four departments:

Department of Natural Resources—land, recreation, water resources, energy and mineral resources, and marine resources.

Department of Human Resources—health services, income maintenance and security, education, manpower, and social and rehabilitation services.

Department of Economic Development—food and commodities, domestic and international commerce, science and technology, labor relations and standards, and statistical economic development.

Department of Community Development—housing, community development, metropolitan development, and renewal development.[19]

While some of the more modest recommendations of the Johnson and Nixon commissions have been approved by the Congress, most of the far-reaching proposals outlined above have never been realized. To understand why this is so is to appreciate why the President's reorganization power is so severely limited.

Any time a President seeks to transfer, abolish, or consolidate government agencies, he is likely to face formidable opposition from three sources: those within the agency, those congressional committees exercising oversight over the agency, and finally, those clientele groups served by the agency. Lyndon Johnson's experience with the Maritime Administration illustrates the problem. One of his reorganization proposals called for combining this agency along with several others under what was to be a newly created Department of Transportation. This move seemed reasonable enough since the Maritime Administration was concerned with one form of transportation, namely, shipping. Opposition to this proposed change was not long in coming, however. Both organized labor and the shipping industry vigorously opposed the move and lobbied long and hard among members of Congress to defeat it. Their opposition was understandable, for such clientele groups have spent years establishing and cultivating relationships within an agency, and they do not want to see them disrupted by transferring the agency to another jurisdiction. Nor were they enamored of the prospect that their agency would now have to compete with the several other agencies being combined under the umbrella of the Department of Transportation. The move was also opposed by bureaucrats working for the Maritime Administration, since changing its jurisdiction could result in procedural and policy changes that might affect the nature of their jobs. The third major source of opposition came from the House Committee on Merchant Marine and Fisheries, which exercised oversight responsibilities over the Maritime Administration. Their objection stemmed from the fact that transferring the agency over to the

---

[19] *Congressional Quarterly Almanac,* 1971, 27 (Washington, D.C.: Congressional Quarterly, 1972), p. 764.

Transportation Department would take it out from under their committee's jurisdiction. If that were done, a major reason for the committee's existence would be eliminated. No committee's chairman will support a proposal that would result in the liquidation of his committee's power base. Nor are other committee chairmen likely to be receptive to such a proposal, as was made abundantly clear by the chairman of the House Committee on Merchant Marine and Fisheries during debate on the floor of the House: "If LBJ's transportation reorganization puts us out of business this year, then he may send up another proposal which will put your favorite committee out of business next year."[20] Ultimately the alliance of interest groups, bureaucrats, and congressmen succeeded in handing President Johnson a resounding 260 to 117 defeat for his proposal in the House. Another of the President's proposals, notably, combining the departments of Labor and Commerce, faced a similar fate. In this case, however, opposition was so great in both the business and labor communities that the plan never even came to the floors of the House or the Senate for a vote.

Reorganizations that involve transferring or abolishing agencies are the hardest to bring off successfully, for as we have seen, once agencies are created and jurisdictions defined, a variety of interests develop a stake in maintaining things as they are. This is not to say that important reorganizations have never been realized, however. Among recent presidents, Eisenhower succeeded in creating the Department of Health, Education and Welfare, and Lyndon Johnson was able to get through Congress proposals establishing both a Department of Housing and Urban Development and a Department of Transportation. These plans succeeded, however, in large part because committee jurisdictions were not altered by them. In the case of Housing and Urban Development, all of the agencies combined under it remained under the jurisdictions of the same congressional committees after the reorganization as before it. Similarly, all but two of the agencies slated to be combined into the new Department of Transportation were to remain under the jurisdiction of the same congressional committees after the reorganization. The exceptions were the Maritime Administration and the Coast Guard. As noted earlier, the Maritime Administration ultimately was not incorporated into the Department of Transportation, in part because of strong objections from the House Committee on Merchant Marine and Fisheries. On the other hand, Congress did agree to move the Coast Guard primarily because the Coast Guard wanted to be moved. But even though the lack of jurisdictional problems facilitated congressional acceptance of Johnson's two reorganization plans, the job of gaining approval for them was not an easy one. In the words of Johnson's key aid on domestic matters, "The Transportation Department bill had been the toughest legislative fight of the 89th Congress."[21]

It is fair to say that Carter approached government reorganization with considerably more determination than any previous President. As a candidate he made it one of the cornerstones of his campaign. Moreover, two weeks after

---

[20] Califano, *Presidential Nation*, p. 29.

[21] Ibid., p. 51.

taking office, he went on national television and reiterated this commitment. He submitted four reorganization plans to Congress; three were relatively noncontroversial and were promptly implemented. The first involved making several changes in the Executive Office of the President; the second called for combining the U.S. Information Agency and the Bureau of Educational and Cultural Affairs into a new unit called the International Communications Agency; the third was designed to bring about more effective enforcement of equal employment in the federal government. The fourth, which will be examined later in this chapter, involves several reforms in the Civil Service system and is currently under consideration by the Congress as of this writing.

By far the most significant reorganization in the early part of the Carter Administration was Congress's approval of the President's legislation proposing to consolidate the Federal Power Commission, Federal Energy Administration, and Energy Research and Development Administration under a proposed Department of Energy. That this legislation sailed through Congress with relative ease is attributable to several factors. For one thing, the energy crisis had made it apparent to all concerned that a coordinated approach to this problem was essential. In addition, two of the agencies slated for consolidation, ERDA and FEA, had been viewed by Congress as only temporary at the time they were created. Third, since neither of these agencies had been in existence for more than three years, they had not yet built up a loyal clientele group. And last, all three agencies suffered from weak leadership and low morale. Consequently, they were in no position to make an effective challenge to Carter's consolidation effort.[22]

Although Carter has thus far avoided any substantial opposition to his reorganization plans, it hardly seems likely that this will continue. He has several more major reorganizations in the works, and at some point the triple alliance of bureaucrats, interest groups, and congressmen will no doubt be there to resist him, just as they have his predecessors. And while he may try to mobilize public opinion behind his goal of reorganizing the bureaucracy, the task will not be an easy one. People can identify with a presidential plan to cut their taxes, but it is difficult for them to grasp how government reorganization will have any immediate impact upon their lives. Finally, even if Carter is successful in bringing about a restructuring of the bureaucracy in some areas, the price may come high. Major reorganizations are often bloody affairs, and the political capital Carter must expend to win may leave him with little left over for other things.

CENTRAL CLEARANCE

One of the most formidable instruments of presidential control over the bureaucracy is a procedure known as central clearance. Simply stated, it requires that all legislative proposals emanating from departments and agencies be cleared

[22] David Howard Davis, "Establishing the Department of Energy," *Journal of Energy and Development*, 4 (1978).

through the Office of Management and Budget, which is an administrative arm of the President. This procedure was begun in 1921 when President Coolidge issued a directive requiring all departments and agencies to clear their budget proposals with the Bureau of the Budget in order to insure their compatibility with the President's own budget priorities. The clearing requirements became even more inclusive under Franklin Roosevelt, who insisted that not only budget proposals but all legislation coming from the bureaucracy must be subject to screening procedures. Subsequent presidents have followed suit. Given the volume of legislation coming out of the departments and agencies each year, the necessity for some coordinating mechanism seems clear. For example, the Department of Housing and Urban Development alone proposes approximately three hundred different bills annually.

In actuality, central clearance involves a series of clearing points. Following the annual request for budget proposals by the Office of Management and Budget, various agencies and bureaus within departments begin drafting legislative proposals. An agency proposal is then forwarded to the assistant secretary who has line responsibility over the agency. In consultation with the department's legislative counsel, the assistant secretary will decide which bills merit department support. He also recommends changes when necessary. The bills are then routinely sent to the head of the department, but he is not likely to become directly involved unless the bill is of major importance, or unless it has aroused controversy among the agencies within his department, in which case he will act as mediator. After clearance at the departmental level, a proposal will often undergo a form of interdepartmental clearance if its content will have an impact upon the concerns of one or more other departments. At this point, interdepartmental negotiating will take place, and wherever possible the necessary changes will be made in order to reflect the views and suggestions of these other departments.

The bill then moves to the central clearance point in the Office of Management and Budget (OMB). At this stage, OMB has several options open to it. First, it may give its approval, which may range from enthusiastic support to simply an acknowledgement that the bill is acceptable. Such varying degrees of support are to be expected, for even though a particular bill may not be in conflict with the President's program, it may not necessarily be at the top of the Administration's list of priorities. Thus, although the bill will be sent on to Congress, the President is not likely to work actively to secure its passage. A second course of action open to OMB is to return a legislative proposal to the department or agency with suggestions for changes. There then follows a process of negotiation between budget officials and the department in order to put the bill in a form acceptable to both. In some cases, the demand for changes may not come from OMB itself but rather from other departments and agencies. While these changes would normally be worked out at the interdepartmental clearing point, it is not always possible to reach an accommodation, and thus it falls to OMB to try to work out a settlement. The third option open to OMB is to return the proposal to a given department with a notation stating that it is simply not compatible with the President's program. Following such a rejection, the only option open to a department head in the past has been to make a direct appeal to the President. This approach has not proved very fruitful, for presidents have not been willing to undermine the credibility of OMB by frequently overruling it.

Since the early sixties, White House staffs have become increasingly involved in the policy-making process. The net result of this development has been to reduce the role of OMB as the ultimate arbiter of the acceptability of a department's legislative proposals. As one government official notes, following a rejection of their proposals by OMB, departments are now taking their case to members of the White House staff with the hope of gaining a more favorable hearing: "There has got to be a way to go over OMB on a regular basis without going directly to the President. There is. That's the White House staff. Ted Sorensen and Joe Califano, in the Kennedy and Johnson Administrations, respectively, were constantly available to mediate and arbitrate between the secretary of a department and the Director of the Budget."[23]

The End Run

Regardless of whether or not the final clearing point occurs at the level of OMB or the White House staff, rejection of some part or all of a department's proposal in theory means that it may not be submitted to the Congress. In actuality, however, elements within a department or agency will from time to time seek to reverse such a decision by making an end run around OMB and taking their case directly to Congress. Sometimes this ploy will have the tacit approval of a department head and sometimes it will not. There is some risk, however, for the department that makes frequent use of this tactic may find OMB considerably less receptive to its future legislative proposals. For this reason, the end run usually involves working through informal channels. A department, for example, may enlist the support of its clientele groups, asking them to drum up support for the legislation among members of Congress. In addition, bureaucrats within the department may take advantage of their long-time contacts within the Congress by paying them a private visit and pleading their case. Such efforts will often meet with a favorable reception, for departments and agencies take great pains to cultivate a good image in the minds of both Congress and the public. In 1972 alone, for example, departments and agencies spent $164 million on public relations, $37 million of which was spent by the Defense Department.[24] More important, departments attempt to ingratiate themselves with congressmen by providing a variety of services and rewards:

---

[23] Robert Gilmour, "Policy Formulation in the Executive Branch: Central Legislative Clearance," in James Anderson, ed., *Cases in Public Policy Making* (New York: Praeger, 1976), p. 93.

[24] Emmet John Hughes, *The Living Presidency*, p. 159. Copyright © 1973 by Emmet John Hughes. Reprinted by permission of Coward, McCann & Geoghegan.

requests for information are answered within twenty-four hours; drafting assistance is readily provided to a congressman who is sponsoring a bill of benefit to the department; speeches will be written for him upon request; federal facilities may be located in his district; transportation may be provided to him if he wishes to visit a federal installation at home or abroad.[25]

L. Mendel Rivers is perhaps the classic example of a congressman who benefited from such largesse. During his long years of service on the House Armed Services Committee, part of which time he was its chairman, Rivers proved to be a strong and consistent supporter of a strong national defense. In appreciation of this support, the Defense Department made Rivers's congressional district the beneficiary of numerous federal facilities, some of which included: an Air Force base, an Army depot, a Marine Corps air station, an Air Force recreation center, a National Guard office, a Naval hospital, a radar station, an Air Force tank farm, and a national cemetery.[26] Needless to say, these and other rewards did not serve to diminish Mendel Rivers's enthusiasm for Defense Department programs.

It should be noted that the end-run strategy is used by the bureaucracy not only to gain favorable consideration of their own policy proposals, but also to torpedo presidential policies they oppose. Kennedy's ultraconservative Director of the Central Intelligence Agency, for example, happily lent members of his agency to the Senate Armed Services Committee in order to help conservative committee members make their case against the Administration's proposed nuclear test ban treaty.[27]

Richard Nixon faced a similar problem with the Commissioner of the Social Security Administration. According to one Nixon aid, "The President would make a policy and enunciate it but then Ball would go up to Congress, the doors to the committee room would close and he would say what he really thought. He was very persuasive. We couldn't have that."[28]

Determined department heads have tried to check this kind of behavior but have not met with much success. Kennedy's Secretary of Defense, Robert McNamara, became concerned that military officers were making public and written statements that were critical of U.S. military and foreign policies.[29] Accordingly, a procedure was instituted by which any remarks made to a public group by a military officer must first be screened by a committee in the Defense Department. Those parts of the speech that could prove embarrassing to the Administration were then deleted from the prepared text. When the Senate

[25] James Davis, *The National Executive Branch* (New York: Free Press, 1970), pp. 132, 133.

[26] Drew Pearson and Jack Anderson, *The Case Against Congress* (New York: Simon and Schuster, 1968), p. 272.

[27] David Halberstam, *The Best and the Brightest* (New York: Random House, Inc., 1969), p. 190.

[28] *New York Times,* March 6, 1973, p. 20. © 1973 by The New York Times Company. Reprinted by permission.

[29] Louis Gawthrop, *Bureaucratic Behavior in the Executive Branch* (New York: Free Press, 1969), pp. 162–165.

Armed Services Committee got wind of this procedure, it promptly instituted an investigation, asking that the members of the screening committee appear before it. Secretary McNamara refused. The committee persisted in its demand until finally President Kennedy himself intervened and refused to disclose the names on grounds of executive privilege. In spite of the fact that the names were never revealed, the controversy created by the censoring procedure persuaded the Administration to drop it.

HEW's Caspar Weinberger encountered similar resistance when he attempted to implement a slightly different procedure. Disturbed by the fact that career bureaucrats in HEW were going before congressional committees and speaking out against Administration policies, he instituted a system of clearance and chaperones; that is, all career officials in HEW not only had to gain prior approval before going to Capitol Hill but they also had to be accompanied by someone "reliable" to insure that their testimony would not be damaging to the Administration. The policy was quickly dropped, however, when the powerful Chairman of the Senate Finance Committee raised strong objections.[30] That members of Congress would oppose such muzzling procedures is quite understandable, for they put great value on the special expertise that career bureaucrats bring to the analysis of policy issues.

OTHER LIMITATIONS ON PRESIDENTIAL CONTROL

Our discussion thus far has focused upon identifying the three major ways by which the President attempts to exert a measure of control over the bureaucracy. We have made an effort to show how these instruments of leverage are restricted and resisted by the bureaucracy itself as well as by the Congress and organized interests outside government. At this point, however, it is important to note that the limitations on the President's capacity for control are also the result of other equally important factors which have little to do with any intentional efforts by bureaucrats to resist him. They are (1) the size and complexity of the bureaucratic establishment, and (2) the President's inability or unwillingness to make clear what he wants.

Size and Complexity

The bureaucratic establishment consists of nearly three million civilian employees, 87 percent of whom are not even located in Washington, D.C., but rather are spread out in various parts of the country and the world. At the top of this bureaucracy sits the President, and below him are several layers of officials through whom his directives must customarily pass before they are implemented.

[30] Richard Nathan, "The Administrative Presidency," *The Public Interest,* No. 44 (Summer 1976), 44, 45.

While the hierarchy of command varies by department and agency, it is often complex enough to insure that presidential orders will occasionally be short-circuited during the process of transmission. In some instances, the order may be misconstrued, while in others, it is simply not relayed to everyone who needs to know. As one former White House aid noted, " . . . departments are so big that it is difficult for anyone to get the 'message' around even when they want to do something about it."[31] This problem is further compounded when the number of people who need to know transcends the bounds of any one department or agency.

An incident that occurred during the Kennedy Administration may serve as an illustration of the communications problem. In the early stages of our involvement with Vietnam, President Kennedy became increasingly concerned over the Diem government's resistance to Administration policies. Although several of his high-level advisers called for cutting off commodity aid to Vietnam in retaliation for its failure to cooperate, the President made it clear that he did not favor such a step at that time. As the recalcitrance of the Vietnam government increased, however, he finally decided to convene a group to reconsider the possibility of cutting off commodity aid. When the President raised the issue for consideration at the meeting, the AID Director informed the President that the decision had already been made. There followed this exchange:

President: You've done what?
Director: Cut off military aid.
President: Who the hell told you to do that?
Director: No one. It's automatic policy. We do it whenever we have differences with a client government.
President: My God, do you know what you have done?[32]

The Director of AID was not engaged in a deliberate effort to sabotage presidential policy but rather was following the established policy of the State Department. Unfortunately, officials at higher levels in the department apparently had failed to inform him of the President's earlier decision not to halt commodity aid. Such breakdowns can also occur as communications move up the bureaucracy to the President, as Gerald Ford discovered when he was put in the embarrassing position of having to withdraw his support from two sections of an antitrust bill submitted to Congress by his own Justice Department. The President had inadvertently not been informed of its content.[33]

While more efficient organization would reduce the communications problem, it surely would not eliminate it. In a bureaucracy as large and complex as ours, such short circuits in the communications process are inevitable.

[31] Cited in Cronin, *State of the Presidency*, p. 171.
[32] Halberstam, *Best and the Brightest*, p. 346.
[33] *New York Times*, December 26, 1976, p. E1.

Lack of Clarity in Presidential Intent

The President's ability to secure bureaucratic compliance is also hampered by his unwillingness to make his position known. In some cases, for instance, he may intentionally withhold a given policy decision from the bureaucracy because he feels that it may encounter resistance at the lower levels. As former Secretary of State Kissinger has noted, however, such a strategy frequently leads to a situation where the White House and the bureaucracy are working at cross purposes:

> Because management of the bureaucracy takes so much energy and precisely because changing course is so difficult, many of the most important decisions are taken by extra-bureaucratic means. Some of the key decisions are kept to a very small circle while the bureaucracy happily continues working away in ignorance of the fact that decisions are being made, or the fact that a decision is being made in a particular area. One reason for keeping the decisions to small groups is that when bureaucracies are so unwieldy and when their internal morale becomes a serious problem, an unpopular decision may be fought by brutal means, such as leaks to the press or to congressional committees. Thus, the only way secrecy can be kept is to exclude from the making of the decision all those who are theoretically charged with carrying it out . . . There is, thus, small wonder for many allegations of deliberate sabotage of certain American efforts, or of great cynicism of American efforts because of inconsistent actions. In the majority of cases this was due to the ignorance of certain parts of the bureaucracy, rather than to malevolent intent. Another result is that the relevant part of the bureaucracy, because it is being excluded from the making of a particular decision, continues with great intensity sending out cables, thereby distorting the effort with the best intentions in the world. You cannot stop them from doing this because you do not tell them what is going on.[34]

It is precisely this kind of presidential secrecy that accounted for the Nixon Administration's embarrassment during the India-Pakistan War in 1971, when it was discovered that the White House was taking the side of Pakistan, while the State Department was supporting India. This policy conflict immediately brought the famous White House order instructing the State Department to "tilt" toward Pakistan.

Many times, of course, the President does make his position known but does so in a way that invites confusion and misinterpretation. Such ambiguity may result for a variety of reasons. If a given issue is especially controversial, political considerations may require that he phrase his decision ambiguously enough to satisfy those on both sides of the issue. Secondly, he may simply lack the time

[34] Cited in Morton Halperin, with the assistance of Priscilla Clapp and Arnold Kanter, *Bureaucratic Politics and Foreign Policy* (Washington, D.C.: Brookings Institution, 1974), p. 247.

and knowledge necessary to work out the details of a decision. Or finally, he may have made two policy decision that are in direct conflict with each other.

It was this latter situation that in part served to explain what many viewed as a classic case of bureaucratic intransigence. Within two years after he assumed office, President Kennedy ordered the State Department to negotiate the removal of U.S. Jupiter missiles from Turkey, for they had already become obsolete and were easy targets for Soviet missiles. It was not until the Cuban missile crisis in 1963 that Kennedy learned, in a letter from Nikita Khrushchev, that U.S. missiles were still in Turkey. Needless to say, the President was greatly irritated that his order had not been carried out, and even more so because he had to learn of it from none other than the head of the Soviet government. Yet the continued presence of missiles in Turkey was the consequence of bureaucrats' being faced with having to implement two conflicting presidential policies: one called for negotiating the removal of missiles from Turkey, but the other called for strengthening the NATO alliance. Kennedy had, after all, pledged to bolster the alliance during his campaign for the Presidency, and after taking office he instructed the State Department to move in this direction. One former State Department official notes the dilemma faced by the bureaucracy in this situation:

> The officials who received the directive to remove the missiles from Turkey also felt themselves to be operating under a more general presidential directive to strengthen the troubled alliance. They did not believe that the order to remove the missiles from Turkey was meant to contradict the order to strengthen NATO. They raised the issue in a tentative way with the Turkish government. When that government registered strong objections, they held off obeying the order to remove the missiles.[35]

Presidents and their aids have a tendency to see lack of compliance as a deliberate attempt by various elements in the bureaucracy to subvert presidential policies. Such an assessment is understandable, for it is frequently correct. At the same time, however, presidents are far less inclined to acknowledge that problems with policy implementation may just as frequently be a product of their own making.

RICHARD NIXON AND THE BUREAUCRACY: AN ATTEMPT AT GREATER CONTROL

While all of our recent presidents have remarked upon their inability to gain greater control over the reins of the bureaucracy, none made a more concerted and systematic attempt to correct this problem than did Richard Nixon. For this reason, his effort deserves our attention.

[35] Ibid., pp. 241–42.

Richard Nixon came into office claiming that, unlike his predecessor, he was not going to locate all policy making in the White House. Instead, he would appoint competent administrators of independent mind and give them broad policy-making responsibilities:

> I would operate differently from President Johnson. Instead of taking all power to myself, I'd select cabinet members who could do their jobs, and each of them would have the stature and the power to function effectively . . . . Every key official would have the opportunity to be a big man in his field.[36]

> I don't want a Cabinet of "Yes" men and I don't think you want a Cabinet of "Yes" men. Every man in the Cabinet will be urged to speak out in the Cabinet and within the Administration on all the great issues so that the decisions we will make will be the best decisions we can possibly reach.[37]

He further demonstrated their importance by his willingness to allow each department head to fill the sub-Cabinet positions within his department. After his first six months in office, however, the President's enthusiasm for his Cabinet started to wane as he saw his domestic secretaries slowly being captured by the career bureaucrats and clientele groups of their departments. HEW's Robert Finch was being pressured by his staff not to retrench on Johnson's Great Society programs. Equally disturbing were the actions of some of the liberal appointees he was placing in sub-Cabinet positions. Secretary of HUD George Romney had been persuaded by his department's housing experts to advocate expensive housing programs, which the President felt were a waste of money. Interior Secretary Walter Hickel had proved to be more responsive to environmental groups than the Nixon Administration had expected or desired.

Developments such as these led the President to make some significant changes in his relations with domestic department heads. Cabinet meetings were held less and less frequently. Some Cabinet secretaries, such as George Romney and Walter Hickel, found it increasingly difficult to gain access to the President. In addition, the White House began to play a much more active role in screening those being recommended for sub-Cabinet level positions in the various departments. Most important, policy making was taken out of the hands of department heads and given to what were called *working groups.*[38] These groups were made up of some members of the White House staff and selected members of the bureaucracy. The White House staff clearly played the dominant role here, since they ultimately decided which individuals in a department would be brought into these working groups. This new procedure caused considerable irritation

[36] Stephen Hess, *Organizing the Presidency* (Washington, D.C.: Brookings Institution, 1976), pp. 112, 113.

[37] Richard Nathan, *The Plot That Failed* (New York: John Wiley, 1975), p. 37.

[38] Ibid., pp. 45–48.

among department heads, for they were not always consulted on the makeup of these groups, nor were they always informed of the policy decisions reached by them.

As the White House staff became increasingly involved in policy making, it quite naturally grew in size. This expansion continued as the staff also began to involve itself in the actual administration of White House policies and programs. Thus, more and more decisions that would normally have been made within a given department or agency now had to receive clearance from the White House staff. Two consequences followed from these developments. First, the White House staff had become so large and unwieldy in the process of trying to control one bureaucracy that Richard Nixon had in effect created another one on top of it. Second, as the President's staff became increasingly involved in administering and overseeing programs, it ultimately found less and less time for the formulation of policy. Consequently, policy making gradually shifted back to the bureaucracy, which was precisely what President Nixon was trying to prevent. One former government official speaks to this phenomenon:

> Operational matters flow to the top—as central staffs become engrossed in subduing outlying bureaucracies—and central policymaking emerges at the bottom. At the top minor problems squeeze out major ones, and individuals lower down the echelons who have the time for reflection and mischief-making take up issues of fundamental philosophical and political significance.[39]

A Change In Approach

At the end of his first four years, President Nixon found that his attempts to get a handle on the bureaucracy had not proved successful. Following his reelection, therefore, he decided to deal with the problem in a more vigorous and systematic fashion. His decision to do so was further encouraged by the fact that he had been returned to office with an overwhelming mandate from the people; accordingly, he was determined that no bureaucracy was going to frustrate the implementation of his policies.

His first goal was to populate the bureaucracy with people he could trust. To this end, he summoned his Cabinet shortly after the election and asked them to submit pro forma resignations, some of which he accepted. Transportation Secretary Volpe, for example, was approached and told he had one half hour to decide if he wanted to become the next American ambassador to Italy. He accepted. His departure from the Cabinet was occasioned by his frequent policy disputes during the previous four years with the President's chief domestic aid, John Ehrlichman. The Secretary of Commerce was told that he was going to be made a roving ambassador specializing in U.S. trade relations. Although he

[39] Ibid., p. 52.

suggested that it would be beneficial for him to remain in Washington for six months in order to work out his responsibilities with the State Department, he received word that he was to leave Washington as soon as possible. Only later did he learn that he was being replaced because he had been traveling in social circles known to be antagonistic to the President.[40] Other Cabinet members— Romney, Laird, and Rogers—were leaving because they wished to do so.

The vacancies were to be filled by individuals who had little national following, thereby reducing their ability to act independently of the President. There was also some reshuffling within the Cabinet. Suspicious of Elliot Richardson's cordial relationship with the HEW career bureaucracy but impressed nevertheless with his managerial skills, President Nixon decided to move him from HEW to Secretary of Defense. Richardson's replacement at HEW was Caspar Weinberger, who was transferred from his position as Director of the Office of Management and Budget.

The change in Richard Nixon's attitude toward the Cabinet proved to be remarkable. Whereas he had come into office stressing his desire to be surrounded by Cabinet secretaries of independent mind, he now sought men who would give him unquestioning loyalty. This new attitude was best captured by Nixon's chief domestic aid, John Ehrlichman: "There shouldn't be a lot of leeway in following the President's policies. It should be like a corporation, where the executive vice presidents (the Cabinet officers) are tied closely to the chief executive, or to put it in extreme terms, when he says jump, they only ask how high."[41]

In addition to reshuffling his Cabinet, Nixon also asked for the resignations of some two thousand other political appointees, including those at the deputy and assistant secretary level, as well as some high-level bureaucrats who enjoyed civil service status but whose jobs were not protected by statute. Some of these were simply fired outright, while others were transferred to positions where they could do little harm. The more important vacancies created by these firings were to be filled with people from the President's already bloated White House staff and also by individuals from the Committee to Re-elect the President (CREEP). It was felt that these Nixon loyalists could more effectively monitor the activities of the bureaucracy from positions within that bureaucracy rather than from the White House. In all, some eighty-four White House staffers and CREEP workers were strategically located in various departments and agencies throughout the bureaucracy. Even with these replacements, however, the firings had been so sweeping that many positions were still vacant several months later.[42]

Besides personnel changes, the President's plan for control also included a reorganization effort. In January of 1973 he announced that three of his Cabinet

[40] Theodore White, *Breach of Faith* (New York: Atheneum, 1975), pp. 176, 177.

[41] Cited in *Watergate: Its Implications,* p. 46.

[42] Lewis Beman, "President-Less Government in Washington," *Fortune* January 1974, p. 84.

secretaries—all with demonstrated track records of loyalty to the President— would enjoy the additional title of Counsellor to the President. In this capacity, each would become responsible for coordinating policy areas that transcended the concerns of his own department. Thus, Secretary of Agriculture Earl Butz was given the area of *natural resources,* Secretary of HEW Caspar Weinburger, *human resources,* and Secretary of Housing and Urban Development James Lynn, *community development.* Secretary of the Treasury George Shultz had earlier been given an additional responsibility as Special Assistant to the President for *economic affairs.* These four "super" secretaries would see to it that the actions of departments involved in these four general areas were consistent with the policy goals of the President. Operating at a level above these super secretaries were four individuals whom the President designated his principal White House assistants—Henry Kissinger, Roy Ash, John Ehrlichman, and H. R. Haldeman. Their responsibility would be "to integrate and unify policies and operations throughout the executive branch . . . and to oversee the activities for which the President is responsible."[43]

The Results

Unfortunately for President Nixon, he never had an opportunity to see how all of these changes would have affected his control over the bureaucracy, for shortly after they were implemented, the scandals of Watergate engulfed his administration. His most important White House aids were forced to resign, and so too were some of the loyalists whom he had just appointed to positions in the bureaucracy. The President and his reconstituted White House staff soon became so preoccupied with avoiding impeachment that little attention could be directed toward monitoring the activity of the bureaucracy. With such a vacuum in leadership at the top, members of the Executive branch, from the Cabinet on down, found themselves with greater freedom of action.

Although the Watergate developments effectively cut short, and thus precluded any definitive evaluation of Richard Nixon's strategy for control, the early indications were that it was meeting with less than complete success. Those White House staffers whom the President had sent out to colonize the bureaucracy were proving no match for the political and substantive expertise of the high-level career bureaucrats.

Nor did the President's attempt to coordinate and oversee departmental activities through the use of super secretaries prove workable. His Transportation Secretary, for example, made it quite clear that he was not going to take his marching orders from James Lynn, Secretary of HUD and super secretary for *community development.*[44] Such a reaction on the part of Cabinet members should not have been surprising, for as one former White House aid has noted,

---

[43] Cited in Nathan, *Plot That Failed,* p. 69.

[44] Woll and Jones, "Bureaucratic Defense," p. 19.

"cabinet officers regard themselves as equals in their access and responsibility to the President and take seriously those laws that vest jurisdiction over certain matters to their department. . . . Nixon did not realize that cabinet officers will not take orders from one of their peers."[45] If Nixon was not initially sensitive to this fact, he soon became so, for he abolished the positions of super secretaries only four months after creating them.

INCREASING PRESIDENTIAL CONTROL OVER THE BUREAUCRACY

Appointments

One scholar expressed a conclusion reached by many when he noted that "the key to the establishment of some measure of managerial control over the executive establishment is in one word—appointments."[46] But in order for appointments to have an impact, presidents must make them in a judicious manner. In the past, presidents have too often been guided by political considerations when making high-level appointments: Did he support me during my campaign? Is he acceptable to business, farmers, labor, minorities, or some other organized interest in the society? While these factors cannot be completely ignored, it is argued that they should not take precedence over the two more fundamental criteria: Are his policy views thoroughly compatible with the President's? Does he have demonstrated managerial skills? To be sure, compatibility of views is not likely to prevent political appointees from being responsive to interests in Congress, the bureaucracy, and the society, but it may at least reduce the impact of these interests.

In addition to the factors already mentioned, presidents might also benefit from taking several other factors into consideration in filling positions within the bureaucracy. For one thing, a greater effort could be made to choose Cabinet secretaries with demonstrated expertise in the substantive concerns of their respective departments, thereby reducing to some extent their dependence upon those below them. Second, greater care should also be taken to insure compatibility between a department head and the deputy and assistant secretaries serving immediately under him. This goal could quite obviously be accomplished by giving Cabinet secretaries a greater say in personnel decisions at the sub-Cabinet level. Third, it takes approximately two years for department heads to become versed in the internal operations of their departments, and by that time many are ready to leave. Thus, presidents might do well to extract some kind of commitment from their high-level appointees to serve at least three to four years. Finally, the transition from one administration to another should be approached

---

[45] Califano, *Presidential Nation*, pp. 30, 31.
[46] Nathan, "Administrative Presidency," p. 53.

more systematically. This would include briefing a President's Cabinet nominees on the programs, operations, and personnel of the departments they are to manage, thus reducing the length of the on-the-job orientation process. The Carter transition team appears to have been more successful than most in this regard. For the transition effort to be successful, however, the incoming President must decide on his appointments fairly early, and also a spirit of cooperation must exist on the part of the outgoing administration.

Some would contend that the above proposals do not go far enough, for the problem of presidential control does not lie merely with the criteria and procedures for making appointments, but also with the number of appointments the President is able to make. As noted earlier in this chapter, a President has effective control over approximately 3,500 positions in the bureaucracy. The rest are occupied by career civil servants who are protected by the Civil Service Act. Many of these positions carry with them important policy-making responsibilities. Furthermore, they may be filled by individuals who, for a variety of reasons, may choose to frustrate rather than facilitate a President's policy goals. Accordingly, it has been suggested by some that many of these positions be removed from the career civil service classification and given to the President to fill as he wishes. It is pointed out that Presidents are, after all, elected with a mandate to implement their programs and thus should not be impeded from doing so by career bureaucrats who are not held directly accountable to the people for their actions.

It is difficult to characterize the nature of an election mandate with any precision, for people choose their presidents for various reasons. Some may support part but not all of a candidate's program, while others may not vote on the basis of issues at all. Thus any conclusion that bureaucrats are automatically violating the people's mandate when they frustrate a presidential objective is risky at best. Leaving aside this problem, however, some may contend that any attempt to broaden greatly the President's appointment power would seriously erode three inestimable benefits provided by the civil service system, one of which is *competence.*

For nearly one hundred years Presidents were accorded the right to fill all the positions in the Executive branch under what came to be known as the *spoils system.* Such a system inevitably resulted in positions being filled on the basis of such considerations as partisanship, personal connections, and pay offs, while little attention was paid to the matter of competence:

> The spoils system was more fruitful of degradation in our political life than any other that could possibly have been invented. The spoils-monger, the man who peddled patronage, inevitably bred the vote-buyer, the vote-seller, and the man guilty of malfeasance in office.
>
> *Theodore Roosevelt, 1895*

Every four years, the whole machinery of government is pulled to pieces. The country presents a most ridiculous, revolting and disheartening spectacle. The business of the nation and the legislation of the Congress are subordinated to the distribution of plunder among eager partisans. Presidents, secretaries (of departments), senators, representatives are dogged, hunted, besieged, besought, denounced, and they become mere office brokers. The country seethes with intrigue and corruption. Economy, patriotism, honesty, honor, seem to have become words of no meaning.

George Curtis, 1870

Reacting to this unseemly process, Congress passed the Pendleton Civil Service Act in 1883, which created the Civil Service and a Civil Service Commission to administer it. Subsequent amendments to this act have bestowed several responsibilities upon the commission, one of which is to provide competitive examinations for job openings in the bureaucracy. The purpose behind these examinations is to insure that only individuals with the required level of competence are hired for a given position. Critics of the Civil Service maintain, however, that positions are not in fact awarded solely on the basis of meeting certain standards of competence:

As for selection on pure merit from all applicants, that is not done now in the civil service. . . . the present civil service is a patronage machine that instead of being run on a political basis is run on the basis of friendship. You get a civil service job by knowing someone who is in the agency where you want to work. He gives you an advance tip on the opening, writes a job description tailored to fit your experience, and then requests your name from the Civil Service Commission. Isn't it possible that a job might be filled better by politicians who are interested in putting together an administration that will do a good enough job to get them re-elected?[47]

A former Executive Director of the Civil Service Commission readily acknowledges these and other abuses of the merit system. At the same time, however, he points out that investigations conducted in 1973-74 indicate that some of these abuses were motivated by a desire to hire personnel on the basis of ideological compatibility with the incumbent administration rather than on the basis of merit: "Responsiveness in personnel matters was translated into systematic efforts to politicize the career civil service and nearly make a mockery of the merit system concept. Not only did some agency officials, career and noncareer, participate in this effort, but they also had the cooperation of the Office of

---

[47]Charles Peters, "A Kind Word for the Spoils System," *Washington Monthly* 8 (September 1976), 28.

Management and Budget, and the understanding, if not the encouragement, of some White House officials."[48]

Even where administrations could legitimately fill positions with their own personal choices, their record has not been overly impressive. By use of the re-organization power, for example, recent presidents have succeeded in having several high-level positions in the bureaucracy switched from a "career" to a "noncareer" classification, thus permitting them to be filled by appointment. Not only have vacancies in some of these positions been allowed to lapse for considerable periods of time, but also they have not been filled with individuals of uniformly high caliber.[49] Thus, it may well be argued that maintaining competence in the bureaucracy is not to be gained by expanding the President's appointment power but rather by maintaining the current civil service system and at the same time eliminating the abuses that have occurred under it.

Defenders of the civil service system contend that, in addition to providing competence, it provides an important element of *continuity* in government. Presidents and their cabinets come and go in four or eight years. The mainte-nance of a career civil service, which transcends the life of any given administra-tion, insures stability and continuity—elements that would be compromised if presidents could sweep more widely with the broom when they came into of-fice. Critics point out, however, that continuity comes at a high price, for permanent bureaucrats become increasingly protective of the status quo, and thus innovation and risk-taking are discouraged:

> At the beginning of the cycle, when the bureau is young, there is a lot of mobility in an expanding organization, promotions are frequent, and young, ambitious bureaucrats compete either to aggrandize their positions and themselves or move on to new opportunity. As bureaucrats and organizations get older, organizational expansion slows, and promotion possibilities shrink. Bureaucrats then concern themselves with maximizing security and convenience. They avoid risk, follow the written procedures to the letter, and resist change. In short, conserving officials become more difficult to control, particularly when innovative policy is called for.[50]

The problem is a very real one, but the solution does not necessarily lie in providing the President with the option of replacing more people when he comes into office. Rather, it may be more appropriate to institute reforms that furnish greater opportunities for advancement within the bureaucracy. At the moment, unfortunately, such opportunities are unusually low. The most prized senior

---

[48] Bernard Rosen, *The Merit System in the United States Civil Service*, a monograph pre-pared for the Committee on the Post Office and Civil Service, House of Representatives (Washington, D.C.: Government Printing Office, 1975), p. 25.

[49] Ibid., pp. 23, 24.

[50] Eugene McGregor, "Politics and the Career Mobility of Bureaucrats," *American Political Science Review* 68 (March 1974), 19.

positions (grades 16, 17, 18, for example) are thought by many to be too few in number.[51] And to make matters worse, several of these jobs have been reclassified to noncareer positions in order to allow the President to fill them by appointment. While a career bureaucrat could certainly be appointed to such positions, there is little incentive for him to accept, for in doing so he would be surrendering the benefits he has built up over the years as a career bureaucrat.[52] Providing greater mobility for bureaucrats would increase morale and furnish an incentive for creativity, thus reducing the tendencies toward stagnation.

A third major benefit to be derived from a career civil service is *integrity*. Individuals whose jobs are not threatened by the prevailing partisan winds can administer public services with a greater degree of impartiality:

> . . . neutral competence contributes a quality of impartiality to be set against other, more sectional appeals in government. Its viewpoint is no more pure or unbiased than anyone else's, but the axes it has to grind are broader than most. Its analysis is less concerned with the short-term political ramifications of who believes what how strongly, and more concerned with the substance of the policy issues themselves. . . . It cares about good form and the use of discretionary authority in a more even handed way than might be preferred by individual contending parties. Thus its advice and analysis provide a useful counterweight to those more interested in a given subject matter or immediate advantage and less interested in brokerage, continuity, and staying around to pick up the pieces.[53]

The importance of integrity in the bureaucracy was especially highlighted during the Nixon Presidency, when an attempt was made to use the resources of the federal government to harass as well as violate the constitutional rights of various segments of the population. In 1970, for example, one Nixon aid had drawn up a proposal that in effect called for the establishment of a secret police unit that would be authorized to read the private mail, intercept communications going overseas, and break into the homes of any individuals who were deemed a threat to the national security. Although this plan was actually in operation for five days, it was quickly abandoned when J. Edgar Hoover expressed his outrage. While Hoover was himself a political appointee, his own strong base of support in and outside government afforded him an independence equal to that of any career bureaucrat.

In 1971, the Nixon Administration embarked upon another course of action designed to harass its political opponents. John Dean was quite explicit about its purpose in a memorandum that he wrote and circulated to various members of

---

[51] *Watergate: Its Implications,* p. 119.

[52] Cronin, *State of the Presidency,* p. 284.

[53] Hugh Heclo, "OMB and the Presidency–The Problem of 'Neutral Competence,'" *The Public Interest,* No. 38 (Winter 1975), 82, 83.

the White House staff: "This memorandum addresses the matter of how we can maximize the fact of our incumbency in dealing with persons known to be active in their opposition to our Administration. Stated a bit more bluntly—how can we use the available federal machinery to screw our political enemies."[54] Dean encountered bureaucratic resistance, however, when he tried to pressure the Internal Revenue Service into investigating the tax returns of newspaper reporters, Hollywood personalities, and institutions known to harbor unfriendly attitudes toward the Nixon Administration. Nor did the bureaucracy prove any more cooperative when asked to help cover up the misdeeds of Watergate. The Central Intelligency Agency, for example, refused to comply with an Administration request for secret CIA funds which were to be used to pay hush money to the defendants arrested during the Watergate break-in. Similarly, the Justice Department refused requests by Nixon aids to "arrange" the release from jail of Watergate burglar James McCord.[55]

Had the upper levels of the career bureaucracy been subject to appointment and removal by President Nixon, their ability to resist such outrageous demands would undoubtedly have been more difficult. It should be noted, however, that in some instances even political appointees—to their credit—also rejected Administration attempts to subvert the political process. And it is probable that their behavior was motivated in part by a recognition of the fact that the career civil servants below them would not have tolerated acquiescence to such demands.

Reorganization

Many individuals with recognized expertise in the area of management have been calling for reorganization of the federal bureaucracy since 1937, when the Brownlow Committee issued its report on the Executive branch. Furthermore, while Republican and Democratic presidents might disagree on who ought to head restructured departments and agencies, they have nevertheless been in basic agreement on the need to reorganize. The reasons for doing so are compelling. First, combining agencies that perform similar programmatic functions will lead to greater policy coordination and accountability. Second, with several departments and agencies involved in the administration of programs in a given policy area, jurisdictional disputes arising between them are frequent. The resolution of these disputes has been pushed up to the White House staff, which, in attempting to perform this mediation function, has become unduly large and cumbersome. Combining functionally similar agencies into one department would certainly not eliminate jurisdictional disputes, but in most cases it would allow them to be settled by the head of the department. Third, it has been argued that domestic departments have become unduly influenced by, and

---

[54] Cited in White, *Breach of Faith,* p. 152.

[55] For a discussion of attempts by the Nixon White House to use the bureaucracy to harrass political enemies and cover up criminal wrongdoing, see White, *Breach of Faith,* pp. 146–68.

responsive to, the organized interests over which they have jurisdiction. This situation frequently results in departments advocating policies that may be in the interests of their clientele groups but adverse to the greater public interest. If agencies, and in some cases whole departments were combined, "constituent groups would be forced to deal with new departments—often in competition with other interests dealing with the same departments."[56] To the extent that they were required to do so, the influence of each would be lessened.

Proposals for reform rarely command unanimous support, and reorganization is no exception. Indeed, there are those in and outside the government who are not yet convinced that extensive reorganization will yield all the benefits that have been promised. They point out, for example, that while combining all functionally related agencies under the umbrella of one super department may make for a more rational organization chart, it may do little to improve managerial efficiency. Cabinet secretaries already have a difficult enough job trying to manage their departments. Expanding them still further may only compound the difficulty. Certainly the departments of Defense and Health, Education and Welfare bear out this point. Both are very large departments encompassing a variety of different interests, and they have earned themselves the reputation for being the most unmanageable departments in the Executive branch.

Others assert that the reduction of interagency disputes through reorganization may also be a mixed blessing. All agencies attempt to portray their own performance in the most favorable light possible, and often the only way a President learns of its failures is from competing agencies. The conflict that results from agency competition may prove time-consuming for those who must mediate it, but such disputes may also serve to flush out needed information as well as new ideas.

Nor is it clear that the influence on the bureaucracy of organized interest groups would be lessened by combining the agencies that service them under one or more super departments. The more powerful interest groups have enough political clout to insure their continued influence regardless of the structural changes made in the bureaucracy. Indeed, in the judgment of some, the only groups likely to have reduced influence are the less-powerful interests (poor, aged) that can least afford it.[57] Finally, some observers of the political process doubt that reorganization can have any major impact unless it is also accompanied by a major reorganization of committee jurisdictions within the Congress:

> . . . some of the eccentricities you find in administrative structure are only mirror images of the congressional committee structure. It's no accident that we have four different water and sewer programs, because these come out of four separate committees of Congress. These are very im-

[56] *National Journal*, May 8, 1971, p. 977.

[57] Douglas Fox, "The President's Proposals for Executive Reorganization: A Critique," *Public Administration Review* 33 (September/October 1973), 405.

portant programs for a congressman's constituency, and a congressman wants to be sure that it will remain in an agency under the jurisdiction of his committee.[58]

Thus, without redefining committee jurisdictions, restructuring departments and agencies in the Executive branch can only eliminate irrationalities of the past. It cannot prevent them in the future.

It is clear that credible arguments can be made both for and against reorganization of the bureaucracy. Resolving the issue in favor of one side or the other cannot be undertaken with any certainty, however, because hard evidence on the effects of reorganization is still lacking. In the words of one scholar intimately involved with this matter during the Johnson Administration, "One of the difficulties we have is that in dealing with reorganization matters we're sailing on an unknown sea. We're dealing here with mythology—we expect that reorganization will produce miracles, as a matter of faith. We've had almost no systematic analysis to determine what in fact reorganizations achieve."[59]

Civil Service Reform

In an effort to increase the responsiveness and efficiency of the bureaucracy, President Carter submitted a reorganization plan to Congress in April 1978 that called for major changes in the federal Civil Service system. The first of these proposals would establish a Senior Executive Service encompassing the top administrative jobs in the government (excluding those of Cabinet rank). This amounts to some 9,200 positions. The members of this Senior Executive Service could be moved in and out of various departments and agencies depending upon where their administrative talents were most needed. Carter also would alter the criteria by which these top administrators receive salary increases. Under current regulations, pay increases are a function of length of service and inflation, a practice that provides little incentive to improve one's performance. Carter would replace these automatic pay increases with a salary bonus based upon performance. These bonuses would not become a permanent part of their salary, but rather would be a one-time payment. If one of these top administrators gave another outstanding performance the next year, then he or she would receive another bonus. In addition, those members of this Senior Executive Service who failed to perform satisfactorily could be dropped from it; however, they could still return to a regular position in the Civil Service.

The President also proposed a change in the pay increase procedures just discussed for those occupying the 72,000 managerial positions that come immediately below the top administrators. Rather than having their pay boosts determined by length of service and the inflation factor, these managers would

---

[58] Seidman, "A Mini-Symposium," p. 489.
[59] Ibid.

instead receive only 50 percent of the increase due them for inflation, and the rest of their increase would be based upon job performance.

The second part of Carter's reorganization plan contained proposals designed to facilitate the removal of incompetents from the bureaucracy. Under current procedures, a civil servant faced with removal may first appeal to the review process established within his own agency. If he is not happy with the result, he may then go to the Civil Service Commission, which appoints an appeals officer to review his case. If he is dissatisfied with the finding of the appeals officer, he may then take his case to the Appeals Review Board, which is directly responsible to the Civil Service Commission. Should he be unhappy with the verdict of the Review Board, he can still make one final appeal to the Civil Service Commission itself. Since this lengthy appeals process can consume up to three years, rather than seeking to remove an employee, his superior will more likely try to get rid of him by transferring, or even promoting, him. Not only is the removal process unduly cumbersome, but it also places the Civil Service Commission in a conflict of interest as well, for the Commission is charged with protecting federal employees on the one hand, and promoting the efficient management of federal personnel on the other.

To overcome these problems, Carter proposed that the Civil Service Commission be abolished and be replaced by two new entities: (1) an Office of Personnel Management charged with such responsibilities as administering Civil Service exams and making policy concerning salaries and benefits; and (2) a Merit Protection Board consisting of three members appointed by the President and confirmed by the Senate to serve staggered seven-year terms. This board would have final authority to rule on recommended firings. Thus, an employee faced with removal would submit his case to a review process within his own agency. If dissatisfied with the outcome, his only other avenue of appeal would be the Merit Protection Board. To insure protection of federal employees who "blow the whistle" on questionable practices in the bureaucracy, the President also proposed that a special counsel be appointed to the Merit Protection Board who would be responsible for prosecuting political abuses and violations of the merit system.

Facilitating the removal process and making salary increases contingent upon performance should serve to make recalcitrant bureaucrats more responsive to presidential policies provided, of course, that their superiors are also sympathetic to the President's programs. As we have seen, however, this is not always the case. Tying pay increases to job performance may also serve to encourage more creativity and risk taking on the part of bureaucrats. But offsetting these advantages are some legitimate concerns, especially when Carter's reform proposals are viewed alongside his legislation calling for repeal of certain restrictions of the Hatch Act. This act, passed in 1939, prohibits civil servants from participating in political activity. Its purpose was to insulate the civil service from politics as much as possible. Today the Hatch Act is considered excessive, and the President's legislation eliminating these restrictions has already passed the House.

With these provisions repealed, federal employees would be free to run for office as well as contribute to campaigns in financial and other ways. Since Carter's civil service reforms would give a President's department and agency heads greater ability to reward and punish civil servants, those with political leanings contrary to the President's might well find themselves in a precarious position.

Whether or not Carter's Civil Service reforms will be blocked by Congress remains to be seen. Under current regulations, bureaucrats find themselves in a situation where pay increases are assured and firings a rarity. Moreover, they may not be inclined to surrender this kind of security. If this does indeed prove to be the case, then the President's reforms will face stiff resistance, for the bureaucracy has powerful allies both in and outside of Congress.

Zero-Base Budgeting

In considering how the President's control over the bureaucracy can be increased, mention must be made of one other proposed reform of potentially far-reaching significance. It involves a procedure known as *zero-base budgeting.* Under existing central clearance procedures, a department or agency is required to submit and justify to OMB only new expenditure proposals. Thus there is no systematic review of those programs already in existence. Some of these existing programs may have been poorly conceived to begin with, while others may simply have outlived their usefulness. Yet since departments and agencies are not likely to call for the elimination of programs that benefit their own clientele groups, they continue to be funded. It is for this reason that President Carter announced his intention to implement zero-base budgeting. Under this plan, a department or agency not only would be required to justify new expenditures but also would have to rejustify *each year* all current expenditures. Through this kind of annual reevaluation, hopefully, inefficient and obsolete programs could be detected and eliminated from the budget.

This system is not new in government. Indeed, more than a dozen states have already adopted it, and surveys suggest that nearly half of the states will do so by 1980.[60] While such a procedure makes good sense and may well be practicable at the state level, there is considerable doubt about whether it can be successfully implemented at the federal level. Departments and agencies are already presented with a time-consuming task in seeking to justify new expenditures, and both OMB and congressional committees have their hands full in trying to evaluate them. Thus, the additional burden of annually reviewing all current expenditures as well could not be undertaken effectively unless there were substantial increases in the staffs of all those involved in the budgetary process.

Some appreciation of the task involved here can be gained by looking at

[60] Advisory Commission on Intergovernmental Relations, *Information Bulletin,* No. 76–5 (December 1976), 6.

the experience of NASA (National Aeronautics and Space Administration). At the request of the House Appropriations Committee, it was asked to prepare just *a small part* of its 1978 budget using zero-base budgeting. In terms of man-hours, the cost to the agency for employing this procedure was approximately $300,000. In addition, their budget report had to be increased by five hundred pages.[61] Finally, it should be pointed out that the job of eliminating programs after they have begun is considerably more difficult than getting them started in the first place. Benefits withheld may raise cries of protest, but they are not likely to be as loud as those raised when what has been given is suddenly taken away.

[61] This information was provided to the author by an official at the National Aeronautics and Space Administration.

5

President,
Public,
and Press

Of all the constituencies with which a President must interact, none is more important to him than the public. For one thing, only the people have the authority to renew or terminate his Presidency, unless of course he is convicted of impeachable offenses by the Senate. And even that kind of drastic action would be highly unlikely unless the public was in favor of it. For another, the President is less likely to encounter resistance to what he wants if the public is firmly behind him. President Lincoln took note of this fact when he remarked, "In this and like communities, public sentiment is everything. With public sentiment nothing can fail, without it nothing can succeed."[1] Although Lincoln overstates the case, few would doubt the fact that public support facilitates the President's ability to act. As was noted in an earlier chapter, most of what a President wants to accomplish requires the acquiescence of Congress in one form or another. Moreover, given the constitutional restrictions on his power as well as the absence of guaranteed support from members of his own party in Congress, the President is forced to enlist congressional support, rather than command it. Since Congress is a popularly elected body, it must of necessity be sensitive to the level of public support the President can generate for his programs. Although public backing is not the only factor that can make a President an effective persuader, it is surely one of his most potent weapons.

In this chapter we shall examine how the public reacts to both the Presidency and the President and consider what, if any, implications these reactions have for presidential power. While for analytical purposes public attitudes toward the office and the man will initially be treated separately, they are in fact interrelated. This interrelationship will constitute a second focus of this chapter. Here

[1] Cited in Jack Valenti, *A Very Human President* (New York: W.W. Norton, 1975), p. 261.

an effort will be made to assess the impact of President Nixon's Watergate involvement upon the public's attitudes toward the institution of the Presidency. Finally, we shall examine how the President attempts to influence the public's attitudes toward himself and his policies. In dealing with this matter, it will be important to discuss the President's relationship with the press, since it is the primary instrument through which he communicates with the people.

PUBLIC ATTITUDES TOWARD THE OFFICE: PRE-WATERGATE

Importance of the Office

That the American people attach extraordinary importance to the Office of the Presidency can be demonstrated in several ways, one of which is the number of people in the population who are able to identify the President of the United States. As Table 5-1 indicates, he is by far the best known public official in the country, with nearly all adults and young adults (98 percent) able to identify him. (While it might be intriguing to speculate why 2 percent of the adult population apparently never got the word, this need not concern us here.) Moreover, not only is the President the most well known political figure on the national scene but, with the exception of the Vice President, other prominent public officials do not even approach his level of public recognition. Although it is not shown in Table 5-1, even school children in the primary grades can identify the President and correctly state his party identification. Furthermore, they also see him as the most important figure in their political world.[2]

It is hardly surprising that the President enjoys such widespread recognition among all segments of the public. He is, after all, the only nationally elected

TABLE 5-1. AWARENESS OF POLITICAL LEADERS ON THE PART OF ADULTS AND CHILDREN, 1969-70

	Percentage Correct by Age		
Office	Adult	17	13
President (Nixon)	98	98	94
Vice President (Agnew)	87	79	60
Secretary of State (Rogers)	16	9	2
Secretary of Defense (Laird)	25	16	6
Speaker of the House (McCormack)	32	25	2
Senate Majority Leader (Mansfield)	23	14	4
At Least One Senator from Own State	57	44	16
Both Senators from Own State	31	18	6
Congressman from Own District	39	35	11

SOURCE: Fred Greenstein, "What the President Means to Americans," in James Barber, ed., *Choosing the President* (Englewood Cliffs, N.J.: Prentice-Hall, 1974), p. 125.

[2] Fred Greenstein, "Popular Images of the President," in Aaron Wildavsky, ed., *The Presidency* (Boston: Little, Brown, 1969), p. 290.

public official in our government. Equally important, he is the focal point of our political process, and thus the media's daily attention to his every word and action far exceeds the coverage given any other public figure.

A further indication of the importance of the Presidency to the American citizenry is reflected in how their attitudes toward this particular institution affect their attitudes toward other institutions. Specifically, an increase or decrease in support for the Presidency appears also to lead to an increase or decrease in support for other institutions such as the Congress and the Supreme Court. One study showed, for example, that as public support for the Presidency declined during the Watergate scandals, so too did support for Congress and the Court, although the declines for the latter were at a much slower rate.[3] Similarly, another study of children done during this same period also demonstrated that their increasingly negative attitudes toward the Presidency were accompanied by increasingly negative reactions toward other political objects.[4] Such a "fallout effect" suggests that for many Americans the Presidency constitutes the most important and fundamental point of identification with the political system.

Finally, the population's reaction to the death of a President may also be taken as an indicator of the preeminent position the office holds in the public mind. Following the death of President Kennedy, for example, substantial numbers of the population reported physiological irregularities that exceeded the levels one would normally expect. A survey made by the National Opinion Research Center found that during the days immediately following the assassination, 43 percent of the adult population reported a loss of appetite, 48 percent experienced insomnia, 25 percent complained of headaches, 68 percent experienced nervousness and tension, 26 percent had rapid heartbeats, and 17 percent noted greater than normal perspiring. These symptoms of emotional strain were experienced by the President's detractors as well as his supporters. And the principle cause of such reactions appears to have had more to do with the fact that he was *the President* rather than with the nature of his death or his youth and personal appeal. Nor was the public's grief over President Kennedy a unique occurrence in our history. On the contrary, the historical evidence suggests that the public reacted in much the same way to the deaths of Lincoln, Roosevelt, McKinley, Garfield, and even to such a marginal President as Warren Harding.[5] That the public has behaved in this way suggests that the President, regardless of who he happens to be, functions as perhaps the most important symbol of

---

[3] Jack Dennis, "Who Supports the Presidency?" *Society* 13 (July/August 1976), 51. See also Roger Davidson and Glenn Parker, "The Pattern of Support for Congress" (Paper presented at the 66th Annual Meeting of the American Political Science Association, Los Angeles, September 8-12, 1970); Kenneth Dolbeare and Phillip Hammond, "The Political Party Bias of Attitudes Toward the Supreme Court," *Public Opinion Quarterly* 32 (spring 1968), 16-30.

[4] Christopher Arterton, "Watergate and Children's Attitudes toward Political Authority Revisited." *Political Science Quarterly* 90 (Fall 1975), 488.

[5] Greenstein, "Popular Images," p. 228.

stability and national unity within our political system. When that symbol is suddenly taken away, the psychological effect upon the population is profound, even if only temporary.

The Office as an Object of Trust and Respect

In the past the population has exhibited a high degree of respect for and trust in the Presidency. Such attitudes have taken root early in the lives of Americans, with grade-school children not only seeing the President as the most important public figure but also assessing him in highly positive terms. According to earlier studies, grade-school children viewed him as "benevolent, dependable, trustworthy and infallible."[6] The following provide some examples of how he was characterized:

"[The President] gives us freedom." (Eighth-grade girl)

"[The President] deals with foreign countries and takes care of the U.S." (Eighth-grade boy)

"[The President] makes peace with every country but bad." (Fifth-grade boy)

"[The President] does good work." (Sixth-grade boy)

"[The President] is doing a very good job of making people safe." (Fourth-grade girl)[7]

These findings were based upon studies conducted during the relative tranquility of the late fifties and early sixties. Even leaving Watergate aside for the moment, most of the sixties and early seventies were characterized by political and social turmoil; there were racial riots in our major cities and student protests against the Vietnam War and, to some extent, against the political system itself. Thus one might expect this turbulent era to have had profound effects upon attitudes toward political authority in general and the Presidency in particular. Yet in a 1969–70 study of British, French, and American children, Fred Greenstein concluded that the white American children "were extraordinarily positive in their spontaneous descriptions of the President."[8] Here are two typical responses:

The President of the United States is a man or a woman or whatever, who is, like, picked by the people to lead the country. And they try to make the person almost perfect. I mean, if he does anything wrong they down

[6]Michael Riccards, *The Making of the American Citizenry* (New York: Chandler, 1973), p. 70.

[7]Fred Greenstein, "The Benevolent Leader: Children's Images of Political Authority," *American Political Science Review* 54 (December 1960), 939.

[8]Fred Greenstein, "The Benevolent Leader Revisited: Children's Images of Political Leaders in Three Democracies," *American Political Science Review* 69 (December 1975), 1385.

him . . . because *if a person is going to be head of a country like the United States for years, he just has to be about perfect.*

The President of the United States is a very important man that is trying to make the U.S. a better place and, well, he takes care of problems that just a few people won't be able to take care of, like the war in Vietnam and like the men who have been over there for a long time. And *he tries to make things equal and fair* so that you know you won't really get mad on the taxes. He's, well, he's trying to make the United States a better place and he's trying to solve a lot of problems.[9]

While the black children in the group were far more inclined to give a negative response about the President than their white counterparts, nevertheless, their responses were still more often favorable than unfavorable. As the following dialogue demonstrates, however, the negative responses were in some cases quite potent:

Respondent: I'd say [of the President] he's stupid and he don't know what he's doing.

Interviewer: What does he do?

Respondent: He doesn't do . . . He doesn't let people do what they want to do. He always putting people in jail or somethin' . . . . He's supposed to keep peace in the world, but he isn't doing that. . . . He isn't trying to stop anything.

Interviewer: Suppose a foreign child asks you what is the President of the United States?

Respondent: A rat.

Interviewer: Okay, try to give the foreign child an idea of what he does. What does he do?

Respondent: I can name a lot of things . . . He prejudiced. . . . He lousy. He picked Spiro Agnew. Spiro Agnew stinks and he ain't no good, none of them.

Interviewer: What is the President's job?

Respondent: To try and make people happy, but he's making them miserable.[10]

Although the reactions of both the black and the white children were generally positive, it is important to note that the children in this study did *not* come from the more depressed areas of their community. The subgroups within our population who have not fared so well at the hands of society have shown demonstrably different feelings toward the Presidency. Especially noteworthy in this regard is a study made of black and white children from grades five through twelve in the economically depressed area of Appalachia. It revealed that these

[9]Ibid., p. 1386.
[10]Ibid.

children saw the President as more malevolent than benevolent. Although in the earlier grades they tended to idealize the President, their attitudes became increasingly negative toward him as they progressed toward the twelfth grade. By their senior year in high school, only 31 percent felt that the President "liked almost everybody while an equal percentage thought that he liked fewer people than most men."[11] Moreover, there was not even one twelfth grader who thought he was the best person in the world; indeed, nearly one-third of them did not think he was a very good person at all. The decline in favorable responses to the Presidency occurred more rapidly among the poor blacks than the poor whites, at least until the ninth grade. At this point, the attitudes of black children began to become more positive, a fact that may reflect their perception of the President as a visible spokesman for civil rights.[12]

In summary, although there are some marked exceptions among certain sociocultural subgroups within our society, nevertheless, taken as a whole the evidence suggests that prior to Watergate the Presidency was trusted and respected by the preadult population.

Not surprisingly, the indiscriminately positive attitudes shown toward the office by the preadult population do not persist into the adult years. Yet even though a more realistic appraisal replaces the idealization of the young, trust in the Presidency has in the past remained quite high, even among adults, In 1966, for example, the Survey Research Center asked a national sample of adults what kinds of work they respected most highly. Included in the choices of occupations were a famous doctor, a bishop or other church official, president of a large corporation like General Motors, a governor, senator, Supreme Court Justice, and several other public officials. Also included, of course, was the President of the United States. The results were decisive, with 52 percent of the sample naming the President as their first choice. The next most respected occupations were those of physician and clergyman, but even these received only a little more than 10 percent of the first-choice responses.[13]

In another study conducted in 1966, 816 people were interviewed on their attitudes toward the Presidency. Once again, the results suggest that in the past the office has been accorded a high degree of respect and trust. Among other things, the authors constructed an "I Like Presidents" index, which appears in Table 5-2. All but two of the statements in the index received the support of a majority of those interviewed. It was also found that scores on the "I Like Presidents" index were affected by certain background and psychological factors as well as by political attitudes about American government. More specifically, those scoring highest on the index tended to be individuals with authoritarian personalities, little education, and positive attitudes toward the American politi-

---

[11] Riccards, *American Citizenry*, p. 77.

[12] Ibid., p. 79.

[13] Fred Greenstein, "What the President Means to Americans," in James Barber, ed., *Choosing the President* (Englewood Cliffs, N.J.: Prentice Hall, 1974), p. 126.

TABLE 5-2. "I LIKE PRESIDENTS" INDEX

	Percent Giving Support Responses
(1) More nearly than any other person, the President stands for our country.	85
(2) One sleeps better knowing that a President one trusts is watching over the country.	72
(3) We are fortunate because our presidents usually make the right decisions.	69
(4) Most people don't appreciate enough how hard Presidents work for the welfare of the country.	63
(5) Since the President has the best information on public affairs, he is more likely than anyone else to know what is the best thing to do.	61
(6) Just seeing or hearing a President makes one feel good.	38
(7) Although he may have been an ordinary citizen before, when he becomes President he should be considered to be the wisest man in the world.	20

SOURCE: Samuel Kernell, Peter Sperlich, and Aaron Wildavsky, "Public Support for Presidents," in Aaron Wildavsky, ed., *Perspectives on the Presidency* (Boston: Little, Brown, 1975), p. 152. © Copyright 1975 by Little, Brown and Company (Inc.). Reprinted by permission.

cal system. This is not altogether surprising. The least educated tend to have little knowledge about the political system, and thus the President constitutes their only visible link to the government. Similarly, in contrast to nonauthoritarian types, those personalities that have a need for authority and order would understandably react more favorably to the authority figure the President represents. And finally, individuals with more positive attitudes toward the political system in general could reasonably be expected to view the Presidency more favorably also.

Once again, however, it must be pointed out that the evidence presented above was gathered prior to much of the societal unrest of the late sixties and early seventies. Several polls taken during this latter period suggest that there was a decline of public confidence in all of our national institutions. In 1966, 1971, and 1972, a Harris Poll asked a national sample of Americans whether they had confidence in "the people in charge of running the Executive branch" (a great deal of confidence/some confidence/hardly any confidence at all). In 1966, 41 percent expressed a "great deal of confidence," but this number dropped to 23 percent in 1971 and rose only slightly to 27 percent in 1972. While only a minority of the respondents ever expressed "hardly any confidence at all," this group nevertheless rose from 8 percent in 1966 to 18 percent in 1971.[14] These

[14] Cited in Everett Ladd, "The Polls: The Question of Confidence," *Public Opinion Quarterly* 40 (winter 1976–77), 545.

data must be viewed with some caution, however, for the question asks about confidence in the Executive branch and not simply the President. Secondly, it is asking for an evaluation of the "current leadership" as opposed to the institution of the Presidency. Despite these limitations, however, one could plausibly argue that declining confidence in the current leadership of the Executive branch during this period could be taken as an indicator of some decline of public confidence in the Presidency itself. But just how much of a decline is unclear.

Attitudes about the Power of the Presidency

Although the public appears to feel that the powers of the Presidency have grown while those of Congress have decreased, people do not have a naive impression of the office as all-powerful. In 1958, the Survey Research Center asked a national sample of Americans, "In general which do you think has the most say in the way our government is run—the Congress, the President, or are they about equal?" Fifty-two percent of the respondents felt that Congress had the most say, only 10 percent felt the President did, and 24 percent thought they were about equal.[15] In another national survey conducted approximately ten years later, only 10 percent of the population felt that the President had the power to get just about anybody to do what he wants.[16] A statewide poll taken in 1973 asked Minnesota citizens which institution had more power and control with the government—Congress or the President. While a substantial number came down on the side of the President (47 percent), Congress was still given the edge (49 percent).[17]

Given the trust and respect that have characterized public attitudes about the Presidency in the past, one would expect that the population would be willing to accord the President considerable freedom of action in what he does. The preponderance of evidence does not confirm this expectation, however. After examining public opinion polls that, over a forty-year period, have dealt with various aspects of presidential power, one scholar concludes:

> A President would have few unchecked prerogatives if it were left to the American public. Whenever given a choice between congressional vs. presidential decision-making, the people tend to trust Congress over the chief executive. Whether the issue pertains to specific domestic or military matters, or to authority in general, seem immaterial. Unsophisticated as the public may be in knowledge of constitutional provisions for the separation of powers, they have systematically given implied consent to the principle

[15] Hazel Erskine, "The Polls: Presidential Power," *Public Opinion Quarterly* 37 (Fall 1973), p. 491.

[16] Cited in Thomas Cronin, *The State of the Presidency* (Boston: Little, Brown, 1975), p. 107.

[17] Cited in Erskine, "The Polls," p. 491.

TABLE 5-3. PUBLIC VIEWS OF PRESIDENTIAL AND CONGRESSIONAL POLICY MAKING RESPONSIBILITIES

	Foreign Policy	Economic Policy	Racial Policy
President	14	7	11
Equal	60	58	63
Congress	23	31	23
Not sure	3	4	3

SOURCE: Louis Harris and Associates, Study No. 1900. Under contract to Roger H. Davidson and financed by the Social Research Council. Reprinted by permission of Professor Davidson.

of checks and balances or, at the least, have shown majority reluctance to grant too much power to one man, the president.[18]

In 1958, for example, the Survey Research Center asked a national sample of Americans the following question: "Some people say the President is in the best position to see what the country needs. Other people think the President may have good ideas about what the country needs, but it is up to Congress to decide what ought to be done. How do you feel about this?" Respondents came down decisively on the side of Congress (61 percent), with only 17 percent choosing the President. Among the remaining respondents, 7 percent said it depends, and 15 percent simply did not know how they felt on the matter.[19] Ten years later, a Harris poll asked a national sample of Americans whether they thought the President or the Congress ought to have the major responsibility in making foreign, economic, and racial policy. The results are presented in Table 5-3. They clearly demonstrate that a majority felt the President and Congress should play an equal role in all three policy areas. Also worth noting, however, is the fact that substantially greater numbers were willing to give Congress, rather than the President, the dominant policy-making role in all three policy areas.

One study in particular must be mentioned that constitutes a notable exception to the findings presented above. In the early sixties, two questions were put to a sample of Detroit citizens on the subject of presidential power. The first was a general question which asked whether they thought the President "should be able to make the people and Congress go along with him," or whether "it is up to the people through their congressmen to find solutions to the problems of the day," with the "President carrying out what the people and Congress have decided." A total of 51.5 percent felt that presidential leadership should be preferred, 39.6 percent opted for the combined leadership of the public and Congress, and 6 percent felt they should all be involved. A second ques-

[18] Erskine, "The Polls," p. 488.

[19] Ibid., p. 492.

tion dealt specifically with a hypothetical matter of foreign policy: Fighting has broken out abroad and "the President thinks it is important to send troops there. Now, what do you think, should he send these troops, which he may legally do as President, or should he follow public opinion and keep them home?" An overwhelming 75 percent felt that he should go ahead and send the troops, while only 20.8 percent felt he should not.[20]

The discrepancy between these results and those of the Harris survey presented in Table 5-3 can perhaps be explained by two factors. In the Harris poll, respondents were being asked to judge the role of the President and Congress in foreign policy, while the Detroit study asked people to choose between the President's judgment and the public's. It may be that the public is sufficiently skeptical about its own knowledge of foreign policy that it is willing to defer to the President. On the other hand, when the choice on making foreign policy is between the President and the Congress, the public does have enough confidence in the judgment of Congress to want to include it in foreign policy decisions. Also, the time when each study was made may also help to explain why the Detroit citizens—unlike those interviewed by Harris—preferred presidential leadership on matters in general and on the commitment of troops in particular. Whereas the Detroit study was done in the early sixties, Harris made his survey in 1968. By this time the Vietnam War had become unpopular, and since the Presidency had been responsible for getting us into it, the public may have concluded that the Congress should have greater say in foreign policy. Similarly, rising inflation, racial unrest in the cities, and a general discontent with busing may also have led them to conclude that Congress should also play a role in the making of economic and racial policy.

If the public is not prepared to give the President the dominant role in the governmental process, it is nevertheless willing to give him strong support when he has made a decision. According to one study, for example, 56 percent of the respondents felt that the President should be supported even if they think he has made a wrong decision. At the same time, however, only 25 percent were willing to go so far as to say that he should be supported *no matter what he does.* During times of crisis, support for the President is even higher, with nearly two-thirds of the respondents feeling that the public should rally behind him. But even under crisis conditions, they do not favor blind and unquestioning support, for only 24 percent felt that people should *not* ask a lot of questions and demand a lot of answers at such times.[21]

To summarize briefly, prior to Watergate the public did not appear to believe

[20] Roberta Sigel, "Image of the American Presidency: Part II of an Exploration into Popular Views of Presidential Powers," in Wildavsky, ed., *The Presidency,* pp. 300, 301.

[21] Samuel Kernell, Peter Sperlich, and Aaron Wildavsky, "Public Support for Presidents," in Aaron Wildavsky, ed., *Perspectives on the Presidency* (Boston: Little, Brown, 1975), p. 153.

that the Presidency was an omnipotent institution. Nor, the evidence suggests, would they want it to be so. On the contrary, a majority of Americans favor a coequal partnership between the President and Congress in the making of policy. These findings suggest that while the public has in the past expressed considerable confidence in the Presidency, this attitude has not overcome what is apparently an even stronger view—namely, that there should be a balance of power and responsibility within the government.

THE PUBLIC'S ATTITUDES TOWARD THE MAN

Thus far our attention has been focused upon the public's pre-Watergate views of the Presidency as an institution, without reference to the individuals who happened to occupy it. We now consider how and why the public reacts as it does to the people who serve in this office.

The Inevitable Decline in Support

Since the midforties, the Gallup poll has periodically tested the waters of public sentiment toward incumbent presidents. The question traditionally put to the public by Gallup has been, "Do you approve or disapprove of the way the President is handling his job?" The answers to this question over an expanse of thirty years allow us to make some generalizations about the patterns of public support for presidents.

One thing is clear. A President's popularity begins to erode fairly soon after he assumes office. An examination of the public approval ratings of our last six presidents is instructive in this regard. Three of them were elected to a first term. The other three served abbreviated first terms because they succeeded to the Presidency upon the death or resignation of the incumbent. As Table 5-4 indicates, three of the five had lower public approval ratings when they started the final year of their first term than they did at the time they first assumed office. The two exceptions were Eisenhower and Johnson. Eisenhower's popularity went up eleven points, which is probably explainable by the fact that he ended the Korean War. In Lyndon Johnson's case, he became President only three months prior to the final year of Kennedy's unexpired term. Thus it is not surprising that his popularity went up one point, to give him an approval rating of 80 percent.

Five of our last six presidents ran for a second term, and four (Truman, Eisenhower, Johnson, and Nixon) did so successfully. As one might expect, they all experienced an increase in popularity following their election victories and inaugurations. Richard Nixon was the only one of the four not to complete his second term, and his public support was disastrously low at the time he resigned from office. As for the other three, they all had a lower public approval rating at the end of their second term than they did at the beginning of it.

TABLE 5-4. DECLINES IN PRESIDENTIAL POPULARITY

	Support upon Assuming Office	Support At Beginning of Final Year of First Term	Support at Beginning of Second Term	Support at End of Second Term	Support at Time of Death, Resignation or Election Defeat
Truman	87	36*	69	31	—
Eisenhower	68	77	79	59	—
Kennedy	72	—	—	—	59
Johnson	79	80	71	49	—
Nixon	59	49	67	—	24
Ford	71	46*	—	—	53

SOURCE: Data from 1945-71 were taken from George Gallup, *The Gallup Poll: Public Opinion 1935-1971* (New York: Random House, 1972). Data from 1972 on were taken from the monthly *Gallup Opinion Index.*

For purposes of this table, "first term" is also being applied to individuals who served out the unexpired terms of those presidents who either died or resigned while in office.

To state the point more generally, all of our last six presidents—regardless of when their presidencies were terminated—left office with a public approval rating substantially lower than the one they received upon assuming the job. To be sure, what a President does or fails to do may retard or accelerate the decline, but the decline itself appears inevitable. On the average, it has amounted to six percentage points a year.[22]

Several factors may help to explain why this is so. In the first place, a President comes into office with the initial support of the majority coalition that gave him his election victory. He also picks up some additional support from those who, although not willing to support him as a candidate, now feel some obligation to unite behind him as President. Thus, in spite of the fact that Jimmy Carter defeated Gerald Ford by only three percentage points in the popular vote, a Gallup poll taken one month after he assumed office showed that 66 percent of the public approved of the way he was handling his job.[23] How long a President's honeymoon lasts depends upon how controversial his actions are, as well as upon the nature of events which he cannot always control. Gerald Ford's honeymoon ended abruptly when, one month after assuming office, he granted Richard Nixon a free and open pardon. This decision brought cries of outrage from the public, and his approval rating fell from 71 to 50 percent.[24]

While Gerald Ford's pardon of Nixon was undoubtedly more controversial than most presidential decisions made during the first few months in office, no President can avoid making controversial decisions for very long. All of the prob-

[22] John Mueller, *War, Presidents and Public Opinion* (New York: John Wiley, 1973), p. 220.

[23] Cited in *Gallup Opinion Index*, April 1977, p. 3.

[24] *Gallup Opinion Index*, September 1977, p. 3; *Gallup Opinion Index*, November 1974, p. 19.

lems that come over his desk are important ones, and they are nearly always controversial as well. Each decision he makes will manage to dissatisfy some segment(s) of the population. As the number of controversial decisions increases, so too will the level of dissatisfaction, producing what one scholar has called a "coalition of minorities" opposed to the President.[25] In office only six months, Jimmy Carter's decisions on policy managed to stir up opposition in several quarters. Farmers were upset by his refusal to seek higher grain price supports. George Meany and the AFL-CIO were upset by his failure to give vigorous support to common situs picketing legislation as well as by his decision to seek a smaller increase in the minimum wage. The shoe industry was offended by his refusal to raise tariffs on shoe imports. Both labor and industry strongly objected to certain portions of his energy program. And the liberal wing of the Democratic Party became increasingly disenchanted by Carter's determination to balance the budget even if it meant holding down expenditures for social programs. The president of the National Urban League charged that Carter had "betrayed" black people. The examples could go on, but these mentioned suffice to show that the necessity for making difficult decisions precludes a lasting honeymoon between the President and the public.

A President's declining public support is a consequence not only of what he does, but also of what he fails to do. All presidential candidates have been prone to making extravagant promises during their campaigns. In part, this is a consequence of their desire to get elected; and in part it reflects a certain naiveté about the magnitude of the problems they must confront as President. After several months in office Jimmy Carter still expressed a commitment to do something about the nation's welfare program but postponed action, acknowledging that the problem was far more complex than he had imagined. While during the campaign he repeatedly asserted that greater controls must be put on the CIA, after becoming President he expressed concern that too many people in government had access to intelligence information. Prior to his election, he told the people of Texas and Louisiana that he would deregulate the price of natural gas, yet his energy program called for maintaining such regulation.[26] He also promised to reduce United States arms sales to other nations and balance the budget by 1980. The former promise has not been kept and the latter is quite simply out of the question, at least for 1980. Regardless of whether it results from political expediency or naiveté, the "over-promising" syndrome has a tendency to elevate public expectations beyond what is within reach. If presidents themselves come to realize the gap between what is promised and what is attainable, so too does the public. The result is a certain amount of disillusionment, which contributes to the decline in a President's support. In assessing his first year in office, Presi-

[25] John Mueller, "Presidential Popularity from Truman to Johnson," *American Political Science Review* 64 (March 1970), 20.

[26] *New York Times*, May 2, 1977, p. 33.

dent Carter acknowledged that "my biggest mistake has been in inadvertently building up expectations too high."[27]

Finally, it has been suggested by Thomas Cronin that a President's declining public support may also be due in part to conflicting public expectations about what kind of man he ought to be. For example, Cronin points out that we seek a *gentle* and decent man in the Presidency, but these qualities must often conflict with our equally strong desire for a man who is *forceful* and *decisive*. We want a man who can exercise *moral* leadership in the office, but we also recognize the necessity of having a man who realizes that *compromise* is essential if one is to get anything accomplished. We look for a President who can provide innovative and creative solutions, yet at the same time our democratic values have imbued us with the belief that presidents should be *responsive to public opinion.* We desire a leader who can *inspire* us, *elevate our hopes,* invite us to reach beyond our grasp, but we also insist that he should *not create false expectations.* We seek a man who can *unify* us, but our desire for creative, decisive, and courageous leadership makes it all but inevitable that he must *divide even as he leads.* These paradoxical expectations place a President in a no-win situation, for in attempting to fulfill some of them, he cannot help but appear deficient in others.[28]

In addition to these general reasons why presidents suffer an overall decline in their popularity, it should also be pointed out that certain circumstances and events appear to be especially important in accelerating or retarding this decline. The President appears to benefit from those situations in which he is acting as the symbolic leader of the nation. President Nixon, for example, experienced increases in his popularity following his trips to China and the Soviet Union (see Figure 5-1), as did President Ford after returning from Europe and China (see Figure 5-2). Perhaps the most marked increases in public approval come on the heels of international crises involving the United States, especially when the President responds with bold and decisive action. Following the Cuban missile crisis President Kennedy's popularity jumped by thirteen points. Likewise, President Ford's daring efforts to rescue the *Mayaguez* brought him an eleven-point rise in public approval, the single largest increase during his entire Presidency (see Figure 5-2). Even when a presidential response to an international crisis appears unsuccessful, the public still exhibits a tendency to come to his support. Thus, following the embarrassing U-2 incident, which led to the collapse of the Paris summit meeting of the major world powers, Eisenhower's popularity still went up six points. The abortive Bay of Pigs invasion proved to be an even greater embarrassment to the United States in general and the Kennedy Administration in particular. Yet despite this fact, Kennedy's approval rating went up by ten points. Even if only temporary, this kind of a supportive public response pro-

---

[27]*National Journal,* January 14, 1978, p. 44.

[28]Thomas Cronin, "The Paradoxes of the Presidency," *Skeptic,* No. 5 (September/October 1976), 20–23, 54–57.

FIGURE 5-1. PRESIDENT NIXON'S PUBLIC APPROVAL RATING, 1969–74

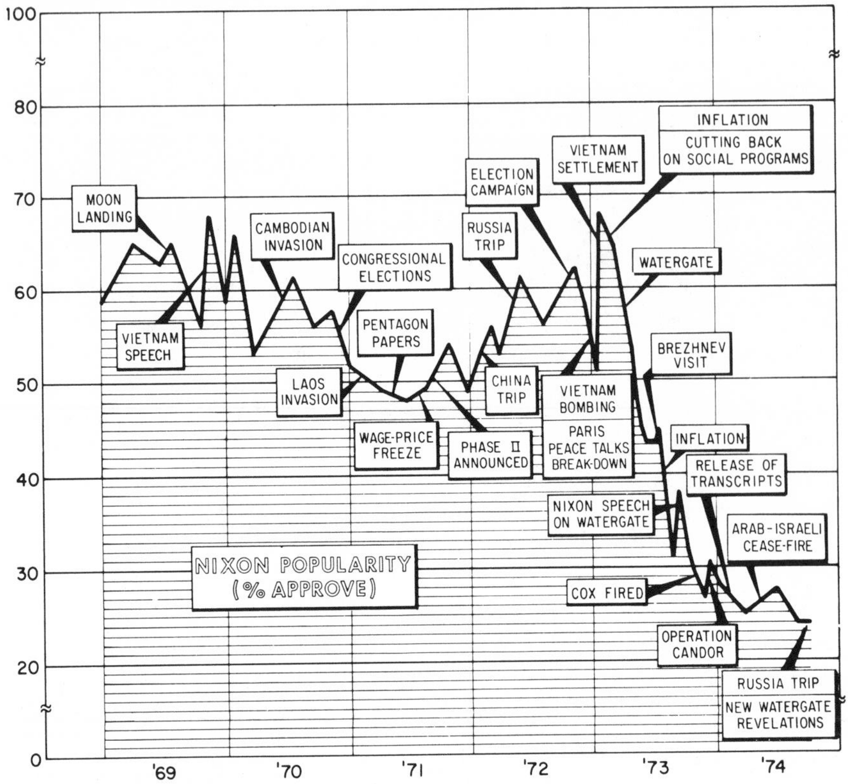

SOURCE: *The Gallup Opinion Index*, September 1974, p. 12.

vides the President with some needed leverage in dealing with his critics. Finally, presidents benefit from events and actions that cannot be neatly categorized, except to say that the public perceives them as "good news."[29] Such good news might take the form of a tax cut, the settlement of an international conflict, or a moon landing (see Figures 5-1, 5-2).

Among the circumstances that have a pronounced effect in the direction of reducing a President's popularity, a declining economy appears to be of major importance. Pollster George Gallup speaks to this point:

Nothing has so devastating an effect upon a President's popularity as do economic troubles. President Truman's popularity plunged 44 percentage

[29] See, for example, Richard Brody and Benjamin Page, "The Impact of Events on Presidential Popularity: The Johnson and Nixon Administrations," in Wildavsky, ed., *Perspectives on the Presidency*, pp. 136–146.

FIGURE 5-2. PRESIDENT FORD'S PUBLIC APPROVAL RATING, 1974-76

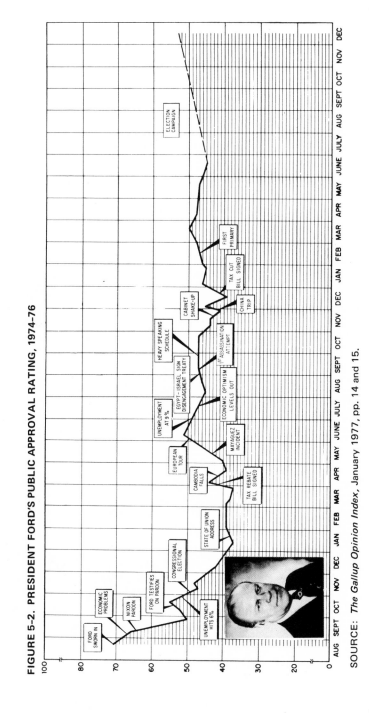

SOURCE: *The Gallup Opinion Index*, January 1977, pp. 14 and 15.

points in just one year, between mid-1945 and mid-1946, largely as a result of the public's concern over economic matters. President Eisenhower's low point in popularity was recorded in the spring of 1958 during a period of recession. And all throughout the Watergate era, the public was actually more concerned about the economy than it was about Watergate.[30]

This relationship between the state of the economy and a decline in a President's popularity is certainly understandable, for economic dislocations have a very immediate and direct effect upon the pocketbooks of the population. What is surprising, however, is that presidents do not appear to benefit significantly from an *improvement* in economic conditions, perhaps because the public views the maintenance of a healthy economy as part of the President's job.

In addition to an ailing economy, a President's popularity will be severely affected by public doubts about his integrity. Of all the qualities that the public is searching for in a President, none appears to be more important than honesty.[31] While it is doubtful that this quality has ever enhanced a President's popularity to any great extent—one assumes, after all, that a President will be honest—its absence can certainly hurt him. In January of 1973, Richard Nixon's popularity was at 68 percent, the highest level it had reached during his entire four years as President. Yet when the Watergate scandals began to unravel, his approval rating started to plummet and finally reached a low of 25 percent shortly before he resigned from office (see Figure 5-1). This forty-three point decline was the sharpest recorded for a President since the Presidency of Harry Truman. A sputtering economy was important in contributing to the rapidity of the decline, but so too was the public's ultimate conclusion that their President could not be trusted. Because it is largely irreversible, no circumstance is likely to be more damaging to a President in the long run than his inability to maintain the public trust. Like innocence, once lost, it cannot be regained.

The impact of war upon presidential popularity is less clear. In his exhaustive analysis of this subject, John Mueller found that the Korean War had a very definite effect in accelerating the decline of President Truman's popularity. On the other hand, while Johnson's declining popularity would appear to have been associated with the intensification of our war effort in Vietnam (see Figure 5-3), Mueller reports that the war actually had no substantial impact on the erosion of his public support. He suggests that one possible explanation for this anomaly is that Johnson managed to keep the Vietnam War above partisan politics, while Truman was not able to do so with the Korean War. Moreover, unlike Truman, Johnson faced a major domestic crisis at home in the form of racial unrest. Thus, it may be that dissatisfaction over this state of affairs was sufficient by itself to

---

[30] George Gallup, "Public Attitudes, Youth, and the Presidency," in John Hoy and Melvin Bernstein, eds., *The Effective President* (Pacific Palisades, Calif.: Palisades Publishers, 1976), p. 84.

[31] Mervin Field, "Public Opinion and Presidential Response," in Hoy and Bernstein, *Effective President*, p. 63. See also Sigel, "Image of the American Presidency," p. 303.

FIGURE 5-3. PRESIDENT JOHNSON'S APPROVAL RATING, 1963–68

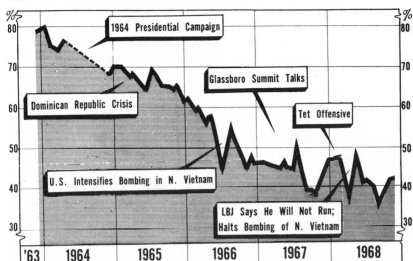

SOURCE: *The Gallup Opinion Index,* December, 1968, p. 1.

produce the marked decline in Johnson's popularity, leaving very little additional impact to be made by public discontent with the war.[32]

In conclusion, in view of the overall downward trend in a President's popularity as he moves through his tenure in office, it would seem appropriate for him to go after what he wants as soon as possible after assuming office. Unfortunately, this is more easily said than done. Presidential candidates have general notions about what goals they want to achieve and what directions they want to move in, but the details of how to do it are not worked out until after they take office. And even then, the process of formulating a major policy will usually require several months of evaluation, consultation, and negotiation. In some cases, it may even be necessary to educate and shape public opinion which, even though generally supportive of the new President, may nevertheless need some persuading on the specifics of what he wants to do.

In addition to acting sooner rather than later, the evidence also suggests that presidents would do well to devote considerable effort toward maintaining a stable economy. Even though economic prosperity may not do much to elevate his popularity, it can nevertheless serve to stave off a precipitous decline in it. Unfortunately, this too is more easily said than done, for many of the factors that affect our highly complex economy are not within the President's ability to control. Richard Nixon, for example, could do little to prevent the OPEC nations from increasing the price of oil in 1974, an event that was instrumental in precipitating a worldwide economic recession. Moreover, in the last few years our economy has been suffering from a unique and curious condition known as stagflation, a disease for which there seems to be no obvious solution.

[32] John Mueller, "Presidential Popularity," pp. 29, 30.

THE INTERPLAY OF PUBLIC ATTITUDES TOWARD THE MAN
AND THE OFFICE: THE CASE OF WATERGATE

Presidents benefit not only from the support the public gives them personally, but also from the more generalized support it gives the Presidency as an institution. As noted in an earlier section of this chapter, this generalized support has been fairly high in the past. How it converts into a President's personal popularity is difficult to say in precise terms, but it certainly helps. For example, the first Gallup poll taken after a President has been elected and reelected to the Presidency has invariably shown a public approval rating substantially higher than the percentage of the popular vote that put him in office (see Table 5-5). While Gallup poll ratings and popular vote percentages are not strictly comparable, nevertheless the comparison does suggest that the public tends to unite around the newly elected leader, in part because he is The President. Even when a President's popularity declines below consensus levels—Truman's and Nixon's at one point dipped down into the twenties and Johnson's into the thirties—the residual support accorded the Presidency itself allows a President to continue governing with at least some measure of effectiveness. This is not to say, however, that support for the institution will always remain constant, unaffected by the actions of those who occupy it. If presidents behave in ways that seriously erode the public's confidence in them, one would also expect that their actions would ultimately have an effect upon the public's confidence and trust in the office itself. And to the extent that the office commands less trust, its occupant

TABLE 5-5. COMPARISON OF POPULAR VOTE PERCENTAGE WITH GALLUP APPROVAL PERCENTAGE

	First Election		Second Election	
	Popular Vote*	Approval First Survey	Popular Vote*	Approval January Survey
Eisenhower	55.1	68	57.4	79
Kennedy	49.7	72	—	—
Nixon	43.4	59	60.7	68
Truman	—	—	49.6	69
Johnson	—	—	61.1	71
Ford	—	71	—	—
Carter	50.1	66	—	—

SOURCE: Figures for Eisenhower through Johnson taken from Elmer Cornwell, "The President and the Press: Phases in the Relationship," p. 60 in volume 427 (September 1976) of *The Annals* of the American Academy of Polical and Social Science. Copyright © 1976 by the American Academy of Political and Social Science. Data for Ford and Carter taken from: *Gallup Opinion Index,* September, 1974, p. 3; *Gallup Opinion Index,* April, 1977, p. 3; Richard Scammon and Alice McGillivray, *America Votes,* 12 (Washington, D.C.: Elections Research Center, 1977), p. 15.

*Percent of total cast for all presidential candidates.

TABLE 5-6. COMPARISON OF 1962, 1973, 1975 STUDIES IN RATING OF THE PRESIDENT FOR "IS THE PRESIDENT YOUR FAVORITE?"

Grade and Year	He Is My Favorite of All	He Is Almost My Favorite of All	He Is More a Favorite of Mine Than Most	He Is More a Favorite of Mine Than Many	He Is More a Favorite of Mine Than a Few	He Is Not One of My Favorites
3rd, 1962	39%	27%	14%	8%	7%	6%
3rd, 1973	8	15	11	4	15	47
3rd, 1975	22	19	6	4	14	35
4th, 1962	28	30	17	11	7	7
4th, 1973	2	5	2	8	13	70
4th, 1975	7	9	22	20	13	30
5th, 1962	21	29	21	13	9	8
5th, 1973	2	3	8	13	11	64
5th, 1975	4	17	18	15	15	29
6th, 1962	22	26	20	14	9	7
6th, 1973	—	—	—	—	—	—
6th, 1975	5	8	18	16	25	29

SOURCE: Adapted from F. Christopher Arterton, "Watergate and Children's Attitudes Toward Political Authority Revisited," *Political Science Quarterly*, 90 (Fall 1975), 481. Reprinted with permission from the *Political Science Quarterly*.

will find it increasingly difficult to mobilize public opinion behind what he wants to do.

At this point, the scandals of Watergate become relevant to our discussion. Beyond any question they disgraced the President involved in them to such a degree that he was compelled to resign from office or else face almost certain impeachment and conviction. But it is also important for us to know whether his actions reflected adversely upon the office as well. There was every reason to believe that they would, for Watergate was the greatest scandal in our political history—directly implicating a President in a systematic abuse of the powers and responsibilities of his office.

The Watergate scandals did indeed have an impact upon the public's attitudes toward the Presidency. Table 5-6 shows the reactions of children in grades three through six to a question posed in 1962, 1973 (after the firing of Archibald Cox), and 1975 (after Watergate had run its course). The question did not refer to any specific President but asked, "Is the President your favorite?" Not surprisingly, in 1962 anywhere from 48 to 66 percent of the children were willing to say that the President was either their "favorite of all" or "almost their favorite of all." In 1973, however, the data available for grades three, four, and five clearly show that Watergate had a devastating effect. Indeed, only 5 to 23 percent were willing to consider him either as their "favorite of all," or almost so. On the other hand, between 47 and 64 percent acknowledged that he was *not* one of their favorites. By 1975, this negative attitude appears to have moderated significantly, but it is still closer to the 1973 reaction than it is to the reaction expressed in 1962. Also, even by 1975, anywhere from 29 to 35 percent of the children still gave the most negative response possible to the question.

Children in these same grades were also questioned on five different components of the presidential image—*attachment, benevolence, dependability, power,* and *leadership.* Predictably, all grades rated the President positively on all these components in 1962, but in 1973 the reaction was strongly negative to all except two—power and leadership. By 1975, attitudes had once again moderated, but the President was just barely rated positively on dependability, continued to be rated negatively on attachment, and for those above the third grade, still received a negative reaction on benevolence. Yet on the dimensions of power and leadership, the President appears to have been rated even more highly than he was in 1962. At the same time, however, the children in all of the grades studied were far less inclined to feel that the President *ought* to have such power.[33]

The immediate effects of Watergate upon adult attitudes toward the Presidency appear to have been equally devastating. According to the Survey Research Center, in 1972 all major subgroups within the population except white Democrats expressed greater trust in the Presidency than they did in either the Congress or the Supreme Court. Yet by 1974 no subgroup rated it above the Supreme Court, and only independents trusted the Presidency more than they did the Congress. Indeed, for practically every major subgroup in the population, the decline in trust for the Presidency was approximately 50 percent.[34] A survey of adults in the state of Wisconsin made in 1972 and again in 1974 also showed erosion in public support for the Presidency. As Table 5-7 indicates, following the Watergate scandals the public appears to have had substantially less confidence in the performance capacity of the Presidency (Question 1). Moreover, their feeling of powerlessness toward the Presidency increased (Question 2), and so too did their belief that the office ought to be reformed (Question 4). While Question 3 was not asked in 1972, nevertheless responses to it in 1974 indicate that respect for the authority of the office was below consensus levels, with only 49 percent believing that the President should be obeyed even if we disagree with him.

If Watergate did have an immediate and negative impact upon the public's attitudes toward the Presidency, it is less clear what its long-range impact will be. Has trust in the office been permanently eroded for those generations of Americans who lived through Watergate; and did Richard Nixon, therefore, hand over a weakened institution to his successor? While an informed answer to this question must await more careful investigation, the existing evidence provides some clues. As already noted, the negative attitude of children toward the Presidency

[33] Arterton, "Watergate and Children's Attitudes," pp. 485, 486.

[34] Arthur Miller, Jeffrey Brudney, and Peter Joftis, "Presidential Crises and Political Support: The Impact of Watergate on Attitudes toward Institutions" (Paper presented at the Midwest Political Science Association Convention, Chicago, May 1–3, 1975), pp. 27, 28.

TABLE 5-7. CHANGES IN PUBLIC EVALUATION OF THE PRESIDENCY BETWEEN 1972 AND 1974

		Nov.-Dec. 1972	Mar.-Apr. 1974
Question 1:	"Office of the President has done some good."	agree—52%* disagree—18	agree—38% disagree—27
Question 2:	"People have a say in what the President does."	agree—19 disagree—58	agree—10 disagree—73
Question 3:	"We should obey the President even if we disagree with him."	agree— — disagree— —	agree—49 disagree—27
Question 4:	"Office of the President should be reformed."	agree—18 disagree—64	agree—45 disagree—35

SOURCE: Adapted from Jack Dennis, "Who Supports the Presidency?" *Society,* 13 (July/August 1976), 51, 52. Published by permission of Transaction, Inc. Copyright © 1976 by Transaction, Inc.

Percentages on each question do not add up to 100% because the "don't know" responses are not included.

had moderated considerably between 1974 and 1975. Moreover, there is some indication that the adult public is also recovering from its doubts about the office. According to a survey made by Potomac Associates, the number of people expressing a "great deal of confidence" in the Executive branch (13 percent) did not change from 1974 to 1976. Yet the number expressing a "fair amount of confidence" rose from 29 to 46 percent; those expressing "not very much confidence" declined from 36 to 30 percent; and finally, those having no confidence at all declined from 19 to 8 percent.[35] A Harris poll taken in March 1977 asked respondents how much confidence they had in the man running the White House, and 31 percent responded a great deal, which constituted an eleven-point increase over the previous year.[36] Of course, this poll was asking the population to react to a particular President rather than to the institution, and thus it is at best only suggestive of a possible increase in confidence in the Presidency. At the close of 1977, the University of Michigan's Institute for Social Research polled high school seniors on their attitudes toward various American institutions, one of which was the Presidency. They were asked to rate them on a scale ranging from "very bad" to "very good." While only 20 percent of the nation's high school seniors had been willing to give the Presidency either a "good" or "very good" rating in a similar poll conducted by the Institute in 1975, 41 percent were willing to do so at the close of 1977.[37] Finally, it should be pointed out that even during the dark days of Watergate, confidence in the Executive branch was far from being completely eroded. According to the Harris surveys,

[35] Francis Rourke, Lloyd Free, and William Watts, *Trust and Confidence in the American System* (Washington, D.C.: Potomac Associates, 1976), p. 22.

[36] Cited in the *Washington Post,* March 14, 1977, p. C9.

[37] *Washington Post,* January 5, 1978, p. A8.

in 1973 only 34 percent of the public stated that they had "hardly any confidence at all" in the Executive branch, and only 18 percent expressed this sentiment in 1974.[38]

All this is to suggest that public support for the Presidency may be robust enough not to be permanently damaged by the actions of one man. Rather, in order for a complete collapse to occur, the public must have profoundly negative reactions toward a series of incumbent presidents. This does not mean that Watergate has left no scars, however. If confidence and trust in the Presidency is restored, it may nevertheless prove to be a more fragile support than previously and thus susceptible to erosion more quickly should Jimmy Carter or his successor foster highly negative attitudes in the minds of the public.

PRESIDENTIAL EFFORTS TO INFLUENCE PUBLIC OPINION

We now shift the focus of our attention to how presidents attempt to influence public reaction to what they say and do. The necessity for them to do so is clear, first, because their reelection is contingent upon generating public approval, and second, because most of what a President wants to accomplish requires the support of other people in government. If his words and actions are perceived as commanding broad public support, they are more likely to be taken seriously.

Before a President can influence public opinion, he must first understand it. This understanding may be gained through a variety of sources, including personal contacts in and outside government and reports by the national polling organizations. In some cases, presidents have even commissioned their own polls. Kennedy, for example, put Lou Harris on his staff. And Jimmy Carter has made considerable use of Pat Caddell's polling organization. All of this information, combined with his own intuitive feel for the public, will give a President some understanding of what is on the minds of the people and what is not.

In many instances, the President does not have to seek public support for what he does because it is fairly clear that his actions will be viewed favorably. It is only necessary that the public be made aware of them—for instance, such presidential activities as a trip abroad or an announcement of a proposed tax cut. Or they may include such seemingly trivial actions as Gerald Ford's calculated effort to phone celebrities and congratulate them on their achievements or Jimmy Carter's decision to spend the night in the private home of an average American citizen. Activities of this kind are designed to enhance the presidential image and build up a reservoir of good will.

Even when a President earnestly desires public support on a given issue, he may deem it appropriate to lead by waiting, hoping that the unfolding of events

[38]Cited in Ladd, "The Polls," p. 546.

will ultimately ripen public opinion to a conclusion he has already reached. Thus, despite recommendations that the United States should enter the Second World War, Franklin Roosevelt held off until events had convinced the American people of the necessity for doing so. While this strategy had its disadvantages, he felt they were outweighed by a more fundamental consideration, namely, that a decision to go to war must have broad public support. There are times, however, when a President cannot afford to wait for public opinion to ripen, either because time will not permit or because the issue he is concerned about has not yet entered the public's consciousness. Under such circumstances, he must ascend the presidential pulpit and seek to shape public opinion by educating it. This approach was best articulated by Theodore Roosevelt when he remarked, "People used to say of me that I was an astonishingly good politician and divined what the people were going to think. This was really not an accurate way of stating the case. I did not divine how the people were going to think. I simply made up my mind what they ought to think and then did my best to get them to think it." A more recent example of this approach was President Carter's decision to go before television cameras and educate the American public to the fact that the energy crisis was genuine and not contrived, and that something had to be done about it now. His speech apparently had some impact, for according to a Gallup poll taken afterward, 54 percent of the American people agreed that the energy crisis was serious, whereas only 43 percent had thought so prior to the speech.[39]

Finally, there will also be occasions when the President must act contrary to public opinion, hoping that hindsight will bear out the wisdom of his decision. Truman faced just such a situation when he decided to fire General MacArthur, and so too did President Ford when he made the decision to pardon President Nixon. Understandably, presidents are least comfortable when faced with having to make an unpopular decision, and thus several factors will be carefully weighed before doing so: (1) Is adverse public reaction likely to have a temporary or a more lasting impact? If the former, he may decide that he can afford to ride it out. If the latter, then he may conclude that such a decision poses an unacceptable threat to his future political leverage on other matters. (2) How critical is public support to the successful implementation of his decision? Gerald Ford's decision to pardon Nixon did not in any way depend upon public support. On the contrary, its success was contingent only upon Nixon's willingness to accept it. At the same time, however, a President might well be inclined to withhold a proposal that required public cooperation—such as gasoline rationing—if it was clear that the public was violently opposed to it. (3) Finally, in deciding whether or not to act, he must also assess what he considers to be his constitutional and statutory responsibilities in a given situation, both of which may preempt the other considerations mentioned above.

[39] Cited in the *Wall Street Journal,* April 27, 1977, p. 1.

The Media as Facilitators of Presidential Influence

Whether the President attempts to generate public support through direct appeals or through the mere reporting of his activities, he must do so through the national media. As one former White House aid put it, the media are "the daily national amplifier of the presidential voice."[40] As such, they can greatly facilitate the President's ability to communicate with and influence the public.

Making News. As noted earlier, one of the ways by which the President seeks to influence the public is by making them aware of what he is doing—a relatively easy task. More than any other public official, the President is assured of constant coverage by the media because the Presidency is where the action is. Of equal importance is the fact that he has considerable leeway in determining *what* that action will be. Much of the information received by the press—both print and broadcast media—is based upon what the President and his Administration choose to release. This is especially so in the area of foreign affairs, where news sources are more limited. In addition to reporting what the White House releases, the press also covers the activities of a President, be they as trivial as a Sunday visit to church or as significant as a trip abroad. Here again, when and how a President chooses to act is to a considerable extent his to control.

Regardless of how he chooses to make news, it is clear the decision to do so is accompanied by careful planning and calculation. If it is bad news, every effort will be made to minimize its impact. Thus, it is common practice for the White House to break bad news on Fridays so that it makes Saturday's papers, which usually have the lowest readership. Or if the bad news comes not from the White House but rather from the President's critics, the Administration may try to overwhelm it by releasing a series of newsworthy announcements. Both Kennedy and Johnson, for example, planned a flurry of White House press releases whenever the Republican National Committee came to Washington to meet. Similarly, on the day that Robert Kennedy chose to deliver a speech critical of the Johnson Administration's Vietnam policies, the White House orchestrated a whole series of news stories designed to minimize the coverage given to Kennedy: (1) President Johnson called an impromptu news conference; (2) he announced that Soviet Premier Kosygin had agreed to negotiate limitations on antiballistic missiles; (3) he delivered an important civil rights speech at Howard University; and (4) he saw to it that both Secretary of State Rusk and General Westmoreland released statements critical of Kennedy's remarks.[41]

When presidential actions are likely to meet with public approval, they are usually orchestrated in such a way as to have the maximum possible impact on both the media and the public. Recognizing that people often do not feel the impact of legislation until long after it has been implemented, President Johnson decided to draw public attention to the truth-in-packaging legislation that he had

---

[40] Joseph Califano, *A Presidential Nation* (New York: W.W. Norton, 1975), p. 102.

[41] William Small, *Political Power and the Press* (New York: W.W. Norton, 1972), p. 114.

proposed and that Congress had just passed. Accordingly, he instructed one of his aids to find the "biggest and most photogenic shopping center in the country" so that he could fly there and sign the legislation into law. A suitable shopping center was finally located in Seattle, Washington. The President arrived and signed the bill, thereby producing an event that received considerable press and television coverage.[42]

Equal care went into the planning of President Nixon's historic visits to China and the Soviet Union. The decision to make the China trip in February 1972 came at a time when President Nixon's popularity was on the decline. Indeed, a Gallup poll taken in early February revealed that in a presidential race between himself and Senator Muskie, he would win by only one percentage point.[43] The Chinese government was persuaded to permit live coverage of the presidential visit. Moreover, the President's schedule was arranged so that he would arrive in Peking during prime time television hours in the U.S. Similarly, on his return, he purposely stopped over in Anchorage, Alaska, for nine hours so that he and his entourage would be arriving in Washington during prime time. Approximately 100 million Americans saw at least some portion of the forty hours of network coverage given to the China trip. Nor was it mere coincidence that all of this was happening as the President's Democratic opponents (Muskie and McGovern) were crossing swords in the New Hampshire primary. The trip to Moscow also came at a propitious time, as both Humphrey and McGovern were campaigning to win the large prize of delegates in California's winner-take-all primary. Once again, both the press and television accompanied the President; and once again, he returned to Washington during prime time, but on this occasion he proceeded directly to the Capitol and went before a joint session of Congress to report on his historic visit. The speech was carried live by all three networks. Not surprisingly, both the trips to China and the Soviet Union brought the President a needed boost in his public approval ratings.[44]

Of course, presidents cannot always be sure that what they propose to say or do will be favorably received by the various publics that comprise the population. Thus in order to avoid taking a position that could subsequently produce a strong negative reaction, they have frequently been known to send up a trial balloon, with the press acting as the vehicle for doing so. This tactic, which originated with Theodore Roosevelt, involves leaking a particular idea to one or more members of the press, who then proceed to report it as an idea rumored to be under consideration by the President. The ventilation of the idea in the press allows the President to gauge reaction to it both in and outside government. If the reaction proves favorable, then the President can go ahead and formally embrace the idea, but if the response is negative, he can disown the idea at no political cost to himself.

---

[42] Califano, *Presidential Nation,* p. 109.

[43] *Gallup Opinion Index,* March 1972, p. 5.

[44] Newton Minow, *Presidential Television* (New York: Basic Books, 1973), p. 67; Martin Nolan, "The Re-Selling of the President," *Atlantic Monthly,* November 1972, pp. 79–81.

Influencing Opinion Makers. In addition to securing the maximum media coverage of his own words and actions, a President also attempts to influence public opinion by trying to win the support of opinion-makers. While those connected with the media do not constitute the only people who influence thinking, they are surely an extremely important segment of that group. Well aware of this fact, President Kennedy embarked upon a policy known as Operation Publisher, which one journalist described as "the boldest and most successful instrument of Kennedy's press policy."[45] It entailed two-hour confidential meetings once a month with newspaper publishers from a given state. The purpose was to allow them to question Kennedy at length and also to provide him with an opportunity to make a case for his policies, in hope of gaining the publishers' editorial support. President Ford appears to have pursued a similar strategy when, during the course of his close primary contest with Ronald Reagan, he invited to the White House journalists and publishers from some of the key primary states. Carter too has repeatedly invited editors and publishers to the White House, and on occasion has used his meetings with them as a forum for making important policy statements.

This kind of presidential lobbying also takes place on a more informal level, with presidents seeking the support of those journalists with whom they enjoy a close personal relationship. Such relationships are not uncommon for politicians whose careers have brought them into close and frequent contact with the press. On one occasion when he was meeting with little success in generating congressional and public support for his economic policies, President Kennedy contacted several of his friends in the press and encouraged them to write about the problems of the economy and his plans to deal with them. As one White House correspondent recalls, ". . . In the final months of 1962 there was a mysterious outbreak of stories about the balance of payments, new ideas for reporting the budget, and the need for tax reduction and reform, and many of them were traceable back to the President."[46] In return for such favors, journalists are also likely to benefit whether it be an exclusive interview with the President, an invitation to dine with him, or early warning of a pending presidential decision.

Press Conference. Unlike his attempts to influence public opinion through the orchestration of news or by appealing to opinion makers, the modern press conference allows the President to convey his views directly to the American people. First formally instituted by Woodrow Wilson, the press conference was originally conceived of as a means by which the press could question the President on current issues facing his Administration. It was also an opportunity for the President to enunciate his views to the press. Hoover, Roosevelt, and Truman continued the practice, but during the Eisenhower Presidency a new wrinkle was introduced. Perceiving that the press conference could provide an effective

---

[45] Taken from Lewis Paper, *The Promise and the Performance* (New York: Crown, 1975), p. 253. © 1975 by Lewis J. Paper. Used by permission of Crown Publishers, Inc.

[46] Ibid., p. 254.

forum for a President to communicate with a wider audience, Eisenhower's press secretary decided to allow filming of the President's press conferences so that they could be run on television. President Kennedy introduced a further twist by deciding to hold *live* news conferences. The decision to do so was based on the fact that he had come into office with most of the press against his presidential candidacy. By going to live news conferences, he would be able to communicate his views directly to the public without having them filtered through the press. Although President Nixon held them infrequently, his news conferences were also televised live, and he took the additional step of moving them to prime time. President Ford continued the practice. President Carter, on the other hand, has held his televised meetings with the press during the morning and afternoon as well as the evening.

The press conference has been viewed as the only means by which the President is formally held accountable for his actions between elections. While that is true, nevertheless, it is still the case that a President risks little by participating. That he holds most of the cards in this confrontation was confirmed by a veteran member of the White House press corps in his assessment of the role of reporters during the Kennedy press conference: "[Reporters] became spear-carriers in a great televised opera. We were props in a show, in a performance. Kennedy mastered the art of this performance early, and he used it with great effectiveness."[47] Even President Ford, who was hardly the equal of Kennedy in speaking ability, was able to use the forum of the press conference to good advantage. Indeed, a study of his news conferences commissioned by the National News Council concluded that they remained largely the "plaything" of the President.[48]

There are several reasons why the President enjoys a decided advantage in this formalized confrontation with the press. In the first place, the initiative for calling a press conference rests solely with the President. Lyndon Johnson's press secretary made this point quite bluntly: "It is the prerogative of the President to decide how he's going to make himself available to the press and how and when he makes certain information known to the press. It's to serve the convenience of the president, not the convenience of the press that presidential press conferences are held."[49]

The frequency of press conferences has varied widely among presidents. Woodrow Wilson stopped having them altogether once the United States became involved in the First World War. Franklin Roosevelt held more than any President in our history, averaging two a week for a total of 1,011 during his presidency. Richard Nixon, on the other hand, held only 37 during the entire time he was in office, and at one point even went a full nineteen weeks without holding

---

[47]Ibid., pp. 323, 324.

[48]Newton Minow and Lee Mitchell, "Incumbent Television: A Case of Indecent Exposure," *The Annals* 425 (May 1976), 77.

[49]Small, *Political Power*, p. 185.

one. President Carter committed himself to holding a press conference at least once every two weeks.

Furthermore, the format of the news conference is also within the President's control. Although the senior Associated Press correspondent is accorded the privilege of ending a news conference with the traditional "Thank you, Mr. President," the fact of the matter is that the President may, if he chooses, terminate it any time he wants. He also determines the questioning procedure. Herbert Hoover, for example, required that all questions be submitted in advance; he permitted no follow-up questions, answered only those he wished to, and even forbade the press from reporting those questions he refused to answer. While no President since Hoover has required the submission of questions in advance, only Roosevelt, Truman, Ford and Carter have allowed follow-up questions. And no President has ever surrendered his right to decide which reporters he will call upon to ask a question.

It should be noted that although the news conference is characterized by spontaneous questions, the President has a good deal more control over the agenda than it appears. He usually begins the conference with an opening statement, which frequently influences the subsequent focus of the questioning. Moreover, it is common practice for the President's press secretary to plant certain questions with friendly reporters to insure that the President will have an opportunity to address the issues that concern him. Most important, he does not come before the press unprepared. On the contrary, he is briefed by his aids on likely questions and appropriate answers. According to Eisenhower's press secretary, James Hagerty, the President and his staff are able to anticipate about 90 percent of the questions that will be asked.[50] Add to this the fact that the President alone decides who will get to ask a question, thus allowing him to avoid calling upon reporters known to be antagonistic to his Administration. (Gerald Ford, for example, committed to memory a set of photographs of reporters classified as "unfriendly.") If the President gets an embarrassing question, he need not respond to it, and if he does not permit follow-up questions, then there is little opportunity for a reporter to pursue an evasive answer. Finally, even in the setting of a press conference, the President benefits from the reverential attitude customarily shown toward the office. This is reflected in the tone of the questions, which more often than not is deferential rather than combative.

All of these factors, then, serve to confirm a conclusion once reached by President Nixon's Director of the Office of Communications, Herbert Klein, "The conference is the President's. This is undisputed."[51]

The Phone-In. With the Carter Presidency has come a major innovation in presidential communication with the public. For two hours one Saturday afternoon the President participated in a national phone-in which was broadcast on

[50]*New York Times,* March 11, 1977, p. A25.

[51] Small, *Political Power,* p. 185.

radio. Some seventy-six different callers got through to the President and questioned him on such wide-ranging subjects as the equal rights amendment, tax reform, consumer protection, the volunteer draft, and rising health costs, to name but a few. This format not only allowed the President to find out what issues were on the minds of the public, but it also provided him with an opportunity to express his views on these issues *directly* to the American people.

The Presidential Address. One final approach to influencing public opinion—considered by many to be the President's most effective weapon—is the television address to the American people. His appearance *live* on *all three networks* during *prime time* assures him an audience of 70 to 80 million Americans to whom he can speak on virtually *any topic* he chooses, for as *long* as he wants, and *without any editing* of his remarks. The presidential address was first used by Franklin Roosevelt in his celebrated fireside chats to the American people. On twenty different occasions during his Presidency, he went on radio both to inform the public of the problems facing the nation and to enlist their support for his programs. The advent of television has added a visual dimension to presidential communication, as well as providing him with access to a much greater audience. Sensing the opportunities here, presidents have taken great pains to insure an effective performance before the television cameras. Jimmy Carter, for example, hired a media consultant at a salary of $45,000 a year.[52] Presidents Johnson and Ford did likewise.

All of our recent presidents have made use of the presidential address to the nation, with Kennedy doing so nine times; Johnson, fifteen; Nixon, thirty-two; and Ford, six.[53] Furthermore, these numbers do not even include the occasions when the networks give live and unedited coverage to presidential speeches before selected audiences, for example, the President's State of the Union Address to Congress, or Jimmy Carter's appearance before a town meeting in Clinton, Massachusetts.

What is the impact of presidential television addresses to the nation? Lou Harris has found that there is a definite "correlation between televised presidential speeches and increased public acceptance of the president's positions."[54] Following Lyndon Johnson's speech announcing his decision to order air strikes against North Vietnam in retaliation for their attacks on U.S. destroyers, public support for his Vietnam policy rose from 42 to 72 percent. During the U.S. bombing pause in 1966, 61 percent of the population favored a resumption of the bombing. But following the President's speech announcing a resumption of the bombing, public support for doing so rose to 73 percent. Richard Nixon also used the presidential address to maintain the support of the "silent majority" dur-

[52] Richard Reeves, "The Prime-Time President," *New York Times Magazine,* May 15, 1977, p. 18.

[53] Denis Rutkus, *A Report on Simultaneous Television Network Coverage of Presidential Addresses to the Nation* (Washington, D.C.: Library of Congress, 1976), Appendix, pp. i–v.

[54] Cited in Minow, *Presidential Television,* p. 19.

ing the period when his Vietnam policies were drawing strong opposition from some segments of the population. He made a total of nine addresses to the nation on Vietnam, all during prime time. One of them, timed to occur just prior to the peace moratorium in 1969, was viewed by 72 million Americans. According to one of Nixon's aids, the speech had precisely the desired impact: "Judging by the results, it was the most effective use of TV that's even been done. You had the massively accelerating peace movement. But after the speech, the balloon just fizzled."[55] Some of Nixon's Vietnam addresses were used to announce and defend dramatic policy decisions. Following his speech announcing the beginning of a phased withdrawal of American troops from Vietnam, support for his Vietnam policy rose from 49 to 67 percent. Similarly, after the speech defending his controversial decision to invade Cambodia, public support for using American troops in Cambodia rose from 7 to 50 percent.[56]

Too Much Access? The President's access to the media in general and television in particular has sparked concern in the political and journalistic communities for some time now. And President Carter's extensive use of television has done even more to focus the spotlight on this issue. In his first eight weeks in office alone, he averaged approximately one and a half hours of live coverage per week.[57] The presidential presence became even more pronounced in the spring of 1977 when the White House orchestrated a media blitz in connection with his energy program. The week of intense exposure began with an hour-long NBC special entitled "A Day in the Life of Jimmy Carter." Four days later the President gave a televised address to the nation outlining the country's energy problems. Two days later he outlined his energy program before a joint session of Congress in a speech covered live by the three television networks. And one day after that, he held a nationally televised press conference to answer questions about his energy proposals.

In the judgment of some, the President's ready access to television may serve to overwhelm and drown out the voices of opposition. In the words of one former Director of the Federal Communications Commission, "Because he can act while his adversaries can only talk, because he can make news and draw attention to himself, and because he is the only leader elected by all the people, an incumbent President always has had an edge over his opposition in persuading public opinion. Presidential television, however, has enormously increased that edge."[58] Given the absence of highly organized and disciplined parties in the Congress, the opposition party has traditionally lacked a single leader who could speak for it with one voice. All of these disadvantages have been compounded by the fact that the opposition party in Congress has not enjoyed the President's ready access to television. While their views are reported in nightly news broad-

---

[55] Paper, *Promise and Performance*, p. 208.

[56] Rutkus, *Report on Television Coverage*, p. 19.

[57] *Washington Post*, March 20, 1977, p. 1.

[58] Minow, *Presidential Television*, pp. 10, 11.

casts, they have experienced considerable difficulty in acquiring television time to address the public the way a President can. For example, from January 1966 up until October 1975, presidents have requested air time from the television networks forty-five times and were given it forty-four. In contrast, the Democratic leadership in Congress requested air time on seven occasions during the Nixon and Ford presidencies and were granted it only three times.[59] Even when the time has been granted, the opposition party in Congress has not always been given prime time; nor has it received coverage by all three networks. In 1977, for example, Republican minority leaders in the House and Senate requested and were granted air time to respond to Carter's media blitz for his energy program. Their impact was severely hampered by several factors, however. First, they were granted the time by only one network (ABC); second, they were allowed only one-half hour on a Friday evening from 10:30 to 11:00 P.M.; third, they were not speaking to the viewing audience directly but were being interviewed by an ABC correspondent.

Come election time, the opposition party is especially disadvantaged, for the President can use his office to gain media coverage in ways that cannot be equalled by his opponents. To be sure, there is the "equal-time" regulation, which states that if a radio or television station permits the use of its air time to one candidate for elective office, it must grant all other candidates for the same office an equal opportunity to be heard. This regulation applies, however, only when the individual using air time has already announced as a candidate. Thus none of an incumbent President's television appearances are subject to a challenge for equal time until he announces that he is a candidate for reelection. Furthermore, the equal-time provision applies only to candidates for the same position. Accordingly, television appearances by a president/candidate before nominating conventions have been held do not necessitate giving equal time to candidates seeking the presidential nomination in the opposition party. Finally, the FCC has ruled that when an announced candidate is appearing on television in what is judged to be a bona fide news event, his opponent cannot make a valid claim for equal time. With specific reference to television appearances by a president/candidate, the FCC has ruled that his national addresses and news conferences fall under the classification of bona fide news events and thus are exempt from claims for equal time.

Finally, it should be noted that the President benefits from a form of media exposure that does not even involve his direct participation. This exposure comes by way of various media materials put out by the government. A report of the Office of Telecommunications Policy found that in 1972 alone government departments spent over $275 million "to produce radio, television and other media materials, much of it supportive of the incumbent administration."[60] Needless to say, the opposition party lacks the resources—financial and otherwise—to gain media exposure of this kind.

[59] *New York Times,* January 18, 1976, p. 43.

[60] Cited in Minow and Mitchell, *Incumbent Television,* p. 78.

The networks have become sensitive to the concerns that have been voiced over the President's access to television, especially his ability to command the air waves to address the American public directly, on any matter he chooses, and without any editing of his remarks. In order to avoid giving the President a totally unchecked forum for the expression of his ideas, networks have for some time now provided analyses of presidential speeches following their delivery. Some would argue that the networks should go further and make a more rigorous determination as to the news value of a given presidential address. Where it lacks such value, live coverage by all three networks should not be given.[61] In actual fact, the practice of always acceding to presidential requests for television time has been followed only since 1966. From January 1964 through September 1965, for example, President Johnson requested television time on eight different occasions but was granted it only three times: "That is, at least one network declined to televise the message simultaneously with other networks or decided against any form of special news coverage."[62] Yet for a third party to decide when the President can communicate with the electorate is itself an unsettling prospect. Moreover, it is difficult to conceive of any presidential address as not being newsworthy, a conclusion the networks have also reached:

> . . . it has become the routine practice of the networks to make television airtime available to a President when he requests it. Statements of network spokesmen suggest two bases for this practice: first, a presumption by the networks that any given Presidential address prepared solely for television almost surely will prove to be sufficiently newsworthy to justify preemption of regular network programming; second, a complementary premise that a Presidential address, regardless of its substance, has a unique inherent news value because of the importance of the Presidential office.[63]

Not only is it inappropriate to contemplate restricting the President's access to television, but there is reason to believe that his ability to command the air waves is not all that alarming. In the first place, presidential television must be used sparingly or else it is likely to lose its chance of having any impact. Franklin Roosevelt was keenly aware of this problem when he observed that "people tire of seeing the same name day after day in the important headlines of the papers, and the same voice night after night over the radio. Individual psychology cannot, because of human weakness, be attuned for long periods of time to constant repetition of the highest note in the scale."[64] President Carter's press secretary was sensitive to this problem during the media blitz on energy: "It's a calculated risk. It's an awful lot of exposure."[65]

[61] See, for example, Rutkus, *Report on Television Coverage.*

[62] Ibid., p. 7.

[63] Ibid., p. 1.

[64] Paper, *Promise and Performance*, p. 234.

[65] *Washington Post,* April 17, 1977, p. A5.

Furthermore, it is not at all clear that television per se is responsible for the dramatic increases in public support for the President's position after some of his speeches. One might well argue that such increases had more to do with the nature of his remarks than with the medium through which he chose to make them. It is not altogether surprising, for example, that approval for President Johnson's Vietnam policies should have risen from 42 percent to 72 percent after he announced his decision to bomb North Vietnam in retaliation for its attacks on American destroyers. Americans have traditionally rallied around presidents at such times. Nor is it especially unusual that support for Richard Nixon's Vietnam policy should have increased after his address announcing the start of American troop withdrawals from Vietnam. Americans were eager to extricate themselves from a war they had grown tired of.

Finally, it should be noted that presidential television has not succeeded in reversing the overall decline that occurs in a President's popularity as he moves through office. Indeed, if the case of Richard Nixon is any indication, presidential television speeches would not appear to have a marked effect upon a President's popularity one way or the other. Nixon made thirty-two television speeches while in office, a figure that far exceeds that of any other President. An examination of Gallup polls taken prior to and following each of his speeches reveals that his popularity went up seventeen times and declined nine times.[66] His average increase was 4.5 points, with his single largest gain registering at 17 points and his single smallest at 1 point. The extraordinary 17-point gain came after his speech announcing the start of American troop withdrawals from Vietnam. If this speech is excluded from the calculations, then his average increase in only 3.7 points. As already stated, there were nine occasions where his approval rating went down. The average decrease was 2.7 points, with the single largest decline registering at 6 points and the single smallest at 1 point. Finally, there were 6 different occasions where two speeches intervened between polls. While one might expect this additional television exposure to give an even greater boost to his popularity, the evidence does not bear this out. In four of these six instances, his popularity went up, but only by an average of 4 points. On the other two occasions, his popularity declined, in one case by 2 points, and in the other, by 4 points.

Two words of caution are in order regarding this data, however. First, the increase or decrease in Nixon's popularity may have been due to other factors besides his television speeches. Second, the evidence presented here does not tell us what would have happened to his popularity had he not given the speeches. It might be argued, for example, that had it not been for the speeches, the increases in his public approval ratings would have been even smaller and the decreases even larger. The fact remains, however, that Nixon's television speeches were not always accompanied by an increase in his popularity. Moreover, even when they were, such increases could hardly be considered substantial.

---

[66] These two figures do not add up to the total of thirty-two speeches because there were six occasions where two speeches intervened between polls.

The Media as Complicators of Presidential Influence

If the media can facilitate a President's efforts to mobilize public opinion behind him, it is equally clear that they can also complicate these efforts. No one is more aware of this than the man in the White House. Indeed, nearly every President in our history has at one time or another vented his spleen against those who reported on his actions and words. So enraged was George Washington by his press critics that he included an attack upon them in the first draft of his Farewell Address, noting that their publications "have teemed with all the Invective that disappointment, ignorance of the facts, and malicious falsehood could invent to misrepresent my politics and affections; to wound my reputation and feeling; and to weaken, if not entirely destroy the confidence you have pleased to repose in me."[67] Only at the insistence of Alexander Hamilton did he finally decide to eliminate these remarks from the final draft of his address. President John Adams became so disgruntled with press coverage of his own Administration that he proposed the establishment of a newspaper that would specifically reflect the views of the government. Even the great libertarian, Thomas Jefferson, underwent a change of heart toward the press. Prior to becoming President he had remarked that "were it left to me to decide whether we should have a government without newspapers, or newspapers without a government, I should not hesitate a moment to prefer the latter." Once in the Presidency, however, he wrote a friend, "even the least informed of the people have learned that nothing in a newspaper is to be believed . . . and I therefore have long thought that a few prosecutions of the most prominent offenders would have a wholesome effect."[68]

Nor has presidential antipathy toward the press been confined to earlier presidents who served at a time when the press was admittedly less responsible than it is today. Woodrow Wilson warned a friend, "Do not believe anything you read in the newspapers. If you read the papers I see, they are utterly untrustworthy. . . . Their lying is shameless and colossal."[69] Having always suspected that the eastern media could not abide a southerner as President, Lyndon Johnson bemoaned the fact that "they warp everything I do, they lie about me and about what I do, they don't know the meaning of truth. They are liars and cheats."[70] Among recent presidents, however, none felt a greater hostility toward the press than did Richard Nixon. It was summed up in one very brief warning to one of his aids: "Remember—the press is the enemy." As a symbolic indication of his low esteem for the press, he initially decided against even assigning the title of "press secretary" to anyone on his staff. While Ron Ziegler prevailed upon the President to grant him the title, the President signalled the low status of the position in another way. When he made his first trip to Europe,

[67]Cited in Small, *Political Power,* p. 58.

[68]Cited in Peter Forbath and Carey Winfrey, *The Adversaries: The President and the Press* (Cleveland: Regal Books/King's Court Communications, 1974), p. 5.

[69]Small, *Political Power,* p. 56.

[70]Ibid., p. 109.

the press secretary was put at the bottom of the protocol list. Ultimately, that too changed, not because Nixon altered his views of the press but because Ziegler became a close adviser to him.[71]

An Adversary Relationship. Although some presidents have enjoyed more cordial relations with the press than others, the relationship remains an adversary one. This is so because the interests of the President and the press are fundamentally in conflict. For his part, the President wishes to present the most favorable possible image of himself and his administration to the public. Doing so requires the orchestration of information and events. In the words of one seasoned Washington columnist, "Any good politician worth his salt will know that he must try to manage the news. An activist President will try to manage the news on the broadest scale of any politician, because his purposes are the largest."[72] Every effort will be made to insure that good news will have maximum impact. Bad news will in some cases be repressed or else minimized. Needless to say, attempts to manage the news do not sit well with the press. Commenting on such efforts by the Kennedy Administration, one noted columnist for the *New York Times* pointed out that its management of the news "was enforced more cynically and boldly than by any previous administration in a period when the United States was not at war."[73] This view was confirmed in a *Newsweek* poll of forty-three top Washington correspondents, forty of whom felt that the Kennedy Administration had attempted to manage the news to a greater extent than any previous one.[74] When Lyndon Johnson became President, the phrase "news management" gave way to a new and more sinister characterization—the "credibility gap." The latter term grew out of such trivial incidents as Johnson's misleading statements about the heroics of his ancestors as well as more important ones dealing with our involvement in the Dominican Republic and Vietnam.[75]

The basic interests of the press are decidedly different from the President's. While his interests require that he put the best possible face on what he says and does, the press feels it has a responsibility to report the negative as well as the positive about the President and his administration; where he has failed as well as succeeded; where he has been inconsistent as well as consistent; when he has been less than candid as well as when he has boldly stated the facts. Similarly, while the White House seeks to control the flow of news so that the timing of an announcement will have maximum or minimum impact, as the case may be, press competition requires that newspapers and television networks report significant developments as soon as they can find out about them. Acquiring

[71] Willian Safire, *Before the Fall* (Garden City, N.Y.: Doubleday, 1975), pp. 70, 351. Copyright © 1975 by William Safire. Used by permission by permission of Doubleday & Company, Inc.

[72] David Broder, "The Presidency and the Press," in Charles Dunn, ed., *The Future of the American Presidency* (Morristown, N.J.: General Learning Press, 1975), p. 264.

[73] Arthur Krock, "Mr. Kennedy's Management of the News," *Fortune,* March 1963, p. 82.

[74] Paper, *Promise and Performance,* p. 327.

[75] David Wise, *The Politics of Lying* (New York: Vintage Books, 1973), pp. 27–75.

information the President does not want released may come from extensive detective work. Or a story may be leaked to some members of the press by a government official who is opposed to a policy currently under consideration by the President. Still another way for the press to pry information from the President is to report his intention not to make it public. Thus when the press learned that President Ford did not intend to make public the Rockefeller Commission Report on the Central Intelligence Agency, it reported this fact. Reaction in Congress was so averse to keeping the report secret that the President was compelled to release it.

If the press reacts negatively to presidential efforts at managing the news, it is equally clear that presidents have been angered by attempts by the press to frustrate these efforts. Given their egos as well as the daily pressures of the office, it is not surprising that presidents have responded to negative or premature reporting as unfair. Nor have they always confined themselves to merely saying so. Reporters who write "unfriendly" stories about the administration may suddenly find their access to White House sources cut off. Theodore Roosevelt even went so far as to ban some reporters from the White House altogether. Occasionally, presidential reaction becomes even more heavy-handed. President Kennedy sought to have a *New York Times* reporter reassigned to another position because his stories from Vietnam were highly critical of administration policies there. In some cases, Kennedy even succeeded in squelching stories he thought would be damaging. He persuaded the *New York Times* not to print a story about U.S. intentions to invade Cuba. Similarly, in an effort to keep from further alienating the business community following his confrontation with the steel companies, he managed to persuade CBS not to air interviews with two members of his administration who were highly critical of business.[76] The press has since become less amenable to such requests, however, as evidenced by Jimmy Carter's unsuccessful attempt to dissuade the *Washington Post* from reporting a story alleging that foreign officials were being secretly paid by the CIA.

Frustrated by leaks, recent presidents from Kennedy on have even gone so far as to order taps placed on the phones of certain reporters in order to determine their sources within the government. But the most concerted effort by an administration to intimidate the press came during the Nixon Presidency. *Washington Post* columnist Joseph Kraft had his phone tapped, not because he was receiving leaked information, but because he was writing columns critical of the Nixon Administration. CBS correspondent Daniel Schorr also felt the force of government intimidation by being subjected to an FBI investigation into his personal life, although he may not have been the first to face this kind of pressure.[77] Columnists Joseph and Steward Alsop claim to have been subject to the

---

[76] Paper, *Promise and Performance*, pp. 254, 255.

[77] Theodore White, *Breach of Faith* (New York: Atheneum, 1975), pp. 121, 122.

same form of harassment during the Eisenhower Administration.[78] Perhaps the most notable difference between the Nixon Administration and its predecessors with respect to influencing press coverage was its willingness to use the government's regulatory power in an effort to extract more favorable press treatment. In an Indianapolis speech, Nixon's Director of Telecommunications warned that local "Station managers and network officials who fail to act to correct imbalance or consistent bias in the networks—or who acquiesce by silence—can only be considered willing participants, to be held fully accountable . . . at license renewal time."[79] The implication was clear.

The Public Broadcasting System (PBS), which is financed in part by the federal government, also became a target because of its allegedly liberal programming. Its director for program activities noted the Nixon Administration's feeling that "until public broadcasting shows signs of becoming what this administration wants it to be, this administration will oppose permanent financing."[80] The White House also attempted to terminate certain of the PBS programs, but most were saved through private funding. Finally, the government's regulatory power was even used to intimidate a newspaper, notably, the *Washington Post.* In an effort to retaliate for the newspaper's repeated stories about the Watergate scandals, the Administration let it be known that it might not renew the license of a Florida television station owned by the *Post.*

A President's efforts to influence the tone of press coverage meets with some success simply because he has something the press wants, namely, information about what he is thinking and doing. And since the networks and newspapers operate in a competitive environment, they are not unaware of the advantage they enjoy when the White House favors them with an inside scoop. But this carrot can only be used sparingly, and even then, it fails as often as it succeeds. However, when a President's attempt to influence reporting moves beyond his legitimate prerogative to grant and deny access to himself and his staff and escalates instead to using the power of government to intimidate, the payoff is likely to be a negative one. Such efforts will themselves be made a public issue by the press, which quite rightly sees them as a threat to its independence.

Elevating Public Expectations. Reporting the negative as well as the positive is not the only way by which the media complicate the President's attempt to maintain a favorable impression with the public. Ironically, they also do so by glorifying the office and—at least initially—the man who occupies it.

While not alone in this practice, the journalistic community has traditionally celebrated the presidential office, pointing to it as *the* source of political and

---

[78] Michael Grossman and Francis Rourke, "The Media and the Presidency: An Exchange Analysis," *Political Science Quarterly,* 91 (Fall 1976), 459.

[79] Cited in Wise, *Politics of Lying,* p. 403.

[80] Cited in Walter Mondale, *The Accountability of Power* (New York: David McKay, 1975), p. 205.

moral leadership. If significant changes are to be made, if we are to be led out of dark times, it is the Presidency that will make it all possible. Even more important, there is also a tendency for the media to paint a highly personalized and favorable image of the newly elected President. Articles appear extolling certain aspects of his character, and even the most trivial of his habits and tastes are somehow made to appear admirable. In a column written shortly after Gerald Ford assumed office, Joe McGinniss took note of this phenomenon with some dismay:

> At this stage of Gerald Ford's Presidency there is only one impression we are capable of receiving, and, unfortunately—both for him and for us—it is unrealistic.
>
> Consider what we know of him: he dances, he prays, he walks onto his front lawn in his bathrobe to get his morning paper. He makes his own breakfast, he swims, he holds meetings, he sleeps in the same bed as his wife.
>
> Hardly the stuff of which legends are made. Yet, since his elevation, each of these acts has been perceived as a source of hope and inspiration for the nation.
>
> And consider, for a moment, his words: Honesty is the best policy, practice the Golden Rule, God will provide. A month ago these were harmless platitudes, greeted with snickers and yawns, of a decent but docile Vice President. Now they are moving, simple, eloquent articulations of concepts so noble as to reduce brave columnists to tears.
>
> It does not matter, for now, who Ford is or what Ford does. He is the President, and simply by not having disgraced himself, or the office, he has become the recipient not only of the adulation and reverence which traditionally have been awarded the President; but also of that potent extra measure which had been repressed during the Nixon reign.[81]

Of course, the media are simply reflecting as well as responding to the national desire to rally behind the newly elected leader. But there is a problem inherent in all of this. During the euphoria that accompanies and immediately follows the installation of a new President, expectations about him and what he can do are elevated beyond what is attainable. Then when presidential action falls short of these expectations—as inevitably it must—the public experiences a sense of disillusionment with the President. In the words of McGinniss, "In selling ourselves an ideal President who does not and never can exist, we are once again repeating the destructive process of buildup and letdown that we have suffered through so often in the recent past."[82] Presidents quite naturally enjoy being the beneficiaries of such adulation—indeed they often encourage it—but they would do well to realize that these unrealistic appraisals may only serve to make

---

[81]*New York Times,* September 8, 1974, p. E19. © 1974 by The New York Times Company. Reprinted by permission.

[82]Ibid.

their relations with the public more difficult over the long run. It should be noted that some members of the media have taken note of their tendency to oversell an incoming President, but if the initial media treatment of Jimmy Carter was any indication, it would have to be said that such warnings have largely gone unheeded.

Media Bias. In the judgment of some, the President's ability to mobilize public opinion behind his policies is complicated by an additional factor—media bias. The charge is not a novel one. Indeed, for years those on the right have accused the media of a liberal bias, while those on the left have been just as convinced that the media suffered from a decidedly conservative bias. Beginning in the late sixties, however, the issue achieved heightened visibility because the White House entered the debate. In essence, the Nixon Administration was contending that the television networks were dominated by individuals whose liberal ideology caused them to be openly hostile to the more conservative policies of the President and, for that matter, hostile to the values of a majority of Americans as well. One of President Nixon's close aids stated the problem this way:

> . . . an incumbent elite with an ideological slant unshared by the nation's majority has acquired absolute control of the most powerful medium of communication known to man. And that elite is using that media monopoly to discredit those with whom it disagrees, and to advance its own ideological objectives—and it is defending that monopoly by beating its several critics over the head with the stick of the First Amendment.
>
> Within the media, many will readily concede this bias and retort, "What else is new?" What is new is not the existence of the liberal bias. What is new, in the last decade, is the wedding of that bias to unprecedented power. Men who are taking an increasingly adversary stance toward the social and political values, mores, and traditions of the majority of Americans have also achieved monopoly control of the medium of communication upon which 60% of these Americans depend as the primary source of news and information about their government and society. And these men are using that monopoly position to persuade the nation to share their distrust of and hostility toward the elected government.[83]

Vice President Agnew acted as the spear carrier for the Administration on this issue as he took after the networks with such colorful phrases as the "supersensitive, self-annointed, supercilious electronic barons of opinion." Nor was the press entirely spared. Certain columnists for the *New York Times, Washington Post,* and national weekly magazines were chastised by the Vice President for their "wild, hot rhetoric" and "irresponsibility and thoughtlessness."[84]

---

[83] Patrick Buchanan, *The New Majority* (Philadelphia: Girard Bank, 1973), pp. 18, 20, 21.
[84] Cited in Small, *Political Power*, p. 138.

While Agnew's remarks at times bordered on demagoguery, it is important to note that his concerns were shared by certain respected members of the journalistic and scholarly communities. Some, for example, acknowledge, and are concerned by, the increasing ideological homogeneity of the Washington press corps. Moreover, they attribute this development to the fact that more and more of the reporters covering Washington are middle- and upper-class individuals who have been educated at our elite institutions. Such institutions, it is argued, promote an idealistic liberalism.[85] Robert Novak, a syndicated columnist, even went so far as to specify some of the liberal attitudes that underlie the bias of the Washington press corps:

1. The immoral war in Vietnam was the result of our obsession with anti-communism.
2. The military-industrial complex is not to be trusted, and defense spending should be cut.
3. We should vigorously enforce pollution standards even at the risk of unemployment.
4. Integration of the races must be made a reality even if it means forced busing.
5. The forces of repression under the Nixon Administration threatened our liberties.
6. National priorities must be reordered to bring about a massive infusion of funds into our cities for "social rebuilding purposes."
7. There must be a redistribution of wealth through reform of both the tax structure and fiscal policy.[86]

Daniel Patrick Moynihan concurs with the charge that the national press is increasingly dominated by individuals of a liberal persuasion, but he also takes note of certain developments in the journalistic community that are likely to disadvantage *any* President. These include:

1. The fact that an increasing number of journalists have taken an indiscriminately hostile view toward power, which has led them to be hypercritical of our institutions in general, and the Presidency in particular
2. A tendency for members of the press to foster unrealistic expectations about what the Presidency can achieve
3. Increased reliance by members of the press upon "clandestine" sources

---

[85] Ithiel De Sola Pool, "Government and the Media," *American Political Science Review* 70 (December 1976), 1236. See also George Will, ed., *Press, Politics and Popular Government* (Washington, D.C.: American Enterprise Institute, 1972); Max Kampelman, "Congress, the Media and the President," in Harvey Mansfield, ed., *Congress Against the President* (New York: Academy of Political Science, 1975), pp. 85–98.

[86] Adapted from Robert Novak, "The New Journalism," in Harry Clor, ed., *The Mass Media and Modern Democracy*, pp. 3, 4. © The Public Affairs Conference Center. Reprinted by permission of Rand McNally College Publishing Company.

of information within a bureaucracy that frequently has interests antagonistic to those of the President

4. A reluctance on the part of the press to correct its errors in reporting
5. Objectively reporting even the most outrageous of statements and happenings and thereby according them a degree of legitimacy

According to Moynihan, all of these factors taken together "have been working to reverse the old balance of power between the Presidency and the press. It is the thesis here that, if this imbalance should tip too far in the direction of the press, our capacity for effective democratic government will be seriously and dangerously weakened."[87]

An assessment of the validity of these criticisms is hampered by the paucity of hard data. However, there have been some attempts to assess the charge that the television networks were biased against the Nixon Administration. In her much discussed book *The News Twisters,* Edith Efron examined the news coverage given to Humphrey and Nixon by all three networks during the 1968 election campaign. Her conclusion was that the news departments of all three networks exhibited a flagrant bias against candidate Nixon.[88] Yet subsequent studies have cast some doubt upon the validity of her conclusion. CBS commissioned International Research Associates to undertake a similar study of its news coverage during the 1968 campaign. These results showed that 63 percent of the news stories mentioned Nixon and 61 percent mentioned Humphrey. With respect to favorable or unfavorable treatment in these stories, it was found that 19 percent of the stories were favorable to Nixon, 19 percent were unfavorable, and the remaining 62 percent were neutral. For Humphrey, on the other hand, 26 percent of the stories were judged favorable, 17 percent unfavorable, and the rest neutral.[89] While these results support Efron's general conclusion, they nevertheless show considerably less bias against Nixon than she found.

In still another study made of CBS coverage during the 1968 election campaign, researchers used the very same transcripts of the CBS evening news that Efron did. But whereas Efron had examined only the commentary about the candidates, these researchers also included the amount of time that the candidates themselves spoke before the cameras during news broadcasts. As Table 5-8 indicates, only with respect to *amount* of coverage did one candidate enjoy a substantial advantage over the other, with Humphrey getting 37.5 percent of the coverage and Nixon 28.6 percent. Converted into time, this amounted to an advantage for Humphrey of about three minutes per week. As for type of coverage, however, there was scarcely any difference between the two candidates (see Table 5-8).

[87] Daniel Moynihan, "The President and the Press," *Coping: On the Practice of Government* (New York: Random House, Inc., 1973).

[88] Edith Efron, *The News Twisters* (Los Angeles: Nash Publishing, 1971), p. 47.

[89] These figures cited in De Sola Pool, "Government and the Media," pp. 1236, 1237.

TABLE 5-8. CBS TREATMENT OF THE 1968 PRESIDENTIAL CANDIDATES

	Nixon	Humphrey	Other
Amount of coverage	28.6	37.5	33.9
Type of coverage			
Favorable	24.5	23.5	17.8
Neutral	17.7	16.8	16.9
Unfavorable	11.7	11.0	15.1
Mixed	8.8	9.0	8.6
Candidate before camera	37.3	39.7	41.6
Total	100.0	100.0	100.0

SOURCE: Adapted from Robert Stevenson et al., "Untwisting the News Twisters: A Replication of Efron's Study," *Journalism Quarterly,* 50 (Summer 1973), 217, 218.

Perhaps the most extensive investigation made of network news bias was Richard Hofstetter's study of the coverage given to Nixon and McGovern during the 1972 campaign. While the studies mentioned above examined coverage only over a seven-week period, Hofstetter's study covered approximately twelve weeks of the campaign. Moreover, like Efron, he analyzed the coverage of all three television networks. His findings, however, do not support Efron's conclusion of a bias against Nixon. On the contrary, he concludes that, "It is not possible to make a persuasive case that partisan political bias was present in network television coverage of the 1972 presidential election campaign. Indeed, based on the evidence in this study, the objective reader would be forced to conclude that partisan bias was not a significant factor in news coverage."[90]

All of these studies, of course, have focused exclusively upon the question of bias in a presidential election campaign. While taken as a whole, they do not support the claim that the television networks showed a *pronounced and systematic* bias against Richard Nixon, it might be argued that these studies still tell us nothing about the presence of bias *after* the election. Yet if the thesis of network bias is correct, it presumably ought to manifest itself during any given period of time. Indeed, one would expect such a bias to be especially pronounced during a presidential election campaign, given its crucial importance.

What of the charge that the *press* is increasingly dominated by those of a liberal persuasion? Such noted publications as the *New York Times, Washington Post, Time,* and *Newsweek* have been cited as constituting the liberal axis of the press. While they have often espoused the liberal side on issues, it would be an oversimplification to say that these publications are characterized by a uniformity of positions. In 1972, for example, the *New York Times* endorsed George McGovern for President while *Time* magazine supported President Nixon. Furthermore, the liberal persuasion does not by any means enjoy a monopoly on

[90] Richard Hofstetter, *Bias in the News* (Columbus, Ohio: Ohio State University Press, 1976), p. 187.

national publications. Publications such as the *Washington Star, Wall Street Journal, Daily News,* and *U.S. News and World Report* are generally considered to have a moderate-to-conservative orientation, and all enjoy a high circulation. Indeed, the *Daily News* has the highest readership of any newspaper in the country. While the *New York Times* and *Washington Post* are quite rightly considered to have considerable influence in governmental circles, it must be remembered that taken together their circulation still constitutes less than 1 percent of the population. The remaining readership is spread out among approximately 1,700 daily newspapers.[91] Moreover, of those newspapers with a policy of endorsing presidential candidates, an overwhelming majority have traditionally supported Republicans over Democrats. In 1976, for example, *Editor and Publisher* found that in a survey of 38 percent of the daily newspapers, 411 (30 million combined circulation) endorsed President Ford. Carter, however, was endorsed by only 30 dailies with a combined circulation of 7.6 million.[92] Finally, it should be noted that most of the nation's daily newspapers get a large portion of their news from the Associated Press and United Press International news services. And as one former presidential press secretary has pointed out, neither of these news organizations can be neatly classified into ideological categories:

> The largest audience remains, as it has for decades, with the Associated Press and United Press International—about 170 editorial employees who are not elitist by any definition other than competence. Neither are they liberal nor conservative. The *New York Times* and the *Washington Post* may dominate academic and governmental discussion, but the stories that move people in the mass usually bear the logotypes AP and UPI. Furthermore, the impact of these two wire services is far greater than the quality of the stories they write and distribute. In a very direct manner, they are more responsible than any other organization or group for establishing the *pattern* of daily news coverage not only for newspapers but for the television industry.[93]

In summary, biases do indeed exist within the nation's press. The First Amendment was not drafted in the belief that newspapers would be objective. Indeed, the purpose of the amendment was in part designed to protect the right of newspapers not to be so. Having acknowledged the existence of bias, however, it is far less clear that it decidedly disadvantages a President of one ideological persuasion over another.

---

[91] Philip Geyelin and Douglass Cater, *American Media: Adequate or Not?* (Washington, D.C.: American Enterprise Institute, 1970), p. 5.

[92] Cited in *Time,* November 1976, p. 13.

[93] George Reedy, "Why Does Nobody Love the Press?" in Harry Clor, ed., *The Mass Media and Modern Democracy* (Chicago: Rand McNally College, 1974), p. 29.

The Future of the President's Relationship with the Press

If it has yet to be proven that the media exhibit a systematic bias against any particular President, nevertheless, there is reason to believe that the relationship between presidents and the press may become even more contentious. Several factors may help to explain why this might be so.

For one thing, there has developed within the press what one noted columnist sees as a shift in attitude from "simple credulity to informed skepticism" about what the government says.[94] Several journalists mark the beginning of this change with the U-2 plane incident in May 1960. A high-altitude aircraft piloted by Francis Gary Powers was shot down over the Soviet Union while gathering intelligence information. The government initially issued a statement saying that the U-2 was probably a weather research plane. But after it was learned that the Russians had captured the plane intact, the Eisenhower Administration acknowledged that it was a spy plane, but also added that the flight had been undertaken without authorization from Washington. This statement also proved to be false, for President Eisenhower had approved both the U-2 program itself and the schedule for its flights over the Soviet Union. The President ultimately reversed his position and acknowledged that the spying flights had been authorized and indeed would continue.[95] The seed of skepticism planted by this incident continued to be nurtured by the lack of candor shown by subsequent presidents in dealing with such matters as the Bay of Pigs invasion, the sending of troops to the Dominican Republic, and the Vietnam War. Consequently, as Max Frankel has noted, the press is increasingly inclined to treat "virtually every official utterance as a carefully contrived rendering that needs to be examined for the missing word or phrase, the sly use of statistics, the slippery syntax or semantics."[96] Needless to say, the Watergate scandals did not do anything to diminish this skepticism.

Other developments related to media organization and personnel may also serve to increase the instability in the President's relationship with the press. The White House is being covered more and more by large news organizations; that is, reporters working for the three television networks, large national newspapers, and the weekly news magazines. Whereas smaller papers—because of limited resources—must rely primarily on what the White House and the wire services provide them, the larger news organizations have the resources to monitor and investigate government activities in greater depth. The *Washington Post,* for instance, is staffed with a considerable number of researchers and librarians, in

---

[94]Max Frankel, "The Press and the President," appearing under "Letters from Readers," *Commentary,* July 1971, p. 16.

[95]Wise, *Politics of Lying,* pp. 47–50.

[96]Frankel, "Press and the President," p. 16.

addition to reporters. The quality of the Washington press corps has also risen substantially. News organizations are not only insisting on higher educational qualifications, but they are also seeking reporters with special expertise in given policy areas. This puts them in a better position to evaluate complex policy issues independent of what the White House says about them.[97]

Finally, legislation passed by the Congress in recent years has greatly facilitated the press's ability to find out what the President and his administration are doing. Of crucial importance in this regard was passage of the Freedom of Information Act (1966). Under this act, the government records of ninety different agencies—except for medical records, security secrets, corporate trade secrets, and the like—were opened up to the public. But the procedures for gaining access to such records were so cumbersome that few attempts were made to do so. In 1975, however, Congress amended the act so as to facilitate access procedures. This action had the desired impact, for in 1975 alone, 89,000 people requested, and in most cases received, files from the departments of Justice, the Treasury, and Defense.[98] Access to Executive branch operations has also been furthered by passage of the "Government in the Sunshine" Act (1976). With certain exceptions, it required that independent agencies in the Executive branch conduct their business in *public* meetings.

Few would dispute the necessity of having a vigorous and independent press. Scanning the governmental process with a watchful eye, it plays a crucial role in drawing public attention to error, inadequacies, and abuse of power. No historical example highlights its contribution in this regard better than the scandals of Watergate. Less appreciated, but equally important, is the role the press plays in preventing some abuses from occurring in the first place. In the words of one former White House aid, "The occasions on which presidents and their staff aides have decided not to cut corners because their action might be discovered by the press are legion."[99] However, in addition to both watching for and pointing out what is wrong in government, the press also has a responsibility to identify the positive. In this connection, some have voiced the concern that for much of the national press, a healthy skepticism about government has given way to a not so healthy cynicism. Such an orientation, it is argued, fosters a climate of negativism in which it becomes increasingly "hard for government to succeed and just as hard for government to appear to have succeeded when, indeed, it has done so."[100] The expression of this concern comes not from the lunatic fringe but rather from thoughtful observers of the political scene. The press would do well to ponder it.

[97] Grossman and Rourke, "Media and the Presidency," pp. 468, 469.

[98] *New York Times,* April 10, 1977, p. E4.

[99] Califano, *Presidential Nation,* p. 102.

[100] Moynihan, "President and the Press," p. 42.

CONCLUSION

If the President's relationship with the public is more crucial to him than anything else, it is equally true that trust is the cement necessary for holding it together. By virtue of his actions, Richard Nixon caused a near total disintegration of this trust. This was his ultimate mistake.

The public has a relationship with the Presidency as well as with the President. This relationship, too, is held together by trust. Having endured over the course of our history, it is a stronger, more durable bond, and consequently not subject to erosion so easily. Thus, even though the behavior of Richard Nixon precipitated a near total erosion of confidence placed in him by the people, he did not manage to completely destroy their trust in the institution itself. But he did damage it all the same, and to this extent, he handed over a weakened institution to his immediate successor. Unfortunately, Gerald Ford's pardon of the President initially contaminated him with some of the fallout from Watergate. Yet, despite this fact, most would probably agree that Ford's conduct in office contributed toward a restoration of the public's trust in the Presidency. But it was only a beginning. The aftermath of Watergate still lingers, as evidenced in a remark by a Carter appointee: "I didn't realize how debased the currency had gotten. You have to spend so much time saying "but I really mean it.' "[101] That President Carter must give top priority to this problem was made clear in a secret memo written by none other than his chief public-opinion analyst, Pat Caddell: "Carter needs to gain personal credibility and restore the trust of the people. If he can do this, he may convince them to give him a chance, to give him the time to solve some of the long-term problems of the country. If we don't buy the time quickly, given the mood today, the American people may turn on us before we ever get off the mark."[102] There was every indication that Carter had taken this advice to heart. Witness the fireside chat, efforts to remove some of the pomp from the office, the phone-in, the appearance before a local town meeting, the overnight visit in the home of an average American family, the invitation to the public to write him letters, and his insistence on a rigorous code of ethics for his appointees. All of these efforts were designed to demonstrate that the Presidency is both of and for the people. Moreover, nearly all of these actions constituted unprecedented presidential behavior.

Yet these efforts to inspire trust and confidence were tarnished somewhat when President Carter permitted friendship to cloud his judgment concerning the questionable banking practices of Bert Lance, Director of the Office of Management and Budget. In a Harris poll taken in October 1977, 51 percent of the American public expressed a negative reaction to the President's handling

---

[101] *Wall Street Journal,* May 5, 1977, p. 1.

[102] *New York Times,* May 7, 1977, p. E1. © 1977 by The New York Times Company. Used by permission.

of the Lance affair, and only 34 percent expressed approval.[103] While Carter's dogged defense of Lance may have been understandable in personal terms, it was nevertheless inappropriate, especially when viewed in the context of the high moral standards set by the President and the public skepticism regarding the nation's political leadership. How seriously the Lance affair impaired the President's efforts to restore trust in the Presidency is unclear. More than likely, it has not made the task any easier.

[103] *Washington Post,* October 14, 1977, p. A11.

6

Decision Making
in
the White House

THE PARTICIPANTS

The President of the United States functions in several capacities in our political system. He is a foreign policy maker, legislator, party leader, manager of the economy, protector of the peace, and Commander in Chief. In performing all of these roles he is confronted with having to make decisions. This task is a formidable one. As Eisenhower informed the incoming President Kennedy, "There are no easy matters that will ever come to you as President. If they are easy, they will be settled at a lower level."[1] Moreover, the President cannot sidestep the problems that come over his desk. This reality was conveyed very poignantly by a sign on President Truman's desk which read "The Buck Stops Here." He may act or refuse to act on a given matter, but in either case he will be making a decision; and whether the consequences be good or bad, he must ultimately accept the responsibility for that decision. Finally, the task of making presidential decisions is a formidable one because "all of the facts are rarely, if ever, available to a President at the time he must make most decisions. Those that are, often turn out to be half-facts or incorrect as they are subjected to careful analysis."[2] Lyndon Johnson demonstrated his sensitivity to this dilemma when he observed that the problem for presidents lies not so much in *doing* what is right, but rather in *knowing* what is right.

In this chapter we shall be examining where and how the President gets the information and advice he needs in order to make decisions on the critical prob-

[1] Taken from *The Promise and the Performance* by Lewis J. Paper (New York: Crown, 1975), p. 138. ©1975 by Lewis J. Paper. Used by permission of Crown Publishers, Inc.

[2] Joseph Califano, *A Presidential Nation* (New York: W.W. Norton, 1975), p. 218.

lems that come to him in the Oval Office. Four specific examples of presidential decision making will then be studied in order to determine how, in each case, the nature of the decision-making process affected the success or failure of that decision.

THE CABINET

There is no provision in the Constitution that calls for the establishment of a formal body known as the Cabinet. The term itself was coined by newspapermen during the Presidency of George Washington and was used to refer to his four department heads, which at that time were the Attorney General and the Secretaries of State, War, and the Treasury. Today the Cabinet consists of thirteen members, one of whom is the U.S. representative to the United Nations. The other twelve members are the Attorney General of the Department of Justice and the Secretaries of State, Defense, the Treasury, Commerce, the Interior, Energy, Labor, Health, Education and Welfare, Housing and Urban Development, and Transportation. The Postmaster General was formerly a member but was dropped in 1971 when the Post Office was changed from a department into an independent agency.

The President's Cabinet has in the past consisted of individuals who have built up considerable reputations based upon clearly demonstrated ability in a given field of endeavor. Accordingly, one would expect it to be a highly suitable group for the President to consult in seeking information and advice on critical problems. In actual fact, however, it has rarely been so. Andrew Jackson, for example, maintained that he could not find the "necessary standards of selflessness and candor" among his Cabinet, and consequently he turned to an informal group of personal advisers who came to be known as his Kitchen Cabinet. Abraham Lincoln showed his lack of concern for Cabinet advice when, upon deciding to issue the Emancipation Proclamation, he convened them and said, "I have gathered you together to hear what I have written down. I do not wish your advice about the main matter. That, I have determined for myself."[3]

Throughout the First World War, Woodrow Wilson declined to include the Cabinet in any major decision making, and when he did summon them together the issues discussed were, according to one Cabinet member, essentially trivial in nature: "Nothing talked of at Cabinet that would interest a nation, a family, or a child. No talk of the war."[4] Nor did Franklin Roosevelt take the Cabinet into his confidence. On the contrary, his Secretary of the Interior noted that "the cold fact is that on important matters we are seldom called upon for

---

[3] Cited in Kenneth Cole, "Should Cabinet Departments and Agencies Be More Independent?" in Charles Roberts, ed., *Has the President Too Much Power?* New York: Harper's Magazine Press, 1974), p. 126.

[4] Emmet John Hughes, *The Living Presidency* (New York: Coward, McCann & Geoghegan, 1973), p. 148. Copyright © 1973 by Emmet John Hughes. Reprinted by permission of Coward, McCann & Geoghegan.

advice."[5] Unlike his predecessor, however, Harry Truman did initially make use of his Cabinet, a fact that can perhaps be accounted for by his lack of confidence upon taking over the reins of the Presidency. As he progressed through his term, however, the purpose of Cabinet meetings became not so much to make important decisions as to insure policy coordination. Among our recent presidents, Eisenhower made the greatest use of the Cabinet. He came into the Presidency believing that the Cabinet should be used to discuss matters of great public concern. Accordingly, he held frequent as well as long meetings with his Cabinet. Agendas were prepared for each meeting, and he even went so far as to appoint a Cabinet Secretary. However, in spite of Eisenhower's effort to elevate the importance of the Cabinet, one of his close advisers argues that he was not well served by it. Not only were the meetings for the most part noncontroversial, but Cabinet members usually came unprepared, which produced "unpremeditated, if not aimless discussions."[6] Kennedy's treatment of the Cabinet provided a marked contrast to his predecessor. Although he began by holding regular Cabinet meetings, he soon became frustrated with them, as his Postmaster General recalls:

> After the first two or three meetings, one had the distinct impression that the President felt that decisions on major matters were not made—or even influenced at Cabinet sessions, and that discussion there was a waste of time. . . . When members spoke up to suggest or to discuss major Administration policy, the President would listen with thinly disguised impatience and then postpone or otherwise bypass the question.[7]

The President ultimately concluded that the nature of the issue should determine which Cabinet members needed to be consulted. It served little purpose, he thought, to convene the entire Cabinet to discuss issues that might be of immediate concern to only one or two members. Thus, he abandoned regular meetings and the few he did convene were for reasons of tradition rather than necessity.

Johnson made a serious attempt to use the Cabinet after he took over the Presidency. Regular meetings were scheduled, and a special assistant was appointed to think up topics for the group to discuss.[8] Like most other presidents, however, he gradually allowed the Cabinet to fall into disuse, convening it only to give department heads "new political or personnel marching orders."[9]

[5] Ibid.

[6] Cited in Charles Hardin, *Presidential Power and Accountability* (Chicago: University of Chicago Press, 1974), p. 38.

[7] Cited in Thomas Cronin, *The State of the Presidency* (Boston: Little, Brown, 1975), p. 166.

[8] From George E. Reedy, *The Twilight of the Presidency*, p. 74. Copyright © 1970 by George E. Reedy. Reprinted by arrangement with the New American Library, Inc., New York, N.Y.

[9] Cited in Cronin, *State of the Presidency*, p. 186.

Of all our recent presidents, none made a greater point of dramatically demonstrating the importance of the Cabinet than did Richard Nixon. Indeed, he took the unprecedented step of having the group sworn in on live television. Moreover, he introduced each member, citing his accomplishments and qualifications for the post. Given such fanfare, it is especially ironic that Nixon ultimately sought to reduce the importance of his Cabinet members, perhaps to a greater extent than any other recent President.

If presidents do not rely heavily upon their Cabinets for advice, it is important to know why. First of all, many critical matters must be discussed in secrecy, and Presidents have found that the best way to maintain secrecy is to limit the number of people who will be privy to such matters. Consequently, they are reluctant to risk the chance of leaks by bringing sensitive issues before a Cabinet consisting of a dozen or so individuals.[10] Second, a President will place his confidence in people he can trust, and these are likely to be individuals whom he knows personally. Cabinet members, however, do not usually fall in this category.

Political reasons often compel a President to settle for Cabinet members who are not necessarily his first choice. Kennedy, for example, wanted McGeorge Bundy as his Secretary of State. He finally decided not to appoint him, however, because he felt his newly appointed Ambassador to the United Nations, Adlai Stevenson, would refuse to serve under Bundy. His second choice for the job was Senator William Fulbright. Again, however, Kennedy was finally dissuaded from choosing him because blacks objected to the Senator's civil rights record and Jewish groups took exception to his views on Israel.[11] Kennedy ultimately gave the position to Dean Rusk who, although highly recommended, was someone the President had never met. Nor had he ever met the men he ultimately selected to fill the posts of Secretary of Defense and Secretary of the Treasury, both of whom were Republicans as well as prominent members of the business community. Their appointments were motivated in part by Kennedy's desire to ease the fears of the conservative financial establishment, which viewed his Presidency with considerable apprehension.

Political considerations also played a part in the choice of several of President Nixon's Cabinet appointees. Daniel Patrick Moynihan was his personal choice for Secretary of Labor, but Nixon also recognized the necessity of appointing someone who would be acceptable to the labor establishment. Accordingly, he decided against Moynihan for the job when he learned that the powerful President of the AFL-CIO objected to Moynihan's lack of administrative experience.[12] The position was ultimately given to George Shultz, a man the President had never met. The Governor of Alaska, Walter Hickel, was picked to be Secretary of the Interior, in part because President Nixon felt the western part of the

[10] Reedy, *Twilight of the Presidency*, p. 11.

[11] David Halberstam, *The Best and the Brightest* (New York: Random House, Inc., 1969), pp. 40, 41.

[12] Theodore White, *Breach of Faith* (New York: Atheneum, 1975), p. 103.

country should be represented in the Cabinet.[13] It was an appointment that Nixon would regret later on when Hickel openly criticized the President's administrative style. In an attempt to represent the liberal wing of the Republican Party in his administration, Nixon appointed his former political opponent, George Romney, as Secretary of Housing and Urban Development.[14] Recognizing that he did not enjoy the full confidence of the President, however, Romney decided to leave the Cabinet at the end of Nixon's first term.

The lack of complete trust that characterizes the relationship between the President and his Cabinet appointees is not due merely to the fact that he does not always get the person he wants. It also stems from the President's awareness of the fact that he does not command the total loyalty of many Cabinet members. We have already dealt with this problem at length in an earlier chapter on the bureaucracy. Suffice it to say here that several departments in the Executive branch (Agriculture, Commerce, Labor, Interior, HEW, HUD, Energy) represent powerful interest groups within our society, and these interests enjoy considerable support in Congress. Accordingly, department heads may be under considerable pressure from these interests to advocate and pursue policies that are not necessarily consistent with the President's program. Reacting vigorously to what he perceived as disloyal department heads, Richard Nixon demanded the resignations of several Cabinet members at the start of his second term. In response to a question on this shake-up, Nixon's chief of staff, H. R. Haldeman, replied: "You're goddamned right we're cleaning house, we're going to have loyal people now, who take their marching orders from the White House, no Cabinet officer is going to be able to make his own deal with Congress."[15]

Finally, if the President is reluctant to trust the counsel of Cabinet members because of the reasons stated above, it must also be acknowledged that Cabinet members are themselves reluctant to provide frank and honest advice.

> There is no such thing as adversary discussion in a cabinet meeting. Men do not pound the table, contradict each other, challenge contrary opinions. . . . What follows is a gentlemanly discourse conducted on an extremely "high" level, and enveloped in the maximum dullness conceivable. And every word is addressed to one man and one man only. A Cabinet meeting is not a marketplace of thought where ideas undergo crucial tests.[16]

More important, Cabinet secretaries are reluctant to disagree openly with the President. Indeed, one of Kennedy's closest aids, Theodore Sorensen, warns that a President must take care not to make his position known too early in such

---

[13] From *Before the Fall* by William Safire. Copyright © 1975 by William Safire. Used by permission of Doubleday & Company, Inc.

[14] Richard Nathan, *The Plot that Failed* (New York: John Wiley, 1975), p. 39.

[15] White, *Breach of Faith*, p. 179.

[16] Reedy, *Twilight of the Presidency*, pp. 77, 78.

meetings, for once it is detected, there is a rush by the others to register their agreement with him.[17] Robert Kennedy described this phenomenon:

> His office creates such respect and awe that it has almost a cowering effect on men. Frequently I saw advisers adapt their opinions to what they believed President Kennedy and, later, President Johnson wished to hear.

> I once attended a preliminary meeting with a cabinet officer, where we agreed on a recommendation to be made to the President. It came as a slight surprise to me when, a few minutes later, in the meeting with the President himself, the cabinet officer vigorously and fervently expressed the opposite point of view, when from the discussion, he quite accurately learned that it would be more sympathetically received by the President.[18]

Even such a forceful and independent personality as Secretary of State Dean Acheson acknowledged that he found it extremely difficult to stand up to President Truman when he disagreed with him.[19]

Cabinet Member Influence

Although we have mentioned several factors that serve to reduce the impact of Cabinet appointees upon presidential thinking, it should be noted that under certain circumstances individual members may come to exercise considerable influence. Specifically, those individuals whose ability, loyalty, and personality are judged favorably by a President will gain entry to his inner circle. Eisenhower, for example, never disguised the fact that he valued highly the judgment of his Treasury Secretary, George Humphrey. Similarly, having developed great respect for the abilities of Defense Secretary McNamara and Treasury Secretary Dillon, President Kennedy frequently sought out their counsel on a variety of matters. On the other hand, while he regarded Secretary of State Rusk as able and hard working, he never felt comfortable around him. Their relationship was a very formal one, and indeed, Rusk was the only member of the Kennedy Cabinet whom the President never addressed by his first name.[20] Johnson, however, had no such difficulty in developing a free and easy relationship with Rusk. In addition, his confidence in the loyalty and judgment of both Rusk and McNamara insured that they would be influential figures in foreign policy deliberations. In the Nixon Administration, John Connally stood out as one of the most influential members of the Cabinet. Although prior to Con-

---

[17] Theodore Sorensen, *Decision-Making in the White House* (New York: Columbia University Press, 1963), p. 60.

[18] Cited in Hardin, *Presidential Power*, p. 41.

[19] Ibid., p. 35.

[20] Paper, *Promise and Performance*, pp. 158, 159.

nally's appointment as Treasury Secretary, the President had only a passing acquaintance with the Texan, Connally's ability, loyalty, and style impressed Nixon to such a degree that he even seriously considered the former Texas governor as a vice presidential running mate in the 1972 election.[21]

Other things being equal, the influence of certain Cabinet members over the President also stems from the nature of their responsibilities. Those members who deal with matters of greatest concern to the President will have greater access to him. Given the fact that presidents have increasingly focused their attention on matters of foreign policy, national security, the economy, and justice, it is not surprising that the secretaries of State, Defense, and the Treasury and the Attorney General are the Cabinet members with whom he has the most frequent contact. Indeed, these secretaries have come to be known as the *inner* Cabinet. The *outer* Cabinet members (notably the secretaries of Agriculture, Labor, Commerce, Interior, Transportation, HEW, HUD and Energy) may from time to time gain access to the President when an important issue arises relevant to their departments, but their access is not likely to be consistent over time. Moreover, as noted earlier, these *outer* Cabinet departments represent strong clientele groups in the population. And to the extent that heads of these departments develop loyalties to such groups, their loyalty to the President is suspect, and consequently he is less likely to take them into his confidence.[22]

THE EXECUTIVE OFFICE OF THE PRESIDENT

Concerned that the administrative responsibilities of the President had become too overwhelming for one man, President Franklin Roosevelt in 1936 established the President's Committee on Administrative Management. It was charged with evaluating the administrative procedures of the Executive branch. It did so and ultimately concluded that "the President needs help."[23] Accordingly, in 1939, the Executive Office of the President (EOP) was established by Executive Order 8248. It was to consist of six administrative assistants to the President along with three advisory bodies—the National Resources Planning Board, the Liaison Office for Personnel Management, and the Office of Government Reports. In the thirty-eight years since its establishment, the Executive Office of the President has expanded steadily and at the time President Carter assumed office housed some 1,712 full-time staff members:

This expansion has occurred for a variety of reasons. In part, it has been a response to crises of one sort or another. Following the abortive Bay of Pigs invasion, for example, President Kennedy concluded that the information that had

---

[21] Safire, *Before the Fall,* pp. 497–508.

[22] Cronin, *State of the Presidency,* pp. 191, 197, 198.

[23] Cited in Clinton Rossiter, *The American Presidency* (New York: New American Library, 1956), p. 122.

guided the planning of this undertaking was seriously deficient, and consequently he decided to expand the size of the National Security Council staff.[24] Similarly, President Ford established the Economic Policy Board, the Council on Wage-Price Stability, and the Labor Management Committee, all of which were designed to assist him in dealing with the economic recession that befell the nation in 1974-75. Likewise, his establishment of the Energy Resources Council was in response to the energy crisis. Another cause for expansion was the realization that certain problems facing our industrialized society are of such complexity that the President needs a group of experts readily available to assist him in dealing with such problems. This consideration motivated the creation of such Executive Office units as the Council of Economic Advisers and the Office of Science and Technology.

Finally, of course, the creation of Executive Office units in the White House has resulted from a desire to bring about greater policy coordination. Given today's large federal programs, which in many cases involve the participation of several departments and agencies throughout the bureaucracy, there has developed a need for a higher-level body which can coordinate their administrative activities as well as settle interdepartmental conflicts.

Having campaigned on a platform of reducing the size and increasing the efficiency of the government bureaucracy, President Carter immediately set about trying to get his own house in order. Accordingly, he ordered the Office of Management and Budget to undertake a study to determine how the Executive Office of the President might be reduced in size, as well as how to maximize the use of the government's resources in presidential decision making. As a means of accomplishing this latter goal, the President's reorganization team undertook an analysis of the decision-making process employed on eight separate issues (food stamps, minimum wage, Social Security financing, shoe imports, rural telecommunications, wiretap legislation, breeder reactors, controls on conventional arms sales) which required presidential action during Carter's first six months in office.

Based upon recommendations from OMB, the President implemented a reorganization of the Executive Office which reduced its staff from 1,712 to 1,459, cut back its operating units from 21 to 12, and created two new EOP operations: the Domestic Policy Staff and the Office of Administration. The current composition of the Executive Office of the President is shown in Figure 6-1. Several units within EOP are of sufficient importance to deserve special mention.

National Security Council

The National Security Council (NSC) was established in 1947 for the purpose of providing the President with advice and policy coordination on matters related to national security. Many congressmen and senators who were upset with Roosevelt's personal direction of the war strategy in the Second World War

[24] Cronin, *State of the Presidency,* p. 121.

FIGURE 6-1. EXECUTIVE OFFICE OF THE PRESIDENT

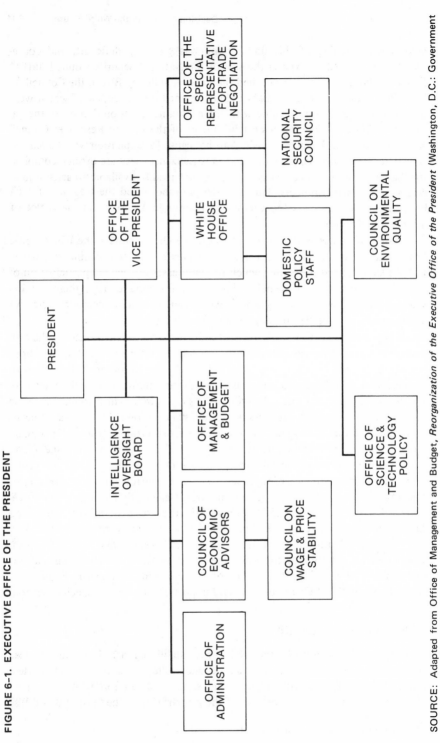

SOURCE: Adapted from Office of Management and Budget, *Reorganization of the Executive Office of the President* (Washington, D.C.: Government Printing Office, 1977), p. 9.

felt the NSC would insure that presidents would be presented with a wider range of views on military and diplomatic matters. Its statutory members include the President, Vice President, Secretary of State, and Secretary of Defense. The Congress also specified certain individuals who would serve as statutory advisers to the Council, notably, the Chairman of the Joint Chiefs of Staff, the Director of the CIA, and the Director of the Arms Control and Disarmament Agency (added in 1975). Presidents were also authorized to appoint additional advisers to the Council as they saw fit. And in fact, the number of advisers has increased considerably over the years.

Like all advisory groups to the President, the National Security Council has been important only to the extent that presidents have been willing to let it become so. Of the presidents serving since Franklin Roosevelt, the Council appears to have received greatest use during the Truman and Eisenhower years. Truman sought the advice of the NSC frequently following the outbreak of the Korean War. His successor called the NSC together almost once a week, not a surprising development given the fact that Eisenhower's military background had accustomed him to operating through formal channels. Yet even though Eisenhower relied on this body more than any President before or since, it was still not the dominant force in shaping foreign policy during his administration. In part, this was because of his desire to have the Council deal with long-range policies rather than the day-to-day happenings in the world; and in part because Eisenhower had a forceful Secretary of State, John Foster Dulles, who was not about to surrender the foreign policy initiative to anyone else in the government.[25]

Although President Kennedy met with the members of the National Security Council during his first few months in office, he ultimately found it to be too large a group for making policy on delicate matters of national security. Johnson shared Kennedy's view, preferring to rely on a few select individuals whom he knew well and felt he could trust.[26] Thus, in planning strategy related to the Vietnam War, he chose to deal primarily with a small group of advisers who met with him every Tuesday for lunch. And on occasion, he would even bring in trusted friends from outside government. A meeting of the full National Security Council was convened by Johnson only for "educational, ratification and ceremonial purposes."[27] Ironically, Richard Nixon came into office criticizing his predecessors for their failure to utilize the NSC, and while he did indeed meet more frequently with the group during his first two years in office, the meetings became increasingly infrequent as the influence of his national security adviser (Henry Kissinger) grew. Moreover, like his two predecessors, Nixon preferred to

---

[25]I. M. Destler, "National Security Advice to U.S. Presidents," *World Politics* 29 (January 1977), pp. 147, 148.

[26]Keith Clark and Laurance Legere, *The President and the Management of National Security* (New York: Praeger, 1969), p. 60.

[27]Ibid., p. 88.

deal with foreign policy crises by bringing together a small group of advisers. Created after a United States reconnaissance plane was shot down over North Korea, this group came to be known as the "Washington Special Actions group." Although the NSC enjoyed some resurgence under President Ford, its role was decidedly secondary to the one played by Henry Kissinger.

If the National Security Council itself has played a limited role in shaping foreign policy, the same cannot be said of its staff. Originally conceived of as a career staff that would carry over from one administration to the next, during the Kennedy Administration the NSC Staff developed into an instrument of the incumbent President, primarily because Kennedy had become increasingly frustrated with the lack of initiative and imagination at the State Department. Accordingly, he sought to move foreign policy making into the White House, and the National Security Council staff provided a ready instrument for developing this capability. He expanded the size of the staff considerably and ordered the creation of a "Situation Room" in the White House which would receive all cable traffic coming into the State Department, CIA, and Defense Department, thus providing the NSC staff with its own intelligence capacity. Finally, he also gave his ambitious national security adviser, McGeorge Bundy, responsibility for directing the activities of the staff.

While the NSC staff continued to be an important force in foreign policy under President Johnson, it had to share the spotlight with Secretary of State Rusk, who stood much higher in Johnson's esteem than he had in Kennedy's. It was in the Nixon Administration, however, that the staff of the NSC came into its own. Three circumstances made this inevitable: first, a President whose primary interests lay in the area of foreign affairs; second, a national security adviser whose foreign policy expertise and sense for bureaucratic politics were unequalled; and third, a Secretary of State whose talents in both of these areas were limited.

Under President Ford, the NSC staff continued in its prominent role, while Henry Kissinger simultaneously held the positions of national security adviser and Secretary of State. But ultimately Kissinger was asked to give up his role as national security adviser, which meant he was no longer director of the NSC staff. While this change did not diminish Kissinger's role in foreign policy, one suspects that it lessened the importance of the NSC staff.

What are the roles of the National Security Council and its staff in the Carter Administration? Thus far Carter has made little use of the National Security Council as a group. Instead, he breakfasts once a week with a small group of foreign policy advisers which includes the Secretary of State, the Vice President, national security adviser Brzezinski, and more recently, the President's top aid on political matters, Hamilton Jordan. The latter was included to insure that domestic political considerations would be factored into foreign policy decisions. (Incidentally, it is for this reason that Carter also decided to make the head of his Domestic Policy Staff a non-statutory adviser to the National Security Council.)

After the President and his advisers have identified a foreign policy issue that requires a decision, a Presidential Review Memorandum is sent to all the departments and agencies involved with the issue. The memorandum defines the issue, specifies questions that need answering, and asks for recommendations. This information-gathering process is coordinated by the NSC staff. After all relevant parties make their input, the NSC staff condenses the recommendations into manageable form and sends them on to the President, along with its own assessment. The purpose of this procedure is to provide the President with input from as many sources as possible.

Whether Brzezinski and his NSC staff become a "little State Department," as was the case in the Kennedy and Nixon presidencies, will ultimately depend upon Carter's relationship with both his Secretary of State and Brzezinski. While the President came into office stating that he wanted Secretary of State Vance to be his spokesman on foreign policy, there have already been indications that Brzezinski might play a more active role; for example, Brzezinski dispensed with his low profile and frequently appeared before the media to articulate the administration's position on various foreign policy issues. Moreover, the President saw fit to send him to China to further explore the improvement of relations between the two countries. Finally, Vance and Brzezinski appear to disagree on how to deal with the Soviet Union. If the President should come down on the side of Brzezinski's more hardline approach, the Secretary of State would suffer a substantial blow to his prestige within the administration.

Council of Economic Advisers

Established under a provision of the Federal Employment Act of 1946, the Council of Economic Advisers was created in response to the belief that the President needed expert advice on such complex economic matters as employment, tax policy, and inflation. While Franklin Roosevelt had several economists on his staff who informally provided him with information and advice about the economy, many members of Congress were not pleased with the advice he was receiving; nor did they appreciate the fact that no attempt was made to share this information with the Congress. Consequently, while the Congress stipulated that the President could appoint the three members of the Council of Economic Advisers, they also required that its membership must be approved by the Senate. Furthermore, they stipulated that the Council must report to the Congress from time to time. In point of fact, however, the Council has had a great deal more influence upon presidential thinking when it has attempted to serve the President alone than when trying to serve both President and Congress.[28]

With the departure of Bert Lance, who, in addition to being Director of the

---

[28] Erwin Hargrove, *The Power of the Modern Presidency* (New York: Alfred Knopf, 1974), p. 85.

Office of Management and Budget also functioned as Carter's key economic adviser, the Council of Economic Advisers now appears to be playing a more formidable role in economic policy making. Yet it must still share this role with other administration officials such as Treasury Secretary Michael Blumenthal, domestic policy assistant Stuart Eizenstat, and the President's special assistant on inflation, Robert Strauss.

Office of Management and Budget

This office is among the most important in the Executive Office of the President. Created in 1921 as the Bureau of the Budget, it was originally located in the Treasury Department and later moved to the Executive Office in 1939. As part of President Nixon's reorganization efforts, the Bureau was renamed the Office of Management and Budget in 1970. Its responsibilities include: (1) assisting the President in drawing up the budget he submits to Congress each year; (2) acting as a clearing house for all legislation coming from the various departments to insure that no department sponsors legislation that might be in conflict with the President's policy objectives; and (3) monitoring the implementation of presidential programs to see that they are administered economically and efficiently. This last responsibility reflected President Nixon's desire to have the Bureau of the Budget focus more directly on managerial efficiency in government—thus the change in name to Office of *Management* and Budget. More specifically, he wanted OMB to become more involved with evaluating and coordinating programs, improving the organization of the Executive branch, establishing more effective information and management systems, and considering ways of developing better executive talent. While OMB made some effort in these areas during the Nixon and Ford administrations, the results were not especially noteworthy.

As stated in an earlier chapter, President Carter came into the Presidency determined to improve the management of government programs and decided to rely on civil service reform, zero base budgeting, and reorganization as the primary instruments for accomplishing this goal. But whereas previous presidents had established special commissions to study government reorganization, Carter decided to give this responsibility to OMB. By making Bert Lance Director of OMB, he assured its commitment to this task. In order to enhance the management focus of OMB, Lance proceeded to divide the office in two, with one half devoted exclusively to budgetary matters, and the other half concentrating on reorganization and certain additional management functions. To the chagrin of those working on the budget side—whose numbers were reduced from 392 to 361—Lance built up the reorganization and management staff to 143. While only 42 of these had reorganization responsibilities, he augmented their number with another 150 people who were either borrowed from other government agencies or brought in from the private sector as consultants.[29]

[29] *National Journal,* October 1, 1977, pp. 1518, 1519.

Despite the ultimate departure of Lance from the Carter Administration, OMB's reorganization efforts have not diminished. On the contrary, it has already submitted four reorganization proposals to Congress, three of which were approved and the fourth (civil service reform) still pending as of this writing. Its future reorganization plans include creation of a Department of Education, consolidation of agencies which provide disaster relief, and consolidation of responsibility for patrolling the nation's borders.

Domestic Policy Staff

One of the changes made as a result of President Carter's reorganization of the Executive Office was the replacement of the Domestic Council by a Domestic Policy Staff. The former was a creation of the Nixon Administration. Viewed as the domestic counterpart to the National Security Council, its function was to formulate and coordinate policy related to domestic matters. The membership of the Council included the President, Vice President, Director of the Office of Economic Opportunity, and all department heads except the secretaries of Defense and Treasury. It was also provided with a staff under the directorship of Nixon's special assistant, John Ehrlichman.

In actuality, the Domestic Council did not function in the manner that was intended. It rarely met as a group, primarily because its size was considered too unwieldy for a fruitful discussion of issues. The Domestic Council staff, on the other hand, did become an important force in the shaping of domestic policy. Under the Direction of John Ehrlichman, the staff grew to 66 people in just two years and devoted most of its time to establishing domestic priorities and providing the President with options for dealing with pressing domestic problems.[30] During those first two years the procedure for handling a given domestic issue typically involved the creation of a Cabinet committee from among the department heads serving on the Domestic Council. In addition, a task force was established consisting of individuals from the various departments and agencies concerned with the issue under consideration. Significantly, Ehrlichman and his staff determined the composition of the task force. Moreover, they were careful to select individuals whose views were clearly in tune with those of the administration. This practice upset some Cabinet members, who saw individuals being picked from their departments whose views were not always consistent with their own. The task force was chaired by a member of the Domestic Council staff, and its final recommendations were presented to the Cabinet committee or frequently to the President himself.

The important role played by the Domestic Council Staff from 1970-1972 was significantly diminished in 1973. Several factors contributed to this development. For one thing, Ehrlichman was elevated to the position of Counselor to the President, and a considerably less influential administration official (Kenneth

[30] Ronald Moe, "The Domestic Council in Perspective," *The Bureaucrat,* 5 (October 1976), pp. 257, 258.

Cole) was placed at the head of the Domestic Council staff. More important, President Nixon realized that the efforts of his staff to supervise the coordination and implementation of domestic policy had resulted in a bloated White House bureaucracy. He decided to shift most of this responsibility to three trusted Cabinet members, giving each the additional title of Counselor to the President. Each of these "super" secretaries would be given responsibility for supervising the formulation and coordination of domestic policy in one of three major areas: natural resources, human resources, and community development. In addition, the Domestic Council would now consist of three committees based upon these three major areas, with the super secretary in charge of each area acting as the committee's chairman.

As noted in an earlier chapter, Nixon's effort to establish super secretaries did not prove workable, and consequently he dispensed with them after a few months. Moreover, it was at precisely this time that the Watergate scandals began to break, and as Nixon became increasingly preoccupied with trying to save his Presidency, he had no time to spend on domestic initiatives. Needless to say, this state of affairs left both the Domestic Council and its staff with little direction.

Upon the recommendation of his transition team, President Ford decided to maintain the Domestic Council, but expanded its membership to include additional representatives from several units within the Executive Office, as well as from certain government agencies. In addition, he also placed Vice President Rockefeller in charge of the council. Neither the Council nor its staff proved to be an effective force in the formulation of domestic policy, however. To some extent this was simply because the Ford Administration undertook comparatively few domestic policy initiatives. Also, some of President Ford's top aids had objected to placing Rockefeller in charge of the Council. Consequently, the relations between the Ford staff and Rockefeller's Domestic Council staff were not as cordial as they might have been. Rockefeller finally asked to be relieved of his supervisory responsibility after concluding that the amount of time he was investing in this endeavor was yielding little payoff.

While Carter's reorganization team recognized the necessity for coordinating domestic policy, they were also aware of his desire to deal with issues through ad hoc groups rather than formal institutions. Accordingly, the Domestic Council was eliminated and replaced with a Domestic Policy Staff headed by the President's assistant for domestic affairs and policy, Stuart Eizenstat. In dealing with domestic issues, the Domestic Policy Staff follows a procedure somewhat similar to the Presidential Review Memorandum employed by the administration on foreign policy issues. The procedure begins with an Issue Definition Memorandum which is drafted by Eizenstat either on his own initiative or at the request of a particular department or agency. This memorandum contains, first, the questions that need to be addressed concerning a given issue; second, it specifies an ad hoc coordinating committee whose membership includes Cabinet or sub-Cabinet members from all of the departments and agencies involved with the issue; third, it designates an agency that will take the lead in analyzing the issue and making recommendations. Before the Issue Definition Memorandum is written up by Eizenstat, however, he first consults with the Vice President, senior White House aids, and the departments and agencies affected. When the memorandum is completed, he takes it to the President for his approval. If Carter gives the go-ahead, then the issue is discussed in the coordinating committee, after which the lead agency prepares a Response Memorandum detailing its recommendations for dealing with the issue in question. Other departments and agencies may also add their own views to the Response Memorandum. The Domestic Policy Staff then summarizes all of these opinions and recommendations and sends them on to the President, along with its own analysis and recommendations.[31]

This rather intricate process reflects the President's desire to give departments and agencies greater input into the policy-making process than they have had in the past. It is also designed to provide Carter with input from a wide range of sources. In the words of Eizenstat, "The notion is to involve all Cabinet Secretaries in the early stages; no one feels left out and can throw a monkey wrench in the review at the last minute. There is a cross fertilization of ideas and the President gets all views."[32] The success of this procedure, of course, is contingent upon the willingness of the Domestic Policy Staff to compile and distill the views of the various departments and agencies in a fair and objective fashion. Thus far at least, Eizenstat appears to command the full confidence of all parties involved in the domestic policy process.

The White House Staff

For the President's purposes, the White House staff (White House Office) is perhaps the most important unit in the Executive Office. It consists of numerous personal advisers, who may hold the title of assistant, counselor, or aid to the President. Usually among the more important staff members are his assistant for national security affairs, assistant for domestic affairs, counsel to the President, appointments secretary, assistant for public relations, assistant for legislative affairs, press secretary, and chief of staff, if he has one. With a few exceptions, individuals holding these positions are largely unknown to the American public. It is doubtful, for example, that most people would recognize the names Buchen, Cheney, Marsh, Hartmann, Baroody, and Cannon, all of whom occupied important positions on President Ford's White House staff. Nor is it likely that people outside of government would have recognized the names of Haldeman, Ehrlichman, Colson, and Dean had it not been for the scandals of Watergate.

---

[31] "Presidential Domestic Policy Review System," *Weekly Compilation of Presidential Documents XIII,* No. 38 (September 19, 1977), pp. 1343–44.

[32] *National Journal,* April 15, 1978, p. 586.

While the personal escapades of top Carter aid Hamilton Jordan temporarily brought him greater visibility than normal, most of the President's other senior advisers (Powell, Eizenstat, Lipshutz, Moore, Watson, Wexler) have consistently maintained a low public profile. The fact that a President's senior staff members operate in relative obscurity should not cause us to view them as inconsequential figures, however. On the contrary, they are among the most powerful people in government. Their importance derives from the fact that they usually have immediate and direct access to the President. They enjoy this access because most of the senior staff, having usually been long-time associates of the President, command his total confidence.

Among the more notable developments in the White House staff has been its gradual expansion over the years. Thomas Jefferson administered the government with a personal staff of one messenger and a secretary, whose services he paid for with his own money. Grant had only three staff assistants and, despite our involvement in the First World War, Wilson maintained a rather small staff of seven. Gradually, however, the White House staff began to expand. Roosevelt had an immediate staff of 11; Truman, 13; Eisenhower, 37; Kennedy, 23; Johnson, 20; Nixon, 48; Ford, 56. But these figures do not tell the whole story, for nearly all of these aids had support staffs of their own.[33] Thus, when we include all the full-time employees serving in the White House Office, the average staff size for each of these presidents becomes: Roosevelt, 49; Truman, 186; Eisenhower, 320; Kennedy, 323; Johnson, 271; Nixon, 461; Ford, 503. Even these figures do not give a complete picture, however, since the White House Office has for a long time made a practice of borrowing employees from the various departments and agencies in the Executive branch and detailing them for service on the President's business. When we add these detailed employees to the regular staff of each of these presidents, then the average size of their staffs becomes: Roosevelt, 173; Truman, 248; Eisenhower, 357; Kennedy, 445; Johnson, 461; Nixon, 567; Ford, 530.[34]

Given the complexity of the problems we face today plus the fact that we look increasingly to the President for solutions, it is not surprising that the White House staff has grown considerably. But there are other important reasons for its expansion. Increasingly frustrated over the unresponsiveness of the bureaucracy, from department heads on down, presidents have moved policy making into the White House and given it to aids they could trust. With some regret, Senator Hollings took note of this development during the Nixon Administration:

---

[33] Arthur Schlesinger, Jr., *The Imperial Presidency* (Boston: Houghton Mifflin, 1973), p. 221. Copyright © 1973 by Arthur Schlesinger, Jr. Reprinted by permission of Houghton Mifflin Company. The figure on Ford comes from *1976 Congressional Directory,* 94th Congress, Second Session (Washington, D.C.: Government Printing Office, 1976), pp. 483, 484.

[34] These figures computed from data which appears in Hugh Heclo, *Studying the Presidency: A Report to the Ford Foundation* (New York: Ford Foundation, 1977), pp. 36, 37. Staff figures for 1945, 1963, and 1974 were credited to Truman, Kennedy, and Nixon respectively.

It used to be if I had a problem with food stamps, I went to see the Secretary of Agriculture whose Department had jurisdiction over that program. Not any more. Now, if I want to learn the policy, I must go to the White House and consult John Price. If I want the latest on textiles, I won't get it from the Secretary of Commerce, who has the authority and responsibility. No, I am forced to go to the White House and see Mr. Peter Flanigan. I shouldn't feel too badly. Secretary Stans [Secretary of Commerce] has to do the same thing.[35]

The increase in staff is also attributable to the President's desire to monitor the activities of the various departments and agencies to make sure they are implementing his policies.[36] This factor in part accounts for the especially large increase in the White House staff during the Nixon Administration. Convinced that the bureaucracy had a liberal Democratic bias, President Nixon wanted to make sure that his more conservative programs were not being sabotaged by the bureaucracy.[37]

The changes in the *size* and *responsibilities* of the White House staff have evoked legitimate concern among people both in and outside of government. A staff grown so large becomes difficult to supervise, with the result that staff members run about demanding action in the name of the President, but not always with the President's authorization. Nor has the transfer of responsibility for policy making and implementation away from department heads and into the White House been viewed as altogether desirable. For one thing, it has been argued that members of the White House staff may lack the administrative perspective that department heads bring to policy issues. Secondly, even with its increased size, the staff cannot hope to oversee the implementation of presidential programs effectively, for there are too many, and they are frequently so complex that several departments and agencies are involved. Finally, there is the issue of accountability. At the expense of department heads, the White House staff has been given a vastly increased role in the formulation and implementation of policy and yet, unlike Cabinet secretaries, they are subject neither to confirmation by the Senate nor to periodic questioning by the Congress.

Candidate Carter shared these concerns and vowed that as President he would take steps to reduce the size of the White House staff and institute "Cabinet government." No longer would members of the President's staff tell Cabinet members how to run their departments. Carter's reorganization of the Executive Office in 1977 did indeed reduce the White House staff from 485 to 351, al-

---

[35]Cited in John Anderson, "A Republican Looks at the Presidency," in Charles Dunn, ed., *The Future of the American Presidency* (Morristown, N.J.: General Learning Press, 1975), pp. 214, 215.

[36]Hugh Sidey interviews Bill Moyers, *The White House Staff vs. The Cabinet* (Washington, D.C.: Washington Monthly, 1969), p. 4.

[37]Nathan, *Plot that Failed,* pp. 37–54, 82.

though 70 of the 134 positions eliminated were merely transferred to the Office of Administration (see Figure 6-1). The President's commitment to this reduction remains in question, however, for he subsequently sent legislation to Congress that would raise the number of supergrade aids on the White House Office staff from the current statutory ceiling of 55 up to 100. In addition, this bill would give the President authority to employ an unlimited number of private consultants and borrow an unlimited number of employees from other departments and agencies within the government. The White House contends that it has no intention of expanding its staff and points out that the purpose of this legislation is merely to provide the President with flexibility in the event of a crisis. This explanation is hardly a compelling one, however, for in the event of a crisis, Congress has traditionally been most accommodating in meeting presidential requests.

As for Carter's effort to establish "Cabinet government," here again his commitment appears less firm than it was at the start of his administration. While he initially met with his Cabinet every Monday, he now does so only once every two weeks. He also became sufficiently concerned over the leaking of Cabinet minutes to the press that he asked one of his aids to investigate the matter. As all presidents have discovered, however, the leaks will continue and President Carter, like his predecessors, will become increasingly reluctant to discuss matters of consequence at Cabinet meetings.

The President's effort to give his department heads a greater role in the shaping of policy has also produced some embarrassing moments. Agriculture Secretary Bergland, for example, announced that increased income supports for wheat farmers would fall somewhere between $3.40 to $3.50 per bushel, when in fact the White House had decided that $3.40 would be the absolute maximum. Treasury Secretary Blumenthal stated in several speeches that there would be no tax reform, and he did so at a time when the White House was putting together its tax reform package. The Department of Housing and Urban Development drew up a set of recommendations for dealing with urban problems, nearly all of which were scrapped by the President because the price tag was so far out of line with his own budget target. These as well as other misfires caused many to wonder, "Who's in charge here?"

In March and April of 1978, President Carter undertook a reassessment of his administration and its personnel. According to one senior White House aid, this reassessment made it abundantly clear to all concerned that henceforth "there will be a fuller realization of the priority of Administration goals over agency goals and an individual's goals."[38] To insure this, Cabinet members were told that they must now check with White House aids before making statements on administration policy. While the President and his staff have insisted that this change does not signal the death knell for "Cabinet government," clearly some effort is being made to rein in the Carter Cabinet. Nor should this come as any

[38] *New York Times,* March 12, 1978, p. 25; see also *New York Times,* April 9, 1978, p. E3.

surprise. As already noted, Cabinet members are not wholly the President's men. Most of their time is spent, not with the President, but rather in their departments, where they are subject to constant internal and external pressures from clientele groups represented by the department. Frequently the objective of these pressures is to move Cabinet members in directions that are not compatible with the President's goals. As the effects of these pressures take a firmer hold, a President turns increasingly to those whose support he can count on most—namely, the White House staff. Thus, we may anticipate that future changes in the nature of "Cabinet government" will be in the direction of less rather than more.

THE WHITE HOUSE STAFF
AND THE PROBLEM OF PRESIDENTIAL ISOLATION

While one may question the increasingly powerful role played by the White House staff in the administrations of our more recent presidents, clearly there are certain critical functions that any White House staff must perform. In the first place, it must see to it that important information and advice gets to the President from people both in and outside of government. A President is constantly besieged by people who wish to see him. In addition, letters, memoranda, and reports are sent to him for his attention. Quite obviously, there are not enough hours in the day for a President to be able to honor all of these requests; consequently, it falls to the White House staff to determine which people and material are important enough to deserve his personal attention. Second, the staff itself should act as a source of information, advice, and ideas for a President. Third, it should function as a critic and evaluator of the President's own ideas and judgments, as well as those coming from other people in and outside government. Finally, it should act as a channel through which the President can convey his own wishes to those in the bureaucracy, Congress, the press, and to opinion leaders within the society.

While all of these functions are important, the first three are especially so, since they bear directly on the acquisition of information and advice—the essential ingredients for informed decision making. The degree to which the staff can perform these three functions successfully depends upon: (1) how the staff is organized, (2) staff attitudes toward the President, and (3) the President's attitude toward his staff. Let us now examine each of these three factors in greater detail.

Staff Organization

The organization of the White House staff defies precise generalization, for its form and structure are inevitably a reflection of the style and personality of the man it is serving. However, we can say that staffs have ranged on a continuum from structured to unstructured. Perhaps the best example of the un-structured type was the White House staff of Franklin Roosevelt. He functioned as his own chief of staff, handing out assignments to staff members and requiring them to report directly to him. There was no rigid chain of command on the Roosevelt staff. On the contrary, all of his staff members had direct access to him. He also sought to surround himself with generalists; that is, people whose breadth of knowledge was such that they would be put to work in a variety of different policy areas. By doing so, Roosevelt avoided the possibility of a staffer developing so much influence in a given policy area that the President would be forced to rely exclusively upon him as a source of information. Nor was he content to delegate a given task to only one staff aid, but would often give the same assignment to several aids. This practice frequently caused compe-tition and conflict among his staff, but it also insured that several channels of information would be open to him on a given problem. While to some, Roose-velt's staff appeared to be in a state of utter chaos, this method of operation accomplished Roosevelt's purpose, namely, to avoid the presidential isolation that can result from restricted channels of information.[39] The Kennedy and Johnson staffs were similar to Roosevelt's. Each functioned as his own chief of staff; each was accessible to staff members who wished to see him, and while both assigned their staff members to a given area or responsibility, they did not hesitate to assign them to a problem outside their specialty area, if the need arose.[40]

Both Eisenhower and Nixon provide examples of presidents who had highly structured staffs, although each had different reasons for making them so. Eisenhower had spent most of his life in the military and thus was accustomed to staffs that operated according to a rigid chain of command with clearly specified rules and procedures. It is not surprising, therefore, that he followed this model upon becoming President. Eisenhower gave his staff members specific areas of responsibility. As his chief of staff he appointed Sherman Adams, who was regarded by many as the most powerful man in government next to the President himself. Adams was charged with handing out assignments to staff members. More important, he ultimately decided which individuals and what materials would gain entry to the Oval Office. Moreover, if reports and memo-randa were to have any chance of gaining the personal attention of the President, they had to be reduced to one page.[41] Thus, whereas Roosevelt had a variety of information channels, Eisenhower had essentially one—Sherman Adams. This rigidity in staff organization and procedures did moderate somewhat in 1958, when Adams was succeeded by the less autocratic Jerry Persons.

President Nixon's staff was perhaps even more structured than Eisenhower's.

[39] Arthur Schlesinger, Jr., "The Dynamics Of Decision," in Aaron Wildavsky, ed., *The Presi-dency* (Boston: Little, Brown, 1969), pp. 133–50; Alex Lacy, "The White House Staff Bureaucracy," *Transaction* 7 (January 1969), 52, 53.

[40] Paper, *Promise and Performance,* pp. 146, 147; Lacy, "White House Staff," p. 55; Cali-fano, *Presidential Nation,* p. 48.

[41] Lacy, "White House Staff," p. 54.

H. R. Haldeman functioned as the President's chief of staff, and the rest of the staff were each given a specific area of responsibility. A staff member who went beyond his responsibilities was severely reprimanded. Jeb Magruder, for example, one day wrote a memorandum proposing a new idea for the President's attention. It was quickly returned with a note from Haldeman saying, "Your job is to do, not to think."[42] Similarly, in drafting a speech for Nixon on Vietnam, one of his speechwriters proposed that no more draftees be sent to fight in Vietnam. He was promptly taken off the speech.[43] Any person wishing to see the President or any material marked for his attention nearly always had to gain the prior approval of Haldeman before gaining entry to the Oval Office. Haldeman was strongly criticized by staffers, members of Congress, and department heads for building a "Berlin Wall" around the President. However, he was merely accommodating himself to the style of his chief, for as one White House aid noted, "Nixon did not like to see many people, and wanted to see still fewer privately."[44]

Even among his personal staff, access was restricted to only a very few aids. Former President Johnson detected the isolation of President Nixon while visiting him at the White House. When Johnson was President he had had a telephone with an elaborate set of buttons which could put him in direct contact with any member of his staff or the Cabinet. Accordingly, he was astounded to observe that President Nixon had one little phone with just three buttons on it which could connect him with only Haldeman, Ehrlichman, and Kissinger.[45]

Haldeman's deputy assistant testified before the Senate Watergate Committee that "60 percent of the time that the President spent with any staff member in 1972 was spent with his chief of staff, and that for 90 percent of that time they were alone."[46] Nixon speechwriter William Safire recalls that the only time the staff saw Nixon was when they were asked to show up for the arrival of Nixon's helicopter on the White House lawn. Thus, more frequently than not, people were told that if they had something to say to the President they should put it down on paper. Contrary to popular belief, some Nixon aids contend that Haldeman, being sensitive to the President's isolationist tendencies, took great pains to see that Nixon was presented with a full range of opinion.[47] However, even if several options were presented to the President, either on paper or by Haldeman himself, such a procedure still foreclosed the opportunity for give and take between the President and his aids, where he could probe and challenge their ideas and vice versa.

Nixon's isolation from his staff no doubt explains why he was unaware of

---

[42] Cited in Paper, *Promise and Performance,* p. 120.

[43] Safire, *Before the Fall,* p. 274.

[44] Ibid., p. 281.

[45] Paper, *Promise and Performance,* p. 113.

[46] John Kessel, *The Domestic Presidency* (North Scituate, Mass.: Duxbury, 1975), p. 114.

[47] Safire, *Before the Fall,* pp. 283, 277; see also Robert Woodward and Carl Bernstein, *The Final Days* (New York: Simon and Schuster, 1976), p. 31.

some of their Watergate-related activities. Whether such activities would have been avoided if Nixon had not remained so isolated seems doubtful, however, for the White House staff takes on the coloring of the man it serves.

Even before taking office, Jimmy Carter had made it clear that his staff would be organized in the tradition of Roosevelt, not Nixon. He would function as his own chief of staff; all of his senior aids would be treated equally, and each would report directly to him. Indeed, in characterizing the organization of the White House staff, Carter spokesmen likened it to a bicycle wheel, with staffers representing spokes which lead directly to the center—namely, the President. The analogy did not originate with the Carter Administration, however. Rather, it was borrowed from President Ford's White House aids who had tried to arrange his staff along the same lines—but failed. In the words of Ford's chief of staff, " . . . the spokes of the wheel concept is a nice concept, but it won't work, . . . Somebody has to make certain that before the President signs off on a decision that he has all the relevant information and that he has taken into consideration economic, political, domestic, foreign, and all other factors involved. Somebody has to police the process."[48]

During his first twelve months in office, Carter remained accessible not only to his nine senior staff aids, but also to the Vice President and the Cabinet. Those members of the staff who could not get in to see him personally were nevertheless able to present their views in writing. In place of a chief of staff, staff coordination was handled by senior staff aids who met three times a week. As time passed, these meetings gradually dropped off to only twice a week and senior aids increasingly sent deputies to attend in their places.

After the first year, however, it became apparent to both the President and his top advisers that the White House staff operation was not functioning as effectively as they had hoped. Carter found himself inundated with detail, and apparently neither he nor anyone else was making any effort to discriminate between matters that could be handled at a lower level and those that could not. In addition, the absence of any single point of coordination frequently resulted in the left hand not knowing what the right hand was doing. This problem was highlighted, for example, when the United States decided to issue a joint communique with the Soviet Union calling for a resumption of Geneva talks on the Middle East. In taking such a step, the United States appeared to be inviting the Soviet Union to play an active role in dealing with the Middle East problem. But despite the fact that this decision had weighty implications in terms of its impact on American Jewish opinion, none of the President's domestic advisers were consulted before the decision was made.

In January 1978 President Carter issued two orders to his senior staff, the first of which authorized his top political adviser, Hamilton Jordan, to become

---

[48]Cited in Robert Shogan, *Promises To Keep* (New York: Thomas Y. Crowell, 1977), p. 202.

more actively involved in the substance of foreign policy decisions. More directly relevant to our discussion here, however, was the second order, which stated that Jordan would henceforth have responsibility for coordinating staff activities. He would chair the weekly staff meetings and hold any additional ones he deemed necessary and report discussions and recommendations directly to the President.[49] While Jordan continues to insist that he is not really functioning as chief of staff in this new role, it is nevertheless clear that an effort is being made to provide more structure to the White House staff operation. Whether this effort will have an impact on who and what comes to the President's attention is not yet clear.

In summary, the Roosevelt approach to the White House staff would appear to be far more conducive to maximizing the flow of information into the Oval Office than were the hierarchically organized staffs of Eisenhower and Nixon. And yet a staff as unstructured as Roosevelt's is probably not feasible in the contemporary Presidency. He, after all, sat at the top of a staff that was relatively *small* because it had limited responsibilities in formulating legislation and overseeing presidential programs. Consequently, the task of functioning as his own chief of staff was more manageable. On the other hand, both Ford and Carter came into the Presidency after the White House staff had undergone a remarkable expansion during the Nixon years. Not surprisingly, both ultimately concluded that they needed a chief of staff. All of this is not to say that presidents must adopt a rigid Nixonian staff organization. Rather, it is to suggest that a balance must be struck, one which on the one hand results in enough structure so that adequate coordination is achieved and the President is freed from unnecessary detail, and yet at the same time has enough flexibility to provide the President with sufficiently varied channels of information and advice.

Staff Attitudes toward the President

A less rigidly structured staff does not by itself maximize the possibility that the man in the Oval Office will get all the information he needs. Those staff members who have access to the President must be willing to speak candidly with him. When necessary, they must be capable of telling him things he may not want to hear. This may take the form of presenting him with disquieting information or being openly critical of his ideas. This staff function is *especially* important, first, because the staff are the people whose judgment he trusts most; and second, because others in government are often reluctant to speak frankly with the President.

In spite of their relatively close relationship with the President, however, staff members do also have a tendency to be overawed by the Presidency. This reaction serves to restrain them from challenging the President. Robert Kennedy

---

[49] *The New Republic,* February 11, 1978, p. 11.

noted that this Office has an "almost cowering effect on men."[50] Another of Kennedy's aids notes its effect in the following way:

> I saw no halo, I observed no mystery. And yet I found that my own personal, highly informal relationship with him changed as soon as he entered the Oval Office.
>
> He was the same human being with the same faults and virtues with whom I had worked, joked, argued, and traveled, almost night and day, for eight years. Yet my attitude was instantly characterized by a greater degree of not only deference but awe. Addressing him at all times, at play as well as work, as "Mr. President" instead of the former Jack was but a symbol of this change. I noted a similar alteration in the attitudes of his other staff members, his old friends, his seniors in the Congress, and even his political enemies.[51]

In a similar vein, Charles Colson admits that, even after he came to know Richard Nixon well, "I never lost my reverent awe of the President, or the Presidency, which for me were synonymous."[52] This attitude could not help but affect what he characterized as his relationship with Nixon. "During the time I served in the White House, I rarely questioned a Presidential order. Infrequently did I question the President's judgment. I had one rule—to get done that which the President wanted done."[53]

There is yet another reason why staff aids are often disinclined to speak candidly with the President. Not unlike other government officials, White House advisers seek to maintain, and hopefully increase, their power, and as a former presidential adviser noted, power is defined in terms of one very important factor:

> Power in Washington is measured by a stern gauge: the direct proportion of access to the President, for the asset of the realm is information that flows only from the President. If you were to fluoroscope the brain and conscience of any top official within the government, you would be able to chart the flight of agony caused by lost intimacy with the President, or denial of access to him.[54]

Daniel Moynihan was not insensitive to the importance of access when he was taken on as a Nixon adviser. Accordingly, he decided to forego a spacious office in the Executive Office Building across the street from the White House and

---

[50] Cited in Hardin, *Presidential Power,* p. 41.

[51] Theodore Sorensen, *Watchmen in the Night* (Cambridge, Mass.: MIT Press, 1975), p. 140.

[52] *Family Weekly,* March 28, 1976, p. 4.

[53] Cited in Paper, *Promise and Performance,* p. 119.

[54] Jack Valenti, *A Very Human President* (New York: W.W. Norton, 1975), p. 66; see also Reedy, *Twilight of the Presidency,* p. 88.

instead took a tiny office in the White House basement because it put him closer to the President. Although Henry Kissinger had considerable access to the President, he nevertheless bemoaned the fact that it was not enough. One Nixon speechwriter recalls an incident in which Kissinger acknowledged his distress:

> I was writing the President's opening toast for the first night in Moscow at the end of the State dinner in Granovit Hall. Henry glanced at my four-page draft and said, "You need two more pages." I said, no, Haldeman told me one thousand words tops, and Kissinger exploded: "Foreign policy decided by flacks." . . . He called Haldeman to get the President to change to fifteen hundred words. . . . The fact that he had to deal with Haldeman and could not go direct to the President irritated him immensely. It was Nixon putting him down again. "A week ago," Henry said with passion, "he would have done anything I asked, he was on his *knees*—God! And now I have to talk to Haldeman."[55]

If power is defined in terms of access to the President, how then do White House staffers gain and maintain such access? By flattering him, agreeing with him, withholding unpleasant thoughts from him. Woodrow Wilson's close aid, Colonel House, frankly admitted that he constantly flattered his boss, on one occasion telling him that he was the "one hope left to this torn and distracted world. Without your leadership, God alone knows how long we will wander in the darkness."[56] During Kennedy's Presidency, one of his closest advisers gave a speech in which he compared the President favorably with such notables as Apollo, Charlemagne, Roland, and St. Francis. Similarly, one of Lyndon Johnson's senior staff members was criticized in the press for giving a rather syrupy speech in which he stated, "I sleep each night a little better, a little more confidently because Lyndon Johnson is my President. For I know he lives and thinks and works to make sure that for all Americans, and indeed, the growing body of the free world, the morning shall always come."[57]

The President's Attitude toward Staff

Staff behavior that takes the form of flattery as well as ready agreement with the President can succeed only if presidents are willing to encourage it. There is, in fact, a tendency for presidents to do so, and the reasons grow out of the effects the Office has upon the man, as well as the effect the man has upon the Office.

To understand how the Office may influence the man, consider for a moment how we treat this institution. For years the scholarly and journalistic communities have sung the praises of this Office, pointing to it as the only place

---

[55] Safire, *Before the Fall*, p. 437.

[56] Hughes, *Living Presidency*, p. 144.

[57] Valenti, *Very Human President*, pp. 95, 96.

in our political system capable of leadership and innovation. Not only have the media romanticized the Presidency, but they have also personalized it, informing us of the President's habits, tastes, and hobbies, many of which become national fads. Nor should we minimize the symbolic trappings surrounding the Office. The President is the only democratically elected Chief Executive in the world who is hailed by a special song ("Hail to the Chief") when he appears at public events. Men and women alike stand when he enters and leaves a room. Upon becoming President, he is henceforth referred to as "Mr. President" even by his closest friends. This fact was impressed upon Eisenhower when, shortly after assuming the Presidency, he placed a call to his friend Omar Bradley, Chairman of the Joint Chiefs of Staff. After the conversation was over, Eisenhower turned to his secretary and with great surprise said, "He called me Mr. President, and I've known Brad all my life."[58] While the Prime Minister of Great Britain is referred to by his Cabinet as "Mr. Prime Minister" on formal occasions, in Cabinet meetings he is called by his first name. Members of the President's Cabinet, however, would never think of referring to him by anything other than "Mr. President," regardless of the circumstances. Yachts, custom-made automobiles, planes, bodyguards, and houses are all placed at his disposal. Extraordinary efforts are made to fulfill his every desire. For example, one day while President Eisenhower was putting on his special green on the White House lawn, a squirrel ran in front of the ball and he casually remarked, "Get that goddamned squirrel out of here." Lo and behold, the next day he discovered the corps of the Parks Department rushing about the White House lawn trapping squirrels. Attention and reverence are accorded presidents even after they leave office. When a former President takes ill, we receive hourly bulletins on his condition, and when he dies, a national day of mourning is declared and he is usually laid to rest in an elaborate state funeral. Clearly the respect for this institution has changed markedly from the time of Thomas Jefferson, who, after being inaugurated, returned to his boarding house for dinner and had to wait in line until there was a vacant place at the table.

It is difficult for a President to escape being affected by the reverential treatment accorded to the office he occupies. One of Kennedy's long-time friends recalls that when sailing on the presidential yacht, Kennedy became quite annoyed if other boats failed to recognize and salute him. On one occasion after giving a speech on a military base, President Johnson headed out onto the landing strip full of planes. While proceeding to where he thought his plane was situated, he was approached by a soldier, who told him his plane was off in the other direction. Johnson took him by the shoulder and said, "Son, I want to tell you something—just so you never forget. *All* of them, those over there *and* those over there—are *my* planes." Only after he was severely ridiculed by the press did Richard Nixon abandon the regal, fancy-dress uniforms he had

[58] Charles Murphy, "Eisenhower's White House," in Nelson Polsby, ed., *The Modern Presidency* (New York: Random House, 1973), p. 89.

ordered for the White House guards. And as Charles Colson notes, he was also quite insistent that traditional symbolic trappings be maintained. One evening, for example, President Nixon decided to pay an unannounced visit to the Kennedy Center to hear a concert given by the military bands. Shortly before entering the presidential box, Colson recalls, "The President turned and said, 'Have you made arrangements for them to play the you-know-what, Chuck?' He didn't come right out and say it, but I knew he meant 'Hail to the Chief.'"[59]

These examples of presidential behavior may seem inconsequential, but they are symptomatic of a more fundamental presidential attitude which is of concern to us. Presidents have a tendency to become intoxicated by the deference and veneration shown to the Office they hold. They begin to see themselves as deserving of praise and come to view challenge and disagreement as an affront. In order to preserve their access to the President, staff members accommodate themselves to this presidential tendency. One of Franklin D. Roosevelt's closest aids contends that those advisers who lasted the longest with him were the ones who did not challenge his thinking, but rather gave unquestioning service.[60] Even the seemingly unpretentious Harry Truman was not enamored of the prospect of having an individual on his staff whose sole job would be to act as a critic of presidential thinking. In fact, one of his advisers had made just such a suggestion, although he noted that such an individual would probably last only six months. Truman replied, "Six *months*? I would not have him around six *minutes.*" Similarly, one of Eisenhower's senior aids notes that in the closing years of the Eisenhower Presidency, the White House staff agreed informally not to bring him any upsetting news.[61]

The isolation of presidents from the disquieting advice of staff members was especially pronounced in the Johnson and Nixon administrations. Both men were lacking in a sense of security, and consequently they were especially susceptible to the arrogance generated by the intoxicating atmosphere of the Presidency. In Johnson's case, his style of bullying staff members and his obsession with loyalty further encouraged advisers not to challenge him. One participant in White House decision making during the Johnson Presidency describes how this timidity manifested itself:

The President, in due course, would announce his decision and then poll everyone in the room—Council members, their assistants, and members of the White House and NSC staffs. "Mr. Secretary, do you agree with the decision?" "Yes, Mr. President!" "Mr. X, do you agree?" "I agree, Mr. President." During the process I would frequently fall into a Walter Mitty-like fantasy: When my turn came I would rise to my feet slowly, look around the room and then directly at the President, and say very

[59] Charles Colson, *Born Again*, p. 53. Copyright © 1976. Published by Chosen Books Publishing Co., Ltd., Lincoln, Virginia 22078. Used by permission.

[60] Hardin, *Presidential Power*, p. 25.

[61] Hughes, *Living Presidency*, p. 143.

quietly and emphatically, "Mr. President, gentlemen, I most definitely do *not* agree!" But I was removed from my trance when I heard the President's voice saying, "Mr. Cooper, do you agree?" And out would come a "Yes, Mr. President, I agree."[62]

As we shall see in the next chapter, those aids who did ultimately stand up and challenge Lyndon Johnson's Vietnam policy either lost their access to him or, more frequently, were let go.

Of all our recent presidents, Richard Nixon was perhaps the most isolated. As noted earlier, he simply did not like to see people. Moreover, like his predecessor, he did not take kindly to disagreeable advice from his staff. Indeed, when possible, he sought to avoid seeing advisers who he knew were about to bring him "bad news or unpalatable recommendations."[63] Those who did challenge him with disturbing facts thought twice before doing so again. One aid, for example, recalls that on one occasion he complimented the President on becoming more accessible to the press. Having held a rather antagonistic attitude toward the press, Nixon proceeded to deny that he was becoming any more accessible. When the evidence was produced to show that he was in fact granting more interviews to newsmen, the President promptly cancelled a news conference that had been scheduled for the next day. As for the aid who brought the disquieting information to Nixon and even refuted the President's challenge to its validity, he recalls that, "for three solid months I did not receive a speech assignment from the President, or a phone call, or a memo, or a nod in the hall as he was passing by."[64] As further punishment, he was one of two long-time advisers not invited to the White House wedding of the President's daughter.

Gerald Ford was quite different from his two predecessors in both style and temperament. He lacked both their powerful ego and their insecurity. Consequently, he appears to have been less influenced by the monarchical trappings of the Presidency, less inclined to feel the need for praise and agreement from those around him. Yet even under Ford, the awe of the Presidency was still there, and according to his former chief of staff, this factor continued to inhibit his advisers from being completely candid with him:

> I can think of many instances where individuals who have been long-time associates and colleagues of the President's have been in a meeting with the President, addressed an issue with him, and then slipped down to my office after the meeting and said, "Now, what I really wanted to say was this." And they took the bark off, and there was something that had a very different feel.[65]

[62] Cited in Russell Baker and Charles Peters, "The Prince and His Courtiers: At the White House, the Kremlin, and the Reichschancellery," *The Washington Monthly,* February 1973, p. 36.

[63] Woodward and Bernstein, *Final Days,* p. 31.

[64] Safire, *Before the Fall,* p. 350.

[65] Interview with Donald Rumsfeld on "Firing Line," telecast on the Public Broadcasting System, November 1975. Transcript from Southern Educational Communications Association, P.O. Box 5966, Columbia, South Carolina 29250.

If accounts thus far are correct about Carter's White House staff, it has behaved no differently from those of previous presidents. Indeed, after his administration was only three months old, Carter received a confidential memo from Hamilton Jordan expressing concern over the tendency of advisers to anticipate what the President wanted to hear, instead of providing him with candid appraisals.[66] While a sense of awe for the office has no doubt contributed to this kind of behavior, there is evidence to suggest that Carter's personality may also have been a contributing factor. Charles Kirbo, who is one of the President's closest confidants, readily acknowledges that the President "has a strong personality that tends to intimidate some people."[67] This assessment is confirmed by another White House assistant: "The office, of course, is so damned intimidating in itself and Carter is such an intimidating man that it's just very difficult to disagree with him."[68] Other individuals in the Carter Administration have remarked about being ignored or receiving an "icy look" from the President when they dissented too strongly from his views.[69] Yet unlike Johnson and Nixon, Carter's impatience with dissent does not appear to be rooted in feelings of insecurity, but rather in a supreme sense of confidence in his own judgments. This aspect of Carter's personality will be considered in greater detail in the next chapter.

OUTSIDE ADVISERS

In discussing whom the President consults for information and advice, we have thus far focused upon individuals and groups within the Executive branch. But it should be noted that he seeks the counsel of people outside of government as well. Such individuals often include former government officials. Lyndon Johnson, for example, sought the advice of former presidents Truman and Eisenhower. Indeed, in the case of the latter, Johnson on many occasions had him flown by a Jetstar from his farm in Gettysburg to Andrews Air Force Base outside Washington. Johnson then helicoptered to Andrews where he met in secret with Ike aboard the Jetstar. He also sought the assistance of former Secretary of State Dean Acheson in dealing with the Cyprus problem.[70] Similarly, President Kennedy included both Acheson and former Secretary of Defense Robert Lovett in the decision making during the Cuban missile crisis.

Presidents also turn to old and trusted friends for advice. Johnson, for example, brought his long-time friend Clark Clifford into the deliberations on Vietnam long before he finally appointed him as Secretary of Defense. Simi-

[66] Shogan, *Promises To Keep,* p. 200.

[67] Ibid., p. 249.

[68] *New York Times,* April 25, 1977, p. 53.

[69] Hedrick Smith, "Problems of a Problem Solver," *New York Times Magazine,* January 8, 1978, p. 38.

[70] Valenti, *Very Human President,* pp. 380, 308.

larly, his lawyer friend, Abe Fortas, was consulted on a variety of matters before, and even after, he appointed him to the Supreme Court. Even a President's family have been reputed to exercise considerable influence over presidential opinion. Eisenhower sought out his brother Milton, and Kennedy was known to consult with his father. In the cases of Roosevelt, Ford, and especially Johnson, the judgment of their wives was frequently solicited on a variety of matters.

Other outsiders consulted by presidents include recognized experts in a given field. Both Kennedy and Johnson, for example, sought the expertise of economist John Kenneth Galbraith and foreign policy expert Henry Kissinger. Moreover, presidents may from time to time bring a whole group of experts together to examine a critical problem or formulate policy proposals. Lyndon Johnson made use of several such informal presidential task forces which were charged with developing legislative proposals for his Great Society program. These groups were made up of academicians, economists, scientists, doctors, businessmen, labor leaders, and lawyers from all over the country.[71] Nixon continued the practice, setting up seventeen different task forces for purposes of developing legislative programs for 1970 and beyond.[72]

In attempting to deal with certain highly visible and controversial issues, presidents may decide to establish more formalized groups known as commissions, whose members are appointed directly by the President. Following the urban riots of the midsixties, for example, Johnson established the National Commission on the Causes and Prevention of Violence and toward the end of his administration, he created the National Commission on Obscenity and Pornography. Similarly, in response to the increasing concern among Americans over the use of drugs, Richard Nixon established the National Commission on Drug Abuse. Following the revelations about CIA activities in and outside of the United States, President Ford decided to clear the air by appointing an eight-member commission which was charged with determining whether or not the CIA had exceeded its statutory authority. Of these eight members, seven were private citizens and the eighth was Vice President Rockefeller, whom Ford designated as chairman of the commission.

Relying upon individuals who are not officially connected with the government can be very beneficial to a President. Given their separation from the machinations of government, as well as the fact that their livelihood is in no way dependent upon the favor of the President, they are more likely to provide him with a candid assessment. Seeking the advice of distinguished private citizens is not without its risks, however, for they may ultimately come up with conclusions and recommendations that run contrary to the views of the President. Thus, it was undoubtedly somewhat embarrassing for President Nixon when he felt compelled to refute publicly the findings of both the National

[71] Califano, *Presidential Nation,* p. 239.

[72] "The Office of the President: Formulation and Implementation of Domestic Policy," *The White House: Organization and Operation,* Proceedings of the 1970 Montauk Symposium, vol. 1 (New York: Center for the Study of the Presidency, 1971), p. 82.

Commission on Obscenity and Pornography and the National Commission on Drug Abuse. Nor was it likely that the distinguished citizens sitting on these commissions were pleased with the fact that he did so.

Finally, it should be noted that presidents may also seek the counsel of individuals who, although not outside of the government, are nevertheless outside of the Executive branch. I refer to members of Congress, many of whom are recognized experts in certain policy areas. President Kennedy had great respect for the foreign policy expertise of former Senator William Fulbright, who was Chairman of the Senate Foreign Relations Committee. Accordingly, he included him in the White House deliberations on the Bay of Pigs invasion of Cuba. Similarly, because of his knowledge of labor relations, Lyndon Johnson always sought the advice of then Senator Wayne Morse on important matters concerning labor. However, according to Lyndon Johnson's former Press Secretary George Reedy, the counsel provided to presidents by members of Congress is often not what it should be. For them, just as for others in government, frank advice is often muted by their awe for the Office:

> I can recall an occasion about six or seven months after I had left the White House, when I met Senator Russell at a party in Washington. I said to him: "Senator, do things look as bad as I think they do?" and he said "Yes they do, George." And I said, "Senator you used to be quite effective in talking to the President. Why don't you make a trip down to the White House and have a heart-to-heart talk." And his response was, "George, I can't talk to a President the way I can talk to a Senator." And this to me was the key. There *is* a difference in status which separates the President from his peers because if a United States Senator is not the peer of a President, who is?[73]

Reedy also notes his surprise at the behavior of Senator Barry Goldwater and Governor George Wallace when they came to the White House in 1964. As presidential candidates, they had been travelling about the country excoriating the President and his policies, and Reedy fully expected that they would have some strong words for the President. Yet when these two rather independent and blunt individuals were confronted with his presence, "They were the mildest, meekest Casper Milquetoasts I've ever seen in my life. Those men were not afraid of Lyndon Johnson. It was the President who overawed them."[74]

PRESIDENTIAL DECISION MAKING

Quite obviously the essential ingredients for informed decision making are information and advice. The latter includes varying perceptions as to how the facts ought to be interpreted, judgments about what options are available for

[73] George Reedy, *The Presidency in Flux* (New York: Columbia University Press, 1973), p. 30.

[74] Ibid., p. 32.

dealing with a particular issue, and finally, judgments about what consequences are likely to follow from the implementation of any given option. Of course, even if the President is in possession of the best information and advice he can hope to get, there is still no guarantee that he will make the right decision. The facts and advice he receives may prove to be wrong. Or his own biases may be so strong that he misperceives the realities of a situation and thus ignores the advice he receives. Or perhaps circumstances may arise that could not have been anticipated at the time a decision was made. Yet even if access to information and advice do not always insure the right decision, it is even more likely that the lack of them will produce a bad one.

Whether or not the flow of information and advice to the President is maximized will depend most directly upon two factors, the first of which is the number of sources he is willing to reach out to. To the extent that he restricts his information channels, he risks becoming the captive of what a few people tell him. For not only are government actors capable of misjudgments but in most instances they have a stake in how a given policy issue is to be resolved, and thus, consciously or unconsciously, they may provide the President with a biased assessment. Though by no means foolproof, the President's willingness to expose himself to a variety of sources acts as a corrective against biased or faulty information.

The accumulation of the necessary facts and advice for informed decision making is also dependent upon the degree to which the President encourages a frank and open exchange of views from among those he does consult. Indeed, he must make a special effort in this regard, for as already noted, presidential advisers are too much inclined toward ready agreement with their boss. Moreover, if scholars such as Irving Janis are correct, there is still another reason for him to do so, since cohesive decision-making groups have a tendency to engage in "groupthink." Among other things, this phenomenon involves an effort by the group to maximize amicable relations by minimizing differences and emphasizing areas of agreement: "The group leader and the members support each other, playing up the areas of convergence in their thinking, at the expense of fully exploring divergences that might disrupt the apparent unity of the group. Better to share a pleasant, balmy group atmosphere than to be battered in a storm."[75] Both the excessive deference and "groupthink" phenomena can only be further encouraged if the President conveys the impression that he does not take kindly to those who dissent from his and the group's point of view.

Having stressed how important it is for the President to consult widely, it is also important to recognize that this task is rendered either easier or more difficult by the nature of the decision. The decisions he makes may be viewed along two dimensions, one dealing with their *substance* (foreign ←——→ domestic) and the other with their *importance* (routine ←——→ crisis).

[75] Irving L. Janis, *Victims of Groupthink* (Boston: Houghton Mifflin, 1972), p. 39. Copyright © 1972 by Houghton Mifflin Co. Reprinted by permission.

Substance. If the President is freer to act in the foreign policy area, it is also the case that his informational constraints are greater. To the extent that foreign policy involves issues exterior to the United States, the problems in acquiring necessary information about them are increased. Quite obviously, getting information is much less of a problem in the domestic area, where the proximity of an issue renders its nature and consequences more readily observable.

Also, the President's informational problems are likely to be greater in the area of foreign policy because there are fewer participants in the foreign policy-making process, and thus the sources of information are less. At the upper levels, the participants in foreign policy in most instances include the departments of State and Defense, the CIA, and the National Security Council. While the Congress certainly has an impact upon foreign policy, its role in domestic policy is more direct and persistent, first because the President's information base on foreign policy is superior to that of Congress; second, because the committee organization of Congress is far less developed in the foreign policy area than in the domestic area; and third, because the interests of most congressmen incline toward domestic issues because the political payoff is likely to be greater. While interest groups are more in evidence on those foreign policy issues that have immediate and direct domestic implications, their involvement is far less apparent as the issues become more discreetly foreign in their impact. This is in marked contrast to the domestic policy-making process, where a whole panoply of interests are constantly operating at both the executive and congressional levels.

Finally, it should be noted that, unlike the domestic policy-making process, the limited number of actors in foreign policy will often be reduced still further because many foreign policy issues involve delicate matters of national security.

Importance. The President's problems with information relate not only to the substance of a given issue but also to its importance. While in the strict sense every issue that requires a presidential decision qualifies as important, clearly some issues are more important than others; and given the considerable demands on his time, the President must reserve his own energies for the more critical ones. Thus on the more routine issues—whether domestic or foreign—he is not likely to become directly involved in the decision-making process until the final stage. This means that he is far more reliant upon what his advisers tell him regarding the deliberations up to that point. On the other hand, when dealing with issues of great moment, the President's involvement in the decision-making process is likely to be more persistent and direct. Consequently, he is in a position to hear *firsthand* the facts presented, the options considered, and the consequences weighed. Moreover, as the most prominent actor in the decision-making process, he is in a better position to force consideration of all possibilities—*if* he is of the mind to do so.

Yet if he has the advantage of more intimate involvement on the more critical issues, it should also be pointed out that such issues may impose an informational constraint that is not likely to be present on more routine matters. For among the more critical issues he must confront are those characterized as "crises." By their very nature, crises customarily require timely action, which may sometimes prevent him from making as extensive a search for information as he might like.

FOUR CASES IN PRESIDENTIAL DECISION MAKING

In the remainder of this chapter, we shall examine four examples of presidential decision making. The first three attempt to show how and why the flow of information to the President was not maximized, while the other demonstrates an apparently successful effort at information maximization. Before looking at these examples, however, the reader should be apprised of their limitations. First, three of the four decidedly fall in the realm of foreign policy. The absence of more examples on the domestic side is dictated by the state of the literature on presidential decision making, which unfortunately has focused almost exclusively on the analysis of foreign-policy decisions.[76] Second, while it is hoped that the following examination of these four decisions identifies the major factors that bear on the decision-making process, this cannot be said with complete certainty. As one President himself admitted, "There will always be the dark and tangled stretches in the decision-making process—mysterious even to those who may be most intimately involved. . . ."[77]

The Bay of Pigs Invasion

The plan to invade Cuba had its genesis in the Eisenhower Administration. Acting upon a proposal made by Vice President Nixon, Eisenhower instructed the Central Intelligence Agency to organize and train Cuban exiles for the purpose of engaging in guerrilla warfare against the government of Fidel Castro. As the plan began to take shape, the CIA's confidence grew to the point where it decided to abandon the more modest goal of guerrilla warfare and opted instead for a full-scale invasion of Cuba. This invasion, which occurred approximately three months after John Kennedy took office, may be justly characterized as one of the greatest foreign policy blunders in American history.

Upon landing at the Bay of Pigs, the invasion force of fourteen hundred men was put at a severe disadvantage, for Castro's air force sank two of the four ships that were supposed to provide the invaders with munitions and other supplies. Following these sinkings, the other two ships promptly departed the scene and sought safer waters. Although all reports suggest that the invaders fought valiantly, by the third day they were surrounded by Castro's army and

[76] Heclo, *Studying the Presidency*, p. 22.

[77] Sorensen, *Decision-Making in the White House*, p. xiii.

forced to surrender or else be killed. The costs resulting from this debacle were high for both the President and the country. Kennedy and his administration appeared inept. Moreover, charges of American imperialism and aggression were heard in the United Nations and in foreign capitals around the world. After it was all over, President Kennedy turned to an aid and mused aloud, "How could I have been so far off base. . . . How could I have been so stupid to let them go ahead?"[78] Others were asking the same question.

The pressures upon Kennedy to go ahead with the invasion had been considerable. While he personally did not think that Castro posed any security threat to the United States, nevertheless, the presence of a Communist regime only ninety miles off our coast was a constant source of irritation. In addition, during his election campaign he had pledged to support anti-Castro rebels; by refusing to do so, he would not only be reneging on a promise, but also abandoning a tradition of American support for anti-Communist forces around the world. There was also the problem of what to do with the Cuban exiles if the plan were called off. If brought to the United States, they would undoubtedly reveal the plan and make known their dissatisfaction with the President's refusal to go through with it. Lastly, Kennedy was advised that a decision to go ahead or to abort the invasion plan could not be delayed, for the Soviet Union would soon be providing Castro's army with armaments and training, thus making it a more formidable opponent. With all of these factors in mind, the President gave the go ahead but also made one major change in the plan—there was to be no overt United States involvement in the operation. As he would later recount to one of his aids, he thought the United States had everything to gain and nothing to lose. The invasion, after all, had a good chance of succeeding, and even if it failed, the Cuban exiles could retreat to the mountains and carry on guerrilla warfare against the Castro regime.[79] Moreover, all of this could be achieved without any direct involvement on the part of the United States.

Given the nature of the facts and advice he received, it is not surprising that Kennedy's initial skepticism about the invasion plan was ultimately overcome by a more optimistic attitude. Unfortunately, most of the information provided him proved to be erroneous or inadequate. The CIA's Richard Bissell had, for example, assured him that no one would ever be able to trace the invasion plan back to the United States government. The exiles were being trained in secret camps in Nicaragua and Guatemala; and the American B-26s that were to be used for air cover in the invasion would be painted to look like Castro's own B-26 bombers, thus creating the impression that his own men had defected to the other side. Despite these precautions, however, stories about an impending invasion of Cuba began to appear in the press as early as one week prior to the event. That both the invasion and our covert involvement in it could have been kept secret seems naive, considering the fact that the plan was known to some

[78] Theodore Sorensen, *Kennedy* (New York: Harper & Row, 1965), p. 309.
[79] Ibid., pp. 295–97.

fourteen hundred Cuban exiles as well as to officials in the Nicaraguan and Guatemalan governments. This miscalculation may have arisen from the CIA's lack of experience in planning large-scale clandestine operations.[80]

Kennedy's advisers also appeared confident that camouflaged American B-26 bombers could knock out Castro's allegedly ill-equipped air force immediately before the landing of the invasion force at the Bay of Pigs. This assessment also proved to be a gross misjudgment. The B-26s were obsolete, many of them developed engine trouble, and on the first day alone, half of them were shot down by Castro's planes. Contrary to what Kennedy had been told, the Cuban dictator's air force proved to be well trained and well enough equipped to meet the invasion challenge. Even those American planes that managed to escape being shot down proved to be limited in their effectiveness, for their flight from Nicaragua to Cuba had required a considerable amount of fuel; consequently, in order to insure enough fuel for the return to Nicaragua, the planes were limited in the amount of time they could spend over the combat area.

Kennedy had repeatedly inquired about the morale of the invasion brigade, and CIA officials assured him that it was high. This evaluation represented an exaggeration of considerable proportions, however. Many of the Cuban exiles had little use for their commanding officers. The latter were left over from the Batista regime, which had governed Cuba ruthlessly before Castro came to power. At one point prior to the invasion, there was a full-fledged mutiny among the Cuban exiles, and the ringleaders were spirited off to a Guatemalan prison camp by CIA agents. The morale of the invasion brigade would no doubt have been even lower had not the CIA deceived them into believing that other brigades were also being trained for the invasion, that American Marines would be assisting in the operation, and finally, that other landings would be made on other parts of the island so as to draw some of Castro's forces away from the Bay of Pigs.[81] These false promises apparently were made without the knowledge of President Kennedy.

The ability of the invasion brigade to establish a beachhead on the shores of Cuba was predicated on the assumption that it would be facing a poorly trained and ill-equipped Cuban army. While Kennedy had received assurances from the CIA that Castro's army would pose no serious threat to the invaders, in actual fact the training and military equipment of Castro's forces proved to be more than adequate to the task of thwarting the invasion. The CIA had been told as much by experts in the State Department and British Intelligence, but chose to ignore these estimates and also failed to pass them along to the President.

Certainly one of the most costly miscalculations concerning the Bay of Pigs invasion dealt with the role of the Cuban underground and the likelihood of a revolt against Castro by the Cuban people themselves. Given the small number of

[80] Janis, *Victims of Groupthink*, pp. 20, 21.
[81] Ibid., p. 22.

people in the invasion force, the overthrow of Castro would be contingent upon carefully coordinated sabotage efforts by the Cuban underground and also upon armed uprisings among the populace. As one Kennedy adviser noted, this view was universally shared by those advising the President: "We all in the White House considered uprisings behind the lines essential to the success of the operation; so, too, did the Joint Chiefs of Staff. . . ."[82] The CIA reported that the Cuban underground consisted of some twenty-five hundred individuals plus another twenty thousand or so sympathizers. Once the invasion force landed, these indigenous anti-Castro forces would swing into action and internal uprisings would follow.

Here too, this CIA assessment was more a reflection of hope than of the realities of the situation. In actuality, the CIA had not made any hard intelligence estimates as to the capability of the Cuban underground or the likelihood of popular uprisings. Indeed, CIA Director Allen Dulles later admitted that his agency never really expected much support from the Cuban underground, for as it turned out, the underground distrusted the CIA and vice versa. Consequently, there was little coordination between the invasion planners and the leaders of the underground. Moreover, the CIA never provided the underground with the supplies they needed to carry out their sabotage operations. These factors alone made it all but inevitable that the internal resistance movement would lack any substantial punch. Furthermore, after the invasion began, Fidel Castro proved to be highly efficient at rounding up potential dissidents, and his support among the Cuban people proved to be far greater than the CIA had estimated. Thus, the possibility of overthrowing the Castro regime through indigenous uprisings was doomed to failure.[83]

The safety of the invasion brigade had been a constant source of concern to Kennedy. In the event that the invasion did not succeed, he wanted to be sure that the exiles would be able to escape. On several occasions the top men at the CIA assured the President that they would, noting that if necessary, the brigade could retreat into the Escambray Mountains, which were only a short distance from the landing site. Once in the mountains, they could join up with other anti-Castro forces and assist them in guerrilla operations against his regime. Unfortunately, this plan would work only so long as the brigade landed at Trinidad, which was the original site selected for the invasion. On the grounds that Trinidad was too conspicious for such a landing, the site was later changed to the Bay of Pigs. With this change, the Escambray Mountains were now some eighty miles away, and in order to get to them, the invading force would have to traverse terrain consisting largely of swamps and jungle. Consequently, the CIA made no preparation for an escape to the mountains, and instead instructed the exiles to fall back on the beaches if the invasion effort failed. While Kennedy

[82] Ibid., p. 24.
[83] Ibid., pp. 24–26.

knew of the change in the landing site, he was not told that this change eliminated the possibility of an escape to the mountains.[84] Nor, it should be noted, did it occur to Kennedy or any of his advisers to look at a map of Cuba, or they would have seen immediately that the escape option was not feasible.

In the decision-making process that led up to the Bay of Pigs invasion, Kennedy was clearly the victim of faulty and inadequate information. In part this resulted from the fact that he had to rely almost exclusively upon one channel of information—the CIA. Since this agency had planned the invasion, it is not altogether surprising that it proved to be a forceful advocate of the benefits and less than forthcoming on the risks involved in such a venture. Had other units in the government been more intimately involved in evaluating the plan, its limitations may well have been exposed. Unfortunately, the operations division of the CIA kept close control over the operation. Neither the Cuban desk at the State Department nor even the intelligence-gathering division at the CIA was consulted on the invasion plans. Moreover, when the head of the State Department's intelligence branch later asked permission to scrutinize the plan, he was refused.[85] The severe restriction put on the number of people involved in the planning and evaluations of the invasion was motivated by a desire to maintain complete secrecy, but as one Kennedy adviser noted, "The 'need-to-know' standard—i.e., that no one should be told about a project unless it becomes operationally necessary—thus had the idiotic effect of excluding much of the expertise of government at a time when every alert newspaperman knew something was afoot."[86] Thus, with the cat out of the bag, the continued concern for secrecy served little useful purpose in this particular case.

Of course, a President may indeed be forced to restrict his channels of information when he is dealing with highly sensitive matters, but it is precisely on these occasions that both he and his advisers must be especially vigilant in probing and challenging the few experts on whom they are relying. In this respect, both Kennedy and some of his key advisers failed. During the deliberations with the CIA and the Joint Chiefs of Staff, Kennedy's advisers expressed few doubts about either the feasibility or desirability of the invasion. There appears to have been no serious examination of the most fundamental question of all, namely, was the invasion necessary in the first place? Also absent was any serious probing of the CIA as to how it knew that Castro's army was ill-equipped and poorly trained, or on what grounds it concluded that his political strength was weak. Nor were the Joint Chiefs thoroughly questioned on the military aspects of the invasion. That key advisers failed to raise vigorous challenges should not be interpreted to mean that no doubts existed, however. In fact, one of the participants in the group, Arthur Schlesinger, wrote a lengthy memorandum to the President arguing that Castro was too strong to be over-

[84] Sorensen, *Kennedy*, p. 302.

[85] Roger Hilsman, *To Move a Nation* (Garden City, N.Y.: Doubleday, 1964), p. 31.

[86] Arthur Schlesinger, Jr., *A Thousand Days* (Boston: Houghton Mifflin, 1965), p. 248.

thrown by this small-scale invasion. Yet at no time did he voice these misgivings during the deliberations. Likewise, according to one State Department official, Secretary of State Rusk raised incisive questions about the plan with his aids at the State Department but declined to do so during meetings at the White House. Moreover, one undersecretary who had attended one of the meetings in Rusk's place subsequently wrote an extensive memorandum criticizing the proposed invasion. But when he asked Rusk's permission to present these arguments to the President, he was refused. Even the CIA and the Joint Chiefs apparently had some doubts regarding the plan's feasibility after the President stipulated that there could be no *overt* United States involvement, yet they too failed to voice them to the President.[87] They might have, however, had they been pressed more forcefully by Kennedy and his advisers.

Thus, despite lingering doubts, the meetings took place in what Arthur Schlesinger describes as a "curious atmosphere of assumed consensus." Several factors may help to explain why this occurred. For one thing, to the *newly* installed President and his advisers, the CIA and the Joint Chiefs appeared as formidable and impressive advocates of the plan, thus discouraging any serious challenge to their assessments. As Kennedy later remarked, " . . . you always assume that the military and intelligence people have some secret skill not available to ordinary mortals."[88] Second, some Kennedy advisers apparently felt that opposition to the plan would be interpreted as being "soft on communism," a label that might destroy their credibility in future White House councils.[89] Finally, Kennedy's own handling of the deliberations was not as effective in encouraging debate and thorough analysis as it might have been. In the interest of security, he permitted the printed information distributed by the CIA to be collected at the end of each session; thus there was little opportunity for advisers to digest and critically evaluate it. He made no effort to circulate the memo he had received from Schlesinger criticizing the plan. Nor was he especially vigilant in encouraging those in attendance to voice their opinions. Undersecretary of State Chester Bowles attended one of the meetings in Rusk's place and was appalled by what he heard. Unfortunately, the President did not call upon him to express his views; nor could he volunteer them, since protocol dictates that undersecretaries may not speak at meetings unless asked to by the President. The President also knew of Arthur Schlesinger's misgivings about the invasion, but apparently made no effort to force him to voice them before the group. To his credit, it should be noted that Kennedy did invite Senator William Fulbright to come before a final meeting of the group and express his strong opposition to the plan, a view he had already communicated to the President in a memorandum. After the senator finished his presentation, however, Kennedy failed to stimulate a discussion about it. Instead, he continued what he had begun before

---

[87] Janis, *Victims of Groupthink*, p. 42; Sorensen, *Kennedy*, p. 306.

[88] Schlesinger, *Thousand Days*, p. 258.

[89] Sorensen, *Kennedy*, p. 306.

Fulbright came into the meeting, namely, going around the table and asking each member of the group for a final opinion on whether to go ahead with the plan.[90] Following a unanimous vote in favor of the invasion, Kennedy gave the final go-ahead, assuming a consensus among his advisers that proved to be far less real than it appeared.

The Cuban Missile Crisis

As a foreign policy problem, the Cuban missile crisis differed from the Bay of Pigs invasion in two important respects. For one thing, the stakes were much higher. The United States was now in a direct "eyeball-to-eyeball" confrontation with the second greatest nuclear power in the world. President Kennedy estimated the chances of a resulting nuclear war at one in three. Second, while there was ample time to consider the plan for the Bay of Pigs invasion, the placing of missiles in Cuba by the Soviet Union was unexpected and required some kind of an immediate response by the United States.

The Soviet Union had repeatedly asserted that there was little reason for it to place nuclear weapons on foreign soil. As the Soviet news agency put it, " . . . there is no need for the Soviet Union to shift its weapons for the repulsion of aggression, for a retaliatory blow, to any other country, *for instance Cuba.* Our nuclear weapons are so powerful in their explosive force . . . that there is no need to search for sites for them beyond the boundaries of the Soviet Union."[91] Yet the increase in the shipment of Soviet arms and personnel to Cuba caused Kennedy considerable concern. Through private diplomatic channels, he sought and was given assurances by the Soviets that no offensive missile capability would be placed in Cuba. But as the build-up in arms continued, the President felt it necessary to issue a public warning to the Russians, noting that if Cuba became an "offensive military base of sufficient capacity for the Soviet Union, then this country will do whatever must be done to protect its own security and that of its allies."[92] At this point, the United States still had no hard evidence that the Russians had in fact placed offensive missiles in Cuba. Indeed, in September 1962, a National Intelligence estimate concluded that it was unlikely that the Soviets would make such a move. This assessment proved to be inaccurate, however, for one month later photographs taken by a U-2 reconnaissance plane provided incontrovertible evidence that missile sites were indeed being constructed there.

The President summoned a group of advisers to the Cabinet Room, informed them of the news, and stated that under no conditions could the United States accept the Soviet Union's bold action. He then instructed the group to consider a course of action that would lead to the removal of the missiles from Cuba.

[90] Janis, *Victims of Groupthink,* pp. 43–46.

[91] Cited in Graham Allison, *Essence of Decision* (Boston: Little, Brown, 1971), p. 40.

[92] Ibid., p. 41.

That Kennedy immediately eliminated one option—doing nothing—was dictated by several considerations. He saw the Soviet's action as a probe designed to test American will in general, and more specifically, his own. He feared that Premier Khrushchev had perceived him as a man lacking in resolve; and there were indeed some grounds for Khrushchev's thinking so, for when the two met in Vienna in June of 1961, Kennedy appeared indecisive and intimidated by the Soviet leader.[93] Moreover, Khrushchev apparently had been surprised that the United States did not respond more forcefully when the Soviet Union erected the Berlin Wall in August 1961. If Kennedy once again appeared weak in the face of this latest Soviet initiative, the Russians would feel free to become even more daring in the future. Also, Kennedy felt that regardless of whether or not the missiles in Cuba would significantly alter the balance of power, the fact is they would appear to have done so; and as he himself remarked, "Appearances contribute to reality." Finally, he also had to take domestic political considerations into account, for if he failed to take action, the Republicans would be handed an explosive campaign issue in the upcoming midterm elections. Nor could he ignore the possibility that inaction might even lead to his impeachment.

Rather than relying essentially upon the National Security Council as he had done in the Bay of Pigs invasion, this time Kennedy reached out to a wider group, which would later be dubbed the Executive Committee of the National Security Council (ExComm). From his White House staff he included not only his Special Assistant for National Security Affairs, but also his close aid, Theodore Sorensen. In addition, his appointments secretary and personal confidant, Kenneth O'Donnell, was also invited to some of the meetings. While neither of these two aids had any special expertise in foreign policy matters, the President nevertheless respected their judgment. Besides, the Bay of Pigs fiasco had already taught him that experts could be wrong. Naturally, the Chairman of the Joint Chiefs, the secretaries of Defense and State, and the Director of the CIA were also included in ExComm. But this time Kennedy also made a special effort to reach out for capable individuals further down in the bureaucracy. Thus, from the Department of State he brought in Undersecretary George Ball, Deputy Undersecretary Alexis Johnson, Assistant Secretary Edwin Martin, the U.S. Ambassador to the United Nations Adlai Stevenson, and Soviet expert Llewellyn Thompson. Likewise, he included both the deputy and assistant secretaries of Defense. Although neither the Justice nor Treasury departments had any direct involvement in the crisis at hand, the President asked his Attorney General (Robert Kennedy) and Treasury Secretary (Douglas Dillon) to attend the meetings—again, because he valued their judgment. Also tapped for the group was the Deputy Director of the U.S. Information Agency. In addition to reaching down into the government, Kennedy sought the wisdom of prominent

---

[93] James Nathan, "The Missile Crisis: His Finest Hour Now," *World Politics,* 27 (January 1975), 266.

individuals outside of government. Included were Dean Acheson (former Secretary of State), Robert Lovett (former Defense Secretary), and John McCloy (former High Commissioner of Germany), all of whom were present at several of ExComm's meetings. Moreover, Kennedy also communicated by phone with former presidents Hoover, Truman, and Eisenhower, although none of them participated in the deliberations.

In summary, in dealing with the Cuban missile crisis the President was clearly seeking to expand his channels of information and advice. In contrast to the group that had deliberated on the Bay of Pigs invasion, ExComm included more people from his White House staff, more from the various departments and agencies, and a third group of individuals from outside the government. While the numbers involved increased the risk of a leak, Kennedy apparently felt that an even greater risk lay in limiting his sources of information. At this point it is worth noting that the President sought to enhance his access to information in still another way. Following the Bay of Pigs debacle, he decided to set up a Situation Room in the basement of the White House which would be tied into all of the cable traffic coming into the departments of State and Defense and the CIA. The White House would thereby gain the information in these cables firsthand, rather than having to rely on the departments to relay it.

In order to avoid the illusory consensus that had developed in connection with the Bay of Pigs invasion, President Kennedy took several steps to insure that ExComm would rigorously consider all the options available to his administration. First, he absented himself from several of the earlier meetings. Robert Kennedy later commented, "This was wise. Personalities change when the President is present, and frequently even strong men make recommendations on the basis of what they believe the President wishes to hear."[94] When the President was present, he took special pains to elicit the views of lower-level advisers, for he had learned that "lower-ranking advisers. . . . would not voluntarily contradict their superiors in front of the President, and that persuasive advisers such as McNamara unintentionally silenced less articulate men."[95] In his absence, Kennedy charged his brother and Theodore Sorensen with the responsibility for drawing out the views of all members of the group and encouraging a contentious discussion of the issues. To further foster a free exchange of opinion, the members of ExComm were told not to confine their remarks only to their own area of expertise. Instead, military experts, for example, were to feel free to comment on the political aspects of the issue and political experts were to feel equally free to address the military aspects. In addition, the group was told that the customary rules of protocol would be set aside, thus freeing under- and assistant secretaries from having to wait until they were called upon before offering their views. Lastly, the meetings were conducted without prearranged

[94] Robert Kennedy, *Thirteen Days* (New York: W.W. Norton, 1969), p. 11.

[95] Sorensen, *Kennedy*, p. 679.

agendas so that members of the group would feel free to raise any issue they thought appropriate.

Virtually all recollections of the ExComm deliberations suggest that the President's efforts to avoid a premature consensus were successful. Theodore Sorensen, for example, has noted:

> Indeed, one of the remarkable aspects of those meetings was a sense of complete equality. Protocol mattered little when the nation's life was at stake. Experience mattered little in a crisis which had no precedent. . . . We were fifteen individuals on our own, representing the President and not different departments. Assistant Secretaries differed vigorously with their Secretaries; I participated much more freely than I ever had in an NSC [National Security Council] meeting; and the absence of the President encouraged everybody to speak his mind.[96]

In commenting on the nature of the deliberations, Robert Kennedy wrote, "It is no reflection on them that none was consistent in his opinion from the very beginning to the very end. . . . For some there were only small changes, perhaps varieties of a single idea. For others there were continuous changes of opinion each day."[97] Despite the fact that in his initial charge to ExComm the President appeared to have ruled out a nonmilitary response to the situation, some members of the group forced a consideration of it anyway. McNamara, for example, initially raised the possibility that perhaps no action was necessary at all, for the presence of the missiles did not materially alter the nuclear balance of power. Moreover, whether we were killed by a missile from the Soviet Union, or from a Russian submarine, or from Cuba made little difference. The end result was the same. This view was rejected by the others on several grounds. Missiles launched from Cuba would give us less warning time to react; moreover, the accuracy of offensive missiles would be substantially increased if launched from nearby Cuba rather than from thousands of miles away in the Soviet Union. McGeorge Bundy and Adlai Stevenson argued that our response should be diplomatic rather than military. Their reason was that he had nothing to lose by taking the diplomatic route first, for it might work. Moreover, even if this approach failed, it had the advantage of not foreclosing other options. At least in Bundy's case, it is not clear that he really favored this approach so much as he wanted the President to consider all options: "I almost deliberately stayed in the minority. I felt that it was very important to keep the President's choices open."[98] Although Stevenson proved to be an advocate of the diplomatic approach throughout the deliberations, others rejected that approach on the grounds that it

---

[96] Ibid.

[97] Kennedy, *Thirteen Days*, p. 9.

[98] Allison, *Essence of Decision*, p. 196.

would allow Khrushchev to stall long enough to permit the missiles to become operational.

Thus there developed a consensus on the necessity for military action, but the group was still sharply divided as to what form it should take. Six options were considered:

1. Blockade Cuba and thereby deny entry to Soviet ships carrying armaments.
2. Bombard the missile sites with pellets that would neutralize the missiles without causing casualties.
3. Surgically bomb the missile sites but forewarn the Cubans and Soviets in the area.
4. Surgically bomb the sites without any forewarning.
5. Bomb all military targets in Cuba.
6. Undertake a full-scale invasion of Cuba.

The military argued that a surgical strike was not feasible and pushed for a bombing of all military targets in Cuba. During the second week of deliberations, however, civilian experts learned that a surgical strike was in fact possible, and it was restored as an option. The group continued to debate the blockade option versus some kind of attack upon Cuba itself. Indeed, ExComm appeared to be so far from reaching a consensus on what to do that President Kennedy became irritated. Accordingly, he instructed both his brother and Sorensen to bring the group to a recommendation. Their efforts were not successful, however, as the group continued to debate the possibilities. Finally, eight of the fourteen agreed that the blockade was the most desirable course of action to follow.[99] It had several advantages. First, it was drastic enough to convey our determination, and yet not so drastic as to invite a military response from the Soviet Union. Second, even if the blockade should produce a military confrontation off the coast of Cuba, our naval superiority would be overwhelming. Third, a blockade would leave the next move up to the Russians, while still providing them with some time to consider what that move should be. Fourth, the blockade did not foreclose other more drastic options. Finally, this response was more appealing to the President when viewed against the alternative of a military strike. Both he and some others were troubled by the morality of a sneak attack on Cuba. In addition, the Air Force could not guarantee that a strike on the missile sites would incapacitate *all* of the missiles. Then too, a direct strike on Cuba would be drastic enough to possibly elicit a military response from the Soviets in a place such as Berlin where their conventional forces were superior to our own.

Whether or not President Kennedy handled the Cuban missile crisis deftly is a matter of some debate. Some would contend that it was indeed his finest hour—that he judiciously selected a course of action that, while forceful enough

---

[99] Nathan, "Missile Crisis," p. 260.

to convince the Russians we meant business, was nevertheless not so reckless as to precipitate a military response from the Russians. Others argue that the President needlessly took us to the precipice of nuclear war—that domestic political considerations caused him to adopt a stance far more severe than was warranted by the presence of missiles in Cuba. Still others point out that the blockade did not in and of itself prove sufficient to force the Russians into removing their missiles from Cuba; rather, they ultimately agreed to do so only after Robert Kennedy privately warned Soviet Ambassador Dobrynin that, unless the Soviet Union removed the missiles, we would. Yet if President Kennedy did make the wrong decision, it was not for want of having the necessary facts and options placed before him. On the contrary, not only did he reach out to a variety of sources for information and advice, but he also structured the deliberations so as to maximize the expression and evaluation of all points of view. Clearly the President who faced the Cuban missile crisis was far wiser in the ways of decision making than the man who, one year earlier, had ordered the abortive Bay of Pigs invasion. In short, he had learned from his mistakes.

The Vietnam War

Regardless of what standard one chooses to employ, the Vietnam War qualifies as perhaps the greatest foreign policy blunder in American history, for not only did it fail, but the costs exacted upon the nation during the process were extraordinary. First and foremost was the cost in lives, with some forty-six thousand Americans killed and three times as many wounded. Moreover, there were social and political costs as well, for as the war became more unpopular, protests grew increasingly more violent and public confidence in government began to erode. The war also imposed a heavy burden on our economic resources as hundreds of millions of dollars were diverted into an ever-expanding war effort. And to all of this must be added the loss in our international prestige, especially among nations of the third world.

While United States involvement in Vietnam had its beginnings in the Kennedy Administration, the full-scale commitment of our human and material resources to this Southeast Asian country was made under the stewardship of President Johnson. As he prepared for the election campaign of 1964, he found himself confronted with a rapidly deteriorating situation in South Vietnam. Its government was unstable; the rising number of desertions in their armed forces was a clear indication of declining morale; the North Vietnamese had increased the movement of troops and arms into the South; and the Viet Cong (South Vietnamese Communists) had become more daring in its military operations there, the most recent of which had been their attack on an American military base at Bien Hoa. Having been apprised of these developments, Johnson ordered his advisers to review our policy toward Vietnam and recommend a course of action. Since his own energies were focused on the election campaign, he did not involve himself directly in these policy discussions, but ultimately accepted the recommendation that flowed from them, namely, a continuation of retaliatory strikes.

The most critical decision came in 1965 when Johnson sent the Chairman of the Joint Chiefs and Defense Secretary McNamara to South Vietnam on a fact-finding mission. Their report to the President pointed out that the South Vietnamese were in desperate straits. Reinforcements for the Viet Cong were pouring into the South, and without a substantial commitment of U.S. forces, the South Vietnamese army would be incapable of preventing a takeover of its country. It was clear to the President that he was now at the crossroads. To assist him in deciding which way to turn, he summoned together a vast array of individuals from inside the government: Dean Rusk, George Ball, and William Bundy from the State Department; Robert McNamara, Cyrus Vance, and John McNaughton from Defense; members of the Joint Chiefs and the secretaries of the Army, Navy, and Air Force representing the military; Admiral Raborn and Richard Helms from the CIA; Carl Rowan, Director of the U.S. Information Agency; McGeorge Bundy, Special Assistant for National Security Affairs and his aid, Leonard Unger; and Jack Valenti and Bill Moyers from his White House staff. From outside the government, Johnson brought in Henry Cabot Lodge, who had recently retired as U.S. Ambassador to South Vietnam, and also Clark Clifford, who had been an adviser to several presidents. While not all of these individuals were present at all of the meetings, which took place from July 21 to 27, each attended at least one of them.

At the first meeting, Secretary McNamara proceeded to inform the group of recommendations made by William Westmoreland, the general in charge of U.S. military operations in South Vietnam:

1. An initial commitment of 175,000 troops would be necessary by the end of 1965 in order to repel the advances of the enemy.
2. Another 100,000 troops would be necessary in 1966 so that the U.S. would be able to take the offensive.
3. Still another increment of troops (*unspecified*) would be necessary if war were to be brought to a successful conclusion by the end of 1967.

McNamara noted that he concurred with these recommendations and suggested that Johnson call up 235,000 reservists.[100] Following this presentation, the President put some tough questions to the group:

Have we wrung every single soldier out of every country that we can? Who else can help us here? Are we the sole defenders in the world? Have we done all we can in this direction? What are the compelling reasons for this call-up? What results can we expect? Again, I ask you what are the alterna-

[100]Herbert Y. Schandler, *The Unmaking of a President: Lyndon Johnson and Vietnam,* p. 28. Copyright ©1977 by Princeton University Press. Reprinted by permission of Princeton University Press.

tives? I don't want us to make snap judgments. I want us to consider all our options. We know we can tell the South Vietnamese we are coming home. Is that the option we should take? What would flow from that?[101]

The President then asked for reactions from those who disagreed with McNamara. George Ball said he thought we were getting ourselves into a quagmire which would inevitably lead to a greater and greater expansion of the war. Carl Rowan allowed as how more troops would do no good as long as the South Vietnamese government remained so unstable. In the afternoon session, the President began by asking Ball to elaborate on his opposition to increased U.S. involvement. Ball argued that American conventional forces could not successfully fight a guerrilla war against Orientals in an Asian jungle, and he noted also that as we became bogged down, the temptation to expand the war into North Vietnam would become irresistible. In a protracted war, he said, world opinion would ultimately turn against us. After he finished, the other side began to weigh in. First, there was Secretary of State Rusk, who pointed out that our failure to stand firm in Vietnam would only serve to further encourage Communist aggression in other parts of the world. Ambassador Lodge concurred with Rusk, reminding the group that our lack of resolve in Vietnam would be analogous to the capitulation to Hitler at Munich. After further discussion, the President adjourned the group and told them that tomorrow he wanted them to hear what the military had to say on the matter.

At the opening of the next meeting, Johnson outlined to the military his own view of what the alternatives were: (1) cut our losses and leave the country, (2) continue at our current level of commitment and slowly lose, or finally, (3) increase our commitment with the risk that the war might escalate and last a long time. All of the military spokesmen appeared confident of our ability to win if our troop commitment was significantly increased. The President probed them further, asking if we were starting something that in two or three years we would not be able to finish. Wouldn't the Chinese and the Russians come in on the side of the North Vietnamese?[102] They did not think either of these possibilities likely. Johnson then asked his Special Adviser for National Security Affairs to present some disquieting arguments that were being made by some congressmen and senators: "What Bundy will now tell you is not his opinion or mine, but what we hear. I think you ought to face up to this too."[103] Bundy proceeded to raise the following concerns:

1. Everything we have done in Vietnam thus far has failed.
2. How can conventional forces be sent to fight a guerrilla war?

[101] Valenti, *Very Human President*, pp. 326, 327.

[102] Ibid., pp. 346, 348.

[103] Ibid., p. 351.

3. We are ignoring General McArthur's long-accepted warning that the United States should never become involved in a land war in Asia.
4. How can we win a war for a country that does not appear to want to help itself?
5. Is not the problem in Vietnam essentially political rather than military?

Johnson asked the group to ponder these questions and be prepared to discuss them at the next meeting. In the subsequent meetings these doubts were apparently answered to his satisfaction.

In the final analysis he seemed strongly persuaded by the argument that if we backed down in Vietnam, the Communists would be encouraged to become aggressive in other parts of Asia, Africa, the Middle East and Latin America.[104] No doubt this view took on added credibility for Johnson because it was shared by the two advisers he respected most: secretaries Rusk and McNamara. He therefore decided to increase our troop commitment by one hundred thousand, as General Westmoreland had suggested. At the same time, however, he refused to go along with the recommendation to call up the reservists, fearing that such drastic action would both alarm the country and perhaps force the Russians and Chinese to enter the conflict. At the final meeting, which was held at Camp David, the President went around the table asking his advisers if they were in agreement with his decision. Only George Ball and Clark Clifford expressed skepticism. He then called the congressional leadership together to get their reaction to his decision, and while they posed several questions, only Senator Mansfield expressed serious doubts about the President's proposed course of action.

In retrospect, it is clear that both Johnson and his advisers made a grave miscalculation, for the North Vietnamese and Viet Cong proved to be a far more formidable foe than they had anticipated, and the South Vietnamese less capable and committed than they had hoped. But if this initial decision to increase our involvement in Vietnam was a bad one, it cannot be attributed to Johnson's failure to reach out for information, nor to his unwillingness to push for examination of all points of view. At this stage anyway, he appears to have encouraged consideration of the costs and benefits associated with getting out, continuing what we were doing, or else escalating our involvement. The short circuit in the decision-making process lay, rather, in the kind of information and advice he was given.

Several factors may help to explain why it proved inadequate. Some would surely argue that Johnson and his advisers were captives of an outmoded anti-Communist ideology, which called for the United States to stop the spread of communism anywhere in the world. So strong was this view, it is argued, that it blinded them to both the political and the military realities of the situation in

---

[104] Lyndon Johnson, *The Vantage Point* (New York: Holt, Rinehart and Winston, 1971), pp. 148, 151, 152.

Vietnam. Second, those advising the President may have fallen victim to over-confidence. In the words of Johnson's close aid, Bill Moyers, "There was a confidence, it was never bragged about, it was just there—a residue, perhaps of the confrontation over the missiles in Cuba—that when the chips were really down, the other people would fold."[105] Third, the quality of advice that Johnson was getting was hampered by the lack of expertise on Southeast Asia. As Dean Rusk would later point out, the government had few experts on this area of the world, for most had left the State Department after being discredited as a result of our problems with China in the fifties.[106] Fourth, the information base on which Johnson and his advisers were operating may not have presented an altogether accurate appraisal of the military picture in Vietnam. Those in the field were committed to the view that the United States belonged in Vietnam, and the information relayed back to Washington was frequently designed so as not to discourage this belief.

David Halberstam, for example, tells of assessments submitted in 1965 by the CIA regarding future prospects in Vietnam. One was written by an individual who had been studying that country for over ten years. Among other things, he pointed out in his conclusions that the enemy was possessed of an enormous capacity to escalate the war if the United States decided to bomb; it was his judgment that the enemy would not hesitate to make full use of this capability. However, before this CIA assessment was sent back to the United States, the pessimistic portions were deleted from the report by Ambassador Taylor's office in Saigon. The other assessment had been requested by General Westmoreland, who wanted a study on the ability of the North Vietnamese to reinforce their troops in the South. When the study was completed, he voiced amazement at the results and asked that the figures be rechecked. After being informed that the figures were indeed accurate, he replied, " . . . if we tell this to the people in Washington we'll be out of the war tomorrow. We'll have to revise it downward."

One final respect in which the advice received by Johnson proved to be inadequate lay in the failure of the military to voice their objections to the nature of his escalation decision. While firmly supportive of an increased commitment to Vietnam, the Joint Chiefs did not feel that the President had gone far enough. In addition to dispatching 100,000 troops, they felt a successful prosecution of the war required calling up the reserves as well as placing the country on a war footing. Yet when Johnson, during that final meeting at Camp David, asked the Chairman of the Joint Chiefs if he agreed with the decision, General Wheeler answered yes.[107] Had Wheeler voiced his strong doubts about Johnson's decision on the grounds that it was not enough, the President might have heeded this advice by further escalating our commitment. On the other hand, he may also have

---

[105] Janis, *Victims of Groupthink,* p. 125; see also Halberstam, *Best and Brightest,* pp. 640, 774.

[106] Hargrove, *Modern Presidency,* p. 152.

[107] Halberstam, *Best and Brightest,* pp. 610, 661, 728.

concluded that the costs of our involvement were going to be too high and thus moved toward a reduction in our commitment. Why Wheeler failed to voice his objections is unclear. Possibly he feared he would be overruled anyway, or perhaps he was afraid that by calling for more drastic action he would scare Johnson out of making any increase at all in our commitment to Vietnam.

Unfortunately, the lengthy review of our Vietnam policy during July 1965 was really the only one to take place until the Viet Cong launched their famous Tet offensive in 1968. After the initial commitment to increase our efforts, subsequent decisions were largely tactical in nature and involved little reevaluation of underlying objectives and costs; this despite the fact that greater and greater involvement on our part seemed to have little impact upon bringing the war to a successful conclusion. While it may indeed be argued that the failure to reconsider our Vietnam policy was simply a reflection of the fact that both Johnson and his advisers were convinced of its soundness, other factors appear to have been at work, also. For one thing, President Johnson himself can hardly be said to have encouraged an atmosphere conducive to a reexamination of our policy toward Vietnam. As the war began to go badly and public criticism mounted, Johnson became more irascible and increasingly prone to equate dissent with disloyalty. On one occasion, for example, when the White House was holding a banquet for students who had been selected as Presidential Scholars, Johnson sought to bar the parents of one girl from attending the banquet because they had spoken out against the war.[108] It is not surprising, therefore, that he appeared to be equally distraught with those inside the government who voiced similar doubt about our presence in Vietnam. As a result of this attitude, many aids were reticent about disagreeing with the President openly. John McNaughton, the chief assistant to Defense Secretary McNamara, repeatedly voiced his opposition to the bombing in the presence of his boss at the Defense Department; he even went over to the White House in the evenings to secretly argue his point of view with a White House aid. Yet when Johnson on one occasion went around the table asking aids if they agreed with the decision to bomb oil depots in North Vietnam, McNaughton merely replied, "I have nothing to add sir."[109] According to George Ball, even McNamara himself harbored doubts about the bombing long before he voiced them publicly. As David Halberstam notes:

> When it came right down to it, McNamara had doubts about the bombing in his mind, but those doubts were not reflected in the meetings. He was forceful, intense, tearing apart the doubts of the others, almost ruthless in making his case. . . . He was, Ball found, quite different in private sessions than in the major meetings where Johnson presided. When Ball prepared paper after paper for Johnson, he would first send them to the other principals, and occasionally McNamara would suggest that he come by and

[108] Eric Goldman, *The Tragedy of Lyndon Johnson* (New York: Alfred Knopf, 1968), pp. 501, 502.

[109] Halberstam, *Best and Brightest,* pp. 447–49.

talk the paper over before they went to see the President. Ball would find McNamara surprisingly sympathetic....[110]

Those within the administration who did voice disagreement with Vietnam policy might find themselves frozen out of the decision-making process or else invited to leave. At one of the strategy meetings in 1965, for example, Vice President Humphrey voiced strong opposition to the bombing; thereafter, he was systematically excluded from discussions on the war and bypassed in the memo traffic relating to Vietnam policy. Similarly, in an appearance before a Senate committee in 1967, Secretary McNamara for the first time publicly voiced his doubts about the bombing. Subsequently, he was progressively bypassed in the deliberations. To one senator, the President remarked, "No don't go see Bob— he's gone dovish on me."[111] The final straw came when McNamara delivered a speech in Montreal in which he voiced his misgivings about our whole involvement in Vietnam. To his surprise, he read in the papers a few days later that President Johnson had appointed him to head the World Bank.

Despite Johnson's apparent disdain for dissent, there were a few within his administration—Bill Moyers, Harry McPherson, George Ball—who were willing to voice their criticisms. But apparently they were tolerated because they kept their views within the "family" and never challenged the fundamental assumptions of our Vietnam policy.[112] Yet one suspects that the role of critic within the administration was not a pleasant one, for both Moyers and Ball resigned their positions in 1967.

In addition to Johnson's own failure to encourage an atmosphere conducive to independent thinking, the apparent unwillingness to reassess our Vietnam policy may have also been fostered by the development of "groupthink" among the President's senior advisers. These individuals, who typically met with the President every Tuesday for lunch, became known as the Tuesday Cabinet. The membership included Dean Rusk; Robert McNamara; Earle Wheeler, Chairman of the Joint Chiefs; Richard Helms, Director of the CIA; Bill Moyers, press secretary; and the President's Special Adviser for National Security Affairs, McGeorge Bundy (later to be replaced by Walt Rostow). Several factors may help to explain why this group sought to minimize differences and maximize agreement. For one thing, their relationships with each other appear to have become personal as well as professional. As Bill Moyers recalls:

> ... the men who handled national security affairs became too close, too personally fond of each other. They tended to conduct the affairs of state almost as if they were a gentlemen's club, and the great decisions were often made in that warm camaraderie of a small board of directors

[110] Ibid., p. 625.
[111] Ibid., p. 783.
[112] Janis, *Victims of Groupthink*, p. 120.

deciding what the club's dues are going to be for the members next year.
. . . So you often dance around the final hard decision which would set
you against . . . men who are very close to you, and you tend to reach a
consensus.[113]

Second, the inclination toward group cohesion may also have been enhanced
by the fact that the group's policy decisions on Vietnam were coming under
severe attack from people in Congress and the country at large. In his analysis
of the Tuesday Cabinet, for example, Henry Graff notes that as members of
the group "felt increasingly beleaguered, they turned toward one another for
reassurance."[114] Perhaps most important of all, Johnson insisted on making
decisions by consensus—an idiosyncrasy that was in evidence even during his
years in Congress. This desire to have everybody on board could only serve to
further increase the pressures toward a convergence of views.

In addition to the factors already mentioned, Johnson's failure to reconsider
our commitment to Vietnam—at least up until 1968—may also have been due in
part to the fact that he was not being given a fully accurate picture of how the
war was going. Perhaps the President's most critical source of information on the
war was his national security adviser, Walt Rostow. Himself an avowed hawk,
Rostow's briefings to the President were frequently selective, as he sought to
accentuate the positive and minimize the negative. Moreover, he was also successful in persuading the CIA officer (George Carver) charged with briefing the
White House to become more optimistic in his reports. Indeed, by 1967 it had
become quite clear that Carver's briefings on the war appeared far more optimistic than assessments by other intelligence analysts with the CIA.[115]

That Johnson had not been told all became painfully apparent during the
deliberations in 1968. It was in January of that year that the enemy launched its
Tet offensive—a massive, coordinated assault upon the major population centers
of South Vietnam, including Saigon. Needless to say, the ability of the enemy to
strike at will in areas that were thought to be safely in the control of the South
Vietnamese stunned Washington. No less was the shock when the President
learned that General Westmoreland was now asking for an additional 200,000
American troops. Quite obviously this would represent a substantial increase in
our commitment, necessitating a call-up of the reserves and placing the country
on a semiwar footing. Before taking such a drastic step Johnson asked his newly
appointed Secretary of Defense, Clark Clifford, to undertake a study as to the
desirability of such a course of action.

Clifford was in a unique position among Johnson's advisers. As the new man
on board, he was able to view Vietnam more objectively than the others. In addi-

---

[113] Ibid., p. 105, 106.

[114] Ibid., p. 105.

[115] Ibid., p. 775; see also Townsend Hoopes, *The Limits of Intervention* (New York: David
McKay, 1969), p. 218.

tion, since he had reluctantly accepted the job of Secretary of Defense and was already a man of considerable stature, he felt no pressure to temper his own views to those of Johnson. Clifford's own soundings within the bureaucracy as well as the studies made by his task force convinced him that the United States was accomplishing neither its military nor political objectives in Vietnam. The Clifford task force concluded that additional troop commitments would serve no useful purpose unless the South Vietnamese government was able to win the support of its people and carry the fight to the Viet Cong more aggressively. The pessimism of the report startled the President and consequently, for the moment, he decided to give Westmoreland only an additional 22,000 troops.[116]

Clifford became convinced that the United States should now move in an entirely different direction, namely, negotiations; moreover, a halt to the bombing might prove to be a necessary first step in leading to them. Rusk had proposed a limited bombing pause (no bombing north of the twentieth parallel) on the grounds that the rainy season was approaching in North Vietnam and thus the bombing would achieve only limited results anyway. While Clifford argued for a more extensive halt to the bombing, he was outnumbered by those who believed that such action would not bring the North Vietnamese to the negotiating table. Although the President decided to scrap the idea of a bombing pause, Clifford was able to prevail upon him to hold off on a final decision until he met with a group of distinguished citizens. "I thought it was going to take something very substantial to shift the president's attitude. I needed some stiff medicine to bring home to the president what was happening in the country."[117]

This group of citizens, dubbed the Wise Men, included first of all individuals who had been involved in earlier policy decisions on Vietnam: George Ball, McGeorge Bundy, Henry Cabot Lodge, and Maxwell Taylor. Also brought in were respected individuals who had served in earlier administrations: Dean Acheson, Douglas Dillon, Arthur Dean, John McCloy, Cyrus Vance, and Robert Murphy. Representing the military were retired generals Omar Bradley and Matthew Ridgway. Finally, the President also invited both his close friend Abe Fortas, who was currently sitting as a member of the Supreme Court, and Arthur Goldberg, the U.S. Ambassador to the United Nations.

At the first meeting, the Wise Men met with senior officials in the government, but not with Johnson present. Questions were asked about the viability of the South Vietnamese government, the capability of their armed forces, the success of the pacification program, etc. The senior officials then left and the group was briefed by individuals from the departments of State and Defense and the CIA. When the Wise Men finally met with the President the next day, all but three expressed grave concern over the course of the war itself as well as the divisions it was causing among the American people. They felt that a further increase in American troops was out of the question. On the contrary, the consen-

---

[116] Schandler, *Unmaking of a President,* pp. 174, 177, 180.

[117] Ibid., pp. 254, 255.

sus of the Wise Men was that the South Vietnamese should shoulder a greater share of the burden, thereby allowing for a substantial cutback in our commitment. The pessimism of the group stunned the President and, according to Clifford, his first reaction was that "somebody had poisoned the well."[118] The next day he insisted on meeting with the government officials who had briefed the Wise Men and, according to Townsend Hoopes, Johnson wanted to know, "What did you tell them that you didn't tell me?" The briefers insisted that there were no discrepancies. But the President continued, "You must have given them a different briefing; you aren't telling me what you told them because what you're telling me couldn't account for the inferences they drew."[119] No explanations were forthcoming.

The advice of this distinguished group of American citizens appears to have been instrumental in causing Johnson to alter his approach, for only one week later he went before the American people and announced a halt to the bombing of North Vietnam (except in the area north of the Demilitarized Zone). Furthermore, he informed the North Vietnamese that he was designating a special representative who would be willing to meet with them at any time and at any place in order to discuss an end to the conflict. Clearly the efforts of an independent-minded Clark Clifford had paid off, but it is worth noting that they came at a cost to his personal relationship with the President.[120] While Johnson was ultimately willing to alter an unsuccessful policy, his ego would not permit him to honor the man who had been instrumental in bringing him to do it.

In summary, the President's initial decision to increase our commitment to Vietnam was probably an unwise decision, but it resulted not from his failure to reach out for information, but rather from the kind of information and advice he was given. Yet once our policy toward Vietnam was set in motion, the President's demeanor and style did little to foster a frank and rigorous reexamination of this policy. Of course, we cannot be sure that a less intimidating presidential style would necessarily have caused Johnson and his advisers to alter their course any earlier, but it certainly would have made such a possibility more likely.

Shoe Import Quotas

The decision-making problem that the Carter Administration faced on shoe import quotas differs from the previous cases in two important respects. In the first place, it involved an issue that is domestic in nature every bit as much as it is foreign. Thus, there were many *more interests in and outside government participating in the decision-making process* than was the case in the decisions just analyzed. Second, unlike the Bay of Pigs, the Cuban missile crisis, or the

---

[118] Ibid., p. 264.

[119] Hoopes, *Limits of Intervention,* pp. 217, 218.

[120] Schandler, *Unmaking of a President,* p. 267.

Vietnam War, the issue of shoe import quotas was relatively *routine* in nature, and thus the President's involvement was less direct.

Since the time that tariffs on shoes were lowered in 1968, countries such as Taiwan, South Korea, Spain, Italy, and Brazil have been exporting large quantities of shoes to the United States. Because the cost of labor in these countries is substantially cheaper than it is here, they have been able to sell their products at prices well below those of American shoe companies. Consequently by 1976, these countries had managed to corner 46 percent of the American shoe market—up from 22 percent in 1968.[121] This development led to the closing of some three hundred shoe factories in the United States as well as a loss of 70,000 jobs. In the early part of 1976, the American Footwear Industries Association sought relief from the International Trade Commission. Created by Congress under the Trade Act of 1974, this commission is charged with considering trade complaints and making recommendations for dealing with them. After receiving the commission's recommendations, the President has sixty days in which to accept or reject its report. If he should decide to reject their recommendations and come up with his own, they are still subject to a congressional override by concurrent resolution. In this particular case, the International Trade Commission ruled by a three-to-two vote that import quotas should be raised in order to provide some relief to the beleaguered shoe industry. Given the closeness of the vote, however, as well as pressure from the departments of State, Commerce, and the Treasury, President Ford decided to reject the commission's recommendation. Instead, he decided to provide "trade adjustment assistance" to the shoe industry. In essence, this amounted to raising the benefits to unemployed shoe workers and increasing loans to the shoe industry so that it might modernize and diversify.

Upset with President Ford's decision, in September 1976 the Senate Finance Committee asked the International Trade Commission to reopen its inquiry into the financial plight of the shoe industry. The commission did so and issued its report on January 6, 1977, this time solidly backing the imposition of import quotas on shoes. Specifically, it recommended that for the next five years, some twenty different countries be permitted to export 265 million pairs of shoes at a tariff rate of 10 percent. For all shoes over this amount, however, the tariff rate would be raised to 40 percent. Rather than acting on the commission's recommendations, President Ford decided to leave the matter to the man who would be succeeding him on the twentieth of January.

Clearly the issue of quotas posed a dilemma for the incoming President Carter. For one thing, he had campaigned on a free-trade plank, declaring that if industries were hurt by imports then they should be helped with federal aid. In addition, the United States was on record as wanting to help the economies of the underdeveloped countries by reducing trade barriers. Third, a decision by the

---

[121] *Washington Post,* March 21, 1977, p. A1.

largest free trader in the world to raise tariff barriers would serve to trigger a similar reaction among other nations. And finally, President Carter had pledged to do everything he could to bring inflation under control. Yet by putting a tariff on foreign shoes, he would be forcing Americans to pay higher prices for the shoes they bought. If all of these points constituted compelling reasons for not instituting quotas, there were also some strong reasons why he should. Most important of all was the fact that a significant part of his electoral support had come from labor, a group to whom he had promised more jobs. Furthermore, there was strong support for quotas among those members of Congress who represented the thirty-nine states where shoes were produced.

The day after he took office, Carter received Presidential Review Memorandum No. 7 from the National Security Council. Its substance consisted of an analysis of trade issues in general as well as the foreign policy implications of shoe import quotas in particular. On February 4, the Office of the Special Trade Representative—a unit within the Executive Office of the President charged with advising the President on trade matters—sent a background memo to President Carter's Economic Policy Group which was to meet on February 7. Chaired by Treasury Secretary Michael Blumenthal, this group was responsible for coordinating Carter's economic policy. The other members of the group were the Vice President, five Cabinet officers, and the heads of five different units within the Executive Office of the President. The memo sent to this group outlined five options for dealing with the shoe problem. Three involved the imposition of some kind of tariff or quota; the fourth called for the continuation of our free-trade policy, but with an increase in "trade adjustment assistance" to the shoe industry; the fifth option was to negotiate Orderly Marketing Agreements (OMAs) with the major exporters of shoes. OMAs are formal contracts between an importing and exporting country. While they are more stringent than voluntary restraints, they are less so than quotas. In addition to reviewing the substance of this memo at their February 7 meeting, the Economic Policy Group also examined a second memo which contained State Department objections to the recommendations of the International Trade Commission. In essence, the State Department argued that the commission's quota recommendations were too restrictive and thus potentially damaging to our relations with the countries involved.[122]

Throughout February and March, interested parties made their case to various government agencies, including the Economic Policy Group. The shoe producers spoke out strongly in favor of quotas, and they had a strong ally in the person of George Meany. Speaking for the AFL-CIO, Meany insisted that without quotas on shoes, the industry would face "slow but certain death." The President received further pressure to move in this direction from the nation's governors,

---

[122] Office of Management and Budget, *Decision Analysis Report: Case Study, Footwear Import Agreements,* pp. 84, 85. This study was supplied to the author by Robert J. Cunningham of the Office of Management and Budget.

thirty-six of whom signed a petition asking the President to "provide effective import relief to the footwear industry before more jobs are lost, more plants are closed and more communities are afflicted by the current tidal wave of footwear imports." These sentiments were also echoed by various congressmen and senators. Weighing in against quotas, however, were other industry officials, consumer groups, major U.S. allies, the Chairman of the Federal Reserve Board, and the President's national security adviser. Speaking on behalf of U.S. retailers, the Volume Retailers Association of America cited a study they had commissioned, which showed that quotas would cost the American consumer $500 million annually. In an address to the National Press Club on March 22, the Japanese Prime Minister voiced grave concern over the possibility that the United States might move in a protectionist direction: "Surely we have learned that such a course can only exacerbate world economic conditions."[123] Similar sentiments were also voiced on the same day by Federal Reserve Board Chairman Arthur Burns in testimony before a Senate committee. In a memo sent to the President on March 16, national security adviser Brzezinski added his voice to the chorus, noting the importance of a "free trade" position to our relations with other nations.[124]

On March 21, the President's Economic Policy Group met to consider a course of action. While all agreed that the shoe industry should be provided with some additional federal relief assistance, they were divided on what other steps should be taken. Those within the group representing the departments of State, the Treasury, HUD, and the Council of Economic Advisers were opposed to any kind of quotas, whereas those from the departments of Labor, Commerce, Agriculture, the Office of Management and Budget, and the Office of the Special Trade Representative came down on the side of a three-year Tariff Rate Quota. While the middle option—Orderly Marketing Agreements—was raised by Stuart Eizenstat as a possibility, apparently it was not given very serious consideration.[125] Following the meeting, Special Trade Representative Robert Strauss sent the President a memo outlining the views of the Economic Policy Group, but he failed to even mention the possibility of OMAs as an option. In addition, through inadvertence the Strauss memo was not sent to the head of Carter's domestic policy staff, and thus he was not able to provide the President with an assessment of the memo. Fortunately, a Strauss aid, who was apparently disturbed by what he had heard at the meeting of the Economic Policy Group, happened to send a memo to the Vice President in which he pointed out that a no-relief stance on the part of the Carter Administration could seriously jeopardize the President's relations with Congress. He further noted that the OMA option might well be the best compromise under the circumstances. On Monday, March 28, the President met with the Economic Policy Group, and the OMA

[123] *Wall Street Journal,* March 23, 1977, p. 44.

[124] Office of Management and Budget, *Decision Analysis Report,* p. 88.

[125] Ibid., p. 88.

option was raised as a possible solution. While this course of action seemed most appealing to Carter, the group had neglected to give it serious consideration in the prior meeting, and consequently there had been no staff work done on it.[126] Thus, the President found himself in a meeting where he lacked the information necessary to make a decision on the OMA option. Accordingly, he immediately instructed his Special Trade Representative to prepare a memo on the feasibility of OMAs.

Strauss's memo came to the President on March 30, and it recommended the OMA approach. It was preceded by another memo from the head of his domestic policy staff which also came down on the side of OMAs. On the same day, President Carter also received considerable advice from other interested parties. The State Department, for example, sent the President an extensive memo criticizing the OMA option as too protectionist and potentially damaging to U.S. relations with other nations. In addition, a communication came to the President from an American official who was planning the President's upcoming economic summit in London. Fearing that any form of trade restrictions might hamper trade discussions with Western leaders, he asked the President to reject OMAs and instead to request that other nations voluntarily restrict their shoe imports. Finally, the Labor Department also chimed in with a memo that argued that voluntary restraints were inadequate and the OMA approach not much better.[127]

Having been pressured in and outside of government by those who were either for or against instituting quotas, it is not surprising that President Carter ultimately chose a middle course, namely, Orderly Marketing Agreements (OMAs). Specifically, these agreements were to be negotiated with Taiwan and South Korea, the two countries that had been exporting the largest number of shoes. Carter also decided to increase federal aid to the beleaguered shoe industry. Pursuant to this decision, the Commerce Department decided to spend $56 million in the form of advice, loans, and loan guarantees to American shoe producers.

The shoe import quota decision serves to highlight two important points. First, it is essential that a President's advisers carefully consider all of the options available to him on a given issue. In this instance, Carter's Economic Policy Group did not appear to have done so. Indeed, the option which the President finally chose (OMAs) had been quickly dismissed at the group's second meeting. While the OMA option was reintroduced into the deliberations at a later meeting, the President was not able to make a decision on it at that time because his advisers had not prepared any assessment of OMAs. Second, this case study also serves to illustrate the fact that on more routine decisions the President is more dependent upon his advisers—at least to the extent that he must rely upon their characterizations of the deliberations on a given issue. Since the Bay of Pigs invasion, Cuban missile crisis, and the Vietnam War were issues of considerable

[126] Ibid., pp. 89, 90.
[127] Ibid., pp. 90–92.

magnitude, the President's involvement in the decision-making process was more persistent and direct. Thus, he had a greater first hand knowledge of the deliberations. In contrast, as we pointed out earlier, the issue of shoe import quotas was certainly a more routine issue, and consequently President Carter was not directly involved in the deliberations until their final stage. For this reason, he was dependent upon what his advisers relayed to him concerning what had transpired during the earlier stages of the decision-making process. In this particular case, he was not adequately informed in this regard. Indeed Strauss's memo to the President summarizing the meeting of the Economic Policy Group failed to even mention the OMA option, let alone explain why the group did not seriously entertain it as a possible solution.

MAXIMIZING THE FLOW OF INFORMATION TO THE PRESIDENT

In the last several years, numerous proposals have been put forth to expand the President's sources of information. Many, no doubt, have been motivated by our dismal experience with the Vietnam War. The common theme running through these proposals is the establishment of some kind of advisory council to the President. This approach, it should be noted, is not a novel one. Indeed, the Founding Fathers considered, but ultimately rejected, the proposal to establish a Council of State whose membership would possibly include the Speaker of the House, President of the Senate, Chief Justice of the Supreme Court, and the heads of the various executive departments. Samuel Rosenman, an adviser to two presidents, recalls that he and Bernard Baruch tried unsuccessfully to persuade presidents Roosevelt and Truman to create a "think board" whose purpose would be "to consider the future, travel the country and come back to the White House to say: 'There is this or that situation. I think it is serious or critical. You should consider taking some action.'"[128]

In 1975, two separate groups came up with recommendations that an advisory group be established to advise the President on matters of foreign policy. The one group consisted of scholars, jurists, and other respected figures, all of whom had come together for a conference on "The Powers of the Presidency." They called for the establishment of an executive council made up of four or five distinguished private citizens, who would be appointed by the President and subject to confirmation by the Senate. Another group, The Commission on the Organization of the Government for the Conduct of Foreign Policy, called for the establishment of a Council on International Planning. It too would be composed of private citizens knowledgeable in foreign affairs and would be available to the President to use as he saw fit.

One other proposal deserves our attention here, for unlike those already men-

---

[128]Cited in John Stegmaier, "Toward a More Effective Presidency," *Presidential Studies Quarterly* (Spring/Summer, 1977), 149.

tioned, it calls for bringing together certain individuals already in government. Graham Allison and Peter Szanton have proposed that the National Security Council be abolished and replaced by a group they call ExCab. Its permanent membership would include the secretaries of State, Defense, the Treasury, and HEW as well as the head of either the Labor or Commerce Department. In their judgment, such a group would be more reflective of the overriding reality of today's world, which is that issues of foreign and domestic politics are increasingly intertwined. They point out that ExCab would hopefully "widen the circle of advisers that the President normally consulted before taking major decisions, thus improving the odds that major decisions would be taken with an eye to both their domestic and foreign effects. It would put those advisers directly in touch not only with the President but with each other, helping to generate a collegial comprehension of the varied dimensions of the issues confronting the President."[129]

While all of these proposals have merit, they all suffer from a common weakness. In the final analysis, presidents make decisions as they wish to make them. Thus, the mere creation of an advisory body is no guarantee that it will be used. Moreover, proposals that call for establishing advisory councils of *outside* experts suffer from an additional disadvantage. Few would doubt the desirability of a President's consulting knowledgeable people outside government. Since their interests are not directly tied to his, and given the fact that they have no stake in the decision, it is more likely that their views will reflect greater objectivity and candor. Indeed, the group of Wise Men consulted by Johnson in 1968 served a highly useful function in this regard. But if we institutionalize such a group within the government, do we not thereby tie its interests more directly to those of the President? Of course, one might argue that provisions could be made for the group's independence, but surely presidents would strongly resist any efforts in this direction.

With respect to the matter of whom the President should consult, we might also suggest that he seek to include in the decision-making process more people whose political experience has been rooted in domestic *politics.* According to Richard Neustadt, this need is especially critical in the foreign policy area, where for years important decisions have been dominated by nonpolitical experts, thus resulting in a lack of appreciation for the domestic implications of foreign policy decisions.[130] In this connection, it is heartening to note that President Carter has decided to involve both Hamilton Jordan and Vice President Mondale in the formulation of foreign policy—two men who in the past have been steeped in domestic politics.

Other suggestions for improving presidential decision making have focused not so much on creating additional sources of information as they have on making

---

[129] Graham Allison and Peter Szanton, *Remaking Foreign Policy: The Organizational Connection,* p. 79. © 1976 by Basic Books, Inc., Publishers, New York.

[130] *Washington Post,* September 7, 1977, p. A15.

better use of the ones that already exist.[131] For one thing, presidents should avoid getting themselves into a position where they are dependent on only one source of information. Second, while it may be appropriate for the President to have policy advocates on his White House staff, this role should not be performed by staffers whose major function is to provide the President with facts and advice coming in from other sources. Clearly, Johnson was not well served by his national security adviser, Walt Rostow, whose position on the Vietnam War was decidedly hawkish and who allowed this view to influence the kinds of information he chose to pass along to the President. Third, given the tendency of presidential advisers to adopt what they perceive to be the President's position on an issue, it may be advisable for presidents to refrain from making their own inclinations known initially. Fourth, it may also be desirable for presidents to absent themselves from deliberations during the early stages of the decision-making process. Truman, for example, on the grounds that his presence might hamper frank discussion, absented himself from meetings of his National Security Council when it was deliberating on possible responses to the Berlin blockade. Similarly, those close to the decision-making process during the Cuban missile crisis have noted that Kennedy's absence from the earlier meetings made for a much more candid discussion among the participants. Of course, if a President chooses to employ this tactic, it is absolutely essential that his advisers provide him with a complete picture of what took place in his absence. Theodore Sorensen and Robert Kennedy, both of whom were highly attuned to the President's interests, performed this function well during the Cuban missile crisis. Fifth, in the interests of preventing a premature consensus, the President (and in his absence, someone from his staff) should foster an atmosphere that is conducive to a thorough airing of views. Among other things, this means encouraging the participation of all those present, accentuating the disagreement that arises among the various participants, taking care to see that someone presents the case for what may be an unpopular position, and perhaps most important of all, avoiding any impression of impatience with views that do not coincide with his own. Presidential advisers, who often are overly deferential to begin with, will only become more so if they see that their boss is not comfortable with dissenting points of view.

Of course, it is one thing to suggest how presidents may better maximize the flow of facts and advice from the people around them, and quite another to persuade them to implement such suggestions. A President's decision-making style is to a considerable extent a reflection of his personality, and consequently, it is not readily subject to change. Thus, given Johnson's intimidating style, his intolerance for those who disagreed with him, and his obsession with reaching a consensus, it is difficult to imagine that he would feel comfortable with several of

---

[131] See, for example, Irving Janis, *Victims of Groupthink,* pp. 209–19; Alexander George, "The Case for Multiple Advocacy in Making Foreign Policy," *American Political Science Review* 66 (September 1972), 751–85.

the suggestions made above. Moreover, even presidents who are more open and flexible in their decision-making styles are likely to become less so the longer they remain in office. One reason for this may be that presidential egos, which are usually considerable to begin with, are bolstered still further by the undue reverence accorded to the office they hold. Consequently, they become increasingly arrogant and less tolerant of those who would challenge their judgments. The other reason may be that as pressures build and opposition mounts, presidents have a tendency to turn toward those who will provide unquestioning support. As Stephen Hess has noted, "Outside opposition generally forces internal consensus as administration officials begin to huddle together for comfort. And a President, feeling increasingly threatened, turns more and more to those who give him the most loyal support."[132]

Given these realities, one final and more drastic proposal may be in order—namely, *requiring* the President to appear before Congress periodically and answer questions in much the same way as the Prime Minister is compelled to do in the British House of Commons. This proposal would have several benefits, the first one being to reduce the regal, "untouchable" nature of the Presidency. Presently, the only time the President is held accountable for his actions between elections is when he holds a press conference. Even here, however, he is not being questioned by his peers; nor is he even required to hold press conferences. Second, appearances before Congress might serve to reduce the isolation that results as presidents increasingly surround themselves with people of like mind. Finally, the fact that a President would be compelled to justify his actions before Congress in person might also provide some additional incentive for him to consult more systematically with the legislature on important policy issues.

As for the weaknesses of this proposal, one may question whether members of Congress would be any less deferential than presidential advisers. Certainly no serious challenges were raised against President Ford when he voluntarily testified before the House Judiciary Committee concerning his pardon of President Nixon. But perhaps that was to be expected, since presidents have rarely appeared before Congress to justify their actions. If such appearances were institutionalized, as this proposal suggests, the tendency to be overly deferential to the President would probably decrease considerably after the first several encounters. A more serious objection to this proposal, however, might be that very little in the way of meaningful interaction could take place in an encounter between the President and five hundred and thirty-five members of Congress. (As a way around this problem, it might be more appropriate for the President to meet with a smaller group of individuals selected from the total membership of Congress. This group should probably not exceed forty people; the President should meet with it once a month on Capitol Hill; its membership should consist of an equal number of Republicans and Democrats from the House and an equal

---

[132] Stephen Hess, *Organizing the Presidency* (Washington, D.C.: Brookings Institution, 1976), p. 163.

number from the Senate; finally, to insure that all would have an opportunity to participate in the meetings, the membership of the group would be determined each month through a system of random selection.) One final objection to this proposal may be raised on the grounds that it is simply out of touch with reality. After all, to require presidents to appear before Congress would necessitate a constitutional amendment, and such a process is customarily a long and tedious one. Moreover, while students of the Presidency may be properly concerned over the potential for presidential isolation in decision making, it is highly doubtful that this concern has yet permeated the national consciousness.

Alas, all of the proposals suggested here may be found wanting in terms of their feasibility, desirability, or both. Thus, in all probability, we shall have to content ourselves with identifying the problem areas in presidential decision making, hoping all the while that the man in the Oval Office may take cognizance of them.

7

Personality
and
the Presidency

So far, we have been concerned with how the President interacts with the environment around him. The major components of his environment include the international situation; political, social, and economic conditions in our own society; institutional actors such as the Congress, the bureaucracy, the courts, the press, and organized interests; and finally, the general public. In assessing how he interacts with these various elements, we have dealt with the role of his personality in only a passing fashion. We shall now deal with it directly, first by considering to what extent an understanding of a President's personality can help us to explain his behavior as he attempts to shape and respond to his environment. Second, we shall address the question of whether some personality types may be more suited to the demands and responsibilities of the Presidency than others. Finally, we shall consider if it is possible to do a better job of screening the personalities of candidates who seek the office. Of course, all of these considerations presume that the personality variable can have a major impact upon presidential conduct—a matter to which we now turn.

Conditions Conducive to the Expression of Personality

The likelihood that an individual's behavior will give expression to his personality depends not only upon the degree to which a given circumstance elicits his strong beliefs, feelings, and needs, but also upon whether he finds himself in a structured or unstructured situation. That is, to the extent that certain norms and expectations prescribe what is expected of an individual in a given situation, the opportunity for personality to have an impact is lessened. This is especially so when a violation of prescribed behavior results in sanctions. These expectations may be formalized to the point where they are codified in law—a fifty-five-mile-an-hour speed limit on interstate highways, for example. Or they may be of an informal nature. Thus, although it is not written into the rules of the United States Senate that each member must treat his colleagues with utmost courtesy, there does exist an informal institutional consensus that requires it. Regardless of whether expectations operate at a formal or informal level, sanctions may result from noncompliance. If caught exceeding the fifty-five mile-an-hour speed limit, a driver will be subject to a traffic ticket. Similarly, if a senator fails to adhere to the norm of senatorial courtesy, he is likely to be ostracized by the rest of the membership.

Where an individual is put into a less structured environment, there is greater likelihood that personality will surface in his behavior. Thus, he might find himself faced with a new situation which may be largely free of any expectations or cues regarding behavior; or he might be involved in circumstances where there are indeed expectations for behavior, but they are contradictory; or finally, he may find himself in a situation where the cues from the environment allow for a variety of different, yet acceptable, modes of conduct.[1]

Of the three branches of government, the presidential environment is perhaps the most unstructured of all. Within both the Congress and the Supreme Court there have evolved numerous informal norms of behavior which the ongoing membership instills in its new members. But the Presidency is something quite different. Since only one man occupies the office, there is no ongoing membership there to socialize him into any particular set of behavior patterns. Rather, the expectations for presidential conduct are, to a considerable extent, the creation of the man who happens to occupy the office at any given time. Of course, his behavior is circumscribed by constitutional requirements as well as by public expectations, but both tend to be rather broadly defined, allowing him considerable leeway in responding to his environment. The style he chooses to adopt in dealing with such constituencies as the Congress, the bureaucracy, the public, and the press is largely his to determine. So too is the manner in which he organizes and interacts with his staff. Furthermore, while he is charged with making decisions, *how* he does so will be largely shaped by his own needs and inclinations. Moreover, *what* he decides may also invite the intrusion of personality, for in some cases the issue he faces may be new, or ambiguous, or possibly one on which there is sharp disagreement.

Analysis of Presidential Personality

There have been numerous attempts to psychoanalyze historical figures. Among the more notable efforts have been Freud's analysis of Leonardo da Vinci and Erik Erikson's case studies of Martin Luther and Gandhi. Only within the last ten years or so, however, have scholars begun to focus their attention

[1] Fred Greenstein, *Personality and Politics* (Chicago: Markham, 1969), pp. 46–47.

on assessing the personalities of presidents. Indeed, prior to this time the only systematic analysis of a President's personality was the psychobiography of Woodrow Wilson by Alexander and Juliette George. Not surprisingly, the especially fascinating personalities of Johnson and Nixon have spawned several attempts to fathom their psychological makeup: Doris Kearns, *Lyndon Johnson and the American Dream* (1976); Bruce Mazlish, *In Search of Nixon* (1973); Eli Chesen, *President Nixon's Psychiatric Profile* (1973); David Abrahamsen, *Nixon vs. Nixon* (1977). These and several other psychoanalytic case studies have attempted to construct a President's personality by looking for persistent behavior patterns as he responds to his environment over the course of his private and public life. These psychobiographies also make an effort to explain *why* an individual's personality develops as it does. Since psychoanalytic theory posits that personality is shaped by psychological needs that develop during the formative years, such explanations have necessitated piecing together a President's childhood experiences.

It should be noted at this point that psychoanalytic inquiries into presidential behavior are not without their limitations. For one thing, there is the problem of data. No President has ever surrendered himself to the psychoanalyst's couch and submitted to prolonged in-depth questioning. (The closest we have come to this were the extensive conversations Doris Kearns had with Lyndon Johnson over a four-year period. Those took place after Johnson left the Presidency.) Thus, the researcher is forced to rely upon biographies, letters, diaries, interviews with family, friends, and associates, and finally, upon what presidents may write about themselves. Richard Nixon's book *Six Crises* provides valuable insights into how he attempted to cope with his environment. But most presidents have not chosen to write books of this kind. Nor have they chosen to write their own life story—Jimmy Carter being a notable exception. The data problem may be especially acute when the scholar is attempting to reconstruct the formative years of a President's life. While biographies may be of assistance, there is no way of knowing that a biographer has recorded all the facts that a psychoanalyst might deem important. Interviews with family and friends may fill in the gaps, but even here one is faced with the problem of recall.

In addition to the problem of adequate data, there is also the matter of its interpretation. One observer, for example, may see rigid or inflexible behavior as a sign of some underlying insecurity, while another may view it as a dedication to principle. Since there is an absence of agreed-upon standards of evidence and inference within psychoanalytic theory, no interpretation can be demonstrated with certainty.

Finally, some object to the fact that psychoanalytic theory places such great stress on childhood experiences as the determiner of an individual's personality. Such reductionism, it is argued, fails to take account of adolescent and adult experiences that may also influence the development of personality. While all of these limitations should not cause us to dismiss the psychohistorical approach out of hand, they should invite us to view such explanations as suggestive rather than definitive. Much of what follows in the remainder of this chapter should be viewed in the same light.

Barber's Analysis

James David Barber's work *The Presidential Character: Predicting Performance in the White House* deserves our special attention for several reasons. First, his analysis of the personalities of thirteen twentieth-century presidents shows a careful concern for marshaling evidence. Second, the inferences made from this evidence are, for the most part, formulated with appropriate caution. Third, while Barber's analysis of presidential personalities places considerable stress upon childhood experiences, he does not ignore the impact of adolescent and adult experiences on the development of personality. Fourth, his work represents the first attempt to move from a case-study examination of individual presidents to an attempt at classifying presidential personalities into types. Finally, he has suggested what factors may account for the development of each type, thus providing us with some assistance in predicting presidential personalities.

Barber's conceptualization of personality consists of three components, the first of which is *character*. Character is "the way the President orients himself toward life—not for the moment—but enduringly"; how he "confronts experience" and how he views himself. This facet of personality is largely determined during the formative years of life. Of the three personality components, it is clear that Barber views this first one as the most important for understanding presidential behavior. The central message of his book, he states, is, "Look to character first." The second component of personality is *world view,* which consists of the individual's "primary, politically relevant beliefs, particularly his conceptions of social causality, human nature, and the central moral conflicts of the time." This belief system, according to Barber, takes its shape during the period of adolescence. The third component is *style,* which he defines as the way a political leader performs three roles: "rhetoric, personal relations, and homework." How an individual's style develops will be a function of his needs, skill, and the opportunities that present themselves. Barber is quick to point out that personality does not operate in a vacuum. Rather, the manner in which character, world view, and style influence presidential behavior will also depend on what kind of "power situation" the President finds himself in as well as on the "climate of expectations" existing within the population.[2]

Barber's personality types are derived from what he considers to be two fundamental orientations toward life. The first is an *active-passive* dimension and is concerned with how much energy an individual expends on what he does.

---

[2] James David Barber, *The Presidential Character: Predicting Performance in the White House,* 2nd ed. (Englewood Cliffs, N.J.: Prentice-Hall, 1972), pp. 7, 8, 445. ©1972 by James David Barber.

FIGURE 7-1. BARBER'S CLASSIFICATION OF THE PERSONALITIES OF AMERICAN PRESIDENTS (TAFT-CARTER)

	Positive	Negative
Active	Franklin Roosevelt Harry Truman John Kennedy Gerald Ford Jimmy Carter (?)	Woodrow Wilson Herbert Hoover Lyndon Johnson Richard Nixon
Passive	William Taft Warren Harding	Calvin Coolidge Dwight Eisenhower

Does he seek to influence his environment, or is he largely content to be influenced by it? The second dimension is one of *positive-negative* affect, and it relates to how an individual feels about what he does. Specifically, is he happy and optimistic or sad and pessimistic? Combining these dimensions, Barber comes up with four personality types, which he uses to classify thirteen twentieth-century presidents from Taft to Carter (see Figure 7-1).

The major attributes that Barber finds present in each of these four types are briefly summarized below:

Active-Positive: self-confident; flexible; creates opportunities for action; enjoys the exercise of power; does not take himself too seriously; optimistic; emphasizes the "rational mastery" of his environment.

Active-Negative: compulsive; expends great energy in what he does but derives little enjoyment from it; preoccupied with self in terms of whether he is failing or succeeding; low self-esteem; has problems with self-definition; inclined toward rigidity; pessimistic.

Passive-Positive: compliant; low self-esteem, which he attempts to overcome by being an ingratiating personality; reacts rather than initiates; reluctant to act decisively; superficially optimistic.

Passive-Negative: involved in politics out of a sense of duty and not because he enjoys it; compensates for low self-esteem by being of service to others; responds rather than initiates; avoids conflict and uncertainty; emphasizes principles and procedures and demonstrates an aversion to engaging in politicking.[3]

Of course, personalities are rarely so discrete that they can be neatly identified as wholly one type or another. Barber readily admits this, noting that some presidents may manifest the characteristics of more than one of his four types. Thus the classification of presidents is based upon the general tendency for a President's behavior to conform to the attributes of a given type, although it must be recognized all the while that the fit may not be a perfect one.

[3] Ibid., pp. 12, 13, 95–97, 146, 172, 174, 206, 210, 211.

In this chapter, we shall focus primarily on the active-positive and active-negative types since—as we hope will become apparent—the one (active-positive) shows the greatest promise of successfully coping with the responsibilities and pressures of the Presidency, while the other (active-negative) has the potential for doing the greatest harm. This is not to say that the passive-positive or passive-negative President cannot be either harmful or beneficial. But we shall defer a discussion of these matters until later in the chapter.

LYNDON JOHNSON AS AN ACTIVE-NEGATIVE

Many of the problems that surrounded the Johnson Presidency may be traced back to a psychological state that appears to be characteristic of all active-negative presidents, namely, a profound sense of insecurity. Before discussing its impact upon Johnson's presidential behavior, however, it is first helpful to know what factors may have engendered this condition.

Johnson's Youth

The environment in which Johnson grew up was not an altogether happy one. Throughout most of his childhood, the Johnson family experienced hard times financially, with his father going bankrupt three different times. All of Lyndon's clothes were homemade, and the food on the table was characteristic of the rural poor: bacon fat on cornbread, grits, turnip greens, and the like. To his father's apparent embarrassment, young Lyndon at one point even became a bootblack in order to earn extra money.[4]

His relationship with his parents was another source of unhappiness during his early years. His attachment to his mother was a strong one. Indeed, in later years he would characterize her as "a saintly woman, I owe everything to her."[5] Rebekah Baines Johnson was a cultured and intelligent woman whose father had at one time been editor of a newspaper and later became the Secretary of State for Texas. Her marriage to Sam Johnson was a step down for her on the social ladder and the financial situation of the Johnson family was a source of disappointment and concern to her. She was determined that young Lyndon would do better. By the time he was two years old she had already taught him the alphabet, and at the age of four she had him reading and enrolled him in the first grade. He was also taught to recite the poetry of Longfellow and Tennyson, and by the time he was seven, she had him taking dancing and violin lessons. When Johnson excelled in the tasks his mother had laid down for him, he received an outpouring of love and affection from her. "I'll never forget how much my mother loved me when I recited those poems." By the same token,

---

[4] Ibid., pp. 129, 130.
[5] Ibid., p. 129.

when he failed to live up to her expectations, her love was withdrawn completely. "For days after I quit those lessons she walked around the house pretending I was dead. And then to make it worse, I had to watch her being especially warm and nice to my father and sisters."[6] Later on when Lyndon initially decided not to attend college, his mother once again retaliated with a freeze out of affection: "We'd been such close companions, and, boom, she'd abandoned me."[7] When he ultimately did decide to go to college at San Marcos, his mother even travelled there to help him study for his math entrance exam. All of this suggests that the pressures on Lyndon to succeed were considerable, and the consequences that followed when he did not were often traumatic.

If Lyndon's relationship with his mother imposed a psychological strain on him, so too did his relationship with his father. In first grade, Lyndon wrote a poem entitled, significantly perhaps, "I'd Rather Be Mamma's Boy." None of the evidence on Johnson's youth suggests that he felt close to his father. Sam Johnson's drinking as well as his failure to provide adequately for the family caused considerable suffering for the person Lyndon loved most—his mother. He would never forget the time he came across his mother crying in the living-room because Sam had been out drinking all night. Lyndon put his arms around her and told her not to worry because he would always be there to take care of her. Another source of tension grew out of the fact that Sam Johnson was constantly raising doubts about his son's manliness. Lyndon Johnson vividly recalled the time his father accused Rebekah of making a sissy out of their son because he was still wearing curls at the age of four. Finally, after she had repeatedly refused to cut his hair, Sam Johnson took it upon himself to do so one day while Rebekah was at church. As a youth, the matter of masculinity appears to have preyed upon Lyndon's mind. He was noticeably concerned when his school friends began making fun of him because he was engaging in such "feminine" activities as dancing and playing the violin.[8] Of greater concern, however, were the gnawing doubts raised by his father. Lyndon would often go hunting with his friends but always returned empty handed because he could not bring himself to pull the trigger. One day his father asked him if he was a coward. Lyndon promptly picked up his gun and went out and shot a rabbit. On another occasion, he wrecked the family car and was afraid to return home and tell his father about it. Instead, he went to his uncle's house where he received a call from his father on the following day. Sam said he had bought a new truck and wanted Lyndon to go get it. He then added, "I want you to drive it around the courthouse square, five times, ten times, fifty times, nice and slow. You see there's some talk around town this morning that my son's a coward, that he

---

[6] Doris Kearns, *Lyndon Johnson and the American Dream* (New York: Harper & Row, 1976), p. 25. Copyright ©1976 by Doris Kearns. Reprinted by permission of Harper & Row, Publishers, Inc.

[7] Ibid., p. 40.

[8] Ibid., p. 33.

couldn't face up to what he'd done, and that he ran away from home. Now I don't want anyone thinking I produced a yellow son. So I want you to show up here in that car and show everyone how much courage you've really got."[9]

So determined was Johnson about demonstrating his manliness to his father that it appears to have been his major reason for initially deciding against continuing with his education after high school. He feared that if he decided to go to college, "It would make me a sissy again and I would lose my daddy's respect."[10]

Considering the tensions that existed in his relationship with both parents, it is not surprising that Lyndon ran away from home after he finished high school. But after spending two difficult years out in California, he grew weary of fending for himself and returned home. His mother continued to press him on going to college, but to no avail. Instead, he turned to working on a road gang and began drinking heavily. He got into several fights, and on one occasion returned home with a bloodied face. Reduced to tears at the sight of her son, his mother remarked, "To think that my eldest born should turn out like this."[11] Such a statement of dispirited resignation from the one person he loved and admired most weighed heavily on Lyndon. He decided to go to college.

In describing the environment of Johnson's youth, a plausible argument can be made that his experiences fostered the development of a low sense of self-esteem. He received little love and affection from his father. Nor could he always count on receiving it from his mother. At times she gave it effusively, but at other times she denied it to him completely. In addition, there were self-doubts concerning his ability to meet the high expectations his mother had for him. Finally, there were the gnawing uncertainties Johnson experienced concerning his own masculinity. All of these factors created within him an emotional tension, which could not be released against a father whom he feared or against a mother whom he loved. Instead, this emotional energy was directed toward achievement, for in this way he would be able to demonstrate his self-worth.

In college, the driving, self-disciplined, achievement-oriented Johnson began to show. He got a part-time job at Southwest Texas Teachers College collecting trash. Despite the menial nature of the job, he tried to collect more trash than any of his fellow workers. When this job did not prove challenging enough, he went to the college president's office and asked for something better. He was then given the position of assistant janitor, but that did not satisfy him for long either. He returned to the president's office and said he wanted to help him. The president obliged by making Johnson an assistant in his office. Lyndon was ultimately given the responsibility of answering some of the president's mail, assisting him with his reports, and accompanying him to the Texas legislature. Nor were his college activities confined only to working for the president. When

[9] Ibid., p. 38.

[10] Ibid., p. 40.

[11] Barber, *Presidential Character*, p. 135.

he failed to gain entry into the prestigious campus honorary known as the Black Stars, he created his own honorary and dubbed it the White Stars. He became editor of the college newspaper and developed into a prize debater. While he never managed to become president of the student body, he was nevertheless instrumental in picking the president and helping him win. Finally, even with all of this activity, he still managed to graduate from college with honors.

Johnson Enters Politics

That Johnson would ultimately have entered politics is understandable. His mother had always had a keen interest in national politics, and his father was involved in politics on both a local and state level. Furthermore, Johnson's involvement in campus politics had demonstrated a real talent for dealing with people. But his own explanation suggests a more profound reason for choosing a political career:

> I still believed my mother the most beautiful, sexy, intelligent woman I'd ever met and I was determined to recapture her wonderful love, but not at the price of my daddy's respect. Finally, I saw it all before me. I would become a political figure. Daddy would like that. He would consider it a manly thing to do. But that would be just the beginning. I was going to reach beyond my father. I would finish college; I would build great power and gain high office. Mother would like that. I would succeed where her own father had failed; I would go to the Capitol and talk about big ideas. She would never be disappointed in me again.[12]

Thus, a political career would serve to confirm Johnson's feeling of manliness; but just as important was the fact that politics would also provide him with the power necessary to achieve, and through achievement he would gain the love and respect of his mother and ultimately of others as well. The need for affection and respect ran deep in Johnson, but since his own sense of self-esteem appears to have been low, this respect and affection of necessity had to come from others. He craved and revelled in the cheers of approval he received while campaigning: "Oh boy, listen to that." Following lengthy speeches, he was always able to state correctly the number of times he had been applauded.[13] Especially revealing in this regard were the feelings he expressed about his landslide victory over Goldwater in 1964: "It was a night I shall never forget. Millions upon millions of people, each one marking my name on their ballot, each one wanting me as their President. . . . For the first time in all my life I truly felt loved by the American people."[14] But if politics carried with it the oppor-

[12] Kearns, *Lyndon Johnson*, p. 44.

[13] Eric Goldman, *The Tragedy of Lyndon Johnson* (New York: Alfred A. Knopf, 1968), p. 47.

[14] Kearns, *Lyndon Johnson*, p. 209.

tunity to receive approval from others, it also brought the possibility of losing it. So strong was his fear of rejection and failure that periods of despondency set in before nearly all of his decisions to run for or seek reelection to public office.[15]

World View and Style

It was during his years in Congress that two other facets of the Johnson personality began to manifest themselves, namely, his world view and style. If he was determined to achieve, it is equally clear that the direction of his achievements would be guided in part by a genuine compassion for the less fortunate. While it is probable that his hero, Franklin Roosevelt, influenced this aspect of Johnson's world view, a more significant factor was his own first-hand experience with poverty. Although the Johnson family had not been dirt poor, life had not been easy. More important, he saw the full impact of real poverty when he taught Mexican-American children in Cotulla, Texas: "My students were poor and they often came to class without breakfast, hungry. They knew even in their youth the pain of injustice. . . . I often walked home late in the afternoon, after the classes were finished, wishing there was more I could do."[16] His view of the world beyond the boundaries of the United States was to a considerable extent determined by his experience of living through the Second World War; a war that he thought might have been avoided had political leadership been more resolute against aggression.[17] His actions in Congress and later in the Presidency would reveal his firm conviction that the surest way to stop aggression was to challenge it head on and without delay.

Johnson rose quickly to positions of power in Congress, with the crowning achievement being his selection as Senate Majority Leader. It was in this position that his political style became apparent. Like all active-negative types, his inner drive to achieve created an almost inexhaustible reservoir of energy. Johnson worked longer and harder than others. He expected the same from his staff, which was generally acknowledged to be the most overworked and harassed group of individuals in the Senate. He learned to master the detail of both legislative procedure and substantive policy issues, a talent no doubt helped by his unusually keen intelligence. Perhaps his greatest talent was an uncanny ability to decipher the motives, needs, strengths, and weaknesses of others. Having done so, he would then play upon them in order to achieve the result he wanted. As one aid noted, "The senator was indeed persuasive, to say the least, but the principal reason he prevailed so often was that when he talked to a

[15] Booth Mooney, *LBJ: An Irreverent Chronicle* (New York: Thomas Y. Crowell, 1976), pp. 112, 156, 157. Copyright © 1976 by Booth Mooney. Reprinted by permission of Thomas Y. Crowell, Inc. See also Kearns, *Lyndon Johnson*, p. 49.

[16] Kearns, *Lyndon Johnson*, p. 65.

[17] Lyndon Johnson, *The Vantage Point* (New York: Holt, Rinehart and Winston, 1971), pp. 46, 47.

man he almost invariably knew more about him than the man himself knew."[18] He was most effective in one-to-one situations, and his tactics nearly always included excessive flattery and, when the occasion warranted it, tears or anger. Although the following description by Johnson relates to members of the press, it nevertheless provides some indication of the care and calculation that went into the "Johnson treatment":

> You learn that Stewart Alsop cares a lot about appearing to be an intellectual and a historian—he strives to match his brother's intellectual attainments—so whenever you talk to him, play down the gold cufflinks which you play up with *Time* magazine, and to him, emphasize your relationship with FDR and your roots in Texas, so much so that even when it doesn't fit the conversation you make sure to bring in maxims from your father and stories from the Old West. You learn that Evans and Novak love to traffic in backroom politics and political intrigue, so that when you're with them you make sure to bring in lots of details and colorful description of personality. You learn that Mary McGrory likes dominant personalities and Doris Fleeson cares only about issues, so that when you're with McGrory you come on strong and with Fleeson you make yourself sound like some impractical red-hot liberal.[19]

In addition to hard work and the manipulation of others, there were several other dimensions to Johnson's style. He had an obsession with secrecy and a passion for developing a consensus around issues. According to one aid, "He loved unanimous committee reports."[20] Finally, he insisted upon complete and total loyalty from those immediately around him and sought to insure it through fairly persistent intimidation.

These particular elements of his style are perhaps explainable to some extent by the active-negative's belief that he lives in a dangerous world. Certainly those who knew Johnson best acknowledged that he viewed other people with a certain degree of suspicion.[21] Accordingly, secrecy could provide him with the option of surprise and the room to maneuver right up to the time of decision. The careful search for consensus forestalled the possibility of an ambush against what he wanted to accomplish. And a staff whose loyalty was beyond question provided him with at least a few people whom he could trust implicitly. In short, all of these stylistic qualities enhanced his sense of control over an otherwise uncertain and dangerous world.

---

[18] Mooney, *LBJ*, p. 31.

[19] Kearns, *Lyndon Johnson*, pp. 127, 128.

[20] Mooney, *LBJ*, p. 101.

[21] Ibid., p. 276.

The Johnson Presidency

The Johnson Presidency was characterized by extraordinary activity. The rigorous schedule he had maintained during his Senate years continued in the White House. Any attempts to get him to relax occasionally were to no avail. The results of his driving energy were evident in the myriad legislative proposals sent to Congress. Among others, they included programs dealing with the cities, civil rights, education, medical care, crime, consumer protection, jobs, housing, and conservation. Indeed, it was one of the most formidable legislative records of any President in our history, although some argued that in his effort to accomplish things, he sacrificed quality for quantity.

Yet there were several unsettling aspects to the Johnson Presidency, and these were ultimately traceable to the nature of his personality. The active-negative seeks to confirm his self-worth through achievement, but in order to achieve one must have control. Fear of losing control had always preoccupied Johnson. He frankly admitted that throughout his political career he frequently had dreams with a recurring theme—*paralysis*. Following the heart attack he had while serving as Senate Majority Leader, he dreamed that he was paralyzed in bed and could hear others in the next room deciding how to divide up his power. As Vice President, he dreamed of being seated at a desk where, once again, he was paralyzed.[22] In the White House, his obsession with control manifested itself in the trivial as well as the important. When a member of his staff undertook the task of putting together the President's speeches for publication in a book, Johnson insisted on approving such aspects of the book as the margins, the type, and the cover design. One day while cruising down the Potomac on the presidential yacht *Sequoia,* he passed Vice President Humphrey who was cruising on another one of the presidential yachts. The President promptly informed Humphrey that henceforth, if he wanted to take out one of the yachts, he must first receive permission from Marvin Watson, the President's aid.[23]

The desire to control extended to more important matters as well. He held a close rein over the personnel and budgets of the various executive departments. He would not permit any of his Cabinet to make disclosures to the press. Rather, all information released by the government would come from the White House. As in his Senate days, Johnson insisted upon complete subservience from those around him, Cabinet as well as staff members. Attempts to challenge or question his politics brought either a "freeze out" or dismissal. Everybody had to be on board. On one occasion, for example, when a member of his staff presented Johnson with the name of a possible staff replacement, the first question asked

---

[22] Kearns, *Lyndon Johnson,* pp. 33, 167.

[23] David Halberstam, *The Best and the Brightest* (New York: Random House, Inc., 1969), p. 648.

by the President was, "How loyal is that man?" His aid replied, "Well, he seems quite loyal, Mr. President." Johnson responded, "I don't want loyalty. I want *loyalty.*"[24]

While his penchant for loyalty, secrecy, and consensus may have given him a greater sense of control over his environment, these aspects of his style did not serve him well when he confronted the issue of Vietnam. His insistence upon loyalty and consensus stifled debate and encouraged others to tell him only what he wanted to hear. And the demand for secrecy often restricted the consultation process to only a small group of individuals.

One of the most disturbing features of the Johnson Presidency was his inclination to sacrifice means for ends. This aspect of his political style may also be rooted in the active-negative's sense of insecurity. Since a confirmation of self-worth is dependent upon achievement, the risk of failure becomes intolerable. Consequently, he may go to extraordinary lengths to avoid it. Johnson was apparently so determined that nothing would get in the way of his election to the Presidency in 1964 that he sent a group of FBI agents to the Democratic Convention. Ostensibly, their purpose was to collect information on militants, but in fact it was to provide him with political intelligence on his political opponents.[25] Even though he was well ahead of Goldwater in the polls, it now appears that he practiced some of the "dirty tricks" that would later be repeated in spades by the Nixon Administration.[26]

His lack of concern for *means* was also reflected in his willingness to play freely with the truth. As was often the case, this behavior pattern manifested itself in trivial as well as important matters. While in Texas he pointed to a Lincolnesque log cabin and told reporters that he was born there. On another occasion, he told a group of soldiers that his ancestors had fought at the Alamo. Whether he was attempting to add some glitter to his roots—about which he had always felt insecure—is not clear. But the fact of the matter is that both statements were totally false. More damaging, of course, was his tendency to mislead on issues of consequence. Thus, when he came under heavy criticism for sending 22,000 American troops into the Dominican Republic, he justified his actions on the grounds that he was protecting American lives, and at a news conference he proceeded to paint a tragic picture of the situation Americans found themselves in there. Both the description and the justification proved to be false. There was no evidence to suggest that American lives were in grave jeopardy. Moreover, as he acknowledged privately, his real reason for committing the troops was to prevent a Communist takeover of the government.[27]

[24] Ibid., p. 526.

[25] Nick Thimmesch, "The Abuse of Richard Nixon," *The Alternative* 9 (April 1976), 7.

[26] Theodore White, *Breach of Faith* (New York: Atheneum, 1975), pp. 99, 100, 325.

[27] David Wise, *The Politics of Lying* (New York: Vantage Books, 1973), pp. 60, 61. See also Arthur Schlesinger Jr., *The Imperial Presidency* (Boston: Houghton Mifflin, 1973), p. 178.

At no time was Johnson's deception more clearly shown than in dealing with the Vietnam War. He knew that the major achievement of his administration would be its vast array of social programs. As Johnson later recalled, the passage of this legislation would realize his "youthful dream of improving life for more people and in more ways than any other political leader, including FDR. . . . I was determined to keep the war from shattering that dream."[28] Fearing that the Congress would cut back money for his Great Society programs if the projected cost of the war was too high, Johnson informed Congress that the war's projected cost for 1967 would only be $10 billion. In actuality, his Secretary of Defense had told him that the cost could run as high as $17 billion. It happens that at this particular time Congress was considering the possibility of a tax increase as a means of cooling down the economy. Had Congress known that the war might cost $17 billion, it would certainly have decided in favor of a tax increase. Operating on the $10 billion figure, however, Congress decided that the tax increase was not necessary. As it turned out, the cost of the war came closer to $21 billion, and for want of a tax increase, the economy was started on an inflationary spiral that still plagues us today. In addition to deceiving Congress about the cost of the war, the President misled the country on the extent of our involvement as well. Secretary McNamara, who had been sent to Vietnam on a fact-finding mission, returned to Washington and informed the President that the United States would have to commit anywhere from 100,000 to 125,000 men. Johnson gave the go-ahead for the 100,000 troops, but he also realized that such a massive infusion of troops might spark a negative reaction in the country. Accordingly, he decided to tell the American people about only 50,000 of the 100,000 or so troops he intended to send.[29]

Johnson's handling of the Vietnam War brought out two other disturbing aspects of the active-negative's personality, namely, a tendency toward rigidity and the displacement of personal frustrations upon others. No doubt, Johnson's decision to commit American troops to the defense of South Vietnam grew out of a world view that was shaped by the belief that aggression must be met head on. Yet he persisted in his Vietnam policy even when it became apparent that it was failing and that it was exacting extraordinarily high human, economic, and psychological costs on the American public. This kind of inflexibility appears to be rooted in the active-negative's self-esteem, which is so impoverished that he finds it extremely difficult to admit the possibility of failure. Johnson's associates had long observed his reluctance to admit error, even when it merely involved apologizing to someone for something he had done.[30] Acknowledging the possibility of failure becomes even more unlikely on an issue concerning which the active-negative has invested so much of himself. Vietnam appears to

[28]Kearns, *Lyndon Johnson,* p. 282.

[29]Halberstam, *Best and Brightest,* pp. 727, 736–38.

[30]Mooney, *LBJ,* p. 27. See also Jack Valenti, *A Very Human President* (New York: W.W. Norton, 1975), p. 273.

have been such an issue for Johnson, for any sign of retreat would have signalled his failure to measure up on a quality about which he had always been highly sensitive—his manliness. In the following statement he reveals this concern:

> For this time there would be Robert Kennedy out in front leading the fight against me, telling everyone that I had betrayed John Kennedy's commitment to South Vietnam. That I had let a democracy fall into the hands of the Communists. That I was a coward. An unmanly man. A man without spine. Oh, I could see it coming all right. Every night when I fell asleep I would see myself tied to the ground in the middle of a long, open space. In the distance, I could hear the voices of thousands of people. They were all shouting at me and running toward me: "Coward! Traitor! Weakling!" They kept coming closer. They began throwing stones. At exactly that moment, I would generally wake up . . . terribly shaken.[31]

Thus he steadfastly pursued his policy of expanding troop commitments and accelerating the bombing of North Vietnam. As the picture grew bleaker, he began to blame his problems on others. Most notable among the villains was the eastern establishment. As he later recalled, he thought they were deliberately creating dissension over his Vietnam policy because of his Texas background, because he had never gone to Harvard, because his Great Society programs had far outshone the accomplishments of the Kennedy Administration. "You see, they had to find some issue on which to turn against me and they found it in Vietnam."[32] Then there was the press, which, he reasoned, had turned against him because they were more interested in winning Pulitzer Prizes than in printing the truth. Then too there was his most vocal and articulate critic in Congress, Senator William Fulbright, who had turned dovish only because Johnson failed to make him Secretary of State.

In no instance did Johnson entertain the possibility that dissent might be grounded in any motive other than self-interest. Nor, as he would later recall, was he above ascribing Communist influence to the thinking of his critics, and even his advisers:

> Two or three intellectuals started it all, you know. They produced all the doubt, they and the columnists in the *Washington Post,* the *New York Times, Newsweek* and *Life.* And it spread and it spread until it appeared as if the people were against the war. Then Bobby Kennedy began taking it up as his cause and with Martin Luther King on his payroll he went around stirring up the Negroes and telling them that if they came out into the streets they'd get more. Then the Communists stepped in. They control the three networks, you know, and the forty major outlets of communi-

[31] Kearns, *Lyndon Johnson,* p. 253.
[32] Ibid., p. 313.

cation. It's all in the FBI reports. They prove everything. Not just about the reporters but about the professors too.

Isn't it funny that I always received a piece of advice from my top advisors right after each of them had been in contact with someone in the Communist world? And isn't it funny that you could always find Dobryinin's [Soviet Ambassador to the United States] car in front of Reston's house the night before Reston delivered a blast on Vietnam?[33]

Dovish senators were also perceived by Johnson as being under the Communist spell. He noted, for example, that they frequently attended receptions at the Russian Embassy, that some of the senators' daughters were dating the sons of embassy officials, and that some of the senators were even having their dovish speeches written at the embassy. Indeed, so suspect did he become of his critics' motives that he ordered various government agencies to keep dossiers on certain members of Congress, journalists and various other critics.[34] As protest to his politics mounted, so too did his paranoia. Aids who expressed disagreement with his Vietnam policy were let go. To one he remarked, "I can't trust anybody! What are you trying to do to me? Everybody is trying to cut me down, destroy me!"[35] On another occasion, he opened up a Cabinet meeting by asking, "Why aren't you out there fighting against my enemies? Don't you realize that if they destroy me, they'll destroy you as well?"[36] In short, as Lyndon Johnson surveyed his environment, he increasingly saw himself as a man under siege by conspiratorial elements whose only purpose was to do him in.

In 1968, Johnson was finally prevailed upon to make an important change in his Vietnam policy. His intensive bombing of North Vietnam had not brought the North Vietnamese to the negotiating table as he had hoped it would. Therefore, with great reluctance, he finally accepted the advice of those who argued that the North Vietnamese would be more likely to negotiate if the bombing were halted. Does this change in position not indicate that he could be flexible? Certainly it does. Rigidity is not a condition like pregnancy, where one is either pregnant or not pregnant. Rather it may be spoken of in terms of degrees. To the extent that Johnson was ultimately able to alter his position, he appears less rigid, for example, than Woodrow Wilson, who refused to compromise on any aspect of his proposal for a League of Nations. But if the active-negative's rigidity results from an unwillingness to admit failure, was not Johnson's reversal of position on the bombing in effect an admission of failure? Apparently he was ultimately able to convince himself that he had not lost the love and respect of the American people, despite his disastrous Vietnam policy: "No matter what

[33] Ibid., pp. 316, 317.

[34] Halberstam, *Best and Brightest,* pp. 757, 758.

[35] Barber, *Presidential Character,* p. 53.

[36] Kearns, *Lyndon Johnson,* p. 317.

anyone said, I knew that the people out there loved me a great deal. . . . Deep down I knew—I simply knew—that the American people loved me. After all that I'd done for them and given to them, how could they help but love me?"[37] Of course, the true test of whether or not he was still liked would have been his reelection in 1968. But at the very time he announced a halt to the bombing, he also stated that he would not seek reelection. While he maintained that his decision was based upon a desire to keep politics out of our Vietnam policy, one cannot help but wonder if it was also motivated by a fear that he might be rejected.

RICHARD NIXON AS AN ACTIVE-NEGATIVE

Nixon's Youth

Like Johnson, Richard Nixon did not have a very happy childhood. As he would later recount, "We were poor. We worked hard. We had very little. We all used hand-me-down clothes. I wore my brother's shoes and my brother below me wore mine and other clothes of that sort."[38] There was little time for play.

Young Nixon also experienced problems of a physical nature. As a baby he had fallen out of a buggy and severely gashed his head and thereafter appears to have suffered constantly from motion sickness. At the age of four he contracted a severe case of pneumonia and nearly died. He was also plagued by hay fever, and in high school he contracted a case of undulant fever, causing him to miss most of the school year. Finally, he also went through the traumatic experience of watching two brothers die of tuberculosis and feared that he too would succumb to the same fate.[39]

With respect to his family relationships, young Richard did not find in his father a man with whom he could easily identify. It is fair to say that Frank Nixon had never been very successful at anything he did. He lost his job as a trolley car operator after crashing a trolley car into an automobile. His father-in-law gave him the land to plant an orange grove, but this venture failed. He became foreman of a citrus ranch, but this job lasted for only a few months. Once again, his father-in-law stepped in and helped him to purchase land for another orange grove, but Frank Nixon chose property with depleted soil, and this venture fizzled out also. He finally ended up supporting the family by operating a small grocery store.

Frank Nixon was an irascible sort, prone to violent outbursts of temper and ridicule of other people. Richard and his brothers often bore the brunt of his

---

[37]Ibid., p. 315.

[38]David Abrahamsen. *Nixon vs Nixon*, p. 50. Copyright © 1976 by David Abrahamsen. Reprinted with the permission of Hill and Wang (now a division of Farrar, Straus & Giroux, Inc.).

[39]Ibid., p. 142.

wrath. Indeed, one of the neighbors recalls that Frank "could be hard and he could be beastly . . . like an animal. He could be very hard on the children— spank them freely and give them cracks."[40] Thus, if young Richard was to be the object of affection, it would have to come from someone other than his father.

Nixon's mother appears to have been the most significant figure in his life while growing up. In his final public remarks as President, he harkened back to the memory of both parents, but his warmest remarks were reserved for his mother: "Nobody will ever write a book probably about my mother. Well, I guess all of you would say this about your mother: my mother was a saint."[41] In stark contrast to her husband, Hannah Nixon was the epitome of self-control, and she sought to instill this quality in her children. Moreover, it was from her that Richard received care and affection. But the security gained from her affection could not always be counted on, for there were extended periods when they were separated from each other. At one point, for example, Hannah Nixon was away from the family for two years when she took one of their tubercular sons to Arizona. On another occasion, when Richard was twelve, he was sent away from home to live with his aunt for six months. Precisely what necessitated his departure is still obscure. Despite these separations, however, the relationship between Nixon and his mother was a very close one. He was constantly helping her with chores around the house and as a teenager spent considerable time assisting her in the family store. But the closeness of the relationship also appears to have caused him some anxiety about his masculinity. His brothers teased him for being a mama's boy. Thus, when he helped his mother with "women's work" around the house, he took the precaution of closing the blinds so that no one would see him.[42] This concern also manifested itself in school, where he made a point of stressing his dislike for girls. Especially noteworthy in this regard is an essay he wrote about his brother Arthur, who had died of tuberculosis. As the following excerpts demonstrate, the essay is replete with references to Arthur's distaste for things feminine. That Richard chose to emphasize this aspect of a brother he greatly admired suggests that establishing a masculine identity was much on his mind:

> There was one time when he was asked to be a ring bearer at a wedding. I remember how my mother had to work with him for hours to get him to do it, because he disliked walking with the little flower girl. Then I remember the grief he experienced over his hair. My parents had wanted him to be a girl in the first place; consequently, they attempted to make him one as much as possible. Each day he begged my mother for a boy's haircut, and when he finally did get it, there was not a happier boy in the state

---

[40] Ibid., p. 91.

[41] *New York Times,* August 10, 1974, p. 4. ©1974 by The New York Times Company. Reprinted by permission.

[42] Earl Mazo and Stephen Hess, *Nixon: A Political Portrait* (New York: Popular Library, 1968), p. 10.

. . . He was doing exceptionally well in all things except drawing. He absolutely would not take interest in anything he thought common to girls.[43]

As with the case of Johnson, one can hypothesize that the seeds of Nixon's insecurity were sown within his childhood experiences: lack of affection from a dominating and ridiculing father; sporadic affection from a mother who was separated from him for extended periods of time; doubts about his masculinity arising from a close identification with his mother, and perhaps also from his physical frailty as a youth. The confluence of all these factors produced in Nixon a low sense of self-esteem. Consequently, since his self-worth could not be confirmed by what he was, it would have to be confirmed as a result of what he did.

Achievement requires self-discipline and hard work. Hannah Nixon had instilled in him the necessity for self-control, and his own determination to demonstrate his worthiness provided the energy to work hard. Indeed, Nixon approached every task with extraordinary intensity. One college classmate recalls that "it wasn't uncommon for him to work himself ill." According to the recollections of his history professor, "He was out to win. . . . He was a brute for discipline."[44] While his lack of coordination prevented him from making the first football team, what he lacked in physical prowess was made up for by his competitive spirit. Although athletics did not turn out to be his forte, Nixon did discover that he had a way with words, a talent he put to good use on the college debating team as well as in the classroom. He also took up acting and became sufficiently proficient at it to be able to produce tears when a given scene required it. Apparently he commanded the respect of his fellow students for he helped found, and became the first president of, a college club known as the Orthogonians. More important, he also managed to get himself elected student body president. But respect did not convert to close personal friendships. Nixon was an intensely private person and did not relate to others easily. One classmate recalled him as "lonely, and so solemn at school. He didn't know how to mix."[45]

Despite the fact that he graduated second in his class from college, his strong desire to succeed caused him considerable anxiety when he went to law school: "I'm scared. I counted thirty-two Phi Beta Kappa keys in my class. I don't believe I can stay un top in that group."[46] At the completion of his second year in law school, he was afraid that his grades would not be good enough to retain his ranking of third in his class and his scholarship as well. Indeed, so great was

---

[43] Bela Kornitzer, *The Real Nixon: An Intimate Biography* (Chicago: Rand McNally, 1960), p. 79.

[44] Abrahamsen, *Nixon vs. Nixon*, pp. 28, 110.

[45] Ibid., p. 103.

[46] Barber, *Presidential Character*, p. 409.

his anxiety on this matter that he and some other students broke into the dean's office to sneak a look at the grades. Had he been caught, he almost certainly would have been dismissed from school, but his compulsive fear of failure apparently outweighed the possibility of expulsion. Ultimately, his fears of not achieving in law school proved to be unwarranted, for he graduated third in his class. Once again, it was success born of hard work, with little apparent enjoyment. As his roommate recalled, "Nixon had a quality of intensity in him, worked hard, pretty intense guy—he had a sense of privacy and not terribly strong on humor."[47]

Nixon Enters Politics

After law school Nixon tried to secure a position with a prestigious New York law firm but was turned down. He took a job with the Office of Price Administration in Washington but tired of it and decided to enlist in the Navy. Unlike Johnson, Nixon does not appear to have consciously planned a political career. While stationed in Maryland, he received a call from a banker friend in California who asked him if he wanted to run for Congress. Nixon accepted. Certainly his intelligence, capacity for hard work, and rhetorical ability would suit him well to politics. But as Nixon himself noted, he was an "introvert in a highly extroverted profession."[48] Yet this aspect of his personality was evidently overcome by a deep psychological need to confirm his self-worth. As one long-time associate later recalled, "It's a case of cold respect, he wants respect."[49] The respect he so earnestly sought would be gained by facing up to political challenges and meeting them successfully. Indeed, one cannot read the comments and writings of Richard Nixon without coming away with the clear impression that he viewed life in general, and politics in particular, as a struggle, a battle in which he was to be *tested:*

> I believe in the battle, whether it's the battle of the campaign or the battle of this office, which is a continuing battle. It's always there wherever you go. I perhaps, carry it more than others because that's my way.[50]

> Anybody in politics must have a great competitive instinct. He must want to win. He must not like to lose, but above everything else, he must have the ability to come back, to keep fighting more and more strongly when it seems that the odds are the greatest. That's the world of sports. That's the world of politics. I suppose you could say that's life itself.[51]

[47] Abrahamsen, *Nixon vs. Nixon,* p. 116.

[48] Ibid., p. 148.

[49] Theodore White, *The Making of the President 1968* (New York: New American Library, 1969), p. 177.

[50] Cited in Erwin Hargrove, *The Power of the Modern Presidency* (New York: Alfred A. Knopf, 1974), p. 47.

[51] Abrahamsen, *Nixon vs. Nixon,* p. 83.

[To members of the press] . . . . Don't give me a friendly question. Only a hard, tough question gets the kind of an answer—you may not like it—but it is the one that tests the man. And that is the responsibility of members of the press to test the man . . . I can only say I benefit from it.[52]

Eisenhower demonstrated a trait that I believe all great leaders have in common: they thrive on challenge; they are at their best when the going is hardest.[53]

No one really knows what he is capable of until he is tested to the full by events over which he may have no control.[54]

I don't know what the future brings, but whatever it brings, I'll be fighting.[55]

As Nixon noted in his book *Six Crises,* facing up to the struggle and the challenge is a difficult emotional experience for him, something he does not enjoy doing. In addition, when confronting the difficult decisions that challenge brings, he inevitably sees himself as doing the difficult but also the *right* thing. In discussing his Vietnam decisions, for example, he pointed out that "the President of the United States, when he was under unmerciful assault at the time of Cambodia, at the time of May 8th, when I ordered the bombing and mining of North Vietnam . . . still went ahead and did what he thought was right."[56] Later on when he first went on television to discuss Watergate, he would make the same point:

Who then is to blame for what happened in this case? For specific criminal actions by specific individuals, those who committed those actions must of course bear the liability and pay the penalty. For the fact that alleged improper actions took place within the White House or within my campaign organization, the easiest course would be for me to blame those to whom I delegated the responsibility to run the campaign. But that would be a cowardly thing to do.

I will not place blame on subordinates, on people whose zeal exceeded their judgment and who may have done wrong in a cause they desperately believed in to be right. In any organization the man at the top must bear the responsibility.

That responsibility, therefore, belongs here in this office. I accept it.[57]

[52] William Small, *Political Power and the Press* (New York: W.W. Norton, 1972), p. 126.

[53] Richard Nixon, *Six Crises* (Garden City: Doubleday and Company, 1962), p. 169.

[54] Bruce Mazlish, *In Search of Nixon* (Baltimore: Penguin Books, 1972), p. 110.

[55] *Washington Post,* May 26, 1977, p. A13.

[56] *New York Times,* October 27, 1973, p. 14. ©1973 by The New York Times Company. Reprinted by permission.

[57] *New York Times,* May 1, 1973, p. 31. ©1973 by The New York Times Company. Reprinted by permission.

His emphasis on lack of enjoyment in facing up to challenges and his stress upon taking the difficult but correct course of action in resolving them seem designed to convince himself that he is genuinely being tested.

World View and Style

In certain respects, the Nixon world view is elusive, for it was often adapted to what the political circumstances required. In fact, a close adviser to President Eisenhower maintains that this was one of the reasons Ike considered dropping him from the ticket in 1956. He seemed "too political without holding a genuine point of view."[58] Yet two dimensions of Nixon's world view stood out glaringly: strong anticommunism (although this too would moderate) and a pessimism that was rooted in a suspicion of other people. So apparent was this latter facet of his personality that his classmates in law school gave him the nickname of Gloomy Gus. Nixon did not take an optimistic view of his fellow man. He expressed the belief that most people are "mentally and physically lazy." Moreover, people in politics were seen by him as ingrates and opportunists: "One of the hardest lessons for those in political life to learn is that the rarest of all commodities is a political friendship that lasts through times of failure as well as success."[59] The depth of his suspicion comes through most clearly, however, in an interview he gave to Stewart Alsop while Vice President:

Nixon: The more you stay in this kind of job, the more you realize that a public figure, a major public figure, is a lonely man—the President very much more so, of course. But even in my job you can't enjoy the luxury of intimate personal friendships. You can't confide absolutely in anyone. You can't talk too much about your personal plans, your personal feelings. I believe in keeping my own counsel. It's something like wearing clothing—if you let down your hair, you feel too naked.

. . . You know I try to be candid with newspapermen, but I can't really let my hair down with anyone.

Alsop: Not even with old friends, like Jack Drowns, say?

Nixon: No, not really with anyone, not even with my family.[60]

As for political style, his campaigns reflected one of its hallmarks—hard work. Nearly all campaigns appear to have been grueling experiences, with Nixon working himself almost to the point of exhaustion. He prepared carefully and mastered the details of issues. The rhetorical skills he had demonstrated in college were incorporated into his political style. His speeches were hard hitting and

---

[58]Cited in Arthur Woodstone, *Nixon's Head* (New York: St. Martin's Press, 1972), p. 33.

[59]Nixon, *Six Crises,* p. 394.

[60]Stewart Alsop, *Nixon and Rockefeller: A Double Portrait* (Garden City, N.Y.: Doubleday, 1960), p. 195.

were able to touch the underlying concerns—and frequently fears—of the public. Indeed, it was his rhetorical talents that came to his aid in facing up to some of the events he labelled as "crises" in his political career—his emotional television defense of his political slush fund in the 1952 election campaign, his famous "kitchen debate" with Nikita Khrushchev. Later on, he would once again employ rhetoric—this time unsuccessfully—in his attempt to explain away the scandals of Watergate.

Still another manifestation of the Nixon political style was his insistence on being in complete control of things. In writing about Nixon's bid for the Presidency in 1960, Theodore White observed that "no other candidate of the big seven operated in 1960 with fewer personnel or kept more of the critical decisions in his own hands."[61] This assessment is confirmed by one of Nixon's closest political advisers, who recalls that "he was the hardest candidate of all to manage."[62] This feature of the Nixon style was once again in evidence during the 1968 campaign when he restricted his television appearances to formats over which he had complete control. There were no appearances on talk shows or public affairs programs such as "Meet the Press" and "Face the Nation." Given the Nixon character, this aspect of his style is quite understandable, for if one is obsessed with avoiding failure, he must maintain his power to control his environment, especially when that environment is perceived as dangerous and uncertain.

Considering Nixon's introverted and suspicious nature, it is not surprising that reclusive tendencies were also manifested in his political style. One of his close aids during the vice-presidential years recalls that only rarely did he meet with Nixon. Most of the time the Vice President preferred to communicate with him through memoranda. Similarly, during Nixon's presidential campaigns, he would not join the politicians and reporters who were travelling on his plane but preferred to sit at the back of the plane by himself. If someone had something to say to him, the message was conveyed through a close aid. Of course, if a candidate wants to get elected, he must quite obviously get out and meet people. Nixon did so, but the experience was not an enjoyable one for him. During the 1968 campaign, one aid recalls that "on the way out, as we were landing, I asked Nixon if he was enjoying the campaign. 'Never do,' he said, looking out at the crowd lined up along the fence, the signs, the mike on the podium, the local politicians waiting to shake hands. 'Campaigns are something to get over with.' "[63] This reaction is in stark contrast to a Johnson or a Humphrey, both of whom experienced a sense of rejuvenation from getting out to meet the people.

One final aspect of Nixon's pre-Presidency style deserves mention here, namely, his willingness to "play rough." Even his closest aid, H. R. Haldeman, has

[61] Theodore White, *The Making of the President 1960* (New York: New American Library, 1961), p. 81.

[62] Cited in Barber, *Presidential Character,* p. 374.

[63] William Safire, *Before the Fall* (Garden City, N.Y.: Doubleday, 1975), p. 70. Copyright © 1975 by William Safire. Used by permission of Doubleday & Company, Inc.

readily acknowledged this facet of the Nixon personality: "Nixon rarely spared the rod or the knife in his speeches and, to put it mildly, he wasn't averse to using all possible means to try to defeat his opponents. I believed in tough campaigning too, but even from my hard-line standpoint, Nixon went too far at times."[64] In one way or another, this trait insinuated itself into nearly all of his campaigns for public office. In his first campaign for Congress, he ran against a moderate liberal by the name of Jerry Voorhis. Making the most of his rhetorical ability, he gave a series of hard-hitting speeches in which he accused Voorhis of being associated with an organization alleged to have Communist ties. Apparently voters were also called on the phone and actually told that Voorhis was a Communist. While it was never demonstrated that there was any substance to Nixon's charges, his scare tactics worked. He was elected by a 15,000-vote margin. He took the same tack in his subsequent campaign for election to the United States Senate, but this time his opponent was Helen Gahagan Douglas. Once again, his rhetoric implied that his opponent had Communist sympathies; he sarcastically dubbed her the "Pink Lady" and noted that her voting record was written on a pink piece of paper. His margin of victory this time was 680,000 votes. Even as Eisenhower's runningmate in 1952, the cloud of questionable tactics hung over him. Not only was there the issue of his secret "slush fund," but many people were shocked by the nature of his attacks against the incumbent administration. He took after the State Department, characterizing it as the "Kollege of Kommunism, Kowardice, and Korruption." He also accused Secretary of State Acheson of "colorblindness—a form of pink eye toward the Communist threat to the United States."[65] By the time he ran for governor of California in 1964, public fears of communism had subsided, and thus he made no effort to play upon them in his campaign. Yet even in that campaign there was some doubt raised about his tactics, as evidenced by the fact that a California court found the Nixon campaign organization guilty of violating the state's election laws.

Nixon himself once remarked that "I play to win."[66] But the pattern of conduct described here suggests that the desire to win took precedence over *how* he won. Several features of his personality may help to explain why this was so. First, the active-negative's self-esteem, impoverished to begin with, cannot tolerate failure; consequently, he may be under especially strong pressures to sacrifice means for ends to avoid it. Second, Nixon's view of the world may also have been a contributing factor here. If an individual perceives himself as surrounded by a hostile world, then he must play rough or else be victimized by others. Finally, one cannot help but wonder if Nixon's rough tactics were also designed

[64] H.R. Haldeman, with Joseph DiMona, *The Ends of Power* (New York: New York Times Books, 1978), p. 50. Reprinted by permission of the New York Times Book Co. Copyright © 1978 by H.R. Haldeman, with Joseph DiMona.

[65] White, *Breach of Faith*, p. 64.

[66] Safire, *Before the Fall*, p. 601.

to erase doubts about his manliness. Clearly a concern for toughness appears to have been much on his mind throughout his political life. One long-time observer of Nixon's career notes "the captivating iridescence he saw in any invitation to toughness."[67] He was fascinated by New York, in part because it was "very cold and very ruthless." He had great respect for people like Khrushchev, Agnew, Mitchell, and Connally because they were tough. At the same time he expressed reservations about some of his aids—Len Garment and Robert Finch, for example—because he did not think they were mean enough. Even during the darkest hours of his Presidency, his preoccupation with manliness was in evidence. On the eve of his departure from the White House, he met late into the night with Henry Kissinger. It was an emotional encounter. At one point, Nixon broke into tears and asked Kissinger to kneel down and pray with him. Fearful of the impression he might have left, he called Kissinger on the phone afterward and made a request: "Henry, please don't ever tell anyone that I cried and that I was not strong."[68] In his departing remarks to the White House staff the following day, he spoke of Theodore Roosevelt, noting that he too had faced hardship and disappointment during his life. More important, however, he pointed out that Roosevelt had "served his country, always in the arena, tempestous, strong, sometimes right. But he was a *man*."[69]

The Nixon Presidency

Whereas Johnson retreated into isolation only when things started to go badly for him, reclusiveness was a persistent element of the Nixon style. He came into the Presidency believing that "I must build a wall around me."[70] He did precisely that. Only Haldeman, Ehrlichman, and sometimes Kissinger had ready access to him. When faced with important decisions, he frequently went into seclusion and pondered his options. Had he consulted more widely, had he taken more people into his confidence, might he have avoided the scandals of Watergate? Had he reached beyond the counsel of Haldeman and Ehrlichman, might he have decided to respond to the initial Watergate revelations by means other than a cover-up? It seems doubtful, but he might have.

It has already been suggested that the active-negative's special need for control may result from both his obsession with avoiding failure and from his belief that he lives in a dangerous world. While we could see manifestations of this need in Nixon even prior to his taking office, it was most apparent during his Presidency. As with Johnson, it extended to the trivial as well as the important.

[67]White, *Breach of Faith,* p. 163.

[68]Bob Woodward and Carl Bernstein, *The Final Days* (New York: Simon and Schuster, 1976), p. 424.

[69]*New York Times,* August 10, 1974, p. 4.©1974 by The New York Times Company. Reprinted by permission.

[70]White, *Breach of Faith,* p. 63.

In his testimony before the Senate Watergate Committee, one Nixon aid recalled the President's involvement in the following kinds of matters:

> The President was concerned with whether the shades were closed or open. Social functions were always reviewed with him. . . . He debated whether we should have a U-shaped table or a round table. He was deeply involved in the entertainment business, whom we would get for what kind of group. . . . He was very interested in meals and how they were served and the timing of the serving by the waiters.

> He debated receiving lines and whether or not he should have a receiving line prior to the entertainment for those relatively junior people in the Administration who were invited to the entertainment portion of the dinners only and not to the main dinner. . . . he wanted to view the musical selections himself. He was interested in whether or not a salad should be served and decided that at small dinners of 80 or less, the salad course should not be served.

> He was very interested in who introduced him to guests and he wanted it done quite properly. . . . He wanted a professional producer to come and actually produce the entertainment. . . . Guest lists were of great interest to him. . . . he would review all of these lists personally and approve them personally. . . .

> Ceremonies—he was interested in—the details of the drive up the walkway, whether the military would be to the right or left, which uniforms would be worn by the White House Police, whether or not the Secret Service would salute during the Star Spangled Banner and sing. . . .[71]

The desire for control was also evident on more substantive matters. Although all presidents have felt frustrated by their lack of control over the bureaucracy, none made a more systematic effort to correct this problem than did Nixon. Nor was the motive for doing so merely to facilitate the implementation of his policies. Thus, when he learned that the IRS was dragging its feet on investigating his political enemies, he remarked, "I look forward to the time that we have agents in the Department of Justice and the IRS under our control after November 7."[72] He also sought to enhance his control by keeping a tight rein over the flow of information. News releases were to come from the White House and not from other departments and agencies in the government. He held fewer news conferences—some thirty-seven in all—than any President since Herbert Hoover. Furthermore, the ability of Congress to exercise its constitutional responsibility for overseeing the Executive branch was seriously impaired by the President's broad-

[71] Cited in Fred Greenstein, "A President Is Forced to Resign: Watergate, White House Organization, and Nixon's Personality," in Allan Sindler, ed., *America in the Seventies: Problems, Policies, and Politics* (Boston: Little, Brown, 1977), pp. 89, 90.

[72] J. Anthony Lukas, *Nightmare: The Underside of the Nixon Years* (New York: Viking Press, 1976), p. 26.

sweeping use of executive privilege. And as already noted in an earlier chapter, in many cases the Nixon Administration's refusal to provide Congress with requested information was done without even bothering to invoke executive privilege. But, nowhere was Nixon's control over information more evident than in foreign policy, for not only was Congress frequently not consulted, but on several occasions it was not informed as well. The secret bombing of Cambodia was the most glaring example of this. Finally, it should also be noted that in addition to withholding information, Nixon also sought to nullify the constitutional responsibilities of Congress through his abuse of impoundment and the pocket veto.

Unfortunately for Nixon, the gradual unravelling of the Watergate scandals proved uncontrollable, a fact which caused him considerable exasperation: "I hate things like this. We're not in control."[73]

Of all the elements in Richard Nixon's personality, none proved to be more damaging in the Presidency than his inclination to sacrifice means for ends. In the spring of 1972, the Gallup polls had shown Nixon running only slightly ahead of Muskie, while the Harris polls actually gave Muskie a slight lead. Since the election had to be won at all costs, all manner of "dirty tricks" became the order of the day. The sign hanging over the office door of the Committee to Re-Elect the President (CREEP) told it all: "WINNING IN POLITICS ISN'T EVERYTHING, IT'S THE ONLY THING." To this end, the Democratic National Committee headquarters was broken into by members of what was later dubbed the White House "Plumbers" unit. Spies were hired and planted in the campaign organizations of Humphrey, Wallace, and Muskie. Various dirty tricks were played upon the Democratic candidates by CREEP, the most famous of which was their release of a completely false story alleging that Muskie had referred to Americans of French-Canadian extraction as "canucks." Since Ted Kennedy was also perceived as a potential political threat to the President, a member of the Plumbers was charged with investigating his sex, family, and drinking habits in an effort to uncover embarrassing information.

Whether or not Richard Nixon authorized these and other such activities is not of primary importance here. What does matter is that he appears to have fostered an atmosphere among his subordinates that served to encourage this kind of behavior. Moreover, there were other Watergate-related activities that Nixon did approve—none more disturbing than his willingness to use the resources of the federal government to harass his political opponents. Thus shortly before the 1972 election, and despite the fact that Nixon's victory was assured, he issued the following instructions to John Dean:

I want the most comprehensive notes on all those who tried to do us in. They didn't have to do it. If we had a very close election and they were playing the other side I would understand this. No—they were doing this

---

[73]Cited in Haldeman, *Ends of Power*, p. 19.

quite deliberately and they are asking for it and they are going to get it. We have not used the power in this first four years as you know. We have not used the Bureau and we have not used the Justice Department but things are going to change now.[74]

Certain individuals were singled out as special objects of the President's wrath. One such person was Edward Bennett Williams, a noted liberal and lawyer for the *Washington Post*, concerning whom Nixon made the following remark: "I wouldn't want to be in Edward Bennett Williams' position after this election. We are going to fix the son of a bitch, believe me. We are going to. We've got to, because he is a bad man."[75] That Nixon should have taken such a vindictive attitude is not altogether surprising. It has already been noted that he had always been suspicious of other people's motives. But under the pressures of the Presidency, this suspicion increasingly developed into a siege mentality as evidenced by a remark he made to John Dean: "Nobody is a friend of ours. Let's face it." Critics were defined not merely as opponents but rather as "enemies." As such, they posed a threat to the one thing that concerns an active-negative the most— his ability to succeed. Consequently, they had to be dealt with ruthlessly. Nowhere was his determination to do so more disturbingly revealed than in a statement he made in the presence of his close aids: "One day we will get them—we'll get them on the ground where we want them. And we'll stick our heels in, step on them hard and twist. . . . get them on the floor and step on them, crush them, show no mercy."[76]

If Watergate reflected Nixon's willingness to sacrifice means for ends, it also highlighted another dimension of the active-negative personality—namely, rigidity. This may come as somewhat of a surprise, since Nixon often exhibited remarkable flexibility in his views. Given the fact that anticommunism had been the hallmark of his political beliefs throughout most of his public career, few would have expected that Richard Nixon would be the first President to embark upon a policy of détente with both China and the Soviet Union. Nor, given his earlier antipathy toward wage and price controls, would one have anticipated that he would ultimately institute them. Yet as Barber notes, rigidity in the active-negative is likely to set in when he faces a situation that makes him *"seriously vulnerable to public exposure of personal inadequacy"* or that threatens his power.[77] The uncovering of Watergate threatened to do both. Accordingly, in the interests of avoiding failure at all costs, means were once again sacrificed for ends. The immediate solution was a cover-up, which in the first instance was designed to avoid implicating the President and his immediate associates. When that failed, the President decided to blame the scandals on "overzealous" aids,

[74] Gerald Gold, ed., *The White House Transcripts* (New York: Bantam Books, 1974), p. 63.

[75] Woodward and Bernstein, *Final Days,* p. 88.

[76] Charles Colson, *Born Again,* p. 72. Copyright © 1976. Published by Chosen Books Publishing Co., Ltd., Lincoln, Virginia 22078. Used by permission.

[77] Barber, *Presidential Character,* p. 387.

but he continued to insist that he was involved in neither the scandals themselves nor in the efforts to cover them up. As the evidence continued to mount against him, he saw himself as being victimized by those whose only goal was to bring him down. As he would later recount in his interviews with David Frost, "It was a five-front war with a fifth column. I had a partisan Senate committee staff. We had a partisan special prosecutor staff. We had a partisan media. We had a partisan Judiciary Committee staff in the fifth column."[78] It was Richard Nixon once again confronting still another struggle; another challenge in which he saw himself faced off against a constellation of forces whose hatred of him was so great that they were incapable of viewing the evidence objectively. Like all the other challenges in his life, he appears to have viewed this one as another test of his self-worth.

This view was poignantly revealed by him in remarks made at a press conference following one of the most harrowing weeks of his Presidency: a week during which the Senate Watergate hearings were in session; the House Judiciary Committee was preparing for its impeachment inquiry; the President fired Archibald Cox, which in turn led to the resignation of Attorney General Richardson and the dismissal of Assistant Attorney General Ruckelshaus; and to make matters worse, war broken out in the Middle East and the United States armed forces were put on a red alert:

> I have never heard or seen such outrageous, vicious, distorted reporting in twenty-seven years of public life. I'm not blaming anybody for that. Perhaps what happened is that what we did brought it about, and therefore the media decided that they would have to take that particular line. But when people are pounded night after night with that kind of frantic, hysterical reporting, it naturally shakes their confidence. And yet I should point out that even in this week when many thought that the President was shell-shocked, unable to act, the President acted decisively in the interests of peace and interests of the country, and I can assure you that whatever shocks gentlemen of the press may have, or others—political people—these shocks will not affect me and doing my job.

Later in the press conference:

Reporter: Mr. President, Harry Truman used to talk about the heat in the kitchen, and . . .

President: I know what he meant.

Reporter: A lot of people are wondering how you are bearing up under the emotional strain of recent events. Can you discuss that?

President: Well, those who saw me during the Middle East crisis thought I bore up rather well. . . . I have a quality which is—I guess I must have in-

[78] Richard Nixon, the Nixon-Frost interviews, 1977. By permission of Syndicast Services.

herited it from my Midwestern mother and father—which is that the tougher it gets the cooler I get. Of course it isn't pleasant to find your honesty questioned. . . . But as far as I'm concerned, I have learned to expect it. It has been my lot throughout my political life, and I suppose because I have been through so much, that may be one of the reasons . . . I have what it takes.[79]

Nixon remained inflexible on his involvement in the Watergate scandals right up to the end, despite a substantial body of evidence to the contrary. His resignation speech contained no mention of guilt, not even by implication. Rather he was resigning, he said, because he no longer enjoyed enough political support in Congress. Even upon receipt of his pardon, he issued a statement in which he acknowledged certain errors in judgment, but there was no admission of intentional wrongdoing. He continued to maintain this posture two years later when he granted a series of interviews to television personality David Frost. When asked, for example, why he had authorized such illegal actions as wiretappings and burglaries, he responded, "Well, when the President does it, that means that it is not illegal." When invited to explain those portions of the White House tapes that showed him rehearsing Haldeman in the false testimony that would later be given before the Grand Jury, Nixon replied that he was merely playing the role of defense lawyer for a good friend. Only in the final interview (which was the first one to be aired on television) did he begin to come to grips with the full implications of what he had done.

It is ironic that a President who was obsessed with avoiding failure should ultimately be judged as one of the greatest failures of any President in our history. This irony is further increased by the fact that, but for Watergate, the Nixon Presidency might well have received high marks. Certainly the case can be made that much of his foreign policy demonstrated creativity and insight. Even on the domestic side, his program of revenue sharing marked a fundamental—and in the judgment of many a favorable—change in federal-state relations. Unfortunately, his own insecurities gave rise to a pattern of conduct of such disgraceful dimensions that it dwarfed his accomplishments. Moreover, the American people paid an exceedingly high price for these insecurities: presidential abuse of power, obstruction of justice, and governmental paralysis for more than a year as both Congress and the President were preoccupied with impeachment. But the highest price paid was best articulated by Richard Nixon himself: "I let down the country. I let down our system of government and the dreams of all those young people that ought to get into government, but think it's all too corrupt and the rest. . . ."[80]

[79]*New York Times,* October 27, 1973, p. 14. ©1973 by The New York Times Company. Reprinted by permission.

[80]Richard Nixon, the Nixon-Frost interviews, 1977. By permission of Syndicast Services.

FRANKLIN ROOSEVELT AS AN ACTIVE-POSITIVE

Roosevelt's Youth

Concerning Franklin Roosevelt's early years, one scholar of the Roosevelt family has remarked that "in the long shelf of biographies of American presidents, one searches in vain for the story of a childhood more serene and secure." The financial hardship experienced by both Johnson and Nixon was totally absent in Roosevelt's childhood. His family were members of the aristocracy, with a style of living in keeping with their social position: a country estate, servants, horses, frequent trips abroad. More important, young Franklin did not suffer any want of affection from his mother and father; being an only child, he was the center of their attention. At the same time, however, he was not given free rein. Both parents set down definite expectations for his behavior and intellectual development—but they enforced their standards with a sense of understanding. In the words of his mother, ". . . we never were strict merely for the sake of being strict. In fact, we took a secret pride in the fact that Franklin instinctively never seemed to require that kind of handling."[81] While James Roosevelt had an air of formality and reserve about him, this does not appear to have hampered his relationship with his son. Indeed, the evidence suggests that father and son were frequently in each other's company, be it boating, swimming, hunting, riding horses, or touring the family estate. While his relationship with both parents was a close one, he could not become completely dependent upon them since they were frequently travelling and he was not always taken with them.

The Roosevelt who left home to face the outside world was full of self-confidence and optimism—qualities fostered not only by a happy and loving environment but also by the fact that he came from a family of high social position and accomplishment. At fourteen he was sent off to boarding school for four years, where he adjusted to a highly regimented existence without any problem. His gregariousness and personal charm proved of great assistance to him in getting along with his classmates. At Harvard he became involved in a variety of activities ranging from athletics to the Glee Club, Fly Club, Hasty Pudding Club, Boating Club, and writing for the *Harvard Crimson*. While he was elected to official positions in some of these campus organizations, his most significant achievement was his selection as editor-in-chief of the *Crimson*. The key to his leadership ability appears to have been grounded in his winning personality. As one editor of the newspaper observed, "In his geniality was a kind of frictionless command."[82] In his senior year, his class saw fit to nominate him for class marshal and select him as permanent chairman of the Class Committee.

---

[81] Frank Freidel, *Franklin D. Roosevelt: The Apprenticeship* (Boston: Little, Brown, 1952), p. 23.

[82] Erwin Hargrove, *Presidential Leadership: Personality and Political Style* (London: Macmillan, 1966), p. 55.

But there was one profound disappointment for Roosevelt during his college career, namely, his failure to gain entry into Porcellian, Harvard's most exclusive club. Yet it is interesting to note how his reaction differed from Johnson and Nixon, both of whom found themselves in a similar situation. When Johnson failed to be selected into the most exclusive club (Black Stars) on his college campus, he organized another club known as the White Stars. On Nixon's college campus, the most exclusive club was the Franklins, noted for its snobbishness. Nixon was instrumental in forming another club known as the Orthogonians. Roosevelt was undoubtedly hurt over his rejection by Porcellian, but his high sense of self-esteem enabled him to take the disappointment in stride. In the case of Johnson and Nixon, however, it may well be that their fear of rejection spurred each of them to organize his own club and thus insure his acceptance into it.

Entry into Politics, World View, and Style

Following graduation from law school, Roosevelt entered a prominent New York law firm where for four years he worked on matters he found thoroughly uninspiring. Finally in 1910 politics sought him out. A local politician visited him and asked him to run for the New York Assembly, and Roosevelt accepted. Several factors made politics an appealing prospect to him. He was gregarious by nature, a quality that would be highly suited to the extroverted profession of politics. In addition, he appears to have wanted personal power, but unlike the ambitions of Johnson and Nixon, this desire was rooted in self-confidence rather than insecurity. Finally, the attraction of politics was strongly reinforced by a world view that emphasized service. This perspective had been shaped by several forces. First, there were his parents, who had instilled in him the aristocracy's sense of noblesse oblige—the responsibility of the more fortunate to serve the community. And the involvement of James Roosevelt in community activities— many of them charitable—demonstrated that the preachments of service were more than empty words. In addition, his parents' views were powerfully rein- forced by his headmaster at boarding school, a man who apparently had an extraordinary influence upon Roosevelt's thinking: "As long as I live, the influence of Dr. and Mrs. Peabody means and will mean more to me than that of any other people next to my father and mother."[83] Endicott Peabody saw his mission as one of instilling within the well-born of Groton a commitment to both Christian values and service, especially public service. A further incentive to serve was provided in the sample set by Roosevelt's ancestors. While he was at Harvard, Franklin wrote a paper on the history of the Roosevelt family and noted that "they have never felt that because they were born in a good position they could put their hands in their pockets and succeed. They have felt,

---

[83] Barber, *Presidential Character*, p. 218.

rather, that, being born in a good position, there was no excuse for them if they did not do their duty by the community. . . ."[84]

For Johnson and Nixon, politics was fraught with anxieties. The political world was a dangerous one. Both were preoccupied with avoiding failure. On the other hand, Roosevelt's confidence and optimism led him to approach the challenges of politics with joyous expectation. Upon election to the New York State Assembly, he found himself battling the political bosses of Tammany Hall, and he relished it: "There is nothing I love as much as a good fight. I never had as much fun in my life as I am having right now."[85] When he was presented with the opportunity to become Assistant Secretary of the Navy, he approached the job with his characteristic ebullience and confidence. He expressed no hesitation, no doubts about his ability to handle it. While he now found himself dealing with a ponderous military bureaucracy, his enthusiasm was in no way dampened: "I have loved every minute of it."[86]

It was during his stint as Assistant Secretary of the Navy that his political style began to emerge. He was first of all a man of action. Problems were there to be understood and solved; if one solution did not work, he would try something else. At the same time, however, his decisions were preceded by a careful mastering of the details of a problem as well as the political environment surrounding it. This information was garnered through frequent contact with people, another hallmark of his political style. There was a constant flow of people into his office, precisely because he encouraged it: "I want you all to feel free that you can come to me at any time in my office, and we can talk matters over. Let's get together for I need you to teach me your business and show me what is going on."[87] According to the then Secretary of War, the constant meeting with people, the constant probing and listening appeared to have accomplished their purpose: " . . . I should think he'd wear himself out in the promiscuous and extended contacts he maintains with people. But as I have observed him, he seems to clarify his ideas and teach himself as he goes along by that very conversational method."[88] Of course, his frequent contacts with people were designed to persuade as well as to learn. Roosevelt proved highly effective at such persuasion, for like Johnson, he seems to have had a keen understanding of human nature, an ability to read people and appeal to them in terms of their own needs. As one of his White House assistants would later remark: "It is probably safe to say that during 1933, 1934, and 1935 a record-breaking number of men of some political eminence went to the President's office in a state of incipient revolt and left it to declare to the world their subscription to

---

[84] Allen Churchill, *The Roosevelts* (New York: Harper & Row, 1965), p. 180.

[85] Barber, *Presidential Character,* p. 225.

[86] Ibid., p. 230.

[87] Ibid., p. 227.

[88] Frances Perkins, *The Roosevelt I Knew* (New York: Viking Press, 1956), p. 21.

things that they did not subscribe to."[89] No doubt this aspect of his style was greatly enhanced by his special personal charm—congeniality, humor, enthusiasm, and obvious interest in the person he was talking with.

When Roosevelt moved on to become governor of New York, another aspect of his political style surfaced, namely, his rhetorical skills. Faced with a Republican legislature which often proved unreceptive to his programs, he took his case to the people of New York through personal appearances and radio addresses. Just as he had proved effective in appealing to people on an individual level, so too did he have a talent for appealing to them in the mass. His rhetoric conveyed a genuine sense of concern and empathy with his audience, and his points were stated in a manner that made them readily comprehensible to the average citizen.

The Roosevelt Presidency

Whoever stepped into the Presidency in 1933 would find himself confronting an economic crisis the likes of which the country had never experienced before or since. Yet Roosevelt took over the reins of power exuding his customary self-confidence. In the words of Richard Neustadt, "His image of the office was himself-in-office. The memoirs left by his associates agree on this if nothing else: he saw the job of being President as being F.D.R. He wanted mastery, projected that desire on the office and fulfilled it there with every sign of feeling he had come into his own."[90] He enjoyed being President.

Convinced of the necessity for action and confident in his ability to make it happen, he moved with dispatch: ". . . one thing is sure. We have to do something. We have to do the best we know how to do at the moment. . . . If it doesn't turn out right, we can modify it as we go along."[91] The first hundred days of his administration were a bustle of activity, producing the greatest waterfall of legislation of any President in our history. Especially notable among his legislative accomplishments during this initial period were the Farm Relief Act, Banking Act, Economy Bill, Securities Act, Federal Relief Act, Railway Reorganization Act, National Recovery Act, and Agricultural Adjustment Act. His decisions about what to do and when to do it, as well as his assessments of actions already taken, were arrived at through his exposure to wide-ranging channels of information. This necessitated making himself accessible. He met frequently with members of Congress. He met twice a week with members of the press, answering questions but also asking them as well. Approximately one

[89]Cited in James MacGregor Burns, *Roosevelt: The Lion and the Fox* (New York: Harcourt, Brace, Jovanovich, 1956), p. 348.

[90]Richard Neustadt, *Presidential Power,* 1st ed. (New York: John Wiley, 1960), p. 162.

[91]Arthur Schlesinger, Jr., "The Dynamics of Decision," in Aaron Wildavsky, ed., *The Presidency* (Boston: Little, Brown, 1969), p. 139.

hundred people within the government had direct access to him by phone. Nor was it uncommon for him to pick up the phone and summon to the White House some bright young bureaucrat he had heard about. When people came to see him in his office, he would often taken the opportunity to probe their minds on a variety of issues, and not simply on the one they had come to discuss with him. Recognizing that his own staff was one of his most crucial sources of information, he structured it in ways that would enhance its performance of this task. As noted in an earlier chapter, they all had direct access to him. The same assignment was given to more than one person, and he deliberately played personalities off against each other. All of this produced a kind of creative conflict which, though exasperating for his staff, served to maximize the flow of information and ideas to him.[92] Roosevelt was well aware of the provincialism in Washington and thus he exhorted members of his staff to seek out information as he did: "Go and see what's happening. See the end product of what we are doing. Talk to people; get the wind in your nose."[93]

There was also an element of secretiveness in the Roosevelt style. During the process of accumulating information about an issue, he rarely revealed what his own inclinations might be. With one person he might imply that he leaned in one direction, while with the next he would create an entirely different impression. The purpose, of course, was to keep his options open. He was constantly assessing the political realities of a situation, biding his time until the most propitious moment for making a decision. He recognized that success was in part dependent upon timing. Yet it should be noted that, unlike Johnson and Nixon, his secrecy did not extend to restricting the number of people involved in the decision making; nor did it lead to keeping important decisions secret after they had been made. It is unlikely, for example, that Roosevelt would have disguised our increasing commitment to Vietnam, or that he would have secretly bombed Cambodia. Such secrecy would not have been necessary, for it was his custom not to make such crucial decisions until he had prepared both the public and the Congress to accept them.

In seeking to persuade, he drew upon two very effective elements of his political style: his skills in personal relations and in rhetoric. Much of his success with Congress was attributable to his ability to manipulate them: "Roosevelt's leadership talents lay in his ability to shift quickly and gracefully from persuasion to cajolery to flattery to intrigue to diplomacy to promises to horse-trading—or to concoct just that formula which his superb instincts for personal relations told him would bring around the most reluctant congressmen."[94] When necessary, he would exert further pressure by taking his case to the American public. The primary instrument for doing so was the "fireside chat,"

[92] Ibid., pp. 134–38.

[93] Barber, *Presidential Character,* p. 234.

[94] Burns, *Roosevelt: The Lion and the Fox,* p. 348.

and its effectiveness lay in its informality as well as in Roosevelt's ability to convey his ideas clearly and with a sense of genuine concern.

While Roosevelt's personality was to a large extent responsible for his political success, it must be noted that it also led to the major miscalculation of his Presidency—his decision to pack the Supreme Court. We have already noted that he was an activist, a man interested in results. Given this disposition, one can understand his frustration with a conservative Supreme Court which repeatedly declared important parts of his New Deal programs unconstitutional. The legislation voided by the Court included the Railroad Pension Act, Farm Mortgage Law, Agricultural Adjustment Act, Bituminous Coal Act, and a portion of the National Industrial Recovery Act.

A man of great self-confidence to begin with, Roosevelt became even more so following his landslide reelection victory in 1936. Accordingly, he took the brash step of proposing legislation to Congress that would permit the President to add an additional member to the Supreme Court for every judge who reached the age of seventy and did not avail himself of the opportunity to retire. Since there were six judges who fell into this category, Roosevelt would be able to add six additional members and thus break the conservative hold on the Court. He argued that the purpose of this legislation was to allow the Court to operate with greater efficiency. Such a flimsy and demonstrably false justification was, by itself, sufficient to spark outrage from both the Congress and the American public. However, the cold reception given his proposal was further increased by Roosevelt's failure to employ some of the hallmarks of his political style— reaching out for information and advice, carefully assessing the political environment, preparing the public for what he wanted to do. In this particular instance, the proposal came as a surprise to all concerned. Neither the Congress nor the Cabinet was consulted. Moreover, he made no attempt to reveal, let alone explain, his proposal to the people during his campaign for reelection.[95] The result was a stunning defeat for a man who had allowed his overconfidence and impatient desire for results to distort his view of political reality.

Yet if the Court-packing episode highlighted Roosevelt's weaknesses, it also demonstrated his strengths. He did not adopt a rigid stance by converting his proposal into a do-or-die proposition. When failure became apparent, he accepted it and moved on to something else. He was able to joke about his blunder; and apparently he ultimately even concluded that the proposal itself had been ill-conceived, for in putting together his public papers, he titled the volumes in the following fashion: 1935—"The Court Disapproves," 1936—"The People Approve," 1937—"The Constitution Prevails."[96] When the 1938 congressional elections came, he campaigned against those senators who had failed to support his plan, but he did not convert them into "enemies" who must be punished by

[95] Ibid., p. 314.

[96] Barber, *Presidential Character,* p. 245.

any means, fair or foul. In short, Roosevelt responded to his defeat with a sense of proportion, and he was able to do so because of his self-confidence. He was not obsessed with avoiding failure; he did not see his performance in the political world as a constant struggle to test his self-worth. As he once remarked to an aid, "You'll have to learn that public life takes a lot of sweat, but it doesn't need to worry you. You won't always be right, but you musn't suffer from being wrong. That's what kills people like us."[97]

GERALD FORD AS AN ACTIVE-POSITIVE

Ford's Youth

The specifics of Gerald Ford's childhood differ markedly from those of Roosevelt, but the end result appears to have been the same: a happy and loving environment. Christened as Leslie King, Jr., he was still a baby when his mother and father were divorced. Subsequently, his mother moved to Grand Rapids where she married Gerald Ford and the baby's name was changed to Gerald R. Ford, Jr. While the senior Gerald Ford was not by any means a wealthy person, his success in the paint business put the family in a financial position superior to that of most of young Gerald's friends.

His relationship with both parents was a close one. His mother was an energetic and outgoing person who showered her warm-hearted nature on friends as well as family: "Everybody loved her . . . . she just had great compassion for people."[98] But according to Ford himself, it was his stepfather who had the greatest influence upon him: "But I guess Dad was the strongest influence on my life. I've often thought, even nowadays: now how would he have done this?"[99] Ford recalls that the whole family looked up to his Dad. As a father he set down very definite standards of behavior and was the undisputed head of the house, but he could be a friend as well as a father. The affection and concern he showed toward his family was also extended to the community. He organized several programs for poor children, helped create a summer camp, and was active in the Boy Scouts. The care and affection Ford received from both parents seems likely to have fostered within him a high sense of self-esteem and confidence. Nor does there appear to be anything in his high school and college years that would have altered this. In high school he had many friends and was sufficiently adept at football to be selected all-city center and all-state center on the South team. In his senior year in high school he won a prize for being the most popular high school senior in Grand Rapids. He continued to excel in football at the

[97]Schlesinger, "Dynamics of Decision," p. 139.

[98]John Hersey, *The President* (New York: Alfred A. Knopf, 1975), p. 86.

[99]Jerald F. terHorst, *Gerald Ford and the Future of the Presidency* (New York: Third Press, 1974), p. 34.

University of Michigan, where he played on two national championship teams. And in 1934, he was selected as the team's most valuable player. While his academic performance was not exceptional, he managed to get himself into Yale Law School, where he finished in the top third of his class.

Entry into Politics, World View, and Style

After passing the Michigan bar examination, Ford and a friend set up a law practice in Grand Rapids. This was interrupted, however, by a stint in the Navy which took him to the South Pacific. Here he saw action and earned ten battle stars in the process. Upon his return to Grand Rapids, Ford was invited into one of the prestigious law firms in the area and proceeded to become involved in community activities such as Boy Scouts and Red Cross. His stepfather was now chairman of the Republican organization in his county, and the avenue of politics took on greater interest for Ford, as he accompanied his stepfather to the Republican state conventions in 1946 and 1948. The congressman from his district at the time was strongly isolationist on matters of foreign policy. After some prodding from his stepfather and the prominent pro-internationalism senator, Arthur Vandenberg, Ford decided to challenge the incumbent congressman. He went at his campaign with extraordinary energy: "I worked like hell. I really covered those counties."[100] His aggressive yet fair tactics earned him an easy victory over his opponent.

The Ford world view manifests none of the pessimism and suspicion of Richard Nixon. Indeed, even during what was probably the darkest moment of his political career—his concession speech to Jimmy Carter—Ford ended on a positive note: "In the long run the American people have an awful lot more good in them than they have bad. . . . I am an optimist today. I always have been."[101] His ability to look for the best in people was no doubt influenced by the environment in which he grew up. Both parents had provided examples of decency, and they encouraged him to look for it in others. Ford would recall that his stepfather "always saw something good in somebody, even people who had nothing in common with him. We got into a discussion about somebody one time, and I said, 'Oh, he's no good. He does this, or he does that!' And he said, 'Well, but he also does this, which I like—and you ought to like.'"[102] Ford would later maintain that his experience in the Boy Scouts had a great influence upon him, and here again, he encountered what he called "good associations . . . a stream of people that was good, clear, strong."[103] The positive view of people he developed while growing up carried into his political life as well and was

---

[100]Ibid., p. 20.

[101]*Time,* January 10, 1977, pp. 15–16.

[102]Hersey, *The President,* pp. 90, 91.

[103]Ibid., p. 91.

surely one of the reasons why he genuinely enjoyed politics so much: "I enjoy it. I really enjoy people."[104]

Once elected to the House, Ford soon rose to positions of leadership in his party, first winning the chairmanship of the Republican Conference in 1963 and two years later defeating Charles Halleck for the highest position in his party, namely, Minority Leader. His success was rooted in his political style. Described by one colleague as "a workhorse," Ford invested great amounts of energy and effort in his job. But the source of this energy was rooted in a genuine enjoyment rather than in some deep-seated need to prove himself. While he was not noted as either a creative intellect or an effective speaker, he was reasonably adept at personal relations. Yet his style lacked all the subtlety of Johnson and Roosevelt. He was not a manipulator. Rather, his approach to people reflected a combination of geniality and directness: "He's an open tactician. He doesn't look for clever ways to sneak in behind you. He does the obvious, which is usually common sense. He doesn't try to be gimmicky."[105] His winning personality and straightforward approach to dealing with people earned him the respect and affection of both Democrats and Republicans. Democratic Senator William Proxmire, not prone to bestowing compliments freely, acknowledged that he found the Michigan congressman to be a man of "integrity and character."[106] This assessment was generally shared by others as well. The decency that characterized the Ford style should not be interpreted to mean that he was lacking in forcefulness, however. On the contrary, as Minority Leader he proved to be a highly active and persistent critic of the incumbent Democratic Administration.

The Ford Presidency

While Ford had repeatedly said that his ultimate ambition in politics was to become Speaker of the House, a series of untoward events thrust him instead into the Vice Presidency, and shortly thereafter, into the Presidency itself. If he had any self-doubts about his ability to fill the job at this especially critical time, they were not apparent. Indeed, few presidents have appeared more comfortable with themselves than did Gerald Ford. This inner confidence manifested itself in several ways. For one thing, he appeared thoroughly at home in the office—so much so, in fact, that he reversed his earlier decision not to seek a full term in 1976. The fear of failure, which prevented Johnson and Nixon from enjoying the rough and tumble of the Presidency, was totally absent in the Ford psyche. When asked if he liked the job, he replied, "I do. It's mainly the challenge. . . . I always have enjoyed facing up to problems; it's always been

---

[104] *President Ford: The Man and His Record* (Washington, D.C.: Congressional Quarterly, 1974), p. 20.

[105] Ibid., p. 28.

[106] Ibid.

a sort of way of life with me—and you certainly have them here. I really enjoy getting up every morning, looking at the schedule, seeing what the problems are. I don't long for the end of the day."[107] The inner confidence was also apparent when it came to picking his own Vice President. Several of his aids and friends counselled against selecting the dynamic Nelson Rockefeller on the grounds that he would steal the spotlight from the President.[108] Unimpressed by such arguments, Ford went ahead and chose him. Nor did Ford's ego appear to require reinforcement from the symbolic trappings of the office in the way that Johnson's and Nixon's did. When asked whether he thought the perquisites of the Presidency would get to him, Ford responded, ". . . , I don't see why they should. I've had a long sixty years without any of this, so these aren't things that I couldn't get along without in the future."[109] Moreover, he even took some steps to reduce them. Finally, Ford's confidence also came through in his response to speculations that he might not have the mental equipment necessary to cope with the demands of the Presidency. All of Washington was well aware of Lyndon Johnson's uncharitable remark that "Gerry Ford is so dumb he can't walk and chew gum at the same time." Yet there is no evidence to suggest that Ford ever felt intimidated by the brain power that resided in Washington. When a question was directly put to him concerning his intelligence, he responded this way:

> . . . when I was in high school, where the competition was mediocre, I got a little over a B average. When I went to Michigan, I did the same. I think at law school the same. . . .
>
> . . . in the class I entered [law school] with, which had about 125, there were 98 or 99 who were college Phi Betes, of which I was not one. And they were extremely bright. Very able guys. . . . So I seem to have had a capability of competing with whatever competition there was at each level; and yet I could have enough outside activities to enjoy a broader spectrum of day-to-day living than some of them. But I must say I worked damn hard.[110]

There is no sign of defensiveness in this statement; rather it reflects willingness to acknowledge that he was not at the top of the intellectual heap, but it also demonstrates that he felt confident enough to compete with those who were.

When Richard Nixon nominated Ford as his Vice President, Senator Mike Mansfield remarked that "Gerald Ford is the kind of man whom one would

---

[107] Hersey, *The President*, p. 49.

[108] Richard Reeves, *A Ford, Not a Lincoln* (New York: Harcourt Brace Jovanovich, 1975), p. 149.

[109] Hersey, *The President*, pp. 137, 138.

[110] Ibid., pp. 131, 132.

expect the President to nominate—an activist, not a caretaker."[111] His observation proved to be correct. Ford went at his new job with the characteristic energy of an activist, rising every morning between 5:30 and 6:00 A.M. and taking only a very brief period for meals—"Eating and sleeping are a waste of time." While the wisdom of his decisions was questioned by some, it is clear that he was willing to be an assertive President. He acted decisively both in his pardon of President Nixon and in the rescue of the *Mayaguez*. He submitted to the Congress comprehensive programs dealing with the energy crisis and the slumping economy. Nor was he reluctant to take on the Legislative branch through the use of both his persuasive and constitutional powers. He publicly chastised the Congress for spending too much money and went on television to defend his energy program. He wielded the veto power with a vengeance. Indeed, for the relatively brief time he was in office, he used the veto more times than any President since Grover Cleveland.

Given the closed and secretive style of the Nixon Presidency, any individual who took his place would be under considerable pressure to foster a more open administration. But for Ford this approach came naturally, for it was part of his operating style. He dispensed with Nixon's pyramidal staff organization in which access to the President was ultimately determined by Haldeman, and replaced it with a four-layer staff structure. Under this arrangement, certain individuals within each layer had direct access to him. Ford met frequently with members of Congress and even took the unprecedented step of appearing before the House Judiciary Committee to answer questions relating to his pardon of President Nixon. His open style also extended to his relations with the press. Not only were his press conferences frequent, but he was the first President since Truman to allow reporters the opportunity to ask followup questions. The criticism and ridicule from the press, although heavy at times, did not lead Ford to identify a set of "enemies" who must be discredited and harassed. His own sense of confidence made such a tactic unnecessary.

While scholars and journalists may legitimately raise questions concerning Ford's creativity, vision, and ability to inspire, these qualities may not necessarily have been the ones most needed at the time he assumed office. For a country that had just lived through a period of political and moral squalor in high places, the immediate and pressing need was to restore the public's confidence in its leaders and institutions. In this respect, Gerald Ford proved to be the right man at the right time, for his style of openness and decency served to begin this restoration.

JIMMY CARTER: AN ACTIVE-POSITIVE?

Although Jimmy Carter has said that he would like to be an active-positive President, his first term is still too young for us to classify him with any certainty. Yet even at this early stage there are some clues as to how his personality may

[111] *President Ford: The Man and His Record*, p. 29.

affect his Presidency. The evidence is clearest on the active-passive dimension of his personality, with the record thus far clearly demonstrating that he is an *activist*. He has approached the job with an extraordinary investment of energy, rising at 6:00 A.M. and arriving at his desk by 7:00 A.M.[112] His original intention to pace himself by working a fifty-hour week soon gave way to a work week totalling more than seventy hours. Moreover, the impact of his office has already been felt in a variety of areas. In foreign policy, for example, he has adopted a more vigorous stand on human rights, taken an active role in the Middle East conflict, secured passage of the two Panama Canal Treaties, and made a vigorous effort to improve American relations with countries in Africa. In the area of national security, he made the far-reaching decision to scrap construction of the controversial B-1 bomber. Meanwhile on the domestic front, he signed an executive order pardoning draft evaders, called for the elimination of certain costly federal water projects, and sent legislation to Congress dealing with election, tax and welfare reform, hospital costs, energy, and government reorganization.

Carter's Presidency has not been without its difficulties and frustrations, however. While he has been highly active in proposing programs, he has had only limited success in getting them approved. Moreover, he has been subject to numerous charges of presidential ineptitude by both the journalistic and scholarly communities. Yet despite all of this, Carter appears to manifest a *positive* orientation toward his job, as well as a sense of proportion regarding its frustrations:

> I am at ease. When we have difficulties, I don't withdraw. I am not paranoid. I recognize that some of the controversy and difficulties and failures are because of the ambitious nature of some of our undertakings. There has never been an evening when I went to bed that I didn't look forward to the next day.

> If I do the best I can with something and then fail, I don't have any second thoughts or post-regrets. Some of the limitations I have found in the job are frustrating but I have accepted them.[113]

Nowhere in Carter's background does one find the gnawing self-doubt that consumed both Johnson and Nixon. On the contrary, Carter appears to possess that high sense of self-esteem that characterizes the active-positive character. This quality came through most clearly during his campaign for the Presidency. Despite the fact that he was a little-known governor from a small state, he appears to have had little doubt about his ability to win both the nomination and the Presidency: "I don't intend to lose." To those who followed his campaign closely, this sense of confidence was apparent during good times as well as bad: "He was possessed of a quiet self-confidence that could be almost irritating in its stolidness."[114]

[112] Robert Shogan, *Promises To Keep* (New York: Thomas Crowell, 1977), p. 197.

[113] *New York Times,* October 23, 1977, p. 36. ©1977 by The New York Times Company. Reprinted by permission.

[114] Jules Witcover, *Marathon* (New York: Viking Press, 1977), p. 143.

In this connection, some have speculated that Carter may get into trouble in the Presidency, not for want of self-confidence, but rather because he is too confident. More specifically, he may assume an inflexible posture, not from fear of failure, but rather because he is so convinced that he is right. Jody Powell, who has long been one of Carter's closest associates in politics, admits to this stubborn streak: "He's stubborn, that's true, but it's not a stubbornness arrived at lightly. I mean there are a lot of things he doesn't feel strongly about, either way, but once he makes up his mind on something—and that's no simple process—then, generally, that's it."[115] Another Carter aid concedes that the President's relationship with Congress got off to a bad start in part because of his overconfidence: "His flaw is that he thinks he's smarter than they are. In most cases it's true—but it doesn't help his relations with them."[116]

Yet despite all the testimony to Carter's celebrated stubbornness, it must be pointed out that he has thus far demonstrated considerable flexibility. While he came out strongly against funding for thirty federal water projects, strong opposition in Congress persuaded him to reduce the list to eighteen, and finally to nine. Similarly, although he initially threatened to veto a farm bill because Congress had made price supports too high, he ultimately struck a compromise, even though the final figure was still higher than he wanted. Finally, despite the fact that he has made human rights a cornerstone of his foreign policy, he has publicly acknowledged that his position has had a more serious effect upon American-Soviet relations than he had expected. Accordingly, he has since become less strident on the human rights issue.

Some have voiced concern that Carter shows the same propensity toward isolationism that Richard Nixon did. Arthur Schlesinger, for example, characterizes him as a "narcissistic loner."[117] There is indeed some evidence in the Carter background to support this characterization. He has been described by one classmate as a "private kind of guy." Moreover, James David Barber notes that Carter's recollections of his years in the Georgia legislature are free of any mention of collaborative efforts with other politicians; nor are there any references to friendships made.[118] Those who remember him at the governor's conferences note that he was never considered one of the boys. Even in the Presidency, he appears to have no close circle of friends or cronies that he gets together with from time to time. So far, however, there are no indications that Carter's introspective nature has caused him to retreat behind the doors of the Oval Office. On the contrary, openness has been a hallmark of his style, and nowhere has it been more evident than in his relations with the public. In an

---

[115]*New York Times,* June 5, 1977, p. 4E. ©1977 by The New York Times Company. Reprinted by permission.

[116]*Newsweek,* May 2, 1977, p. 45.

[117]William Miller, "The Yankee from Georgia," *New York Times Magazine,* July 3, 1977, p. 16. ©1977 by The New York Times Company. Reprinted by permission.

[118]Barber, *Presidential Character,* pp. 510, 525.

attempt to increase his accessibility, he has participated in phone-ins with the American people and met with gatherings of local citizens. In passing, it should be noted that his open approach has also been shown in his willingness to take the public into his confidence. Thus, holding true to his belief that Americans should be kept informed of American intentions in foreign policy, he made public his initial arms-reduction plan which was presented to the Soviet Union at SALT II, and also publicly announced his "flexible borders" proposal for solving the Middle East conflict. Of course, whether or not diplomacy can be successfully conducted in the public spotlight remains to be seen.

Carter's open style has extended to other constituencies as well. By keeping his campaign promise to hold at least one news conference every two weeks, he has made himself more accessible to the press than any of his immediate predecessors. He has also met frequently with members of Congress, and according to one participant, his weekly meetings with the Democratic leadership have been characterized by unprecedented candor and give and take.[119] Finally, within the White House itself there is also evidence to suggest that Carter wants to maintain his accessibility. While Hamilton Jordan has assumed greater responsibility for coordinating staff activity, there is no evidence to suggest that this change has lessened Carter's accessibility. Rather, he continues to see his staff as analogous to spokes on a wheel, with himself at the center. Yet staff organization alone is not sufficient to avoid isolation, for aids must feel free to talk frankly with their President. On this score, there have been some disturbing reports that Carter does not encourage dissent from his own views. On one occasion, for example, Hamilton Jordan is said to have voiced disagreement with the President on a certain issue and Carter replied, "When you read as much as I do, then maybe you'll have the right to disagree."[120] This kind of behavior may once again be traceable to Carter's confidence in himself. Unlike Johnson, whose intolerance for dissent was rooted in his own insecurities, Carter seems to resist dissent simply because he believes that he knows more than his staff does. Hopefully, this belief will be moderated by the complexity of the issues he must confront as President.

PERSONALITY QUALITIES SUITABLE TO THE PRESIDENCY

While one could no doubt think of a variety of personality attributes which would be desirable in a President, our discussion throughout this chapter suggests that some appear to be especially necessary. In the first place, a President should be an activist in the sense that Barber defines the term—that is, someone who creates opportunities for action, someone who initiates rather than re-

[119] *Washington Post,* June 23, 1977, p. A3.
[120] *New York Times,* April 25, 1977, p. 53. ©1977 by The New York Times Company. Reprinted by permission.

sponds. One might object to this assertion on grounds that the country cannot tolerate a steady diet of activism. Occasionally it needs time to consolidate and take stock of itself, and a President of the more passive type can perform this needed function. This argument has a certain validity to it, but on balance the passive President would seem to be a luxury we can no longer afford. Like it or not, the United States has been thrust into the dominant leadership position on the international stage, and at home we are faced with problems of formidable proportions: energy, race relations, environmental pollution, decaying cities, crime, an uncertain economy, to name but a few. When and if these problems are solved, there is every reason to believe that others will take their place, if only because today's solutions often become tomorrow's problems. Under a passive President we run the risk of being overtaken by events. To be sure, there may also be an element of risk in the activist President, for in his desire to achieve results, he may try to do too much too fast—as Carter did in his first year. But if this should happen, at least Congress has the ability to slow him down—even if it has not always chosen to do so. On the other hand, if we are faced with a passive President, the problem of compensating for this becomes more difficult, since Congress is far better suited to checking overzealous leadership than it is to filling the vacuum that results from its absence.

It would also seem to be desirable to have a man in the White House whose orientation is positive rather than negative. It makes sense, after all, to expect that we are more likely to get a better performance from someone who enjoys what he is doing than we are from someone who does not. Moreover, if the latter is the case, we must ask why? Does he not enjoy the politicking which is the lubricant of the governmental process and so essential to getting things done? Or is his lack of enjoyment rooted in a sense of insecurity arising from self-doubt and/or fears that he is surrounded by a hostile environment?

In this chapter, much has been made of the necessity for having a President with a high sense of self-esteem—a quality that appears to be present in the active-positive and lacking in the active-negative. Here too, however, one might argue that low self-esteem in a President is not without its blessings, for in an effort to confirm his self-worth, such a person would have an especially high motivation to achieve. Unfortunately, the presidencies of both Johnson and Nixon demonstrate that low self esteem may carry costs as well as benefits. More specifically, so impoverished in the active-negative's sense of worth that the prospect of failure becomes intolerable. Moreover, in order to avoid it, he may engage in behavior that can prove detrimental to the political system. Such behavior could include a tendency to seek greater and greater control over his environment, an inclination toward rigidity, and a willingness to sacrifice means to ends. This latter aspect of behavior is perhaps the most disturbing. As already stated, for both Johnson and Nixon it took the form of deliberate deception, and in the case of Nixon, harassment of political opponents as well.

Two qualifications must be attached to what has been said here. First, it is not inevitable that a President with low self-esteem will sacrifice means to ends, for his sense of morality may intrude—an attribute that is also essential in the presidential personality. Woodrow Wilson, for example, is generally regarded as a man who experienced severe self-doubt, yet his deep sense of morality was apparently strong enough to fend off any temptations to employ the heavy-handed tactics characteristic of Johnson and Nixon. Moreover, despite his inflexibility, Wilson's Presidency was one of notable achievement. Thus, we may not want to exclude an individual from the Presidency solely for want of self-esteem, provided that we also discern in his character a strong sense of morality. Second, it should be noted that a President with high self-esteem is not necessarily immune to sacrificing means for ends. John Kennedy, for example, may be viewed as an active-positive President, yet when the steel companies raised their prices in 1962, he threatened to use antitrust laws against them unless they rescinded the increase. Moreover, he took the additional step of sending a personal emissary to Pittsburgh to inform steel executives that their personal tax returns would be audited if they refused to roll back prices.[121] This hardly constitutes an example of admirable presidential behavior, and yet the major point to be made here is this: while there is no reason to believe that the moral standards of the active-positive are any greater or less than those of the active-negative, the active-positive will nevertheless be under much less pressure to compromise those standards because he is not laboring under the compulsive fear of failure.

In considering personality attributes desirable in a President, we should also be attentive to how he relates to people. Does he enjoy interacting with people, and is he effective at doing so? This is an important question for two reasons. First, much of a President's success will depend upon his ability to be an effective persuader. This frequently requires that he meet personally with individuals and groups. Presidents who feel uncomfortable around others are likely to resist interaction to whatever extent possible, and thus are apt to be less effective at persuasion as well. In part at least, Richard Nixon's problems with Congress were the result of his failure to maintain adequate contact with its membership. Johnson and Roosevelt, on the other hand, showed no such reluctance. Moreover, their ability to persuade was enhanced further by a keen understanding of the motives and needs of other political actors.

The President's readiness to interact with others is important for another reason. His primary responsibility, after all, is to make decisions, and in order to do so effectively he needs information. Frequent contact with people constitutes an invaluable means for accumulating information and ideas. No President was more sensitive to this fact than Franklin Roosevelt, and consequently he structured his environment so as to maximize his exposure to others. Of course, doing so came naturally to him since he was by nature a gregarious person. Richard Nixon, on the other hand, provides a stark contrast to Roosevelt. In the words of one Nixon aid, he "did not like to see many people, and wanted to see

[121] Joseph Califano, *A Presidential Nation* (New York: W.W. Norton, 1975), pp. 135, 263.

still fewer privately." Accordingly, he structured his environment in such a way as to minimize his exposure to others. The result was a severe reduction in the channels of information open to him.

In addition to a President's willingness to interact with others, we should be equally concerned about how he perceives them. In other words, does he appear to be trusting of the other people in his environment, or does he view them with suspicion? A President who harbors deep suspicions about his environment may engage in behavior that is damaging to both the office and the political system. For example, if he is already inclined toward isolation to begin with, a suspicious nature may only serve to make him more so. One can also hypothesize that such an attitude would lead to a style of excessive secrecy, with the result that the number of people involved in decision making will be kept small, and those in and outside government will be denied information which they have a right to know. A distrusting nature may also cause a President to become so concerned with the loyalty of those around him that he equates dissent with disloyalty, and consequently the healthy conflict of opposing views becomes stifled. Finally, one cannot help but wonder whether a deep suspicion of the world around him may also encourage a President to sacrifice means to ends. For if he is to succeed in what he perceives as an unscrupulous world, it may be necessary for him to adopt what he perceived to be the tactics of his adversaries.

PREDICTING PRESIDENTIAL PERSONALITIES

If a President's personality can have a considerable impact upon how he conducts himself while in office, then it would appear that we ought to give closer scrutiny to this facet of a presidential candidate. James David Barber has proposed that we do precisely this: " . . . we need a new program of research aimed at assessing—*before* the choice is narrowed to a few—the probable course each emerging candidate would follow in the White House. Such a program could draw on the talents of psychologists, historians, journalists, politicians, political scientists, and others. . . ."[122]

Various proposals have been suggested regarding how this assessment might be made. Two scholars, for example, have developed a quantitative measure for determining a President's *power* and *achievement* need based upon a content analysis of his inaugural address.[123] They have suggested that this approach might also be applied to the campaign speeches of presidential candidates. Yet this proposal is fraught with difficulties. For one thing, candidates do not always write their own campaign speeches. Nor do they always adhere to what they say

---

[122] James Barber. "President Nixon and Richard Nixon: Character Trap," Reprinted from *Psychology Today Magazine,* October 1974, p. 118. Copyright ©1974 by Ziff-Davis Publishing Company.

[123] Richard Donley and David Winter, "Measuring the Motives of Public Figures at a Distance: An Exploratory Study of American Presidents," *Behavioral Science* 15 (May 1970), 227–36.

in them. On several occasions during his campaign for the Presidency in 1968, Richard Nixon stated that he would run an open administration and would show no reluctance to delegate power. Nothing could have been farther from the truth. Finally, while this approach is designed to give us some understanding of a candidate's need for power and achievement, it tells us nothing about what motivates these needs. In the case of Nixon, for example, we would also want to know that these needs were rooted in a deep sense of insecurity.

Other proposals call for subjecting candidates to some kind of psychological testing. As far back as 1948, Harold Lasswell proposed the establishment of a National Personnel Assessment Board which would administer tests to candidates in order to identify those with "nondestructive, genuinely democratic characters."[124] This proposal should also give us pause for thought. Quite obviously, a serious and perhaps fatal blow would be dealt to the candidacy of any individual who failed to receive the stamp of approval from such a board. To whom do we want to give the power to render such a judgment? How would they be selected? What if these experts cannot agree on what interpretation should be given to the evidence? How would they deal with the problem of predicting the *likelihood* that a given candidate would engage in destructive behavior? For remember, these experts will not be studying psychotics whose capacity for irrationality can be predicted with a high degree of certainty. Rather, they will be dealing with individuals who have demonstrated an ability to cope with their environment. While some may demonstrate tendencies toward destructive behavior, these are only possibilities. But how much of a possibility? Do we exclude those with a 50 percent chance of engaging in destructive behavior in the Presidency? Do we include a candidate if there is an 80 percent chance that he will not engage in destructive behavior?[125] Finally, even if all of these problems could be adequately dealt with, there is still the possibility that this kind of screening process could be undermined. Presidential contenders receive expert advice on a variety of matters related to their candidacy. Public relations experts advise them on what appeals should be made to the people; policy specialists advise them on issues; speech coaches help them with their delivery. More than likely, if an assessment board were established some candidates would also hire consultants to advise them on matters related to their psychological examination, notably, what kinds of questions should be anticipated and what kinds of responses would be most appropriate.

For those who eschew any efforts to submit candidates to psychological testing, the psychohistorical approach to assessing candidates may prove more appealing. As noted at the outset of this chapter, the psychohistorical approach attempts to discover the psychological makeup of an individual by scrutinizing his past. But even here we are confronted with some formidable difficulties. As

---

[124]Cited in Alan Elms, *Personality in Politics* (New York: Harcourt Brace Jovanovich, 1976), p. 174.

[125]Ibid., pp. 173–74.

Barber himself has noted, of the three components that make up personality (*character, style,* and *world view*), it is character that appears to be most important to understanding a President's behavior: "Most strikingly for the active-negative (compulsive-tending) presidents, but also for the other types, character is the most important predictor."[126] Barber further states that character takes shape in childhood, and herein lies the problem, for although an examination of a candidate's childhood may provide us with the best clues to his character, the evidence is likely to be the leanest for this period of his life experience. Candidates do not usually write their own biographies. Thus, we have no systematic evidence on how *they* viewed *their* childhood experiences, except as they may choose to discuss them in interviews. While scholars can attempt to reconstruct a candidate's childhood through interviews and biographies—if there are any—the end product is still likely to be a sketch rather than a detailed picture. Thus, the conclusions drawn and the inferences made are of a highly tentative nature.

Despite these limitations, this chapter has tried to show that psychohistorical explanations may be of some assistance in providing another perspective from which to view presidential behavior. Yet it may be argued that it is one thing to make use of a psychohistorical explanation in seeking to gain additional insight into why presidents behave as they do; but it is quite another thing to apply it to candidates in quest of the Presidency. In short, might we do possible injustice to both the candidates and the voters by making use of this approach in the screening process? If the answer is no, there is still another problem to be faced, for Barber has suggested that the assessment of candidates should take place before the field has been narrowed to only a few. But surely his meticulous inquiry into the characters of presidents was a time-consuming task. This raises the following question: will there be enough time between when a candidate declares and when the nomination is made to conduct a careful inquiry into his character? The magnitude of the task becomes even greater if we are faced with the kind of situation we had in 1976, when there were initially fourteen candidates seeking the Democratic nomination for President.

In attempting to gain some kind of insight into a presidential candidate's personality, it may make more sense to focus our attention on his public career, for the evidence here is likely to be easier to come by. Such an approach would involve examining and accumulating information about his behavior in the political arena from the start of his political career right up to and including his campaign for the nomination. Does he invest considerable energy in politics, and does he appear to enjoy doing so? How does he perceive his environment? Does he interact freely with those around him—press, staff, fellow politicians? Is he flexible? How does he respond to criticism and to those who give it? Does he appear to show concern for means as well as ends? Of course, even this approach is not without its limitations. For one thing, its usefulness will depend

[126] Barber, "President Nixon and Richard Nixon," p. 113.

to a large extent upon how long a candidate has been in political life. In the case of Richard Nixon, the record available for examination was extensive. At the time he ran for President in 1968, he had already been in politics for over twenty years—first as a congressman, then as a senator, then as Vice President, then as a presidential candidate, then as a candidate for governor of California. Add to this the book he wrote (*Six Crises,* 1968), which detailed how he coped with the major crises of his political career. In contrast to Nixon is the case of Jimmy Carter, whose only political experience prior to assuming office was four years in the Georgia legislature and four years as governor. This more restricted time span of political activity obviously complicates the task of trying to detect patterns in a candidate's behavior. But even if we are fortunate enough to be presented with a candidate whose political career spans a number of years, there is still no guarantee that he will have revealed the full range of his personality. Barber himself admits that those on their way to the Presidency are likely "to respond more fully to external pressures and demands, to conform more closely to the expectations of those around them. The preliminary roles are all much more restrictive than the Presidency is, much more set by institutional requirements. One need only consider the legislative performance of Senators who became Presidents to see how contradictory and misleading the signs can be."[127]

Yet relative to the other approaches we have discussed, this one would appear to be the most promising. That it may not tell us all we need to know about a candidate's personality is no reason for abandoning it altogether. On the contrary, we should scrutinize the political careers of presidential contenders with far more care than we have shown in the past. Where scholars and journalists uncover behavior patterns that are a source of either concern or confidence, the results of their inquiry should be thoroughly reported. But this effort must be preceded by something else of equal importance—namely, an attempt to better educate the public as to *why* personality is such an important factor in assessing presidential candidates.

[127]Barber, *Presidential Character,* p. 99.

The President
and
Emergency Powers

Consideration of the Presidency and emergency powers has been deferred until this point because it involves the functioning of the office under abnormal circumstances; however, the occurrence of emergencies has not been so rare as to render emergency powers a topic too exotic for consideration. On the contrary, over the course of the last forty years or so, many Americans have lived a good part of their lives under national emergencies of one kind or another. Roosevelt declared a state of emergency in 1933 in order to forestall the collapse of the American banking system. In 1939, he announced a "limited" national emergency in the wake of the outbreak of war in Europe, and still another "unlimited" one in 1941, as the Nazi threat grew more imminent. Truman put the nation on an emergency footing in 1950, following our entry into the Korean War. Thereafter no national emergencies were declared until the country was well into the first term of the Nixon Administration. President Nixon made two emergency proclamations. One came in March 1970 as a result of the halt in the postal service, the other in August 1971, in response to the dangerously high deficit in the United States balance of payments. Since there is no reason to believe that the future will treat us any more kindly than has the past, emergencies of varying severity will no doubt continue to intrude into our national life at one time or another.

There is a second and even more compelling reason why the topic of emergency powers deserves our close attention; namely, the fact that the nature of these powers is indeed awesome. Upon declaration of a national emergency, there are currently some 470 emergency statutes that become operative. Depending upon the nature of the emergency, the President may invoke some or all of these statutes to regulate the political and economic freedoms to which we are normally accustomed. Powers granted the President under these statutes may be broken down into three broad categories: (1) powers over individuals, (2) powers over the control and regulation of property, and (3) powers over communications.[1] Listed below are just some of the relevant powers that fall under each of these categories:

I. Powers over Persons

Can order the confinement of any individual deemed to be a threat to the security of the United States.

Can restrict travel abroad as well as travel to the United States.

Can restrict access to U.S. citizenship.

Can restrict the movement of individuals *within* and *over* (air flight) the United States.

Can require that certain individuals—by nature of their backgrounds, associations, activities, or ownership of certain articles—register with the government.

Can restrict freedom of association, for example, (1) can prevent individuals deemed a threat to the national security from being employed in certain critical industries, (2) can remove any federal employees deemed a threat to the national security.

Can suspend writ of habeas corpus.

Can declare martial law.

Can assign armed forces "to assist in military matters in any foreign country."

II. Powers over the Control and Regulation of Property

Can order the stockpiling of certain strategic materials.

Can impose restrictions on the export of U.S. goods.

Is authorized to allocate materials in ways he thinks necessary in order to promote the national defense.

Can require industries to give priority to government contracts and seize by any means necessary those industries that fail to comply.

Can fix wages and prices.

III. Powers over Communications

In carrying out his reporting obligations to Congress, the President may withhold information he deems damaging to the national security.

If he concludes that the nation is under threat of attack, he may refrain from publishing his regulations in the *Federal Register.*

---

[1] J. Malcolm Smith and Cornelius Cotter, *Powers of the President During Crises* (Washington, D.C.: Public Affairs Press, 1960).

During war or threat of war he may establish procedures for censoring mail, cable, radio, or other means of communication between the U.S. and any foreign country.

Can require those engaging in propaganda activities on behalf of foreign governments to register with the U.S. government.[2]

Given the far-reaching nature of these powers, it is worth considering whether their exercise is ever appropriate in a democracy. If it is, then what safeguards are necessary to protect against the abuse of these powers? Finally, to what extent have these safeguards been present in the American experience with emergency powers? These questions will constitute the major concerns of this chapter.

THE FOUNDERS, THE CONSTITUTION, AND EMERGENCY POWERS

At the time the Founding Fathers undertook the formidable task of constructing a new government, the practice of investing government with emergency powers had not been unprecedented in history. Aristotle, for example, noted in his writings that the Greek city-states had resorted to elective tyrannies on those occasions when civil strife threatened law and order within the community. The elaborate constitutional framework of the Roman republic also made provision for emergency situations. While executive authority was normally vested in two consuls, during times of "grievous wars or serious unrest" the Roman Senate could initiate a proposal asking the consuls to select an individual who would function as a temporary dictator. It was also possible for the consuls themselves to initiate a proposal for dictatorship, which subsequently had to be approved by the Senate.[3] To these historical examples must be added the writings of such eminent political thinkers as Rousseau and Locke, both of whom addressed the appropriateness of granting emergency powers to government. Notwithstanding his strong commitment to a democratic order, Rousseau felt that circumstances might necessitate the suspension of the normal constitutional processes: "The inflexibility natural to laws, which hinders their bending to events, may in certain cases be pernicious, and, in a crisis, even occasion the ruin of the State. The order and slowness of legal forms require a space of time which circumstances sometimes refuse. . . . [F]or this reason it is advisable not to establish political institutions so strongly as to prevent a possibility of suspending their operation."[4]

---

[2] Smith and Cotter, *Powers of the President,* pp. 26–92; see also U.S., Congress, House, Subcommittee of the Committee on the Judiciary Hearings, on H.R. 3884, *National Emergencies Act,* 94th Cong., 1st Sess., 1975, pp. 22, 23.

[3] Clinton Rossiter, *Constitutional Dictatorship* (Princeton, N.J.: Princeton University Press, 1948), p. 19.

[4] Jean Jacques Rousseau, *The Social Contract* (New York: Hafner Press, 1947), p. 110.

Accordingly, he called for the creation of a "supreme magistracy," which in times of grave crisis could exercise dictatorial powers—but only on a temporary basis. Locke took a similar position. While acknowledging that limited government was essential to democracy, he remained cognizant of the fact that dire circumstances might warrant the assumption of extraordinary powers by the government. Specifically, he argued that the sovereign should have the *prerogative* "to act according to discretion for the public good, without the prescription of the Law and sometimes even against it." Moreover, since the legislature was so unwieldy and unable "to foresee, and so by laws to provide for, all Accidents and Necessities, that may concern the public," this prerogative would be most appropriately lodged with the Executive.[5]

As men of considerable learning, it seems likely that the Founding Fathers were acquainted with how earlier peoples had attempted to cope with emergency situations. They certainly were not unaware of what Locke had to say about prerogative, for his writings constituted an important part of the intellectual baggage they brought to the Constitutional Convention. Yet as one peruses the Convention debates, *The Federalist,* and the ratifying debates, there is scarcely any indication that the Founding Fathers felt it would be necessary to *alter* constitutional arrangements in times of emergency. In the Constitution itself there is only one provision that explicitly calls for altering the existing constitutional order in times of crisis: "The Privilege of Writ of Habeas Corpus shall not be suspended, unless when in Cases of Rebellion or Invasion the Public Safety may require it" (Article 1, sec. 9). Aside from this exception, however, the delegates apparently felt that the provisions they wrote into the Constitution were adequate to deal with any crisis the nation might face. Those parts that may be viewed as contemplating emergency situations are (1) the right of the United States to guarantee to every state a republican form of government and to protect each state against invasion, and upon its request, against domestic violence (Article 4, sec. 4); (2) the right of Congress to declare war, raise armies, "provide for calling forth the Militia to execute the Laws of the Union, suppress Insurrections and repel Invasions" and "make all Laws which shall be necessary and proper for carrying into Execution the foregoing Powers" (Article 1, sec. 8). The only constitutional provisions having any direct relevance to the President's ability to act in emergencies are (1) his designation as "Commander in Chief of the Army and Navy of the United States and of the Militia of the several States. when called into the actual Service of the United States" (Article 2, sec. 2); (2) his right to convene one or both Houses of Congress on extraordinary occasions (Article 2, sec. 3); and (3) his right to protect states, upon their request, against domestic violence when the Congress cannot be convened (Article 4, sec. 4). Excepting these provisions, it appears that any additional emergency actions

---

[5] Peter Laslett, *Locke's Two Treatises of Government* (Cambridge: Cambridge University Press, 1967), pp. 392–93.

taken by the President would have to come through a statutory delegation granted to him by the Congress.

ON THE NECESSITY FOR EMERGENCY POWERS

That the Founding Fathers declined to make special provision for suspending constitutional requirements in times of emergencies is not altogether surprising. Their generally skeptical view of human nature as well as their experience with living under a tyrannical British King made them reluctant to concentrate power in any institution. On the contrary, they went to great lengths to create a constitutional structure that would diffuse power. It was first divided between the states and the national government. At the national level, legislative, judicial, and executive power were placed in three separate institutions, and since they considered the Legislative branch the most powerful of the three, they sought to diffuse its power further by dividing it into two chambers, the House and Senate. Nor was this enough, for they feared that each branch might attempt to infringe upon the powers and responsibilities of the other. Consequently, each was given powers (checks) over the other two branches. As Madison noted, each department must be given "the necessary constitutional means, and personal motives, to resist encroachments of the others." Finally, having become convinced that certain additional safeguards were necessary to protect the citizenry from the power of government, the first Congress proposed, and the states ratified, a series of amendments that have come to be known as the Bill of Rights.

While under normal conditions, federalism, separation of powers, checks and balances, and the Bill of Rights all function as formidable and necessary roadblocks to the abuse of governmental power, under conditions of emergency they may function as an impediment to the preservation of the polity itself. All Western democracies have at one time or another faced emergencies that seriously threatened their very existence. In some cases the threat has come from without, in the form of an attack from a foreign power. In other instances, the threat has come from within, perhaps from a severe economic depression or domestic violence and subversion. But regardless of the source, such crises have required swift and decisive action. In a democracy like ours, where power is both diffused and restricted, the government is ill-suited to acting efficiently in times of crisis. Thus, we are confronted with a dilemma that was best articulated by Abraham Lincoln over one hundred years ago: "Is there in all republics this inherent and fatal weakness? Must a government of necessity be too *strong* for the liberties of its people, or too *weak* to maintain its own existence?"[6]

Most would probably agree that this dilemma should be resolved in favor of according the government some additional capacity to deal with crisis situations. This additional capacity must typically involve both a *concentration* and *expan-*

[6] Cited in Rossiter, *Constitutional Dictatorship*, p. 3.

sion of power. Since most major crises are national in scope, this means concentrating power at the national level. But where at the national level? Clearly the Supreme Court, by virtue of its function, is not a suitable agency; nor is the Legislative branch, given its size. Thus, the most logical choice is the Executive, for it alone has the capacity to act with dispatch. In addition to being concentrated, governmental power must also be expanded. To deal successfully with crises of great magnitude, the government must have the capacity to mobilize and coordinate the human and material resources of the nation. This may require that we give government the power to impose restrictions upon certain political and economic freedoms to which we are normally accustomed. Since the nature and scope of these restrictions have already been illustrated at the outset of this chapter, there is no need to do so here.

ON THE NECESSITY FOR SAFEGUARDS

If the government must be accorded expanded powers when the nation faces emergency situations, it is equally clear that appropriate safeguards are necessary to forestall their misuse. Extraordinary powers, after all, create the potential for extraordinary abuses. In this section we shall consider first what scholars have acknowledged as essential safeguards,[7] and second, to what extent these safeguards have been present or wanting in the American experience with emergency powers.

Essential Safeguards

Emergency powers should be invoked only when there is a genuine emergency.

That emergency powers should only be employed in a real emergency is obvious enough. But how does one insure this? One could resort to a definitional safeguard, thus specifying the circumstances that may be defined as emergency situations. In following this approach, however, there is always the risk that such a list will fail to encompass all possibilities. Alternatively, it has also been suggested that a broader definition is more appropriate; specifically, one that would define an emergency as any situation that threatens the continued existence of the prevailing constitutional order. But even this more general definition may prove too restrictive. Suppose, for example, that terrorists were running about the country poisoning the water supply. While such a circumstance might not necessarily pose a threat to the very existence of the nation, one might nevertheless argue that this kind of activity could be classified as an emergency situation.

---

[7]See for example, Rossiter, *Constitutional Dictatorship,* pp. 297–306; Carl Friedrich, *Constitutional Governments And Democracy* (Waltham, Mass.: Blaisdell, 1968), pp. 557–81.

Thus, rather than having to contend with the problems created by attempting to define an emergency, a more suitable safeguard may lie in *who* is empowered to declare that an emergency exists. This leads us to the next point.

The decision to declare an emergency should not rest with the agency that will exercise emergency powers.

As already noted, the exercise of emergency powers must of necessity be lodged in the Executive. At the same time, however, to allow the Executive to make the sole determination as to when they should be invoked is to face the risk that he may resort to them prematurely. Accordingly, the ultimate authority for declaring a national emergency should be vested in the Legislature. The word "ultimate" is an important and necessary qualifier here, since it is possible to conceive of circumstances where the Executive will not have enough time to seek a declaration of national emergency from the Legislature. Thus, he must be free to make the *initial* determination himself, subject to a later ratification or rejection by the Legislature. At the same time, however, not all emergencies are of equal magnitude; consequently, when circumstances permit, he should ask the Legislature for a declaration.

Within the American experience, declarations of national emergency always have been made by the President. Moreover, Congress has willingly passed all kinds of statutes empowering the President to take extraordinary action when, in his judgment, an emergency situation existed. And only in rare instances have these statutes reserved to the Congress the right to review a presidential declaration.[8] In no instance has the President ever asked Congress to issue a formal declaration of national emergency—even when the circumstances would have permitted him to do so. In 1950, for example, circumstances were not so grave that Truman lacked the time to seek a declaration from Congress following our entry into the Korean War. Nor would it appear that the balance of payments deficit was so critical in 1971 that President Nixon did not have time to gain a congressional declaration before he imposed currency restrictions and enforced controls on foreign trade.

The autonomy accorded to the President in declaring national emergencies is in marked contrast to the procedures followed in several other contemporary Western democracies. In both Canada and West Germany, for example, a declaration of national emergency by the Prime Minister is subject to ratification by the Legislature.

Emergency powers should not be initiated without provision for their termination; and the decision to terminate should not rest with the agency exercising such powers.

[8] "The National Security Interest and Civil Liberties," *Harvard Law Review* 85 (April 1972), 1291.

Since the assumption of emergency powers greatly facilitates the Executive's ability to act, there exists the possibility that he will want to hold onto them beyond the time required to meet a given crisis. Thus, when the Legislature itself declares an emergency or else gives its approval to one announced by the President, it should stipulate a termination date. To be sure, emergencies are not always so discrete that one can precisely determine when they shall cease to exist. But if the period of time should prove too short, the Legislature can extend it. Likewise if the grant of emergency authority proves to be longer than was necessary, the Legislature may nullify its original termination date.

In providing for the creation of the role of "dictator," the Romans clearly specified a limitation on it of six months. Similarly, during the Second World War, the British Parliament was even more stringent, allowing Prime Minister Churchill grants of emergency powers for only thirty days at a time. By comparison, the American approach to this issue has at best been shoddy and unsystematic. In none of the six national emergencies proclaimed by presidents over the last half century has a termination date been specified. Nor, with rare exceptions, has the Congress written any provisions for termination into its statutory grants of emergency powers to presidents. This is not surprising, given the fact that the legislation providing these grants of authority has customarily been drafted in the Executive branch and then submitted to Congress for passage. Since the Executive was not interested in stipulating any conditions for congressional review or termination of these powers, no such provisions were included.[9]

Nor was it uncommon for Congress to rush these drafts through to passage, with little careful thought given to their substance. This kind of perfunctory approval reached the outer extreme in an emergency economic measure passed by the Congress in 1933. This particular bill was subjected to a total of only eight hours of debate in both Houses. Moreover there were no committee reports, and when the bill came onto the floor of the Senate for consideration, there was only one copy of it available.[10]

As already noted, there have been six national emergencies declared by presidents over the last half century. Three were declared by Franklin Roosevelt (1933, 1939, 1941), one was declared by Truman (1950), and two by Nixon (1970, 1971). Although in 1952, Truman issued a proclamation terminating Roosevelt's emergencies of 1939 and 1941, the other four (1933, 1950, 1970, 1971) had still not been terminated as of 1976. Finally, in September of that year, Congress passed legislation wiping them off the books. But the point is that during the entire period from 1933 to 1976, the United States was legally in a state of emergency and thus a President could have invoked emergency powers under the 470 emergency statutes on the books. Indeed, in some instances, emergency powers were in fact exercised during nonemergency circumstances,

[9] Hearings on *National Emergency Act,* 94th Cong., 1st Sess., 1975, p. 35.

[10] Frank Church, "Ending Emergency Government," *American Bar Association Journal* 63 (February 1977), 198.

and such actions were judged legal because a national emergency was technically still in effect. In 1970, for example, a United States Court of Appeals upheld the Cuban Assets Control Regulations on the grounds that they were consistent with the authority granted to the Executive under the Korean emergency; this despite the fact that the justification for the Korean emergency had long since passed.[11]

Actions taken in times of emergency should be grounded in constitutional or statutory provisions.

Because the country is faced with a grave crisis does not mean that the Executive may arrogate powers to himself without any regard to their legality. To allow him to do so would, in essence, be to vest in him legislative and judicial as well as executive authority. And as James Madison warned us over two hundred years ago, previous experience has shown that "the accumulation of all powers legislative, executive and judiciary in the same hands . . . may justly be pronounced the very definition of tyranny."[12] Of course it may well be the case that during emergency situations the Legislature will have to delegate more of its own power to the Executive. Moreover, there may also be instances where the severity of the crisis is such that presidential action cannot be deferred, and consequently the statutory grant of authority may have to come after the fact. But regardless of when it comes, if the President's actions cannot be justified on constitutional grounds alone, they must be legitimized by statute. And even then, they may ultimately be subject to review by the courts. Richard Nixon's contention that "when the President does it, that means it is not illegal," is political nonsense.

In seeking to ground their emergency actions in constitutional or statutory authority, some presidents have moved more cautiously than others. Clearly Lincoln's handling of the Civil War stands out as the most arbitrary use of emergency powers. Following the secession of the South from the Union, he unilaterally increased the size of the army, spent unappropriated funds from the U.S. Treasury, and suspended the writ of habeas corpus. The first two actions were in direct violation of the Constitution, for Congress is given the exclusive authority to regulate the size of the armed forces and spend money. While the Constitution does not specify who may suspend habeas corpus, few doubted that this was a power the Founding Fathers had intended to reserve exclusively to the Congress.[13] At the time Lincoln took these actions, the Congress was not in session, and while he could have summoned it into special session, he did not see

[11] Gerhard Casper, *On Emergency Powers of the President: Every Inch a King?* (Andover, Mass.: Warner Modular Publications, 1973), p. 4.

[12] James Madison, Federalist Paper No. 47, in Jacob Cooke, ed., *The Federalist* (Cleveland: World, 1961), p. 324.

[13] This view was upheld in the case of *Ex parte* Merryman (1861). Chief Justice Taney, who was performing in his role as circuit judge, ruled Lincoln's suspension of habeas corpus unconstitutional. Lincoln, however, chose to ignore the ruling.

fit to do so until a full eleven weeks after the South had seceded. This unusual delay was, no doubt, designed to give him a free hand in responding to events. When Congress was finally convened on July 4, 1861, Lincoln did acknowledge some doubt as to the constitutionality of his actions: "These measures, whether strictly legal or not, were ventured upon under what appeared to be a popular demand and a public necessity, trusting then, as now, that Congress would readily ratify them. It is believed that nothing has been done beyond the constitutional competency of Congress."[14] In short, he was espousing John Locke's doctrine of the sovereign's prerogative—the right to act, when necessity requires it, in the absence of the law and sometimes even against it. Having been presented with a fait accompli and sympathetic with his purposes besides, the Congress readily blessed Lincoln's actions: "All the acts, proclamations and orders of the President respecting the army and navy of the United States . . . are hereby approved and in all respects made valid . . . as if they had been issued and done under the previous express authority and the direction of the Congress of the United States."[15]

While Congress proceeded to grant the President additional statutory authority, there were nevertheless many instances where Lincoln continued to act independently. In some cases he took initiatives that clearly fell within the purview of the Legislative branch. These included the issuance of the Emancipation Proclamation; the making of rules and regulations for the armed forces, a power explicitly reserved to Congress in the Constitution (Article 1, sec. 8); the declaration of martial law behind the lines; seizure of property; suppression of newspapers; arresting without a warrant; and prohibiting the use of the postal service for "treasonable correspondence."[16] The extent of the powers assumed by Lincoln was vividly captured in a remark made by his Secretary of State to the British Minister: "My Lord, I can touch a bell on my right and order the imprisonment of a citizen of Ohio, I can touch a bell again and order the imprisonment of a citizen of New York; and no power on earth, except that of the President, can release them. Can the Queen of England do so much?"[17]

In justifying his authority to take such extraordinary actions, Lincoln cited several parts of the Constitution, most notably, the President's authority as Commander in Chief; his obligation "to take care that the laws be faithfully executed"; and the oath of office, which pledges the President to "preserve, protect, and defend the Constitution of the United States." That any or all of these provisions entitled him to arrogate such far-reaching powers to himself is highly

---

[14] Rossiter, *Constitutional Dictatorship,* p. 229.

[15] Cited in John Roche, "Executive Power and Domestic Emergency: The Quest for Prerogative," *Western Political Quarterly* 5 (December 1952), 598–99.

[16] Arthur Schlesinger, Jr., *The Imperial Presidency* (Boston: Houghton Mifflin, 1973), p. 58. Copyright © 1973 by Arthur H. Schlesinger, Jr. Reprinted by permission of Houghton Mifflin Company.

[17] Ibid., pp. 58, 59.

questionable, to say the least. But because his actions enjoyed broad support in both Congress and the general population, no challenges were forthcoming— at least not until after the war. In his defense, it must be noted that no President before or since has faced a crisis of such magnitude as the Civil War, and thus in this particular instance swift and extraordinary action may well have been necessary. Yet, as Clinton Rossiter observed, "There is, however, this disturbing fact to remember: he set a precedent for bad men as well as good. . . . If Lincoln could calmly assert: 'I conceive that I may, in an emergency, do things on a military ground which cannot constitutionally be done by Congress,' then some future President less democratic and less patriotic might assert the same thing."[18]

In the twentieth century the most notable crises have been precipitated by either war or a faltering economy. In meeting these crises, however, the approach of both Presidents Wilson and Roosevelt was decidedly different from that of Lincoln. In preparing the country to cope with the First World War, Wilson did not strike out on his own as Lincoln had done, but rather, with rare exception, he sought statutory authorization for what he wanted to do. Congress promptly responded by passing the Overman and Lever Acts, which together provided him with a variety of emergency powers. These included the authority to take over and operate the railroad, water systems, and telephone and telegraph networks; redistribute the functions of agencies in the federal government; regulate the foreign language press and censor communications into and out of the United States; regulate or seize all shipbuilding operations; regulate exports; and establish restrictions on the actions of enemy aliens. Roosevelt was also careful to gain Legislative authorization for dealing with the Great Depression, although such grants of authority did not always precede his own actions. In 1933, for example, he declared a national emergency and immediately suspended all financial transactions by ordering all banks to close their doors to the public. While he based his authority on the Trading with the Enemy Act (1917), this justification was dubious at best, since the act authorized the President to regulate trade and financial actions between the United States and foreigners, and only in time of war. Yet this justification, questionable though it was, nevertheless demonstrated Roosevelt's concern for cloaking his actions in legality. Moreover, he quickly asked Congress to pass legislation that would provide a more solid legal base for what he had done. This legislation came just three days later in the form of the Emergency Banking Act.

Either because of increasing confidence or a greater sense of urgency, Roosevelt behaved far more independently of the Congress as he faced up to his second major crisis. In 1939 he declared a "limited" national emergency, thereby clearing the way for invoking certain statutes that would enable him to pre-

---

[18] Rossiter, *Constitutional Dictatorship*, p. 239.

pare the nation for almost certain involvement in a Second World War. The term "limited" was used to prevent the population from becoming unduly alarmed. By May 1941, however, the situation in Europe had steadily worsened, and Roosevelt elevated the emergency to an "unlimited" one. In the months ahead he proceeded to create more than twenty government agencies whose purpose was to deal with the domestic impact of the war. Moreover, he did so without receiving any authorization from Congress. Aware that there was no constitutional precedent for this action, he attempted to skirt the constitutional issue by grouping agencies under the Office of Emergency Management, an agency that had been authorized by Congress in 1940.[19]

His exercise of prerogative was also apparent in other areas. From the time the war began up to 1943, he seized no fewer than eleven industrial facilities and justified his action in "the Constitution and the laws."[20] Precisely what part of the Constitution and what laws he had in mind was never made clear. In February 1942, he issued an executive order removing Americans of Japanese ancestry from the West Coast on the grounds that they posed a threat to the security of the United States. While his action was ultimately ratified by Congress one month later, it is far from clear that circumstances required him to act prior to congressional authorization. There had, after all, been no known instances of sabotage by Japanese-Americans. Roosevelt's most far-reaching claim to presidential prerogative by far came in a speech given to Congress in September 1942. He asked the membership to repeal a certain provision of the Emergency Price Control Act (1942) dealing with farm parity and then went on to warn that unless Congress did so, he would repeal it himself! In asserting his authority on this matter he noted that "the President has the powers, under the Constitution and under congressional acts, to take measures necessary to avert a disaster which would interfere with the winning of the war. . . . When the war is won, the powers under which I act automatically revert to the people—to whom they belong."[21] Quite obviously, if one accepted this line of reasoning, it would be difficult to conceive of any limits that could be imposed upon presidential actions in time of war. Not even Lincoln, who frequently acted in the absence of congressional authorization, ever contended that he could unilaterally nullify legislation that had been duly passed by Congress and signed into law by a President. As it turned out, Roosevelt's preposterous warning was never put to the test, for Congress quickly took action to repeal the parity provision. Indeed, given Roosevelt's astuteness in political matters, it hardly seems likely that he would have issued such a challenge unless he was certain that the votes were there for repeal.

[19] Edward Corwin, *The President: Office and Powers,* 4th ed. (New York: New York University Press, 1957), pp. 242, 243.

[20] Roche, *Executive Power,* p. 607.

[21] Ibid., p. 609.

Emergency Powers and the Courts

We have noted that the exercise of emergency powers should be grounded in constitutional or statutory authority. With the exception of Lincoln, who acknowledged the doubtful constitutionality of his *initial* actions taken after the South seceded, in all the cases cited above, presidents attempted to legitimize their actions through appeals to the Constitution or the statutes, or both. While this should hardly come as a surprise, nevertheless the mere assertion of legality does not necessarily make it so. In the American political system, the final judgment on the legality of presidential as well as congressional acts rests with the Supreme Court. Thus the Court functions as the ultimate safeguard against the abuse of emergency powers. As we shall see below, however, its record in this area has been mixed.

As one peruses American constitutional history, only two cases stand out as attempts by the Supreme Court to limit the President's emergency powers. The first case was *Ex parte* Milligan (1866), and the circumstances surrounding it were the following: L. P. Milligan and his associates were arrested in Indiana on October 5, 1864, by the military commander of the district. Shortly thereafter he was tried in Indianapolis by a military commission that had been created by the sole authority of President Lincoln. The commission found him guilty of aiding a group of rebel forces who were preparing to invade Indiana. Although Milligan was sentenced to be hanged in May 1865, President Andrew Johnson commuted his sentence to life in prison. In the meantime, however, Milligan sued the government on the grounds that his constitutional rights had been violated. The Supreme Court finally heard the case in 1866, and in a unanimous opinion ruled that President Lincoln had been without the constitutional authority to set up military commissions behind the lines as long as the civil courts were still operating. In this particular instance the civil courts were still functioning (in fact, Indiana had not been invaded by rebel forces). In its opinion, the Court set forth a stinging indictment of the right of the President to act independently of the Constitution:

> The Constitution of the United States is a law for rulers and people, equally in war and in peace, and covers with the shield of its protection all classes of men, at all times, and under all circumstances. No doctrine, involving more pernicious consequences, was ever invented by the wit of man than that any of its provisions can be suspended during any of the great exigencies of government. . . . the theory of necessity on which it is based is false; for the government, within the constitution, has all the powers granted to it, which are necessary to its existence . . .

> . . . It could well be said that a country, preserved at the sacrifice of all the cardinal principles of liberty, is not worth the cost of preservation.[22]

[22]*Ex parte* Milligan, 71 U.S. (4 Wall.) 2, 18L. Ed. 281 (1866).

Yet one cannot help but wonder whether the vigor of the Court's decision was not in large part a consequence of the circumstances under which it was rendered. In the first place, the justices heard the case after the crisis of the Civil War had been ended; second, President Lincoln was dead by this time. Would the Court have so readily challenged Lincoln's authority had they been forced to decide the case while he was still President, embroiled in the greatest national crisis of our political history, and with a public and Congress strongly supportive of the actions he took? The opinion of the Court itself causes one to be doubtful:

> During the late and wicked Rebellion, the temper of the times did not allow that calmness in deliberation and discussion so necessary to a correct conclusion of a purely judicial question.
>
> . . . [F]eelings and interests prevailed which are happily terminated. *Now* that public safety is assured, this question, as well as all others, can be discussed and decided without passion. . . .[23]

The case of *Youngstown Sheet and Tube Co.* v. *Sawyer* (1952) provides a more meaningful effort by the Court to challenge the President's exercise of emergency powers, since the decision was rendered against a sitting President. Briefly, the circumstances surrounding this historic case were these: On December 31, 1951, the contract between the major steel companies and their employees ran out before agreement was reached on a new one. At President Truman's behest, the steelworkers continued to work without a contract while the matter was turned over to the Wage Stabilization Board. The negotiating process continued for over three months, but to no avail. Finally the frustrated United Steel Workers of America announced that they would strike on April 9, 1952. Two hours before the announced strike deadline, however, President Truman issued an executive order authorizing the Secretary of Commerce to seize the steel mills. The steelworkers were asked to resume work—this time as government employees—and they complied. Truman contended that the seizure was absolutely necessary, since a strike would have seriously impaired the war effort and damaged the economy as well. Yet he took this extraordinary action in the absence of any statutory authority. Both the Selective Service Act (1948) and the Defense Production Act (1950) authorized presidential seizure of industrial facilities, but only if industries failed to give priority to defense contract orders. Neither of these acts granted the President any seizure authority in the event of an unresolved labor dispute. To deal with this latter problem, the Congress had passed the Taft-Hartley Act (1947), part of which authorized the President to seek an eighty-day injunction against a strike. Moreover, in drafting this legislation, the Congress had specifically considered and rejected the option of providing the President with authority to seize industrial facilities in the event of a

[23] Ibid., p. 109.

strike. Notwithstanding all of this, Truman went ahead and took over the steel mills "on the authority vested in me by the Constitution and laws of the United States, and as President of the United States and Commander in Chief of the armed forces of the United States."[24] In a later defense of his decision, he put the matter more bluntly, noting that, "The President has very great inherent powers to meet national emergencies."[25]

Upon issuing his executive order, the President promptly informed Congress of what he had done and acknowledged its right to overrule him if it so chose. Congress failed to respond, however, and this led Truman to write a letter to the Senate once again asking Congress to act either to support or to oppose what he had done. There was still no response. Meanwhile, the steel companies decided to take the government to court and sue for the return of their property. In the lower courts, the government boldly argued that the President had "inherent" emergency powers, and that was that. This defense was not received sympathetically by the District Court, however, so when the case reached the Supreme Court, the government changed its tack. It contended that a genuine emergency did indeed exist and now argued that "the aggregate of his constitutional powers" as President and Commander in Chief entitled Truman to act in the absence of congressional authorization until such time as Congress itself decided to act. The government brief also noted that there were abundant historical precedents for presidential seizure of industrial facilities.

In arguing their side of the case, the steel companies acknowledged the President's right to take emergency actions and even took cognizance of the fact that in some cases his actions might have to precede congressional authorization. But they went on to insist that the President cannot act at such times without at some point gaining congressional ratification; nor can he act contrary to the expressed or implied will of Congress. In this particular instance, they argued, not only had the President's actions failed to be ratified by Congress, but he had failed to employ the remedy (Taft-Hartley Act) that had been legislated by Congress for dealing with labor disputes.

In a six-to-three decision, the Supreme Court found in favor of the steel companies. Writing the opinion for the majority, Justice Black rejected the notion that a President had *any* inherent prerogative in times of emergency; nor did he feel that the role of Commander in Chief invested the President with any special domestic powers. Therefore, in the absence of any valid constitutional justification for his actions, the President's authority would have to come from a statutory authorization. In this instance, Black noted, there was "no statute that expressly authorizes the President to take possession of property as he did here," and thus his seizure of the steel mills constituted a usurpation of the legislature's power.

---

[24] Smith and Cotter, *Powers of the President,* p. 134.

[25] Schlesinger, *Imperial Presidency,* p. 142.

While Truman lost in this particular case, it is far less clear that the Court was rejecting *any* presidential claim to prerogative in times of emergency. Indeed, each of the five justices who sided with Black wrote a concurring opinion, suggesting that while they agreed with his overall conclusion, they did not fully share his reasoning. Four of the six justices on the majority side either implied or explicitly stated that the President did indeed have some degree of executive prerogative in times of emergency.[26] By far the most thoughtful concurring opinion came from Justice Jackson, who delineated three major types of presidential action:

1. When the President acts in accordance with the implied or expressed will of Congress; in this situation his authority has the greatest presumption of legitimacy, "for it includes all that he possesses in his own right plus all that Congress can delegate. . . ."

2. "When the President acts in the absence of either a congressional grant or denial of authority"; in this instance, he must rely solely on his own independent powers, and thus his actions would have to be judged on "the imperatives of events and contemporary imponderables rather than abstract theories of law."

3. When the President acts contrary to the implied or expressed will of Congress; here Jackson argued, the President's power "is at its lowest ebb, for then he can rely only upon his own constitutional powers minus any constitutional powers of Congress over the matter. . . ." Accordingly, under these circumstances, his action must be subject to the most careful judicial scrutiny, for "what is at stake is the equilibrium established by our constitutional system."[27]

Since Truman's seizure of the steel mills violated the expressed will of Congress embodied in the Taft-Hartley Act, his action fell into the third category.

In addition to their being troubled by Truman's failure to comply with the expressed will of Congress, another, perhaps more telling, current of thought ran through the opinions of the justices. Specifically, they simply were not convinced of Truman's claim that the steel crisis represented one of the gravest crises this nation had ever faced. Nor for that matter, was the country as a whole. Indeed, during the two months that intervened between the time of the seizure and the hearing of the case by the Supreme Court, it had become abundantly clear that neither the Congress, the public, nor the nation's leading newspapers felt the strike was grave enough to justify Truman's drastic actions. On the contrary, in many quarters the steel seizure was viewed as an abuse of power sufficient to warrant impeachment.[28] On the other hand, had there existed a national

---

[26] *Youngstown Sheet and Tube Co.* v. *Sawyer,* 343 U.S. (1952), pp. 582–589.

[27] Ibid., pp. 635–638.

[28] See, for example, Roche, *Executive Power,* p. 613; Maeva Marcus, *Truman and the Steel Seizure Case* (New York: Columbia University Press, 1977), pp. 83–101.

consensus on the presence of a genuine emergency, the Court would more than likely have ruled in Truman's favor, given the fact that several of the justices acknowledged some degree of executive prerogative.

While the Court's decision in the steel seizure case served notice that the President's powers were not limitless in times of emergency, it is important to note that Truman's actions lacked the support of both the public and the Congress. Would the Court be equally willing to challenge a President's exercise of emergency powers if his actions had the strong backing of both Congress and the American people? The case of *Korematsu* v. *United States* (1944) provides a possible—and disturbing—answer to this question. This particular case had its origins in an executive order issued by President Roosevelt in February 1942. It instructed the "Secretary of War, and the Military Commanders who he may from time to time designate . . . to prescribe military areas in such places and of such extent as he or the appropriate Military Commander may determine, from which any or all persons may be excluded, and with respect to which, the right of any person to enter, remain in, or leave shall be subject to whatever restrictions the Secretary of War or the appropriate Military Commander may impose in his discretion."[29] This order was specifically aimed at the large concentrations of Japanese-Americans on the West Coast. Since many of the nation's defense industries were located in this area of the country, it was feared that Japanese-Americans might engage in sabotage and other subversive activities out of loyalty to their homeland. This fear—bordering on hysteria—was dramatically revealed in the final recommendation made by the General of the Western Defense Command to the Secretary of Defense in which he called for the removal of the Japanese from the West Coast:

> In the war in which we are now engaged, racial affinities are not severed by migration. The Japanese race is an enemy race and while many second and third generation Japanese born on United States soil, possessed of United States citizenship, have become "Americanized," the racial strains are undiluted. . . . It therefore follows, that along the vital Pacific Coast over 112,000 potential enemies, of Japanese extraction, are at large today. There are disturbing indications that these are organized and ready for concerted action at a favorable opportunity. The very fact that no sabotage has taken place to date is a disturbing and confirming indication that such action will be taken.[30]

As a consequence of Roosevelt's executive order, 112,000 individuals of Japanese descent, 70,000 of whom were full-fledged American citizens, were summarily separated from their homes, jobs, and property and relocated in

[29]Cited in Roger Daniels, *The Decision to Relocate the Japanese Americans* (Philadelphia: J.P. Lippincott, 1975), p. 113.

[30]Cited in Eugene Rostow, "Our Worst Wartime Mistake," *Harper's,* September 1945, pp. 195, 196.

detention camps, where they were held for periods of up to four years. Even if one allows for the fact that the United States was at war, this action still constituted an appalling abuse of emergency powers. Not only had the Japanese-Americans historically been model citizens, but more important, there was no evidence to suggest that they had or were about to engage in sabotage. As is apparent above, the recommendation of the General of the Western Defense Command was able to cite no evidence of sabotage by Japanese-Americans. Rather, he was reduced to arguing that "The very fact that no sabotage has taken place to date is a disturbing and confirming indication that such action will be taken." This was a curious bit of logic, to say the least.

Instead of presuming guilt by reason of race, surely a more judicious approach would have been to handle each individual on a case-by-case basis whereby only those found to be disloyal would be detained. Although the government argued that time would not permit such an approach, this justification is far from persuasive. In the first place, thousands of enemy aliens throughout the country had already been investigated on a case-by-case basis. Second, Japanese-Americans of questionable loyalty were in most cases already known to both the FBI and military intelligence, and thus they could have been weeded out from the rest of the group by the same procedure the government was using with German-American and Italo-American minorities. Finally, it is worth noting that even the British, who were considerably more hard-pressed than the United States, managed to investigate some 74,000 enemy aliens within a period of a few months.

By the time the Court was called upon to rule on the constitutionality of President Roosevelt's executive order, it was abundantly clear that his action commanded broad support in and outside of government. Congress had passed legislation ratifying the executive order one month after it was issued. Moreover, the nation's leading opinion makers had called repeatedly for some kind of government action against the Japanese-American community. Such an eminent and respected columnist as Walter Lippmann, for example, felt compelled to write a column entitled "The Fifth Column on the Coast" in which he noted that ". . . the Pacific Coast is in imminent danger of a combined attack from within and without. . . ." Another one of his newspaper colleagues was even more direct: "The Japanese in California should be under armed guard to the last man and woman right now—and to hell with habeas corpus."[31]

The case that came before the Court was *Korematsu* v. *United States*. It involved a Japanese-American who had been convicted of remaining in a region from which the Japanese had been excluded. In a six-to-three decision the Court upheld the exclusion order. Speaking for the majority, Justice Black argued that the government's action was well within "the combined federal war powers of Congress and the Executive." He went on to note that military necessity required that the army be able to take such action in wartime. While acknowledging that the exclusion of Japanese-Americans from the West Coast created considerable

[31] Cited in Daniels, *Japanese Americans,* pp. 47, 48.

hardship for them, he pointed out that "hardships are a part of war and war is an aggregation of hardships." In short, life is tough. He said nothing at all about the constitutionality of detaining Japanese citizens in camps, a matter he did not consider to be at issue in this case. Three of the justices issued strong dissents from Black's ruling. Justice Roberts contended that the issue of exclusion could not be divorced from the issue of detention. Moreover, he also reminded the Court that it was upholding the conviction of Korematsu in the absence of *any* evidence demonstrating his disloyalty. Justice Murphy argued that the exclusion policy was, by itself, one that "goes over the 'very brink of constitutional power' and falls into the ugly abyss of racism." Justice Jackson's dissent was not motivated by a repulsion over what the government had done, but rather by the belief that the Court should not be ruling on cases of this sort. He saw war as an extra-constitutional activity and thus not subject to constitutional constraints.[32]

On the same day that the Court ruled on this case, it also rendered another decision that bore directly on the constitutionality of *detaining* Japanese-Americans. In this particular case, *Ex parte* Endo, the Court found that since the loyalty of Mitsuye Endo had already been established beyond any doubt, the War Relocation Authority had no right to detain her at the Tule Lake War Relocation Camp. Yet in rendering the majority opinion, Justice Douglas refused to confront the issue of whether detention itself was constitutional. This can only be viewed as an astonishing bit of judicial behavior, given the fact that neither Roosevelt's executive order, nor the legislation subsequently passed by Congress ratifying the order, specifically authorized the creation of detention camps. It is even more astonishing when viewed in the context of the *Ex parte* Milligan decision. As the reader will recall, the Court ruled here that an individual accused of a crime could not be arrested by the military and tried by a military tribunal unless the civil courts were not functioning. Was it not also unconstitutional, then, to confine individuals who had not committed any crime at all, and who had not had the benefit of any trial, military or otherwise? Douglas contended that the Milligan case was not applicable here since the Japanese were being confined by civil authorities rather than military. However, it may well be argued that Douglas was making a distinction without a difference here since the civilian authorities were acting pursuant to orders given by the military.[33] The Court's failure to come to grips with the obvious and fundamental constitutional issues in the case was more than likely motivated by a desire to avoid a direct confrontation with the President and Congress. While this strategy may have been astute politically, this was hardly the Court's finest hour as defender of the Constitution.

In summary, the effectiveness of the Court in checking the possible abuse of emergency powers is likely to depend upon the circumstances. If the Congress

[32] *Korematsu* v. *United States,* 323 U.S. (1944), pp. 215–248.
[33] *Ex parte Endo,* 323 U.S. (1944), pp. 284–307.

and the public remain unconvinced that the exercise of the presidential preroga-tive is justified by circumstances, the Court is not likely to be convinced either. On the other hand, if the public and the Congress are firmly persuaded that an emergency does indeed exist, and if they are strongly supportive of whatever ac-tions the President may take to meet it, the Court is not likely to risk a confron-tation with the President, Congress, and the public at such a critical time. Thus, there is considerable merit in Clinton Rossiter's observation that "the Court's power of judicial review is least useful when most needed."[34] For it is in times of grave emergency that the government will be most prone to taken drastic ac-tion, and as the relocation and detention of Japanese-Americans demonstrates, such action may on occasion stray far from both the letter and the spirit of the Constitution.

RECENT CONGRESSIONAL ACTION ON EMERGENCIES

In June 1972, the Senate decided to create a Special Committee on National Emergencies and Delegated Powers. The impetus for this action came as a result of testimony given by Secretary of Defense Laird before the Senate Foreign Relations Committee. His appearance had been occasioned by the recent intro-duction of United States troops into Cambodia. At one point in the hearings Secretary Laird was asked what would happen if the Congress voted to cut off funds for the Cambodian invasion. To the astonishment of all, he replied that the President could continue the funding under a Civil War emergency statute passed by Congress in 1861 and still on the books. Known as the Feed and Forage Act, it allowed the President to spend unappropriated funds for purposes of clothing, feeding, and otherwise supplying the cavalry in the American West. In actuality, Laird was wrong about the date, for the act was not a Civil War statute but in fact dated all the way back to 1799.[35] Erroneous or not, his testi-mony threw a scare into the senators present, and consequently the Senate decided it was time to investigate precisely what emergency powers the Congress had granted to the President over the course of our political history. To its sur-prise, the special committee discovered that nowhere in the government was there a catalogue of the emergency statutes passed by Congress. Instead, the statutes were scattered throughout the voluminous United States Code along with all the other federal statutes. With the assistance of the Air Force, which fortunately had put the entire United States Code on computer tapes, the com-mittee was finally able to track down some 470 emergency statutes. During the course of their inquiry, they also learned that four separate national emergencies

[34]Clinton Rossiter, *The American Presidency,* 2nd ed. (New York: New American Library, 1960), p. 53.

[35]See Louis Fisher, *Presidential Spending Power* (Princeton, N.J.: Princeton University Press, 1960), p. 240.

were still in effect as of the time of their investigation. Having apprised itself of the sloppy handling of national emergencies as well as of the scope of powers granted to presidents under such conditions, Congress concluded that corrective legislation was necessary. No doubt the intervening events of Watergate further heightened its commitment to act. Accordingly, it passed the National Emergencies Act, which was signed into law by President Ford in September 1976. The major provisions of this legislation are outlined below:

I. Termination of Existing National Emergencies

Terminates two years from the date of enactment of this act emergency powers and authorities possessed by the President or any other federal officer or executive agency which were still in effect as a result of previously declared emergencies.

II. Declaration and Termination of Future National Emergencies

All future national emergencies declared by the President can be terminated by Congress through a concurrent resolution (not subject to presidential veto) or by a presidential proclamation.

Not later than six months after an emergency has been declared, and not later than the end of each six-month period thereafter, Congress shall be required to consider whether that emergency shall be terminated.

If the President has declared a national emergency, and if it has not been terminated by Congress (in accordance with the provision stated above), it shall be terminated at the end of one year unless the President informs Congress that it is still in effect.

III. Procedures Relating to the Use of Emergency Powers

When the President declares a national emergency, he must specify to Congress the provisions of law under which he will act.

The President and all federal agencies shall keep and report to Congress a record of all rules and regulations issued during an emergency. The same applies to all expenditures for emergency actions.[36]

In order to eliminate the possible use of dilatory tactics as a means of preventing a vote on termination, the act specifies the following procedures for handling the concurrent resolution:

1. It shall be referred to the appropriate committee in the House and reported out within fifteen calendar days.

[36]*Public Law* 94–412 (National Emergencies Act), 94th Cong., Sept. 14, 1976, p. 1.

2. It shall then become the pending business on the floor of the House and must be voted on within three calendar days.
3. The resolution will then be sent to the other House where the same procedures shall be followed.
4. If the two Houses should disagree on the concurrent resolution, a conference committee will be formed, which shall report a recommendation back to both Houses within six calendar days.

Unlike the War Powers Act, this one makes no provision for any kind of presidential consultation with the Congress *prior* to the declaration of a national emergency. To set down an absolute requirement that he consult Congress would quite obviously be unrealistic, for the necessity of timely action may preclude that possibility. Yet it might be argued that not all emergencies are of equal severity and thus it would have been appropriate to call upon the President to at least consult with Congress when the circumstances permit. While this argument has some merit, given the fact that Congress may terminate the emergency at any time, it seems likely that any prudent President will seek its advice prior to making his declaration.

Clearly the provisions of this act do indeed render the President more accountable in the exercise of his emergency powers. At the same time, however, it should be noted that neither this act nor anything else one might contemplate is likely to prevent an abuse the likes of which was inflicted upon Japanese-Americans. If the President, Congress, and the American people are convinced that the circumstances are so grave as to require drastic action, that action will be taken, and in all probability it will be upheld by the Court as well. James Madison was well aware of this political reality when he observed that it is "vain to oppose constitutional barriers to the impulse of self-preservation."[37]

[37] James Madison, Federalist Paper No. 41, in Cooke, *The Federalist,* p. 270.

Presidential
Leadership

In a society as competitive as our own, it is not surprising that considerable effort is expended in evaluating performance. We face such evaluation throughout our years of schooling. We face it again as we pursue our careers. While such assessments take place on a daily basis as we interact with those around us, more formalized mechanisms will be used periodically to evaluate our on-the-job performance. Therefore it comes as no surprise that public officials face a similar scrutiny. The importance and visibility of the Presidency, however, make the evaluation process far more intense and persistent. Almost from the day he assumes office, newspapers, magazines, and periodicals carry articles and editorials that seek to assess whether the President is leading well or poorly. Moreover, in addition to assessments by the journalistic and scholarly communities, George Gallup, Louis Harris, and other pollsters provide the nation with almost monthly reports on what kind of job the American public thinks the President is doing. Should a President choose to seek a second term, his performance will once again be subject to the judgment of the American people. Nor does this evaluation process end when his tenure in office is terminated. On the contrary, books and articles then start to appear which seek to assess either his overall performance or some aspect of it. To take just one example, within three years after Kennedy's assassination, some eight books were published on his Presidency. Moreover, as both the passage of time and new information have presumably brought a better perspective, a second generation of books has been published on the assassinated President. These include: Henry Fairlie, *The Kennedy Promise* (1972); Lewis Paper, *The Promise and the Performance* (1975); Bruce Miroff, *Pragmatic Illusions* (1976); Joan and Clay Blair, Jr., *The Search for JFK* (1976); and Carl Brauer, *John F. Kennedy and the Second Reconstruction* (1977). No doubt there will continue to be books written on Kennedy as well as other past presidents, for the judgment of history is an ongoing process.

The evaluation of presidents inevitably leads to a comparison of performances. Indeed, considerable discussion and debate have been devoted to identifying the "great" and "not so great" presidents in our history. Some scholars have written on the subject, and others have polled their fellow academicians to learn what ranking they gave to the men who have occupied the White House. Certainly the most notable effort to rate presidents were the polls conducted by historian Arthur Schlesinger, Sr. (see Table 9-1). In his 1948 poll, he surveyed fifty-five outstanding authorities on American history. He conducted another poll in 1962, this time surveying some seventy-five persons representing a variety of fields, including historians, political scientists, and journalists. As to the standards by which presidents were to be judged, Schlesinger specified only one—namely, performance while in office.

As Table 9-1 indicates, the interest in ranking presidents continues unabated. In 1970, for example, Gary Maranell and Richard Dodder sought the judgments of 571 historians, asking them to rate our presidents on the basis of (1) accomplishment, (2) strength in shaping government and events, (3) an active or passive approach to their administrations, (4) idealism, and (5) flexibility. On the heels of this survey there came another one by Malcolm Parsons in 1972. He asked 146 economists and 120 political scientists to rate presidents—from Franklin Roosevelt to Nixon—on the basis of their (1) idealism, (2) flexibility, (3) activism, and (4) accomplishment. His purpose was, first, to determine whether political scientists as a group differed from economists in their rankings of these five presidents, and second, to see whether the ideological orientation of the respondents influenced their evaluations. In 1975, a random sample of the American public got a chance to express their views when George Gallup asked what three presidents they considered to be the greatest. Finally, the most recent entry into the presidential rating game has been the United States Historical Society, which in 1977 asked ninety-three historians from colleges and universities around the country to pick our ten greatest presidents. No doubt, the fascination with judging and comparing presidents will remain with us.

EVALUATING PRESIDENTIAL LEADERSHIP: THE PROBLEMS

If evaluating presidential performance is something we all do, laymen and scholars alike, it is also important to bear in mind that such an exercise is not as easy as it might appear, for one must confront the difficult question of *how* performance is to be measured. In response to just such a question, one student of the Presidency remarked that "in the final analysis the basic yardstick is the achievement of that individual and his (or her) administration."[1] Although

---

[1] R. Gordon Hoxie, "Presidential Greatness," in Philip Dolce and George Skau, eds., *Power and the Presidency* (New York: Scribner's, 1976), p. 261.

TABLE 9-1. EVALUATIONS OF PRESIDENTIAL PERFORMANCE

Schlesinger Poll 1948	Schlesinger Poll 1962	Maranell-Dodder Poll 1970	Gallup Poll 1975	U.S. Historical Society Poll 1977
Great	*Great*	*Overall prestige*	*What three U.S.*	*Ten greatest*
(1) Lincoln	(1) Lincoln	(1) Lincoln	*presidents do*	*presidents*
(2) Washington	(2) Washington	(2) Washington	*you regard as*	
(3) F. Roosevelt	(3) F. Roosevelt	(3) F. Roosevelt	*the greatest?*	*Votes*
(4) Wilson	(4) Wilson	(4) Jefferson	*(%)*	Lincoln 85
(5) Jefferson	(5) Jefferson	(5) T. Roosevelt	Kennedy 52	Washington 84
(6) Jackson		(6) Wilson	Lincoln 49	F. Roosevelt 81
	Near Great	(7) Truman	F. Roosevelt 45	Jefferson 79
Near Great	(6) Jackson	(8) Jackson	Truman 37	T. Roosevelt 79
(7) T. Roosevelt	(7) T. Roosevelt	(9) Kennedy	Washington 25	Wilson 74
(8) Cleveland	(8) Polk	(10) J. Adams	Eisenhower 24	Jackson 74
(9) J. Adams	(8) Truman	(11) Polk	T. Roosevelt 9	Truman 64
(10) Polk	(9) J. Adams	(12) Cleveland	L. Johnson 9	Polk 38
	(10) Cleveland	(13) Madison	Jefferson 8	J. Adams 35
Average		(14) Monroe	Wilson 5	L. Johnson 24
(11) J.Q. Adams	*Average*	(15) J.Q. Adams	Nixon 9	Cleveland 21
(12) Monroe	(11) Madison	(16) L. Johnson	All others 9	Kennedy 19
(13) Hayes	(12) J.Q. Adams	(17) Taft	Don't know 3	Madison 16
(14) Madison	(13) Hayes	(18) Hoover		J.Q. Adams 14
(15) Van Buren	(14) McKinley	(19) Eisenhower		Eisenhower 14
(16) Taft	(15) Taft	(20) A. Johnson		Monroe 7
(17) Arthur	(16) Van Buren	(21) Van Buren		Hoover 6
(18) McKinley	(17) Monroe	(22) McKinley		McKinley 4
(19) A. Johnson	(18) Hoover	(23) Arthur		Van Buren 2
(20) Hoover	(19) Harrison	(24) Hayes		Arthur 2
(21) Harrison	(20) Arthur	(25) Tyler		Tyler 1
	(20) Eisenhower	(26) Harrison		Buchanan 1
Below average	(21) A. Johnson	(27) Taylor		Grant 1
(22) Tyler		(28) Coolidge		Hayes 1
(23) Coolidge	*Below average*	(20) Fillmore		Taft 1
(24) Fillmore	(22) Taylor	(30) Buchanan		Coolidge 1
(25) Taylor	(23) Tyler	(31) Pierce		Nixon 1
(26) Buchanan	(24) Fillmore	(32) Grant		W. Harrison 0
(27) Pierce	(25) Coolidge	(33) Harding		Taylor 0
	(26) Pierce	(Harrison and		Fillmore 0
Failure	(27) Buchanan	Garfield not		Pierce 0
(28) Grant		included due		A. Johnson 0
(29) Harding	*Failure*	to brevity of		Garfield 0
	(28) Grant	tenure)		B. Harrison 0
	(29) Harding			Harding 0
				Ford 0

SOURCES: Arthur Schlesinger, Sr., "The U.S. Presidents," *Life* (November 1, 1948), p. 65; Arthur Schlesinger, Sr., "Our Presidents: A Rating by 75 Historians," *New York Times Magazine*, July 29, 1962, pp. 12ff; Gary Maranell and Richard Dodder, "Political Orientation and Evaluation of Presidential Prestige: A Study of American Historians," *Social Science Quarterly*, 51 (September 1970), 418; *The Gallup Opinion Index*, February 1976, pp. 14, 15. U.S. Historical Society provided the author with results of its survey.

few would dispute this statement, we are still faced with a variety of factors that complicate the task of determining *what constitutes achievement.* Let us examine some of these factors more closely.

Achievement Is in the Eye of the Beholder

All of us carry around a cargo of values, beliefs, and orientations that influence our perceptions of the world around us—including presidents. These values and beliefs determine the yardsticks by which we choose to measure presidents. For example, in their study of how 571 historians ranked presidents, Maranell and Dodder found that liberal historians valued *flexibility* and *idealism* in presidents, while conservative historians did not.[2] To take another example, Clinton Rossiter suggests that one of the standards for assessing presidential greatness must be a President's philosophy of presidential power. More specifically, he argues that effective leadership is in part dependent upon an activist view of presidential power: "Indeed, if he is not widely and persistently accused in his own time of 'subverting the Constitution,' he may as well forget about being judged a truly eminent man by future generations."[3] Some would readily share Rossiter's expansive view of presidential power. Others, however, would reject it as too permissive and, instead, concur with President Taft, who maintained that the President could exercise only those powers specifically granted or else reasonably implied to him: "There is no undefined residuum of power which he can exercise because it seems to him to be in the public interest." Still others may not be philosophically opposed to an expansive view of presidential power as such, so long as it is used for purposes consistent with their own values and beliefs. No doubt many of those who are opposed to the spending of vast sums of money on social welfare programs applauded Nixon's vigorous use of the impoundment power to cut back on such programs. On the other hand, those who feel that the federal government has an obligation to look after the less-well-off parts of the population surely saw Nixon's bold impoundments as callous and unwarranted. In short, what one sees depends on a considerable extent upon where one stands.

The Situational Problem

The task of evaluating presidential leadership is further complicated by the fact that our presidents have not all entered the White House confronting the same set of circumstances, opportunities, and expectations. On the contrary, if one views the Presidency in a broad time frame, it is clear that during most

[2]Gary Maranell and Richard Dodder, "Political Orientation and the Evaluation of Presidential Prestige: A Study of American Historians," *Social Science Quarterly* 51 (September 1970), 421.

[3]Clinton Rossiter, *The American Presidency* (New York: New American Library, 1960), pp. 138, 139.

of this century presidents have had to function in an environment decidedly different from that faced by presidents in the eighteenth and nineteenth centuries. Our earlier presidents did not have to contend with a large and complex federal bureaucracy or with such a large, culturally diverse, and urbanized population. Moreover, since they served at a time when the role of the federal government was minimal, public expectations regarding the role of the President were limited also. As we have gradually looked more and more to the federal government to solve the nation's economic and social problems, inevitably we have also expected more of our presidents in these areas. Our earlier presidents likewise faced a very different international environment. The United States had not yet had thrust upon it the responsibility of leading the free world; our economic and security interests were not yet so intimately tied to those of other nations; and finally, neither we nor any potential adversary had the capacity to incinerate the planet with nuclear weapons.

If the presidential environment varies over centuries, it may also be said that it varies from one Presidency to the next. George Washington, for example, was faced with the unique task of starting a newly constituted government off on the right foot, In presiding over a divided nation, Abraham Lincoln confronted the greatest internal crisis in the history of our republic. Woodrow Wilson was the first President to take the nation into a world war. Franklin Roosevelt had to guide the nation during another world war abroad as well as lead us through an unprecedented economic crisis at home. Truman had to ponder not only the future of the European nations that had been devastated by the war, but also the use of a weapon whose capacity for destruction was qualitatively different from anything the world had ever known. Eisenhower presided over the nation at a time when we no longer had a monopoly on nuclear weapons. Rather, the new reality of international politics was that the Soviet Union had the capacity to inflict devastating damage upon the United States and its allies. Lyndon Johnson took over the Presidency at a time of rising expectations among blacks and at a time when urban decay had reached crisis proportions. His successor had to find a way to get us out of what had become the most unpopular war in our history, as well as try to bind up the social wounds caused by it. When Gerald Ford took over the reins of power, he too confronted several unique circumstances: he came into office without having been chosen by a national constituency; he had to lead a population whose cynicism about government had reached an all-time high; and finally, he had to grapple with two problems heretofore unknown to presidents, namely, an energy shortage and stagflation.

In judging presidential performance, it may be argued that we must take into consideration not only the nature of the times in which a given President served, but also the political constraints—legal and otherwise—under which he governed. For example, given the fact that a President customarily enjoys a decided advantage by having his own party in control of Congress, should we not expect more from presidents who enjoy this advantage? Likewise, since

1951, all presidents have labored under the twenty-second amendment, which limits a President to only two terms. As noted in an earlier chapter, this limitation undoubtedly has some effect upon his political leverage as he moves through his second term. Given this fact, we may well decide that expectations should be higher for those presidents who did not labor under this restriction. More recently, an increasingly assertive Congress has passed legislation such as the Case Act (1972), Technology Assessment Act (1972), War Powers Resolution (1973), Budget Control and Impoundment Act (1974), National Emergencies Act (1976)—all of which were designed to provide greater congressional involvement in areas previously dominated by the President. Whether or not these acts accomplish their purposes remains to be seen. If they do, then it may be argued that the constraints created by this legislation constitute additional factors that must be weighed in evaluating the performance of those presidents who must function under them.

One final aspect of the situational problem deserves mention here; namely, to what extent is our evaluation of a President's performance conditioned by the momentous nature of the times in which he served? Clinton Rossiter states the answer bluntly: "A man cannot possibly be judged a great President unless he holds office in great times . . . This standard may work unfairly on Presidents who live under sunny skies, but that is the way that history is written."[4] Certainly the available evidence gives some credence to this view. Note that of the top five presidents appearing in each of the polls reproduced in Table 9-1, a majority served during times of great moment. In the case of Washington, it was his fate to be the first to lead the country under a wholly new set of constitutional arrangements. For Lincoln, Wilson, Franklin Roosevelt, and Truman, it was leading the nation in wartime. Yet if governing during a period of great crisis enhances the chances of being judged a great leader, it does not insure it. James Madison, for example, presided over the nation during the War of 1812, and yet his performance in office has generally been appraised as mediocre. Nor did Herbert Hoover benefit from the fact that he occupied the Presidency during the greatest economic crisis in our history. Quite the contrary. He has been roundly criticized for his failure to respond to it. Great times only provide the opportunity for leadership. The wherewithal necessary to meet such challenges must come from the man in the White House.

Of course, our discussion here presumes that the greatest test of leadership comes during times of crisis. This presumption is open to some question. Indeed, it may be the case that we have every right to expect greater things from the President who serves under "dark" as opposed to "sunny" skies. By their very nature, great crises bind the country and the government together behind the President, thereby greatly facilitating his ability to act. As already noted earlier in this text, both Abraham Lincoln and Franklin Roosevelt took some extra-

[4]Ibid., p. 138.

ordinary initiatives in meeting their respective crises. Some were of doubtful constitutionality, and in the case of Lincoln, others were clearly unconstitutional. But all had the support of both the public and the Congress. In more tranquil times, however, mobilizing support is not so easily accomplished. To do so, therefore, may require that a President be even more skilled and resourceful in seeking to unite the Congress and the public behind his purposes.

The Problem of Perspective

Another factor that complicates the task of evaluating presidential performance is *time*. With its passage inevitably comes the uncovering of new information that may alter judgments of a Presidency in either a favorable or unfavorable direction. Assessments of John Kennedy's performance provide one of the most dramatic examples of this. The appraisals that appeared not long after his death were, for the most part, highly favorable. In the last several years, however, the glitter surrounding Kennedy has been tarnished by a series of revelations. Some concerned his personal life. Others related to certain government activities undertaken during his stewardship: for example, the tapping of Martin Luther King's telephone by the FBI and the CIA's attempt to assassinate Patrice Lumumba as well as its use of Mafia connections in an effort to assassinate Fidel Castro. Even if it has not been firmly established that Kennedy was aware of such activities, the fact is he should have been. These revelations, coupled with claims that the Kennedy years were long on style and short on substance, have led even one of his most ardent admirers to acknowledge, ". . . there's no doubt about it: the idea that Kennedy was a minor figure of limited achievement is widely held today and can be supported in a depth not possible in 1964. . . ."[5] Whether or not this proves to be the final judgment on the Kennedy Administration remains to be seen.

In addition to new information, our initial perspective on a given Presidency may also be altered by intervening events. Thus, when viewed in the context of the Watergate squalor, or when compared with the imperial tones that characterized the Johnson and Nixon presidencies, the openness and simplicity of Truman and Eisenhower assume greater significance. The Vietnam War constitutes still another example of an event that has altered our perspective on the past. The nation was much moved by President Kennedy's inaugural address in which he made a seemingly boundless commitment to the defense of freedom: "Let every nation know, whether it wishes us well or ill, that we shall pay any price, bear any burden, meet any hardship, support any friend, oppose any foe, in order to assure the survival and the success of liberty. This much we pledge—and more." This policy, which was responsible for out initial involvement in Vietnam under the Kennedy Administration, now appears excessive, to say the least.

[5] From *On Press* by Tom Wicker. Copyright © Tom Wicker, 1978. Reprinted by permission of Viking Penguin Inc.

On the other hand, the protracted war in Vietnam appears to have brought some luster to the Eisenhower Presidency. When the French suffered a resounding defeat at the hands of the North Vietnamese in 1954, Eisenhower was under considerable pressure to commit American forces to the area. Fully aware of how large a commitment would be necessary to do the job, Ike decided against any United States involvement. While in the past this decision never loomed large among his accomplishments, in light of our recent experience in Southeast Asia, it now takes on considerably greater meaning. Indeed, in commenting on the reassessment of Eisenhower, one commentator points out that we have only recently begun to appreciate his astuteness in foreign affairs: "We were at war when he came to office, and six months later we were out of it, and we did not enter another war during his tenure. . . . Eight years of Eisenhower: seven and a half of peace. Ten years of Kennedy, Johnson, Nixon: almost ten solid years of war."[6]

The Matter of Unanticipated Consequences

If a given presidential decision proves to be an especially wise one, we are inclined to chalk it up as a plus for his performance record, regardless of what a President's motives might have been at the time the decision was initially made. The purchase of Alaska in 1867 may serve as an illustration of this. At the initiative of his Secretary of State William Seward, President Andrew Johnson authorized the purchase of Alaska from the Russians for the sum of $7.2 million. At the time this decision was made, and for years afterward, it was generally viewed as a waste of money. Indeed, in many quarters the Alaskan territory was derisively characterized by such expressions as "Seward's Icebox" and "Johnson's Polar Bear Garden." Quite obviously, no one would share this assessment nowadays, given the events that have intervened since then. On the contrary, in the words of historian Thomas Bailey, ". . . now that Alaska has panned out with gold, fish, and furs, and has become a state of enormous economic and strategic value, we think more highly of Andrew Johnson's floundering administration for having brought off the coup. It will probably stand as the most significant single act of the ex-tailor's troubled four years, even though it was conceived and carried through by his expansionist Secretary of State. . . ."[7] Yet one may well question whether Johnson should reap the praise for such a decision if only because, as Bailey implies, Seward originated the proposal and was largely responsible for engineering its approval by Congress. But there is an even more fundamental consideration, namely, that the acquisition of Alaska has proven *most* beneficial for reasons that neither Johnson nor Seward could have anticipated. While Seward was aware of some of Alaska's resources, his primary

[6] Cited in Vincent De Santis, "Eisenhower Revisionism," *Review of Politics* 38 (April 1976), 198.

[7] Thomas Bailey, *Presidential Greatness* (Englewood Cliffs, N.J.: Prentice-Hall, 1966), p. 41.

motive for the purchase was to allow the United States to develop its commerce on the Pacific Ocean. As he once remarked, "Japan, China, and Australia are . . . commercially bound to the American Pacific coast"; on another occasion, he noted "the extension of American invention and enterprise into Japan, China, Australia, and India as worthy of consideration equally with international commerce between the United States and the countries of Western Europe."[8] No one at that time could have known that Alaska housed vast oil reserves; nor, more importantly, could they have known that Russia—with whom we enjoyed cordial relations at the time—would one day constitute our major adversary on the international stage.

While we may well want to credit presidents for decisions that demonstrated a sense of vision and foresight, we must also be careful to distinguish such decisions from those that proved highly beneficial largely because of fortuitous circumstance.

Achievement versus Agenda Setting

In assessing presidential performance, we must also consider the question of whether presidents are to be given credit only for what they accomplished, or are we also to recognize them for what they *tried* to accomplish? In 1948, for example, Preisdent Truman addressed the Democratic National Convention and proclaimed that it was time for the government to correct the injustices so long inflicted upon blacks. Accordingly, he announced that he would call Congress into special session to consider civil rights legislation. While no such legislation was ever passed by the Congress, Truman nevertheless began the process of elevating into the public mind an issue that had long been ignored by his predecessors. Moreover, he did so not only by calling for legislation, but also through creation of a Commission on Civil Rights and the issuance of an executive order calling for the desegregation of the armed forces.

Although civil rights legislation was passed in 1957 and 1960, it was not the result of vigorous presidential leadership. Indeed, active presidential involvement in civil rights did not come again until the Presidency of John Kennedy. While he trod gingerly on the civil rights issue at first, in the spring of 1963 Kennedy introduced into Congress the most broadsweeping civil rights bill to date and threw the full weight of the Presidency behind it. Yet at the time of his death, Kennedy had still not succeeded in getting his civil rights legislation passed; nor for that matter, had he been successful in gaining passage of other important pieces of his New Frontier legislation—Medicare, for example. It took instead the subtle political skills of Lyndon Johnson to engineer congressional approval of civil rights legislation, Medicare, and several other Kennedy programs. No doubt Johnson must be given considerable credit for his ability to

[8] Ernest Paolino, *The Foundations of the American Empire* (Ithaca, N.Y.: Cornell University Press, 1973), pp. 117, 118.

get things done. But is Kennedy to receive no recognition merely because he failed where Johnson succeeded? Some will surely argue that credit is also due to those presidents who identify certain crucial issues and raise them to the level of national visibility, thereby compelling the nation to take notice of them. Even though Kennedy was unsuccessful in realizing his goals in such areas as civil rights and health care, he did succeed in placing these issues on the national agenda. Had he not done so, the needed legislation in these areas may well have come later rather than sooner.

The Matter of Who Gets Credit

Given the fact that the Presidency constitutes the focal point of our political system, we have a tendency to identify a given President with whatever successes or failures may have occurred during his tenure in office. In doing so, we may be making judgments about presidents that, in some instances, are either overly generous or unduly harsh. We should not, for example, give credit for an accomplishment that was realized despite a President rather than because of him. In this connection, it is worth noting that the Reconstruction Finance Corporation, though created during the final year of the Hoover Administration, was nevertheless strongly opposed by Hoover himself. Similarly, while the Federal Deposit Insurance Corporation is generally regarded as one of the major accomplishments of Franklin Roosevelt's Administration, the fact is that he came out against the legislation.[9]

There may be other accomplishments realized during a given President's tenure which, though not necessarily opposed by him, nevertheless occurred for reasons having very little to do with his own leadership. Thus, while it so happens that we landed a man on the moon during the Presidency of Richard Nixon, he scarcely deserves any of the credit for such an achievement. Rather, if there is any recognition to be given, it must go to President Kennedy who, back in 1961, committed the resources of the nation to the goal of putting a man on the moon by the end of the decade. Similarly, we generally credit Franklin Roosevelt with pulling us out of the greatest economic crisis in our history, and yet his own programs had relatively little to do with it. To be sure, the economy did improve in 1935-36, but this was only temporary. By 1937, the unemployment rate had reached 20 percent and the index of business activity was down by thirty-five percentage points—the most rapid decline ever recorded. The major factor ultimately responsible for lifting us out of the economic doldrums was our entry into the Second World War.[10] All of this is not to say that Roosevelt deserves no credit for his efforts. If his programs were not successful in taking us out of the depression, many of them did manage to

[9] Bailey, *Presidential Greatness,* pp. 104, 105.

[10] Thomas Cochran, *The Great Depression and World War II* (Glenview, Ill.: Scott, Foresman, 1968), p. 78.

alleviate its consequences. Moreover, the very fact that Roosevelt was doing *something* undoubtedly provided a psychological boost to a population long frustrated by the inaction of his predecessor. The fact remains, however, that our economic recovery was due primarily to events rather than to Roosevelt's own initiatives.

One final aspect of the "who gets credit" problem is also worth considering here. We value the ability of a President and his Administration to come up with new ideas and approaches for dealing with pressing problems. But should the recognition we give to such creative approaches be tempered by a consideration of *where* they originated? In 1950, for example, the Truman Administration sought and received congressional approval of the Food for Peace program. This called for shipping surplus grain to needy countries. In the early sixties the Kennedy Administration established the Peace Corps and secured Senate ratification of the Nuclear Test Ban treaty. Yet the ideas for these efforts did not originate with the Truman or the Kennedy administrations. Rather, they were all first proposed by Senator Hubert Humphrey.[11] Thus, while both Truman and Kennedy may deserve considerable credit for having the discernment to seize upon a good idea, it may nevertheless be argued that whatever points are to be awarded for originality and creativity must go to the late Senator from Minnesota.

QUALITIES OF LEADERSHIP

Thus far we have focused on some of the factors that complicate the task of evaluating presidential leadership in terms of achievement, or if you will, results. I do not propose here to resolve all of these difficulties. Instead, in the remaining pages of this final chapter, I would like to identify a number of qualities and skills that seem necessary to gain results. Before doing so, however, several qualifying remarks are in order. First, one will not find universal agreement on what qualities are deemed essential to effective leadership. Thus, some would no doubt want to add or subtract from the ones I have chosen to identify. Second, given the absence of a firmly based empirical literature on this subject, our discussion is admittedly impressionistic. Third, when viewing the qualities and skills identified here we should bear in mind the enduring context in which a President must function. Under a different set of political and institutional arrangements, some of these qualities and skills might not be necessary in the same degree; others might not be necessary at all. Finally, while the following qualities and skills seem—to this author—essential to effective presidential leadership, it is also the case that some will be needed to a greater extent under some circumstances than under others.

[11] *Congressional Quarterly Weekly Report,* January 21, 1978, p. 111.

Empathy with the Public

In the final analysis, there are two constituencies that are most important to a President—Congress and the public. As already noted, much of what a President wants to accomplish requires the cooperation of Congress. Yet unlike parliamentary democracies, our own does not guarantee that a President will have the support of his party in Congress, let alone have a majority. Thus, in attempting to persuade the Congress to do his bidding, he needs the additional leverage that broad public support can provide. For to the extent that a President is perceived as having a wide following in the population, other elected officials will be considerably more receptive to his programs. In the words of Woodrow Wilson, "Let him once win the admiration and confidence of the country, and no other single force can withstand him, no combination of forces will easily overpower him."[12]

To gain this needed support, however, the President must know the people he seeks to lead. He must have the capacity to understand their hopes and aspirations, their fears and anxieties; he must be able to sense their moods. If he lacks this "feel" for his people, he will have difficulty not only in knowing how to respond to them, but also in getting them to respond to him.

The development of such an understanding is undoubtedly facilitated by the nature of our electoral process. Grueling though they may be, the nominating and election campaigns provide an important means of educating presidential candidates about the nation and its people. Walter Mondale, for example, despite his other objections to our selection process, readily acknowledges this fact:

> A Presidential campaign requires a candidate to speak throughout the nation, to listen carefully, and to learn about the problems of regions and communities. All of this is an essential part of the education of potential Presidents about this country. I think only candidates can realize how incredibly vast and varied America is. It is only this way that candidates can become familiar with this country, with its people and their leaders, with its problems. In this way, they can come to respect the differences that exist in our country. And through this educational process a truly national leader, capable of dealing intelligently, responsibly and respectfully with our nation's problems, can be developed.[13]

This education process cannot end on the campaign trail. It must also continue in the White House. Yet no elective office in this country removes an individual further from the people than the Presidency does. Keeping in touch, therefore, requires a special effort. It will help for a President to surround himself with people of diverse backgrounds, with people who have varied contacts with dif-

[12]Taken from *The Promise and the Performance* by Lewis J. Paper (New York: Crown, 1975), p. 201. ©1975 by Lewis J. Paper. Used by permission of Crown Publishers, Inc.

[13]Walter Mondale, *The Accountability of Power* (New York. David McKay, 1975), p. 260.

ferent segments of the community. It will also help if some of these people have themselves been directly involved in elective politics. Most important, the President must make himself accessible not only to those within his immediate circle, but also to others both in and outside government. No President did so to a greater degree than Franklin Roosevelt, and none was more skillful at sensing the pulse of the nation.

The costs for failing to comprehend the public mood can be high indeed. Woodrow Wilson suffered the major defeat of his Presidency when he stubbornly refused to accept Senate changes in the treaty creating the League of Nations. In so refusing, he insisted that such changes were opposed not only by himself but also by the American people. In actuality, the public overwhelmingly supported them.[14] Hoover was soundly trounced in the 1932 election because he persisted in preaching against government intervention to help a faltering economy, erroneously believing that the American people also shared his view.[15] Although he was usually masterful at gauging public sentiment, Franklin Roosevelt failed to do so accurately when he presented his court-packing proposal. The result was one of the most embarrassing political blunders of his Presidency. Apparently Richard Nixon also failed to grasp the limits of public tolerance when he executed the now famous "Saturday Night Massacre," an act that produced more letters and telegrams of protest to members of Congress than any presidential action in our history.

An Ability to Communicate

William Allen White made a telling point when he observed that, "A democracy cannot follow a leader unless he is dramatized. A man to be a hero must not content himself with heroic virtues and anonymous action. He must talk and explain as he acts—drama."[16] Few would dispute the fact that the towering political figures of this century were exceptionally skillful at communicating with those they sought to lead. In part this skill involves a manner of expression that moves and inspires; in part, an ability to take the people into one's confidence; and in part, a talent for putting issues and goals in a way that makes them readily comprehensible. Of Churchill, for example, it was said that he "marshalled the English language and sent it into battle." Indeed, his skill in this regard both comforted and inspired the British people as they faced the relentless destruction heaped upon them by the Nazi war machine. Among American presidents, Theodore Roosevelt, Woodrow Wilson, and John Kennedy were all captivating speakers; others such as Eisenhower, Johnson, and Ford were notably less so. None excelled in this area more than Franklin Roosevelt, however.

---

[14] Paper, *Promise and Performance*, p. 215.

[15] Ibid., p. 204.

[16] Cited in Emmet John Hughes, *The Living Presidency* (New York: Coward, McCann & Geoghegan, 1972), p. 101. Copyright © 1973 by Emmet John Hughes. Reprinted by permission of Coward, McCann & Geoghegan.

His gift for communicating lay first in his ability to create a sense of intimacy with his audience, whether it was large or small. His radio talks to the American people were indeed "chats" rather than addresses. In addition, he was unusually adept at reducing issues to their essence, so that the public had little difficulty in grasping their meaning. Thus, following Roosevelt's first fireside chat, which announced the bank holiday, Will Rogers commented that "Roosevelt explained the banking situation so well even the bankers understood it." FDR's skill in this regard was best exemplified in the simple but effective analogy he used to explain the Lend Lease program to the American people:

> Suppose my neighbor's home catches on fire and I have a length of garden hose four or five hundred feet away. If he can take my garden hose and connect it up with his hydrant, I may help him to put out his fire. Now what do I do? I don't say to him before that operation, "Neighbor, my garden hose cost me $15; you have to pay me $15 for it." What is the transaction that goes on? I don't want $15—I want my garden hose back after the fire is over. All right. If it goes through the fire all right, intact, without any damage to it, he gives it back to me and thanks me very much for the use of it.[17]

Finally, his communicating style was also characterized by a flair for the dramatic when the circumstances required it. Moreover, Roosevelt was well aware of this talent, noting to one aid that he and Orson Welles were the two best actors in the country. In contrast to FDR, Presidents Taft and Hoover did not seek to dramatize their leadership through words or action. Taft concluded, "I have made up my mind . . . that I will not play a part for popularity. . . . I cannot be spectacular." Similarly, Hoover appeared committed to the belief that the Presidency "is not a showman's job." But as Emmet Hughes has aptly pointed out, in taking this approach to leadership, both of these presidents were ignoring a reality recognized even by our very first President, who once remarked: "The truth is the people must *feel* before they will *see*."[18]

With the advent of radio and television, the ability of a President to communicate effectively through the spoken word has quite obviously assumed even greater importance. But there are also more recent developments that render communication skills even more indispensable for the man who occupies the White House at this point in time. For one thing, in recent years the overall trend in party identification has been downward; even among those who identify with a political party, the "weak" identifiers outnumber the "strong."[19] This trend suggests that the President's hard-core base of support within the population is

---

[17]Cited in Paper, *Promise and Performance,* p. 218.

[18]Cited in Hughes, *Living Presidency,* pp. 94, 101.

[19]Arthur Miller and Warren Miller, "Partisanship and Performance: 'Rational' Choice in the 1976 Presidential Election" (Paper presented at the Annual Meeting of the American Political Science Association, Washington, D.C., September 1-4, 1977), p. 9.

not only smaller but also less committed. Therefore, it may erode even more quickly than in the past unless he is especially effective at explaining and justifying to the people what he has done, what he wants to do, and why.

Second, Carter must compete with the communications media, which in the aftermath of Watergate have become decidedly more skeptical and questioning about what the government is doing. Speaking to the problems he faced during his first year, for example, the President took note of the media's tendency to "separate the component parts of an overall objective, to emphasize failure, that does make it very difficult for me as President to keep before the public consciousness what we hope to achieve."[20] One observer of the Washington scene sees this tendency in even more severe terms: "It is beginning to seem as if, once America elects a leader, it immediately sets about demolishing him, sprawling him across its front pages like an insect on a windshield. How can its allies trust the United States not to pull a President down into the gutter on the smallest pretext?"[21]

Third, in seeking to articulate what he perceives to be in the public interest, the President must speak above the voices of an ever-growing chorus of well-organized and well-financed special interests, all seeking to get their share of government benefits. Moreover, to the extent that domestic and foreign issues are increasingly intertwined, his voice must now compete with those of the special interests in foreign as well as domestic policy.

Finally, while previous presidents have faced crises that essentially spoke for themselves, Jimmy Carter finds himself confronting an energy crisis the major impact of which has yet to be felt. Given the public disposition to focus upon the immediate, persuasive indeed must be the President who is asking for sacrifices *now* so that we may avoid severe energy shortages at some future date.

While there was initially a good deal of optimism regarding Jimmy Carter's ability to communicate with the population, at this writing there is growing concern over his effectiveness in this area.[22] The energy program may serve as an illustration. In his first year in office, Carter gave three nationally televised addresses on this issue. In the first, he sought to demonstrate that the crisis was real, declaring the "moral equivalent of war" on energy. Two days later, he appeared before a joint session of Congress to outline his proposed solutions. This was followed the next day with a nationally televised news conference in which he further elaborated on his previous remarks on energy. While his speeches had some impact initially, the President was still not able to develop sustained public support for his program. Sensing this, he gave still another televised address to the American people some six months later. Unfortunately, by way of both content and style, it proved to be the most ineffective address he has given since taking office. Indeed, Carter's lack of success in dramatizing the

---

[20] *New York Times,* October 23, 1977, p. 36. © 1977 by the New York Times Company. Reprinted by permission.

[21] *Washington Post,* September 18, 1977, p. B8.

[22] *Washington Post,* January 30, 1977, p. A2.

crisis nature of the energy problem was reflected in a Gallup poll taken in February 1978, which found that only 23 percent of the American people felt that the energy shortage was the most important problem confronting the nation.

Credibility

Whatever skills a President may have at expressing his views and purposes, they will do him little good if the people are not prepared to believe what he has to say. In a democracy, trust is the vital link between the leaders and the led. While the citizenry may forgive varying kinds of presidential ineptitude, it will not forgive those who have themselves violated the public trust or who have surrounded themselves with others who did. Nor, apparently, is the judgment of history much more tolerant. Note, for example, that in three of the five rating surveys appearing in Table 9-1, the two lowest rankings are reserved for those presidents whose administrations were characterized by widespread corruption. In the case of President Grant, he freely appointed his own relatives to a variety of different government positions and allowed himself to be manipulated by people around him whose activities ranged from graft to defrauding the government. During the Harding Administration the discovery of bribery in connection with the sale of government-owned oil lands produced the great Teapot Dome scandal. In addition, corrupt practices were uncovered in both the Veterans' Bureau and the Office of the Attorney General. Nor was that all, for three of Harding's Cabinet officers were forced to resign, with one suffering the added indignity of going to prison. Yet given the fact that neither Grant nor Harding was directly involved in the scandals around them, the judgment of history might have been more charitable had there been some overriding achievement in other areas of their administrations. Such was not the case, however.

Although the scandals of the Truman Administration in no way approached those of Grant and Harding, they were significant enough to be made a major campaign issue in 1952. Indeed, a Gallup poll taken in February/March 1952 revealed that 57 percent of those surveyed agreed with the statement that "the Democratic party is loaded down with graft and corruption."[23] Although Truman was not involved in any of the corruption uncovered at the Bureau of Internal Revenue, the Reconstruction Finance Corporation, and the Department of Justice, he was far less sensitive to these problems than he should have been. Thus, despite the fact that he did not discourage investigations into any of these agencies, he nevertheless defended far too long some of the people involved. Truman's popularity ultimately dipped all the way down to 23 percent, and while the Korean War and the firing of MacArthur were important contributing factors, the fact remains that his popularity reached its lowest ebb after the scandals broke into the news. In the words of one Truman scholar, "The moral fiber of the Truman administration had been called into question by the highly

[23] George Gallup, *The Gallup Poll, Public Opinion 1935-1971,* vol. II (New York: Random House, 1972), p. 1051.

publicized revelations of spoilsmongering. The personal authority of the President had been undermined."[24]

History, however, has taken a far more favorable view of Truman than did his contemporaries. No doubt this assessment has been due not only to Truman's lack of personal involvement in the scandals that tarnished his Administration, but also to formidable achievements such as the Marshall Plan, NATO, and the Truman Doctrine.

The scandals of Watergate differ from the others just mentioned in two important respects. First, the primary motive was not a monetary one but rather a desire to use the power of the federal government to harass and intimidate "enemies" of the Nixon Administration. Second, the escapades of Watergate directly implicated the President of the United States. In some instances he gave his approval to certain activities; in others, he tried to cover them up; in still others, he did both. Had Nixon himself not been directly involved, he might well have survived his second term—although in a drastically weakened position, to be sure. But as soon as the public became firmly convinced that he and those around him had violated the public trust on a massive scale, his public support rating underwent one of the most precipitous declines of any President on record. His trip to Moscow and his tumultuous reception in Egypt did little to slow it. Nor were attempts to defend himself in television addresses and televised news conferences enough to reverse it.

In the aftermath of Watergate, we may well ponder whether presidents and their associates will be more hardpressed to maintain the public trust than they have been in the past. Some fear that after having lived through an administration (i.e., Nixon's) in which standards of moral conduct were almost nonexistent, we may now have gone to the opposite extreme and imposed standards that are too high. Irving Kristol speaks to this point:

> Though Americans have always been cynical about political corruption and petty abuses of official prerogatives, they have also been aware—deep down—that it is not really so trivial a matter. . . .
>
> Unfortunately, however, the other side of American political cynicism is American self-righteous moralism. The demand for "clean government" becomes an insistence on a degree of political purity which, in the real world, is either not within human reach or is itself self-destructive. At the moment, this kind of moralistic fervor is in full swing, and is notable in the vigilantelike passion with which the news media track down every sort of misdemeanor committed by officials, no matter how trivial or ambiguous or even nonexistent.[25]

[24] Bert Cochran, *Harry Truman and the Crisis Presidency* (New York: Funk and Wagnalls, 1973), p. 386.

[25] Irving Kristol, "Post-Watergate Morality: Too Good for Our Good?" *New York Times Magazine,* November 14, 1976, p. 35. © 1976 by the New York Times Company. Reprinted by permission.

Gerald Ford, for example, was called to task in several quarters for failing to fire his FBI director (Clarence Kelley), who had apparently accepted a few relatively inexpensive gifts from his employees. Similarly, Commerce Secretary Elliot Richardson found himself being questioned on the propriety of his appearances at fund-raising events held for President Ford. Moreover, Richardson also notes that throughout 1976 he received calls from the press and public interest groups to see if his phone calls to convention delegates were being charged to the government.[26] It hardly seems likely that activities such as these would have raised many eyebrows prior to Watergate.

Jimmy Carter may also have been tarnished because of "post-Watergate morality." While both the Lance and the Marston "affairs" deserved the scrutiny they received, once again one wonders whether the press and other groups would have pursued them with such vigilance in the pre-Watergate era. Of course, Carter himself must shoulder most of the blame for whatever credibility he may have lost as a result of these two incidents. He did, after all, fully embrace the post-Watergate morality during his campaign, noting that his Administration would not tolerate even the *appearance* of impropriety. Whether Bert Lance's bank dealings were improper is a matter of some debate, but clearly they gave the appearance of being so. Yet the President continued to give him his full support. The removal of one William Marston as U.S. Attorney in Philadelphia also raised doubts on at least two scores: first, he was replaced at a time when he was investigating two Democratic congressmen from Pennsylvania; second, while Carter had pledged that he would appoint U.S. attorneys without regard to partisanship, nevertheless he ultimately justified his removal of Marston on the grounds that he was a Republican. Given the fragile nature of the public's confidence in government officials, and given also the fact that Carter had pledged higher standards of conduct, his handling of both the Lance and Marston affairs was inappropriate, to say the least.

A Sense of Timing

Victor Hugo once remarked that "there is no force on earth greater than an idea whose time has come." Those presidents who have been especially successful in realizing their goals were also skillful at knowing when the time was ripe for action. They tested the winds of public and congressional sentiment, and if the winds were blowing in the right direction, they moved ahead. If not, then they would bide their time, perhaps waiting for unfolding events to take hold and push the public to the point of receptivity. Or if events could not speak louder than words, they might take to the hustings and try to educate the population to their purposes. But whether through events or their own actions, or both, when the propitious moment arrived, they acted.

---

[26] Elliot Richardson, "The Sexless Orgies of Morality," *New York Times Magazine,* January 23, 1977, p. 33. © 1977 by The New York Times Company. Reprinted by permission.

By all accounts, Lincoln appears to have been a master at timing. James Russell Lowell, in his essay on Lincoln, testifies to this fact:

> Time was his prime minister, and, we began to think, at one period, his general-in-chief also. At first he was so slow that he tired out all those who see no evidence of progress but in blowing up the engine; then he was so fast, that he took the breath away from those who think there is no getting on safely while there is a spark of fire under the boilers. God is the only being who has time enough; but a prudent man, who knows how to seize the occasion, can commonly make a shift to find as much as he needs. Mr. Lincoln, as it seems to us in reviewing his career, though we have sometimes in our impatience thought otherwise, has always waited, as a wise man should, till the right moment brought up all his reserves. *Semper nocuit differre paratis* is a sound axiom, but the really efficacious man will also be sure to know when he is *not* ready, and be firm against all persuasion and reproach till he is.[27]

Nowhere was his skill in this area more apparent than in his decision regarding the Emancipation Proclamation. Despite constant pressure to free the slaves, Lincoln deferred. There was no doubt in his mind but that such a time would eventually come, however: "I can see emancipation coming; whoever can wait for it will see it; whoever stands in its way will be run over."[28] Indeed, he had drafted the proclamation well before he decided to issue it. But his delay in doing so was motivated by several considerations. For one thing, he wanted to hold off until he was sure that the slave-holding border states would remain in the Union. Second, he wanted to wait until he had firmly cemented the support of the British, for if they had recognized the Confederacy, the Union cause would have been dealt a serious blow. Finally, he was also looking for a dramatic event on the battlefield, which would give greater import to the proclamation. Lincoln ultimately succeeded in gaining the support of the border states as well as the British. Moreover, the Battle at Antietam supplied him with the dramatic event he was awaiting, for even though the casualties were heavy on both sides, this historic confrontation demonstrated Lee's inability to penetrate the North successfully. Shortly thereafter Lincoln issued the Emancipation Proclamation.

Among presidents in this century, few were as adept at identifying the propitious moment as Franklin Roosevelt. He was not speaking lightly when he remarked, "I cannot go any faster than the people will let me." In seeking to determine just how fast that was, he constantly tested the waters of public opinion, with one of his favorite tactics being to get a Cabinet member to give a speech on an idea that was currently under consideration. If the speech produced a favorable reaction, Roosevelt would take the idea and run with it himself. On the other hand, if it fell on deaf ears, he would disown it or else try to educate the public toward acceptance. His sensitivity to the public mood on

---

[27] James Russell Lowell, *Political Essays* (Boston: Houghton Mifflin, 1871), pp. 188, 189.

[28] Cited in Hughes, *Living Presidency,* p. 111.

occasion caused considerable frustration among his advisers, however. In the years 1940–41, for example, several of them pleaded with him to ask the Congress for a declaration of war. Although Roosevelt was well aware that the United States would inevitably have to enter the Second World War, he also recognized that the public was not yet ready for such a bold step. Accordingly, throughout 1940–41, he gradually increased our commitment to the British and the Russians, sensing all the while how much of an escalation the public would tolerate, and helping to prepare them for it as well. Thus, he insured that when we ultimately did enter the war, we would do so as a united nation. As he knew only too well, such had not been the case when we entered the First World War.[29]

Although Lyndon Johnson was hardly the equal of Roosevelt in communicating with the public and preparing them for what he wanted to do, he did have a keen sense for how events could set the stage for what he hoped to accomplish. Moreover, no President in our history had a more subtle understanding of how and when to move on Congress. If the public was Roosevelt's compass, the Congress was Johnson's.

Following the assassination of Martin Luther King, for example, he immediately reintroduced into Congress his legislation designed to prevent discrimination in housing. Whereas this legislation had been defeated on two previous occasions, this time it passed both Houses of Congress and was immediately signed into law by the President. While some may have seen Johnson's timing as a crass attempt to play upon emotions, others no doubt saw it as a stroke of political genius. So too was his timing on the crucially important Voting Rights Act of 1965. Having just achieved passage of the 1964 Civil Rights Act, Johnson initially concluded that 1965 would not be an appropriate year to ask Congress to consider voting rights legislation. In his judgment, both the Congress and the nation needed a breather. The movement of events, however, caused him to alter his appraisal, for on March 7, 1965, Martin Luther King led a march from Selma to Montgomery, Alabama as a protest against infringement upon black voting rights. On the evening news programs, a shocked nation witnessed unarmed blacks being attacked by clubs, cattle prods, and police dogs. The reaction was immediate. Demonstrators assembled outside the White House and demanded that the President take action. And so too did the telegrams and phone calls coming into the White House. Instead, Johnson held off, realizing that a premature use of federal force would make a martyr of George Wallace among the states' rights advocates in Congress and throughout the nation. When he finally did commit troops, it was perceived not as an arbitrary use of federal power but rather as a last-ditch effort to avoid further violence.[30] Moreover, Johnson was now convinced that the brutality of the last several days

[29] See remarks by Samuel Rosenman and Benjamin Cohen in Hughes, *Living Presidency,* pp. 322, 360.

[30] Doris Kearns, *Lyndon Johnson and the American Dream* (New York: Harper & Row, 1976), pp. 228, 229. Copyright © 1976 by Doris Kearns. Reprinted by permission of Harper & Row, Publishers, Inc.

had united the Congress and the American people behind a commitment to guarantee black voting rights. Accordingly, on March 14 he pledged to send a voting rights bill to Congress. On March 15 he took the dramatic step of appearing personally before a joint session of Congress to demand that it act. On March 17 he formally submitted his voting rights legislation, which was signed into law some three and a half months later. Had it not been for the events of Selma and Johnson's ability to discern their meaning, action on the rights of blacks would have been delayed still longer.

While there are some indications that Carter is going to change his ways, at this writing there is genuine concern that he has not yet fully grasped the importance of timing to what he wants to accomplish. In the words of the chairman of the powerful House Ways and Means Committee, "That's one thing I think the President has not understood. Timing is *critical.* It's absolutely essential."[31] In February 1978, for example, Carter's legislation calling for the establishment of a Consumer Protection Agency was soundly defeated in the House of Representatives. Given the fact that he had repeatedly taken a vigorous stand in favor of greater consumer protection during the campaign, the defeat of this bill constituted a significant setback for his legislative program. While several factors were responsible for its defeat, certainly one of the major causes lay in the fact that Carter submitted it without having first generated the necessary support within Congress and among the American people. Indeed, his failure to mobilize public opinion for this particular bill was especially unfortunate since a Harris poll found that Americans were in favor of a Consumer Protection Agency by a two-to-one margin.[32]

Carter might also take a lesson from Lyndon Johnson on how to pace the introduction of his legislative programs to Congress. While Johnson kept the members of Congress extremely busy, he was usually careful to avoid sending them a whole series of major proposals all at once: "It's like a bottle of bourbon. If you take it a glass at a time, it's fine. But if you drink the whole bottle in one evening, you have troubles."[33] In his first year anyway, Carter made the mistake of sending a whole cluster of major proposals to Congress in a relatively brief span of time, thus forcing him to contend with many different pockets of opposition *all at once.* Vice President Mondale expressed the problem best when he noted that Carter's legislative program suffered from "fratricide, the concept in missilery where you fire too many missiles too close together and they kill each other off."[34]

The obstacles to be faced in getting legislation through Congress are formid-

---

[31] *Washington Post,* February 5, 1978, p. A3.

[32] *Washington Post,* February 12, 1978, p. A3.

[33] Cited in Eric Goldman, *The Tragedy of Lyndon Johnson* (New York: Alfred A. Knopf, 1969), p. 259.

[34] Cited in Hedrick Smith, "Problems of a Problem Solver," *New York Times Magazine,* January 8, 1978, p. 33. © 1978 by The New York Times Company. Reprinted by permission.

able enough to begin with. Presidents cannot afford the additional disadvantages that follow from their failure to identify the propitious moment for action.

Courage

Among the qualities necessary for effective leadership, few probably command as much admiration as courage. And for a democratically elected leader, the ultimate test of courage is to go ahead and make a decision knowing full well that he will incur the public's wrath by doing so. It is the President acting as statesman rather than as politician. Of course, presidents must be both. Indeed, in discussing the necessity for a keen sense of timing, we were in fact identifying a skill of an astute politician. At the same time, however, a President cannot always postpone doing what he thinks is right until he has mobilized public opinion, for on some questions the public may not be persuadable. On others, they may not be persuadable soon enough. Thus, while he must always weigh anticipated public reaction, he cannot be eternally ruled by it. As Winston Churchill once observed, "Nothing is more dangerous than to live in the temperamental atmosphere of a Gallup poll, always feeling one's pulse and taking one's temperature. . . . There is only one duty, only one safe course, and that is to try to be right and not to fear to do so or say what you believe to be right."[35]

Over the course of our history several examples may be pointed to which, in varying degrees, qualify as courageous presidential actions: Washington's steadfast commitment to negotiating the Jay Treaty, despite a torrent of public criticism; Lincoln's decision to relieve General McClellan as Commander of the Army of the Potomac; Woodrow Wilson's decision, in the face of widespread prejudice, to nominate the first Jew to the Supreme Court. While several more recent examples could also be identified, two stand out as especially courageous. The first was Truman's decision to remove General Douglas MacArthur from his post as United Nations Supreme Commander in South Korea.

Truman and McArthur. Following the invasion of South Korea by North Korea, American forces succeeded in pushing the invasion force out of the South. In fact, they were so successful that the Truman Administration altered its original goal of simply containing the Communists and decided instead to push ahead into North Korea in the hope of being able to reunify the two countries once again. While there was always the risk that the Chinese Communists would come into the war on the side of North Korea, this was not considered likely. We miscalculated, however, for the Chinese did intervene on the side of the North Koreans, and together they drove the American forces a considerable way down the South Korean peninsula. After four months of heavy fighting, the Chinese and the North Koreans were finally driven out of the South. At this point, the Truman Administration decided that a negotiated

---

[35] Cited in Leo Bogart, *Silent Politics* (New York: John Wiley, 1972), p. 47.

settlement would now be the most judicious course to follow. MacArthur, on the other hand, was now calling for an expansion of the war into China, arguing that we should bomb their major industrial and communications facilities, as well as blockade their coast. When Truman rejected this recommendation, Mac-Arthur decided to go public. On March 25, 1951, he released to the press a statement demanding the surrender of the enemy. This action proved to be especially inappropriate since it was at just this time that Truman had planned to issue a statement implying our interest in a negotiated settlement. Some two weeks later the Minority Leader of the House of Representatives stood up before that body and read a letter from MacArthur, which decried the President's war policy. Five days later, Truman relieved MacArthur of his command.[36]

Both the Joint Chiefs and our European allies agreed that MacArthur's plan to carry the war into China was not feasible. For one thing, by doing so we would run the grave risk of bringing the Soviet Union into the conflict on the side of China. Second, in order to attain the required force levels for such an undertaking, it would have been necessary to take troops from Europe, thereby leaving our allies exposed to any military ventures that the Soviet Union might undertake there. Given the Soviet threat in Europe, neither Britain nor France was prepared to commit any of their military strength to Asia. Thus, we would have to do it alone. But there was another issue at stake here aside from the rightness or wrongness of MacArthur's views. Under our constitutional arrangements, the military is subordinate to civilian authority, a principle reflected in the constitutional provision making the President Commander in Chief of the armed forces. Had Truman permitted MacArthur to continue in his open defiance of the President's policies, civilian control over the military would have been seriously undermined. It was for this reason that Truman relieved him of his command.

There was relatively little Truman could have done to avoid the negative public reaction that followed this decision. MacArthur was, after all, a national hero. Add to this the fact that his "Let's go get 'em" approach toward the Chinese had wide popular appeal. And finally, add also the fact Truman's popularity had been declining even prior to the MacArthur firing. Given all of these factors, it is hardly surprising that MacArthur returned to the United States not in disgrace but rather as a conquering hero. He was given a ticker-tape parade down Fifth Avenue and also accorded the honor of addressing a joint session of Congress. As for Truman, several Republicans in Congress announced that they would seek to impeach him; various state legislatures condemned his action as excessive; and in communities throughout the land he was burned in effigy.[37]

The judgment of history, however, has come down on the side of Truman

---

[36] See John Spanier, *American Foreign Policy Since World War II,* 2nd ed. rev. (New York: Praeger, 1962), pp. 86–93; Richard Neustadt, *Presidential Power* (New York: John Wiley, 1960), pp. 13, 92, 93.

[37] Spanier, *American Foreign Policy,* p. 96.

rather than MacArthur. For not only was he right, but he was willing to be so knowing full well that it would bring him the condemnation of most of the nation.

Ford and Nixon. Gerald Ford's pardoning of former President Nixon provides a still more recent example of extraordinary presidential courage. Surely Ford had little doubt but that such a decision would bring an early end to his honeymoon with Congress, the press, and the public. And that it did, for 61 percent of the American public expressed their disapproval of the pardon. Moreover, this disapproval was also reflected in Ford's popularity rating, which prior to the pardon was 66 percent, and afterwards, dropped to 50 percent. Nor did the population mellow very much on this issue, for as Ford entered the 1976 election campaign, 57 percent of the American public still felt that the pardon was wrong.[38]

If the decision to pardon Nixon for his unlawful behavior created the impression that not all were treated equally before the law, nevertheless there is no evidence to suggest that President Ford's action was guided by any motive other than getting Watergate behind us. The accomplishment of this goal would not have been possible if Richard Nixon had been brought to trial. For one thing, in view of the climate of opinion at the time, he could not have received a fair trial.[39] Thus there would probably have been a delay in the trial of two or three years, and perhaps even longer. Moreover, if Nixon had come to trial and lost, the lengthy appeals process which would have inevitably followed would probably have kept Watergate on the front pages for an additional two years. Certainly a credible argument can be made that another fives years of Watergate would have been debilitating to the national psyche.

While we may still be too close to the happendings of Watergate to assess the correctness of Ford's decision objectively, one suspects that history will judge it to have been not only courageous but also wise.

Decisiveness

There is, to be sure, a relationship between courage and decisiveness. Yet they are not one and the same, for even though acts of courage may also be characterized as decisive, it does not necessarily follow that all acts of decisiveness are courageous as well.

While presidents perform a variety of different functions in our political system, in the final analysis we elect them to make decisions. The President who fails to act resolutely and unambiguously when the occasion requires runs the risk of being overtaken by events; he invites others to misinterpret his intentions;

[38] Miller and Miller, "Partisanship and Performance," p. 72.

[39] Leon Jaworski, *The Right and the Power* (New York: Reader's Digest Press, 1976), pp. 237, 238.

and ultimately he invites a loss of confidence in his leadership as well; for even though decisiveness alone does not insure public support, the appearance of indecision will almost certainly lead to an erosion of it. Thus, as was clearly demonstrated in the 1932 election, the public's perception of Herbert Hoover as indecisive in responding to a rapidly deteriorating economy brought about a loss of confidence in his leadership. On the other hand, even though Franklin Roosevelt's bold new programs were not by themselves sufficient to lift us out of the Great Depression, nevertheless he showed no reluctance to deal with the crisis: ". . . one thing is sure. We have to do something. We have to do the best we know how at the moment . . . . If it doesn't work out right, we can modify it as we go along."[40] His take-charge approach earned him the confidence and admiration of the American people. This same resolve was also evidenced in his successor, Harry Truman, as he faced such difficult issues as the use of the atomic bomb on Japan, the revitalization of Europe, the commitment of United States forces to South Korea, and the firing of General Douglas MacArthur. Indeed, to a greater extent than for any other modern President, decisiveness appears to have been *the* defining characteristic of the Truman leadership style.

While it remains to be seen whether the Carter Presidency will ultimately be characterized by decisive leadership, it would have to be said that his record thus far has been mixed on this score. During his first several months in office, Carter dealt with several key issues unambiguously. Despite the controversial nature of his pledge to pardon Vietnam War draft evaders, for example, once in office he wasted no time in making good on this pledge. This same decisiveness was also apparent in his handling of the B-1 bomber. With powerful forces allied on both sides of this issue, the easiest option for Carter would have been to opt for a middle course that called for the construction of at least a limited number of bombers. Instead, he made a clean, unambiguous decision to scrap production of the plane altogether.

On other important issues, however, Carter conveyed an impression of indecisiveness. Some would surely argue that he waited too long before intervening in the lengthy coal strike. Perhaps most damaging to his image as a decisive leader, however, was the way he handled the neutron bomb issue. While Carter apparently had strong misgivings about producing such a bomb, he was ultimately convinced of its strategic value in the event of a military confrontation with the Soviet Union in Europe. Accordingly, at the President's urging, Congress appropriated the funds to produce the bomb. Carter also instructed his advisers to meet with NATO allies and work out matters related to deployment of the bomb. In March 1978, however, the press reported that Carter had decided not to produce the controversial neutron warhead. This report was then qualified when Carter announced that the United States would not produce the bomb if the Soviet Union made a similar gesture in the direction of arms reduction.

[40]Cited in Arthur Schlesinger, Jr., "The Dynamics of Decision," in Aaron Wildavsky, ed., *The Presidency* (Boston: Little, Brown, 1969), p. 139.

Both the Congress and our European allies were not only bewildered by the President's sudden about-face, but they also feared that it might cause the Soviet Union to perceive the leader of the free world as a man uncertain of what he wants.

Having noted that decisiveness is essential to effective leadership, it must be acknowledged that an assessment of this quality in a President is not an easy task. What some see as decisive, others may view as impulsive and reckless. In addition, what often passes for drift and indecision may in fact reflect a President's conscious effort to wait until the necessary forces have coalesced to produce just the right moment for action. And finally, in assessing this quality of leadership, we must not overlook the significance of negative as well as positive decisions. As Eisenhower's refusal to intervene in Vietnam clearly demonstrates, the decision *not* to act may exhibit decisiveness every bit as much as the decision to act.

Vision

Although presidents lead at a discrete period in time, it cannot be said that their actions are similarly confined. On the contrary, the present is significantly shaped by what presidents have done in the past and the future by what presidents do in the present. Accordingly, it is important for a President to have a sense of vision—an ability to appreciate the implications which present events and circumstances have for the future. Lyndon Johnson made the point well:

> One of the hardest tasks that a President faces is to keep the time scale of his decisions always in mind and to try to be the President of all the people. He is not simply responsible to an immediate electorate, either. He knows over the long stretch of time how great can be the repercussions of all that he does or that he fails to do, and over that span of time the President always has to think of America as a continuing community.

> He has to try to see how his decisions will affect not only today's citizens, but their children and their children's children unto the third and fourth generation. He has to try to peer into the future, and has to prepare for that future.

> . . . Irresistible forces of change have been unleashed by modern science and technology, and the very facts dissolve and regroup as we look into them. To make no predictions is to be sure to be wrong. . . .

> The President of this country, more than any other single man in the world, must grapple with the course of events and the directions of history. What he must try to do, try to do always, is to build for tomorrow in the immediacy of today. . . .[41]

[41] Cited in James MacGregor Burns, *Presidential Government* (Boston: Houghton Mifflin, 1965), pp. 323, 324.

Despite the fact that Wilson's stubbornness prevented Senate approval, nevertheless his forward-looking concept of a League of Nations embodied a recognition of the fact that the world was indeed a community and the preservation of peace a global responsibility. Franklin Roosevelt "grasped at once the political implications of the news of advances in Germany" and thus marshalled the nation's resources for the purpose of developing an atomic bomb.[42] When Europe lay devasted after the Second World War, it was apparent that only the United States possessed the capacity to help it rebuild. Sensing that the military and economic security of our country would continue to be tied closely to that of Europe, President Truman had the foresight to approve the Marshall Plan—a program that called for a massive infusion of American economic aid to help revitalize Europe. Despite subsequent strains in the relationship from time to time, the Marshall Plan was instrumental in creating an enduring bond between the United States and Europe. Considerable credit is also due to President Eisenhower, whose spirit of "rapprochement" with the Soviet Union reflected a belief that the futures of both nations depended upon a reduction in tensions. Kennedy, too, was looking to the future when, despite uncertainty as to how the public would react, he called upon the Soviet Union to join the United States in banning all nuclear testing in the atmosphere, a call that ultimately resulted in the Nuclear Test Ban Treaty. If the initiatives of both Eisenhower and Kennedy did not make the subsequent move toward détente inevitable, they certainly made it more likely.

We must also credit Kennedy for calling upon the nation to probe the frontiers of outer space, a challenge that he issued in his 1961 State of the Union Address to the Congress:

> . . . if we are to win the battle that is now going on around the world between freedom and tyranny, the dramatic achievements in space which occurred in recent weeks should have made clear to us all, as did the Sputnik, in 1957, the impact of this adventure on the minds of men everywhere who are attempting to make a determination of which road they should take.

> . . . Now is the time to take longer strides—time for a great new American enterprise—time for this nation to take a clearly leading role in space achievement which, in many ways, may hold the key to our future on earth.

> . . . I believe that this nation should commit itself to achieving the goal, before this decade is out, of landing a man on the moon and returning him safely to earth. No single space project in this period will be more impressive to mankind or more important for the long range exploration of space.[43]

---

[42] Herman Finer, *The Presidency: Crisis and Regeneration* (Chicago: University of Chicago Press, 1960), p. 130.

[43] *New York Times*, May 26, 1961, p. 12. © 1961 by The New York Times Company. Reprinted by permission.

While neither Kennedy, nor anyone else for that matter, could fully comprehend what lay beyond the confines of our own planet, nevertheless he was able to grasp the fact that no great nation could ignore the challenge to explore it.

In addition to having a sense of vision, effective leadership also requires that the man in the White House have *a* vision. After all, in order to lead a population, *you* must know where you want to take them and you must be sure that *they* know also. For Wilson, this vision was embodied in the "New Freedom"; for Franklin Roosevelt, the "New Deal"; for Kennedy, the "New Frontier"; for Johnson, the "Great Society"; for Nixon, "a generation of peace." Even if phrases such as these could hardly capture all of what these presidents had in their minds, nevertheless they did convey a general sense of direction. The difficulties Jimmy Carter experienced during his first year in office were due, at least in part, to his failure to convey to the Congress and the public where he chose to take us. Carter aid Jody Powell frankly acknowledged this problem: "If there is one area that I see the biggest failure, it is exactly in that area. We haven't clearly enough articulated that overarching, unifying theme or presentation of what we're about or the way we're approaching things. We spent so much time in getting under way on the Administration's work that we did not spend enough time in explaining it in an understandable way to the public."[44] At this point, it is still unclear whether this failure resulted from the absence of any such vision on Carter's part or, as Powell suggested, was merely the consequence of administration neglect in trying to explain it.

Flexibility

Flexibility is used in two senses here—one *cognitive* and the other *tactical.* Regarding the first, it is essential that presidents be open to new ideas and approaches. Circumstances and knowledge change too quickly for a political leader to cement himself into rigid and unalterable views of the world around him. Hoover, for example, had long been philosophically opposed to federal intervention in the life of the nation, believing instead that our economic and social ills could be eradicated most effectively through voluntarism and governmental assistance at the state and local levels. Unfortunately, he clung rigidly to this view even as the economy slid steadily downhill: ". . . each community and each State should assume its full responsibilities for organization of employment and relief of distress with that sturdiness and independence which built a great Nation."[45] This, despite the fact that it had become abundantly clear that neither the states nor voluntary organizations possessed the capacity to combat the widespread unemployment and hunger then befalling the American people.

Richard Nixon, on the other hand—for all of his other shortcomings—demonstrated a capacity for intellectual flexibility. Few political figures on the national

---

[44] Cited in Smith, "Problems of a Problem Solver," pp. 44, 45.

[45] Cited in Harris Warren, *Herbert Hoover and the Great Depression* (New York: W.W. Norton, 1959), p. 193.

scene had been more doggedly anti-Communist than he. Yet he was not so rigidly tied to this view that it prevented him from grasping the changing circumstances in the relationship between China and the Soviet Union as well as how these changes could be exploited in moving toward détente with both countries. Nor did his long-standing opposition to wage and price controls prevent him from instituting them in 1971, after he was persuaded of their absolute necessity.

Presidents must show flexibility not only in their openness to new ideas but also in how they go about trying to realize their goals. The man in the White House, after all, does not hold all the chips in the political game. Rather, more often than not he must compete with the Congress, the bureaucracy, and various organized interests within the society, all of which have formidable resources of their own which may be brought to bear in the policy-making process. Accordingly, at times he must be prepared to compromise with these other power centers, for a rigid insistence upon getting the whole loaf may lead to his getting nothing at all. This is not to say that he must readily abandon his goals and principles. It does mean, however, that he must be prepared to settle for results that move him *closer* to his goals—even though not as close as he might like. The point is well made by James Russell Lowell:

> It is loyalty to great ends, even though forced to combine the small and opposing motives of selfish men to accomplish them; it is the anchored cling to solid principles of duty and action, which knows how to swing with the tide, but is never carried away by it,—that we demand in public men, and not obstinacy in prejudice, sameness of policy, or a conscientious persistency in what is impracticable. For the impracticable, however theoretically enticing, is always politically unwise, sound statesmanship being the application of that prudence to the public business. . . .[46]

Perhaps in no instance were the costs of inflexibility more apparent than in Woodrow Wilson's efforts to gain approval for the League of Nations. The idea to establish such an organization was his own, and he personally attended the Paris Peace Conference where he helped draft the provisions of the League Covenant. When it came before the U.S. Senate, however, several senators expressed some reservations concerning certain provisions. Wilson, unfortunately, would not even entertain the possibility of compromise on any aspect of the covenant. Thus, by rigidly insisting on getting everything, he ended up getting nothing. The Senate refused to ratify the covenant, and Wilson suffered the greatest defeat of his Presidency.

In contrast to Wilson, John Kennedy's actions in the area of civil rights provide us with an example of a President who showed considerable flexibility in pursuit of his goals and principles. He had campaigned strongly on behalf of civil rights for blacks, frequently noting the laxity of the Eisenhower Admini-

---

[46] Lowell, *Political Essays,* pp. 196, 197.

stration in this area. Once in office, however, he began to see that the articulation of such a goal was far easier than its realization, for the civil rights issue now had to be considered within the political context of his Presidency. For one thing, Kennedy's narrow election victory greatly restricted his political leverage over both the Congress and the public. For another, he now found himself confronted with a Congress in which southerners held a disproportionate share of the power. Thus, even if he pushed hard and early for a civil rights bill, there was every chance that he might still fail. Moreover, he would no doubt alienate many southern congressmen and senators whose support was necessary to realize other parts of his legislative program. Accordingly, he temporarily placed civil rights legislation on the back burner.

Even in areas where the cause of the black man could be advanced through executive action alone, Kennedy also compromised. For example, he certainly appointed more southerners to the federal bench than either he or the blacks would have liked, but he felt that building southern support in Congress dictated this necessity. At the same time, however, executive action in other areas clearly demonstrated his concern for blacks. Thus, even though he did not appoint as many blacks to executive positions as some had wanted, the fact remains that from 1961 to 1963 the number of blacks in the upper levels of the civil service rose 88 percent.[47] He ordered the Justice Department to step up its prosecution of cases dealing with school desegregation and voting rights violations. He petitioned the Interstate Commerce Commission to eliminate segregation in those bus terminals that were providing interstate bus service. After some delay, he also issued an executive order prohibiting racial discrimination in the sale or rental of federally financed housing. To be sure, for economic, legal, and political reasons, he decided to exempt some housing from this order. These exceptions included housing already built, houses not in commercially developed areas, and FHA loans given for home improvements. Yet if this executive order did not go as far as many had hoped, it is also important to note that the Eisenhower Administration had not been willing to go any of the distance at all in this area. When blacks seeking entry to the universities of Mississippi and Alabama were harassed, Kennedy dispatched federal marshalls to protect them. Finally, it should also be pointed out that through private persuasion the Kennedy Administration succeeded in bringing about voluntary desegregation in some 256 southern cities and managed to establish biracial committees in 185 of them.[48]

As blacks became increasingly demonstrative in drawing attention to their deplorable condition in American society, the threat of a violent response by whites increased also. Accordingly in June 1963 Kennedy went before the American people and announced that he would shortly submit civil rights legisla-

---

[47] Carl Brauer, *John Kennedy and the Second Reconstruction* (New York: Columbia University Press, 1977), p. 319.

[48] Ibid., pp. 208, 320.

tion to the Congress. Eight days later the Congress received the most comprehensive civil rights bill ever to be placed before it.

The argument that there should be no timetable on civil rights for blacks is a compelling one. If one accepts this principle, then Kennedy's actions may indeed appear to have been overly timid. Yet the fact remains that even with all the compromises, Kennedy still advanced the black man farther toward the goal of full civil rights than had any of his predecessors. Moreover, we cannot overlook the political and social constraints under which he was required to lead. Had he pushed for more, earlier and harder, he may well have accomplished less in the way of civil rights and jeopardized some of his other legislative programs as well. It is well to recall here an observation of the late Hubert Humphrey: "Compromise is not a dirty word. . . . There are times, of course, when it is better to lose than to be partially successful. . . . But to make losing a habit in the name of moral principle or liberal convictions is to fail to govern. . . ."[49]

Despite the fact that Jimmy Carter came into the Presidency with a reputation for inflexibility, the evidence thus far would not appear to support such a characterization. Sensing that his call for the elimination of thirty federal water projects would imperil support from members of Congress on other legislation, Carter settled instead for the elimination of only nine water projects. Similarly, as a price for getting an energy bill, he was willing to accept prices on natural gas that proved to be considerably higher than he had wanted. In the area of foreign affairs, this flexibility has been most apparent in the area of human rights, where, after it became apparent that his public scoldings of the Soviet Union on this matter was adversely affecting their receptivity to further disarmament negotiations, Carter decided to lower his voice.

A Sense for Power

Harry Truman once remarked, "I sit here all day trying to persuade people to do things they ought to have sense enough to do without my persuading them. . . . That's all the powers of the President amount to." This rather simple statement in fact makes a profound point about the role of the President in our political system. For despite the attention focused on the office, despite the powers granted it and the pomp surrounding it, the fact remains that presidents are most often in a position where they must enlist the support of others rather than being able to command it. The separation of powers, checks, and balances, the independent power bases within his own branch as well as in the society at large—all of these insure that it could not be otherwise. At the same time, however, while the President must persuade more often than command, he nevertheless has considerable resources at his disposal, which can make him a formidable persuader. At various points in this text, these resources have been discussed.

[49] Hubert Humphrey, *The Education of a Public Man* (Garden City, N.Y.: Doubleday, 1976), pp. 136, 137.

They include (1) constitutional authority, (2) information, (3) the *status* of the office, (4) control of federal projects and patronage, and (5) ready access to the public through the media. Depending upon circumstances, other resources may include (6) high popularity and (7) the nature of the times. Yet if all of these factors can affect the President's ability to influence outcomes, it must be remembered that they can do so only if he *recognizes* them as such, for power comes to those who sense what power is made of.[50]

But the President's potential for influence does not lie only in the factors identified above. It is also a function of the kinds of decisions he makes. As Richard Neustadt notes, " . . . a President's own choices are the only means *in his own hands* of guarding his own prospects for effective influence."[51] The President with a keen sense for power will be attentive to how any given decision he makes will affect his ability to exert influence in the future. On this score, one may well question how sensitive Jimmy Carter was to the power stakes involved in his decision to invoke the Taft-Hartley Act against striking coal miners in March 1978. This act, after all, had long been anathema to organized labor in general, and to coal miners in particular. Indeed, the miners had been ordered back to work under Taft-Hartley in 1948 and 1950, and on both occasions they had refused to comply. They also made it clear that they would ignore any such order given by President Carter. Yet even though all the evidence indicated that the miners would not obey, the President still went ahead and ordered them back to work under the provisions of the Taft-Hartley Act. Under the best of circumstances, a President should be wary of putting his prestige on the line by giving an order that he knows will not be obeyed and that he knows cannot be readily enforced (it simply was not possible to arrest all of the coal miners who were in violation of the back-to-work order). It is all the more perplexing that Carter would have made this decision at a time when—in the absence of any major successes in his administration—his leadership ability was already being questioned in many quarters. Finally, one cannot help but wonder whether the miners' flagrant violation of Carter's back-to-work order might undermine his leverage in dealing with future strikes.

Of course, to say that a President must be sensitive to the power implications of his decisions does not mean that power considerations can always be uppermost in his mind. At times a President will be forced to make decisions, which though highly unpopular and injurious to future influence, are nevertheless deemed to be in the public interest as he sees it. At the same time, however, there are also many issues concerning which the President has some latitude in how he responds. In the case of Carter and the coal miners, for example, some would surely contend that he should have sought congressional authorization to seize the mines, especially since the miners indicated a willingness to return to work under such an arrangement. Others would argue that more drastic measures

[50] Neustadt, *Presidential Power,* p. 120.
[51] Ibid., p. 57.

could have been avoided had Carter personally intervened in the strike earlier and "jawboned" both parties, much as Johnson did in the 1964 railroad strike.

Up to this point, it has been suggested that a sense for power is the ability of a President to discern what gives him influence. But a sense for power also entails something more, namely, *a willingness to make effective use of that influence.* For the leader who is unwilling to take advantage of the resources at his disposal invites others to conclude there is little to fear from opposing him. The limited accomplishments of the Carter Administration during its first year were in part the result of the President's failure to use all of the resources at his command. In the words of press secretary Jody Powell, " ... we've learned that just being an honest and decent and friendly sort of chap is not sufficient to make things happen the way they're supposed to happen, that people aren't going to do what you think they should do because they think you're a nice guy. It may be to our discredit that it took us a year to learn that."[52]

There is indeed some evidence to suggest that the Carter White House has learned. In December 1977, for example, the House voted (191–161) to appropriate money for the very B-1 bomber that the President had earlier decided to scrap. Fortunately for the President, this bill was defeated in the Senate. The House supporters of the B-1 did not give up, however. Shortly thereafter, they managed to get $462 million for two B-1 bombers written into a $7.8 billion appropriations bill. The Carter Administration was determined to have the appropriation for the B-1 deleted from the bill. In pursuance of this goal, several key congressmen were informed that sewer grants and disaster loans for their districts would be slow in coming unless they voted to delete the B-1 appropriation. The vote to delete carried. As one congressman noted, this application of pressure by the Carter White House was decidedly different from its tactics on previous occasions: "On earlier B-1 votes there was almost a reluctance to use the power of the Presidency. You almost got the feeling that they were somehow not involved."[53] There have also been reports that Carter was willing to make trades in exchange for votes on the crucially important Panama Canal treaties. For example, although the administration had been strongly committed to closing several military bases around the country, some senators who came out in support of the treaties were happy to learn that the bases in their states would probably be taken off the list of closings. Carter also decided to drop his opposition to a $2.3 billion emergency farm bill. Subsequently, Senator Herman Talmadge, a strong advocate of the emergency measure, announced his support for the first Panama Canal treaty. Similarly, Carter gave his approval to government stockpiling of copper—a reversal of his earlier position. And coincidentally, Senator Dennis DeConcini, who represents the copper-mining state of Arizona and whose support of the first Panama Canal treaty was uncertain, came down on the side of ratification.

[52]Cited in Elizabeth Drew, "A Reporter at Large," *The New Yorker,* February 27, 1978, p. 80.

[53]*Washington Post,* February 27, 1978, pp. A1, A7.

To suggest that presidents must have a sense for power will no doubt raise a red flag in the minds of some, for it may certainly be argued that the most dangerous Presidency in our history resulted from a President who was intoxicated by power. This leads us to one final point in our discussion, namely this: to have a sense for power is to appreciate not only its potential but also its *limits*—limits dictated in part by the Constitution and in part by public expectations. Whether due to his own insecurities or lack of moral purpose, the ultimate tragedy of Richard Nixon lay in his inability to discern these limits. And for this failure both he and the nation paid dearly.

CONCLUSION

Of the three branches of government, the Presidency stands out as the institution with the greatest capacity to lead the nation. Clearly the Supreme Court is ill-suited to such a role, for it can speak only when spoken to, and its reply must necessarily be confined to the particular case before it. While Congress may focus upon any issue it wishes, both its size and the multiplicity of its local interests guarantee that it will speak with many voices. The President alone has the ability to speak with one voice on any matter he chooses. However, that does not mean that whoever happens to occupy this office will *ipso facto* be an effective leader. While many of us cling to the notion that the office somehow ennobles the man, this view must remain more a hope than an expectation. To be sure, the presidential experience can develop and refine qualities of leadership, but it cannot create them, for the qualities identified here are, in varying degrees, sown within the individual.

The American people will no doubt continue to look to the President to take the lead in addressing the pressing problems facing our nation, and world leaders are likely to expect no less on matters of international concern. And yet several recent developments promise to make the task of leading a truly formidable one. The Johnson and Nixon presidencies left in their wake a Congress determined to play a more active role in policy making. But within Congress itself, power has become more widely dispersed than ever. The role of political party has become decidedly less important, and organized special interests have stepped in to fill the vacuum. The American public may likewise prove more difficult to mobilize, for even though confidence in the Presidency appears to be on the rise, it has not yet returned to the levels attained in the early sixties. Moreover, for the American people as for Congress, party appears as an increasingly ineffective mechanism. All of these changes have been divisive rather than unifying in their effects, making it more difficult for a President to forge a coalition of support behind his goals and programs.

APPENDIX

The Constitution
and
the Presidency

ARTICLE I/SECTION 3

The Senate shall have the sole Power to try all Impeachments. When sitting for that Purpose, they shall be on Oath or Affirmation. When the President of the United States is tried, the Chief Justice shall preside; and no Person shall be convicted without the Concurrence of two-thirds of the Members present.

Judgement in Cases of Impeachment shall not extend further than to removal from Office, and disqualification to hold and enjoy any Office of Honor, Trust or Profit under the United States: but the Party convicted shall nevertheless be liable and subject to Indictment, Trial, Judgment and Punishment, according to law.

ARTICLE I/SECTION 7

All Bills for raising Revenue shall originate in the House of Representatives; but the Senate may propose or concur with Amendments as on other Bills.

Every Bill which shall have passed the House of Representatives and the Senate, shall, before it become a Law, be presented to the President of the United States; if he approve he shall sign it, but if not he shall return it, with his objections to that House in which it shall have originated, who shall enter the Objections at large on their Journal and proceed to reconsider it. If after such Reconsideration two-thirds of that House shall agree to pass the Bill, it shall be sent, together with the Objections, to the other House, by which it shall likewise be reconsidered, and if approved by two-thirds of that House, it shall become a Law. But in all such Cases the Votes of both Houses shall be determined by Yeas and Nays, and the Names of the Persons voting for and against the Bill shall be entered on the Journal of each House respectively. If any Bill shall not be returned by the President within ten Days (Sunday excepted) after it shall have been presented to him, the Same shall be a Law, in like Manner as if he had signed it, unless the Congress by their Adjournment prevent its Return, in which Case it shall not be a Law.

Every Order, Resolution, or Vote to which the Concurrence of the Senate and House of Representatives may be necessary (except on a question of Adjournment) shall be presented to the President of the United States; and before the Same shall take Effect, shall be approved by him, or being disapproved by him, shall be repassed by two-thirds of the Senate and House of Representatives, according to the Rules and Limitations prescribed in the Case of a Bill.

ARTICLE II/SECTION 1

The executive Power shall be vested in a President of the United States of America. He shall hold his Office during the Term of four Years, and, together with the Vice President, chosen for the same Term, be elected, as follows:

Each State shall appoint, in such Manner as the Legislature thereof may direct, a Number of Electors, equal to the whole Number of Senators and Representatives to which the State may be entitled in the Congress: but no Senator or Representative, or Person holding an Office of Trust or Profit under the United States shall be appointed an Elector. [The second paragraph of this clause was eliminated by the 12th Amendment.]

The Congress may determine the Time of chusing the Electors, and the Day on which they shall give their Votes; which Day shall be the same throughout the United States.

No Person except a natural born Citizen, or a Citizen of the United States, at the time of the Adoption of this Constitution, shall be eligible to the Office of President; neither shall any Person be eligible to that Office who shall not have attained to the Age of thirty-five Years, and been fourteen Years a Resident within the United States.

In Case of the Removal of the President from Office, or of his Death, Resignation, or Inability to discharge the Powers and Duties of the said Office, the Same shall devolve on the Vice President, and the Congress may by Law provide for the Case of Removal, Death, Resignation or Inability, both of the President and Vice President, declaring what Officer shall then act as President, and such Officer shall act accordingly, until the Disability be removed, or a President shall be elected. [See also the stipulations of the 25th Amendment.]

The President shall, at stated Times, receive for his Services a Compensation, which shall neither be encreased nor diminished during the Period for which he shall have been elected, and he shall not receive with that Period any other Emolument from the United States, or any of them.

Before he enter on the Execution of his Office, he shall take the following Oath or Affirmation: "I do solemnly swear (or affirm) that I will faithfully execute the Office of President of the United States, and will to the best of my Ability, preserve, protect and defend the Constitution of the United States."

ARTICLE II/SECTION 2

The President shall be Commander in Chief of the Army and Navy of the United States, and of the Militia of the several States, when called into the actual Service of the United States; he may require the Opinion, in writing, of the principal Officer in each of the executive Departments, upon any Subject relating to the duties of their respective Offices, and he shall have power to grant Reprieves and Pardons for Offenses against the United States, except in the Cases of Impeachment.

He shall have Power, by and with the Advice and Consent of the Senate, to make Treaties, provided two-thirds of the Senators present concur; and he shall nominate, and by and with the Advice and Consent of the Senate, shall appoint Ambassadors, other public Ministers and Consuls, Judges of the supreme Court, and all other Officers of the United States, whose Appointments are not herein otherwise provided for, and which shall be established by law: but the Congress may by Law vest the Appointment of such inferior Officers, as they think proper, in the President alone, in the Courts of law, or in the Heads of Departments.

The President shall have Power to fill up all Vacancies that may happen during the Recess of the Senate, by granting Commissions which shall expire at the End of their next Session.

ARTICLE II/SECTION 3

He shall from time to time give to the Congress Information of the State of the Union, and recommend to their Consideration such Measures as he shall judge necessary and expedient; he may, on extraordinary Occasions, convene both Houses, or either of them, and in Case of Disagreement between them, with Respect to the Time of Adjournment, he may adjourn them to such Time as he shall think proper; he shall receive Ambassadors and other public Ministers, he shall take Care that the Laws be faithfully executed, and shall Commission all the Officers of the United States.

ARTICLE II/SECTION 4

The President, Vice President, and all civil Officers of the United States shall be removed from Office on Impeachment for, and Conviction of, Treason, Bribery, or other high Crimes and Misdemeanors.

AMENDMENTS

Amendment XII(1804)

The Electors shall meet in their respective States and vote by ballot for President and Vice President, one of whom, at least, shall not be an inhabitant of the same State with themselves; they shall name in their ballots the person voted for as President, and in distinct ballots the person voted for as Vice President, and they shall make distinct lists of all persons voted for as President, and of all persons voted for as Vice President, and of the number of votes for each, which lists they shall sign and certify, and transmit sealed to the seat of the government of the United States, directed to the President of the Senate; the President of the Senate shall, in the presence of the Senate and House of Representatives, open all the certificates and the votes shall then be counted; the person having the greatest number of votes for President, shall be the President, if such number be a majority of the whole number of Electors appointed; and if no person have such majority, then from the persons having the highest numbers not exceeding three on the list of those voted for as President, the House of Representatives shall choose immediately, by ballot, the President. But in choosing the President, the votes shall be taken by States, the representation from each State having one vote; a quorum for this purpose shall consist of a member or members from two-thirds of the States, and a majority of all the States shall be necessary to a choice. And if the House of Representatives shall not choose a President whenever the right of choice shall devolve upon them, before the fourth day of March next following, then the Vice President shall act as President, as in the case of the death or other constitutional disability of the President. The person having the greatest number of votes as Vice President shall be the Vice President, if such number be a majority of the whole number of electors appointed, and if no person have a majority, then from the two highest numbers on the list, the Senate shall choose the Vice President; a quorum for the purpose shall consist of two-thirds of the whole number of Senators, and a majority of the whole number shall be necessary to a choice. But no person constitutionally ineligible to the office of President shall be eligible to that of Vice President of the United States.

Amendment XX (1933)

Sec. 1: The terms of the President and Vice President shall end at noon on the 20th day of January, and the terms of Senators and Representatives at noon on the 3d day of January, of the years in which such terms would have ended if this article had not been ratified; and the terms of their successors shall then begin.

Sec. 2: The Congress shall assemble at least once in every year, and such meetings shall begin at noon on the 3d day of January, unless they shall by law appoint a different day.

Sec. 3: If, at the time fixed for the beginning of the term of the President, the President elect shall have died, the Vice President elect shall become President. If a President shall not have been chosen before the time fixed for the beginning of his term, or if the President elect shall have failed to qualify, then the Vice President elect shall act as President until a President shall have qualified; and the Congress may by law provide for the case wherein neither a President elect nor a Vice President elect shall have qualified, declaring who shall then act as President, or the manner in which one who is to act shall be selected, and such person shall act accordingly until a President or Vice President shall have qualified.

Sec. 4: The Congress may by law provide for the case of the death of any of the persons from whom the House of Representatives may choose a President whenever the right of choice shall have devolved upon them, and for the case of the death of any of the persons from whom the Senate may choose a Vice President whenever the right of choice shall have devolved upon them. [See also the 25th Amendment.]

Amendment XXII (1951)

No person shall be elected to the office of the President more than twice, and no person who has held the office of President, or acted as President, for more than two years of a term to which some other person was elected President shall be elected to the office of the President more than once. But this Article shall not apply to any person holding the office of President when this Article was proposed by the Congress, and shall not prevent any person who may be holding the office of President, or acting as President, during the term within which this Article becomes operative from holding the office of President or acting as President during the remainder of such term.

Amendment XXV (1967)

Sec. 1: In case of the removal of the President from office or his death or resignation, the Vice President shall become President.

Sec. 2: Whenever there is a vacancy in the office of the Vice President, the President shall nominate a Vice President who shall take office upon confirmation by a majority vote of both Houses of Congress.

Sec. 3: Whenever the President transmits to the President pro tempore of the Senate and the Speaker of the House of Representatives his written declaration that he is unable to discharge the powers and duties of his office, and until he transmits to them a written declaration to the contrary, such powers and duties shall be discharged by the Vice President as Acting President.

Sec. 4: Whenever the Vice President and a majority of either the principal officers of the executive department or of such other body as Congress may by law provide, transmit to the President pro tempore of the Senate and the Speaker of the House of Representatives their written declaration that the President is unable to discharge the powers and duties of his office, the Vice President shall immediately assume the powers and duties of the office as Acting President.

Thereafter, when the President transmits to the President pro tempore of the Senate and the Speaker of the House of Representatives his written declaration that no inability exists, he shall resume the powers and duties of his office unless the Vice President and a majority of either the principal officers of the executive department or of such other body as Congress may by law provide, transmit within four days to the President pro tempore of the Senate and the Speaker of the House of Representatives their written declaration that the President is unable to discharge the powers and duties of his office. Thereupon Congress shall decide the issue, assembling within forty-eight hours for that purpose if not in session. If the Congress, within twenty-one days after receipt of the latter written declaration, or, if Congress is not in session, within twenty-one days after Congress is required to assemble, determines by two-thirds vote of both Houses that the President is unable to discharge the powers and duties of his office, the Vice President shall continue to discharge the same as Acting President; otherwise, the President shall resume the powers and duties of his office.

Index

Acheson, Dean, 223, 236, 247
Adams, John, 180, 332
Adams, John Quincy, 333
Adams, Sherman, 214
Advisory Council on Executive Organiza-
tion, 120
Agnew, Spiro, 10, 185, 282
Agricultural Adjustment Act (1933), 291,
293
Alsop, Joseph, 182–83, 268, 279
Alsop, Stewart, 182–83, 268, 279
Arthur, Chester, A., 332
Ash, Ray, 134
Aspin, Les, 48

Ball, George, 235, 240–42, 244–45, 247
Barber, James David, 26, 261–62, 301, 304,
306
Bay of Pigs invasion (1961), 228–34
Bayh, Birch, 29
Belmont case, 46
Bentsen, Lloyd M., 13
Bill of Rights, 312
Bituminous Coal Act (1933), 293
Blumenthal, Michael, 206
Bradley, Omar, 247
Brownlow Committee, 118, 200
Brzezinski, Zbigniew, 204–5, 251
Buchanan, James 332
Buckley v. *Valeo* (1976), 15
Budget, 77–83
   Accounting Act (1921) and, 75
   Bureau of the, 124, 206
   Congress's increased responsibility for,
   105
   Control and Impoundment Act (1974)
   and, 77, 92, 335
   zero-base, 144–45 (*See also* Office of
   Management and Budget)
Bundy, McGeorge, 237, 245, 247
Bundy, William, 240–42
Bureaucracy:
   as power center, 3
   President and, 106–45
   size and complexity of, 127
Burns, Arthur, 251
Butz, Earl, 134
Byrd, Harry, 55, 84

Cabinet, 195–200
   influence of, 114–16, 199–200
   "Cabinet government" (Carter's term),
   211–13
Caddell, Pat, 168, 192
Califano, Joseph, 125

Campaigns:
   Congressional, 10–11
   Presidential, 7–31
Candidates, 2, 6–31
   increase in number of, 17–18
   informal criteria for, 8–17
   legal criteria for, 7–8
Carter, Jimmy:
   bureaucracy and, 108–9, 112, 118, 122–
   23, 136, 142–44
   Congress and, 81, 88, 102–5
   decision-making and, 200, 207–8, 211–13,
   216, 222, 248–54
   foreign affairs and, 50–51, 54
   leadership of, 344–45, 347, 350, 354,
   357, 361–62
   personality of, 298–304
   public, press and, 157–59, 164, 167,
   172–78, 182, 189, 192–93
   selection of, 11–12
Case Act (1972), 47–49, 335
Case, Clifford, 47–49
Censure, 102
Central clearance, 108, 123–27
Character of the President, 261
Church, Frank, 86
CIA (Central Intelligence Agency), 49–52,
81, 96
Civil Rights Act (1964), 66–67, 91, 349
Civil Service:
   as career, 136–39
   reform of, 142–44
Civil Service Act, 136
Civil Service Commission, 109, 137, 143
Cleveland, Grover, 298
Clifford, Clark, 223, 242, 246–48
Colby, William, 96
Colson, Charles, 209, 221
Communication skill as quality of leader-
ship, 343–45
Confidential funds, 80–81
Congress:
   as power center, 3
   emergency laws of, 327–29
   "Imperial," 2
   President and, 57–105
      foreign affairs, 32, 41, 44, 47–49,
      52–56
      influence of bureaucracy, 106
   structure of, 59–60
   war powers and, 35–46, 53
Congressional Budget Office (C.B.O.), 77
Connally, John, 199–200, 282
Constitution:
   emergency powers under, 310–12
   President in, 99, 364–69

Contingency funds, 78
Coolidge, Calvin:
  bureaucracy and, 124
  Congress and, 103
  leadership of, 332
  personality of, 262
Council of Economic Advisers, 205-7
Courage as quality of leadership, 351-53
Cox, Archibald, 100, 286
Credibility as quality of leadership, 345-47
Cuban missile crisis (1962), 234-39
Curtiss Wright case, 39

Dean, Arthur, 247
Dean, John, 209
Decision-making in the White House, 5,
  194-257
  Cabinet in, 129, 138-39, 195-200
  Congress in, 66
Decisiveness as quality of leadership,
  353-55
Defense Intelligence Agency, 32, 51
Defense Production Act (1950), 321
Democratic party, selection proposals in, 18
Dillon, Douglas, 235, 247
Direct primary, 72
Dirksen, Everett, 65, 84
Dodder, Richard, 331-32
Domestic Policy Staff, 201, 207-9
Dominican Republic crisis, 38-39, 181, 190,
  270
Douglas Helen Gahagan, 281
Dulles, Allen, 231
Dulles, John Foster, 203

Eagleton, Thomas F., 10-11
Ehrlichman, John, 22, 67, 92, 132-34,
  207, 209, 282
Eisenhower, Dwight D.:
  bureaucracy and, 110, 113, 122
  Congress and, 63-65, 78, 87, 93
  decision-making and, 194, 196, 203, 210,
    214, 216-17, 220-21, 223, 228, 236
  foreign affairs and, 40-41
  leadership of, 332, 334, 336-37, 342,
    355-56, 358-59
  personality of, 262, 279
  public, press and, 156-57, 159, 162, 164,
    172, 182-83, 190
  selection of, 21
Eisenhower, Milton, 224
Eizenstat, Stuart, 208-10
Emergency Banking Act (1933), 318
Emergency powers, 308-29
  list of, 309-10
Emergency Price Control Act (1942), 319
Energy, Department of, 119
Energy problem, 88, 123, 169
"Equal time" regulation, 177
Evaluations of Presidential performance,
  table of, 332
ExCab, 254
Executive agreements, 46-47

Executive Committee of the National
  Security Council (ExComm), 235-38
Executive departments:
  difficulty in coordination of, 120, 128,
    134, 141
  reorganization of, 120-23, 140-42
  table of, 107
Executive Office of the President, 200-213
  (*See also* White House staff)
Executive privilege, 92-96, 284
Ex parte Endo (1944), 326
Ex parte Milligan (1866), 320, 326

"Face the Nation" (TV program), 9, 21,
  280
Fair Housing Act (1966), 62
Federal Election Campaign Act (1974), 15
Federal employees:
  number of, 6, 107
  table of, 107
Federal Employment Act (1946), 205
Federal jobs, Presidential control over, 6,
  85-86, 121
Federal regulatory agencies, 110-13
Fillmore, Millard, 332
Finch, Robert, 10, 131, 282
Flexibility as quality of leadership, 357-60
Ford, Gerald R., Jr.:
  bureaucracy and, 112, 128
  Congress and, 57-58, 60, 69, 87, 90
  decision-making of, 200, 204, 208, 210,
    216, 224, 249, 256
  emergency powers and, 328
  entry into politics of, 294-96
  foreign affairs and, 35, 45, 50-51, 53
  leadership of, 332, 334, 342, 347, 353
  personality of, 262, 294-301
  public, press and, 157, 159, 161, 164,
    169, 172-77, 182, 189, 192
Foreign affairs and the President, 33-56
Foreign Assistance Act (1977), 54
Fortas, Abe, 224
Founding Fathers:
  emergency powers and, 310-12
  foreign policy and, 36-37, 41, 56
  impeachment provision by, 96-97
  legislative powers and, 73
Freedom of Information Act (1966), 191
Frost, David, 286-87
Fulbright, J. William, 1, 72, 82, 197, 216,
  233-34, 272

Galbraith, John Kenneth, 224
Gallup Poll, 16, 33-34, 63, 88, 156, 157,
  160-64, 171, 179, 284, 330, 331, 345,
  351
Garfield, James Abram, 148, 332
Garment, Len, 282
Goldwater, Barry, 7, 13, 16, 26, 225
"Government in the Sunshine" Act (1976),
  191
Grant, Ulysses S., 210, 332, 345
Greer, U.S.S., 39

"Groupthink" phenomenon, 226, 245
Gulf of Tonkin Resolution (1964), 41–42

Hagerty, James, 174
Halberstam, David, 243–45
Haldeman, H. R., 22, 67, 134, 198, 209, 219, 280, 282
Hamilton, Alexander, 36–37, 180
Harding, Warren G.:
  Congress and, 75
  leadership of, 332, 345
  personality of, 262
  public and, 148
Harris Poll, 152–55, 167–68, 192, 330, 350
Hatch Act (1939), 143
Helms, Richard, 240, 245
Hickel, Walter, 131, 197
Hofstetter, Richard, 188
"Honeymoon period," 61, 70, 157
Hoover, Herbert:
  bureaucracy and, 112, 118
  decision-making of, 236
  leadership of, 332, 335, 339, 343, 354
  personality of, 262, 263
  public, press and, 172, 174
Hoover, J. Edgar, 117–18, 139
"Hot pursuit," doctrine of, 37
House Foreign Affairs Committee, 47–48, 50
House Select Committee on Intelligence, 96
Hughes, Emmet, 57, 343
Humphrey, George, 199
Humphrey, Hubert H., 10–11, 13, 171, 268, 284, 360

Impeachment, 96–102
Impoundment, 77, 90–92, 333
Information:
  handling of, 32–33, 74–77, 93–94, 106
  maximizing flow of, 83, 253–57
  Presidential monopoly on, 33, 51
  reliance on for decision-making, 158, 225–28
Issue Definition Memorandum, 209

Jackson, Andrew:
  Congress and, 37, 73, 93, 102
  foreign affairs and, 37
  leadership of, 332
Jackson, Henry, 12, 29
Janis, Irving, 226
Jefferson, Thomas:
  Congress and, 64, 73, 90, 93
  decision-making of, 210, 220
  public, press and, 180
Johnson, Andrew:
  Congress and, 98
  emergency powers and, 320
  leadership of, 332, 337–38
Johnson, Lyndon Baines:
  bureaucracy and, 112, 115, 119–22, 125, 131

Congress and, 59–62, 66–68, 70, 72, 84, 86–89, 93, 104–5
decision-making of, 196, 199, 204, 210, 219–25, 239, 241–48, 254–55
enters politics, 266–67
foreign affairs and, 35, 38–39, 41–42, 44
leadership of, 332, 334, 336–37, 341, 349–50, 355, 357
personality of, 260, 262–74, 299, 301–3
public, press and, 156–57, 162–64, 170, 173, 175, 180–81
world view of, 267–68, 280, 290
youth of, 263–66, 289
Jordan, Hamilton, 204, 216–17, 254, 301

Kennedy, Edward, 76–77, 90, 284
Kennedy, John F.:
  bureaucracy and, 115, 125–26, 128, 130
  Congress and, 59, 65–66, 70–71, 84–88, 93, 104
  decision-making of, 194, 196–200, 203, 210, 214, 219–20, 223–24, 228–34
  foreign affairs and, 33–34, 41
  leadership of, 330, 332, 336–40, 356, 358–60
  personality of, 262, 272, 303
  public, press and, 148, 156–57, 159, 164, 168, 170, 172–73, 175, 181–82
  selection of, 8–9, 14–15, 24
Kennedy, Robert, 170, 199, 217–18, 237, 255, 272
King, Martin Luther, Jr., 22, 62, 336, 349
Kissinger, Henry, 53, 94, 129, 134, 203–4, 219, 224, 282
Kitchen cabinet, 195
Knowland, William, 64–66
Korematsu v. *United States* (1944), 324–25

Laird, Melvin, 133, 327
Lance, Bert, 192–93, 205–7, 347
Leadership, presidential, 63–68, 330–63
Legislative Reorganization Act (1949), 118; (1970), 76
Lincoln, Abraham:
  Congress and, 58, 73
  decision-making of, 195, 204
  emergency powers and, 316–21
  foreign affairs and, 38
  leadership of, 332, 334–46, 348, 351
  public, press and, 146, 148
Lippmann, Walter, 86, 325
Locke, John, 310–11
Lodge, Henry Cabot, 240–41, 247
Lovett, Robert, 236
Lowell, James Russell, 348, 358

MacArthur, Douglas, 101, 169, 242, 345, 351–54
McCarthy, Eugene, 13
McCloy, John, 236, 247
McGinness, Joe, 18
McGovern, George, 10–11, 13, 16, 20–23, 171, 188

McKinley, William, 38, 148, 332
McNamara, Robert, 126–27, 199, 236–37, 240–42, 244–45, 271
McNaughton, John, 240, 244
Maddox, U.S.S., 41–42
Madison, James:
  Congress and, 89, 91
  emergency powers and, 316, 319
  foreign affairs and, 36
  leadership of, 332, 335
Mansfield, Mike, 242, 297
Maranell, Gary, 331–32
Marston, William, 347
Mayaguez, U.S.S., 45, 159–60, 298
Meany, George 158
Media, *see* Press
"Meet the Press" (TV program), 9, 21
Merchandising of candidates, 27–28
Merit system, abuses of, 136–37
Mills, Wilbur, 59
Mitchell, John, 282
Model Cities program, 86
Mondale, Walter, 11, 75, 86, 341, 350
Monroe, James, 37, 332
Moyers, Bill, 243–46
Moynihan, Daniel Patrick, 186, 197
Muskie, Edmund, 171, 184
Myers vs. *United States,* 109

National Emergencies Act (1976), 328, 335
National Industrial Recovery Act (1933), 293
National Opinion Research Center, 148
National primary (proposed), 29–31
National Security Act (1947), 49
National Security Council, 201–5, 254
  ExComm of, 235–38
Nixon, Richard Milhous:
  bureaucracy and, 108, 112, 114–16, 118–35, 139
  Congress and, 58–59, 63, 67–68, 78, 81, 86–87, 101, 105
  decision-making of, 197–98, 203, 206, 208, 210–11, 214, 216–17, 220–24
  emergency powers and, 309, 315–16
  enters politics, 277–79
  foreign affairs and, 33, 35–36, 43–44, 48, 53
  leadership of, 332, 333, 336–37, 339, 346, 353, 357, 363
  personality of, 260, 262, 274–94, 299, 300–303, 305, 307
  public press and, 147–48, 157, 159–64, 166, 169, 171, 173–77, 179–80, 182, 185, 187–88, 192
  selection, 3, 10, 13–14, 16, 21–22, 24, 26–28
  world view of, 279–82, 290
  youth of, 274–77, 289
Novak, Robert, 186

Office of Administration, 201
Office of Management and Budget (OMB), 76, 108, 123–25, 133, 137–39, 144, 192, 200, 206–7, 250–51
OPEC (Organization of Petroleum Exporting Countries), 53, 163
Orderly Marketing Agreements (OMAs), 250–53

Parties, Presidential control of, 68–72
Patronage, 85
Personality of the President, 258–307
Pocket veto, 89–90
Polk, James, 37–38, 58, 336–37
Polls, 27, 31, 155, 168
  (*See also* Gallup Poll; Harris Poll)
Powell, Jody, 210, 357
Power:
  as quality of leadership, 360–63
  Presidency and, 152–56, 253, 304, 313
Presidential image, 166
Presidential Review Memoranda, 209, 250
President's Committee on Administrative Management, 118, 200
Press:
  bias of, 9–10, 185–89
  as power center, 3
  President and, 170–79, 185–89
Primaries, presidential:
  direct, 72
  increase in number of, 17–19, 30
  national, proposed, 29–31
  voter choice in, 28
Public Broadcast System (PBS), 183

Railroad Pension Act (1933), 293
Reagan, Ronald, 20–21
Reedy, George, 225
Regulatory agencies, federal, 110–13
Richardson, Elliot, 116, 286
Rider to a bill, use of 86–87
Rivers, L. Mendel, 126
Rockefeller, Nelson, 13–14, 208, 297
Rogers, William, 94, 133
Romney, George, 7, 13, 20, 25, 131, 133, 198
Roosevelt, Franklin D.:
  bureaucracy and, 107, 112, 117–18, 124
  Congress and, 58, 62, 87–88
  decision-making of, 195, 200–201, 203, 205, 214, 216–17, 221, 224
  emergency powers and, 315, 318–19, 324–25
  enters politics, 289–91
  foreign affairs and, 39
  leadership of, 332, 334–36, 339–40, 342–43, 348–49, 354, 356–57
  personality of, 262, 271, 289–98, 303
  public, press and, 148, 169, 172–75
  world view of, 267, 282, 289–91
  youth of, 288–89
Roosevelt, Theodore:
  bureaucracy and, 136
  Congress and, 57, 73
  foreign affairs and, 38
  leadership of, 332, 342
  public, press and, 169, 171, 182
Rossiter, Clinton, 327, 333, 335

Rostow, Walt, 245–46, 255
Rousseau, Jean Jacques, 310–11
Rusk, Dean, 117, 199, 204, 233, 240–43, 245

Schlesinger, Arthur, Jr., 232–33, 300
Schlesinger, Arthur, Sr., 331–32
Schlesinger, James, 118
Scranton, William, 13–14
Secret funding, 81–82
Senate Foreign Relations Committee, 11, 48, 50, 55, 225, 327
Senate Special Committee on Emergencies and Delegated Powers, 327
Senate Special Committee on Intelligence, 51–52, 81
Separation of powers, 58–59
Seward, William, 337
Shoe import quotas, 248–53
Shultz, George, 134, 197
"Slush funds," 21–22, 281
Sorensen, Theodore, 103, 109, 125, 198, 218, 235–36, 238, 255
Spoils system, 136
Status conferral, 84
Stevenson, Adlai, 13, 257
Supreme Court, and emergency powers of the President, 320–27
(See also specific cases)
Survey Research Center, 151–53
Symington, Stuart, 13–14

Taft, Robert, 64
Taft, William H.:
  Congress and, 86
  leadership of, 332, 333, 343
  personality of, 262
Taft-Hartley Act (1947), 321–23, 361
Taylor, Zachary, 332
Technology Assessment Act (1972), 76, 335
Television, see Press
Timing as quality of leadership, 347–51
Trade Act (1974), 249
Trading with the Enemy Act (1917), 318
Treaties, 46–56
  Panama Canal, 54, 103–4, 362
Truman, Harry S.:
  bureaucracy and, 107
  Congress and 59, 63–64, 74, 87, 101
  decision-making of, 194, 196, 203, 210, 223, 236, 255
  emergency powers and, 314–15, 321–23
  foreign affairs and, 40, 44
  leadership of, 334–37, 339, 345–46, 351–54, 360–61
  public, press and, 156–57, 160, 162, 164, 169, 172, 174
Truman Doctrine, 346

Tyler, John, 93, 332

Udall, Morris, 12, 120

Van Buren, Martin, 332
Veto, 53, 86–87
  pocket, 89–90
Vietnam War, 239–48
  Congress and, 72, 78, 86, 88, 90, 103
  decision-making and, 203, 214–15, 222, 239–48, 252
  foreign affairs and, 35, 41, 43–46, 52–54
  leadership and, 336–37, 354
  personality of the President and, 272, 292
  public, press and, 149–50, 154–55, 160–63, 175–76, 179, 181, 186, 190
  selection process and, 1–2, 20
Vision as quality of leadership, 356–57
Voting Rights Act (1965), 349–50

Wallace, George, 13, 284
War-making power, 35–44
War Powers Resolution (1973), 44–46, 53, 329, 335
Washington, George:
  decision-making of, 195
  foreign affairs and, 36, 46
  leadership of, 332, 334–45
Watergate:
  bureaucracy and, 115, 133–34, 140
  Congress and, 94
  decision-making and, 208
  foreign affairs and, 53
  leadership and, 336, 346–47, 354
  personality of the President and, 283–85, 287
  public, press and, 147, 149, 151, 160–67, 183, 190–92
Watson, Marvin, 210, 269
Weinberger, Caspar, 116, 127, 133
Weiner vs. United States (1958), 113, 116
Westmoreland, William, 240, 242, 246–47
Wheeler, Earle G., 243–45
White House staff, 103, 131–33, 209–23
Wilson, Woodrow:
  Congress and, 74, 97
  decision-making of, 195, 210, 219
  foreign affairs and, 38
  leadership of, 332, 334–35, 341–42, 351, 356–57
  personality of, 260, 262, 273, 303, 318
  public press and, 173, 180

Youngstown Sheet and Tube Co. v. Sawyer (1954), 321

Ziegler, Ron, 180–81